The Apathetic and the Defiant ❧

The Apathetic and the Defiant ⁓

Case Studies of Canadian Mutiny and Disobedience, 1812 to 1919

Edited by CRAIG LESLIE MANTLE

Foreword by MAJOR-GENERAL P.R. HUSSEY

CANADIAN DEFENCE ACADEMY PRESS
KINGSTON

THE DUNDURN GROUP
TORONTO

Published by The Dundurn Group and Canadian Defence Academy Press in cooperation with the Department of National Defence, and Public Works and Government Services Canada.

Editor: Michael Carroll
Copy-editor: Nigel Heseltine
Design: Alison Carr
Printer: Transcontinental

Library and Archives Canada Cataloguing in Publication

The apathetic and the defiant : case studies of Canadian mutiny and disobedience, 1812-1919 / edited by Craig Leslie Mantle.

Issued also in French under title: Les apathiques et les rebelles. Co-published by: Canadian Defence Academy Press. Includes bibliographical references and index. ISBN 978-1-55002-710-5

1. Mutiny—Canada—History. 2. Military offenses—Canada—History. 3. Military discipline—Canada—History. 4. Canada—Armed Forces—History. 5. Canada—History, Military. I. Mantle, Craig Leslie, 1977-

FC226.A63 2007   355.1'3340971   C2007-902055-0

1   2   3   4   5   11   10   09   08   07

We acknowledge the support of the **Canada Council for the Arts** and the **Ontario Arts Council** for our publishing program. We also acknowledge the financial support of the **Government of Canada** through the **Book Publishing Industry Development Program** and **The Association for the Export of Canadian Books**, and the **Government of Ontario** through the **Ontario Book Publishers Tax Credit program**, and the **Ontario Media Development Corporation**.

Printed and bound in Canada.
Printed on recycled paper.
www.dundurn.com

Canadian Defence Academy Press
PO Box 17000 Station Forces
Kingston, Ontario, Canada
K7K 7B4

Dundurn Press	Gazelle Book Services Limited	Dundurn Press
3 Church Street, Suite 500	White Cross Mills	2250 Military Road
Toronto, Ontario, Canada	High Town, Lancaster, England	Tonawanda, NY
M5E 1M2	LA1 4XS	U.S.A. 14150

CONTENTS

Part II: The First World War

FOREWORD

I am extremely pleased to introduce *The Apathetic and the Defiant: Case Studies of Canadian Mutiny and Disobedience, 1812 to 1919*, the Canadian Defence Academy's second volume on misconduct in the military. Following the recently released work that explores the primary foundations of disobedience, entitled *The Unwilling and the Reluctant: Theoretical Perspectives on Disobedience in the Military*, this book provides a number of historical case studies covering more than a century of Canada's early military history.

The Apathetic and the Defiant clearly demonstrates that for more than 100 years, various forms of disobedience have marked all of Canada's conflicts, large or small. Although Canadian soldiers of all eras have served with overwhelming distinction and valour, we must not forget that some did act inappropriately.

I commend this book to anyone who is interested in military leadership, for many of the causes of disobedience are the same today as they were in the past. Failures in leadership and in maintaining a robust military ethos, for instance, have contributed to disobedient acts over time and, if not adequately addressed through training and education, will continue to do so well into the future. With any luck, recognizing where leaders have erred in the past will make us better equipped to avoid similar situations.

The Canadian Defence Academy (CDA) in general, and the Canadian Forces Leadership Institute (CFLI) in particular, welcome your comments on this book and hope that the resulting discussion will further our collective understanding of an issue that can undermine success, in garrison, or more important, on operations at home and abroad.

Major-General P.R. Hussey
Commander, Canadian Defence Academy

PREFACE

The Canadian Forces Leadership Institute is proud to release *The Apathetic and the Defiant: Case Studies of Canadian Mutiny and Disobedience, 1812 to 1919*, the second of a three-volume set on military disobedience. This seminal series looks at military disobedience and its relationship to effective leadership from a philosophical and practical or applied perspective.

The first volume, *The Unwilling and the Reluctant: Theoretical Perspectives on Disobedience in the Military*, assembled and edited by Craig Leslie Mantle, focused on the philosophical and provided a theoretical foundation for understanding indiscipline. This second volume, also edited by Mantle, takes a historical and applied approach. It examines Canadian case studies of military disobedience from the War of 1812 through the First World War. Each case study provides a window into the military and social climate of the day, as well as insight into the definition, and on occasion, the evolving nature of military disobedience and discipline over time.

Significantly, *The Apathetic and the Defiant* is another publication in CFLI's Strategic Leadership Writing Project and is published under the auspices of the Canadian Defence Academy Press. Our intention has always been to create a distinct Canadian body of operational leadership knowledge so that professional development centres, military professionals, civilian members of the defence team, scholars, and the public at large could study Canadian examples instead of relying on the experiences of our allies. After all, our military has a rich history that is more pertinent and relevant to our own military culture, temperament, and character.

This book and its companion volumes fill an important gap because they look at the darker side of military operations. Rather than focus on the heroic and successful, they examine the seedier side of the profession of arms. *The Apathetic and the Defiant* provides great insight into what causes disobedience and seeks to understand the relationship between improper conduct and both leadership and situational factors. But rather than rely solely on theory and scholarly interpretation, it describes real events that professionals can analyze and draw timeless lessons from. The next volume, *The Insubordinate and the Noncompliant: Case Studies of Canadian Mutiny and Disobedience, 1920 to Present*, will provide similar examples from the Second World War onwards.

Overall, the series demonstrates that our effort to increase the body of Canadian-specific military literature is being achieved through the collaborative efforts of CFLI, Canadian Forces personnel, academic institutions, individual researchers, and scholars. The work is providing the necessary examples and reference sources for military and civilian institutions across the country, and internationally.

The Apathetic and the Defiant is a significant addition to the project. I believe you will find this book of great interest and value whether you are a military professional or scholar or simply interested in the study of leadership and the profession of arms. As always, we at CFLI invite your comment and discussion.

Colonel Bernd Horn
Deputy Commander
Special Operations Forces Command
Canadian Forces

ACKNOWLEDGEMENTS

As the old saying goes, "You never know what you have until it's gone." Now, with the publication of this volume, I regret having to part ways with so many excellent colleagues who, through their combined efforts, made my burdens light and my toils enjoyable. I can only hope that I will have the pleasure of working with them all again.

From the outset, Colonel Bernd Horn, the director of the Canadian Forces Leadership Institute, gave his usual support and encouragement to both the editor and the project as a whole. His enthusiasm and eagerness to see this volume through was nothing short of inspiring. Without hesitation, he cheerfully provided every resource that one could possibly ask for. Howard G. Coombs, a constant friend and colleague, freely lent his assistance wherever and whenever it was required. My only fear is that I asked too much and did not give enough in return.

I would be remiss if I did not thank Joanne Simms and Carol Jackson (again) for the excellent administrative support that they provided. This volume, as with much else at CFLI, could not have been realized without their professional advice and timely assistance. Warrant Officer Marc Bourque of the Canadian Defence Academy lent his technical expertise whenever it was required, and, I regret to say, it was required much too often. To them all, as always, I offer my most sincere thanks. Michael Carroll and Nigel Heseltine also deserve mention for their efforts in changing a rough manuscript into a polished book.

I must also offer my earnest appreciation to those who contributed to this collection. Besides their regular military and/or academic responsibilities, they all found the time to provide excellent chapters and to endure my many inquiries and requests. Should I have been a burden in any way,

I apologize. Their passion for "things historic" is commendable and, I can only hope, infectious.

A number of individuals deserve special mention for assisting CFLI in acquiring the visual images used in this book. Ted Zuber offered the original artwork that graces the front cover of this volume. His passion for our project was clearly reflected in his willingness to employ his talents and gifts for our purposes. William Constable lent his excellent map-making skills and I am grateful for his work. Janet Lacroix of the Canadian Forces Joint Imagery Centre and France Beauregard and Maggie Arbour-Doucette of the Canadian War Museum, in addition to staff at the Glenbow Museum and Library and Archives Canada, especially Jean Matheson, all contributed their time, energy, and effort without fail.

Finally, I should like to thank my wife, Angela, for again enduring a seemingly endless flow of demands. Being the voice of escape, and at times reason, this volume would not have been possible without her.

Craig Leslie Mantle
Kingston, Ontario

Introduction

CRAIG LESLIE MANTLE

And We do hereby Command them to obey you as their superior Officer, and you to observe and follow such Orders and Directions as from time to time you shall receive from Us or your Superior Officer, according to the Rules and Disciplines of War.[1]

From the highest rank to the lowest, all are required to obey their superiors. Everyone under arms, be it the chief of the defence staff[2] or the most recent recruit, is compelled to follow the legal orders issued by those set over them.[3] Such conformity, of course, is essential for military success. For a variety of reasons though, ranging from failures in leadership to fear, from elitism to stress, and from neglect to sheer apathy, this expected obedience often fails to materialize or appears in a manner that is less than appropriate.[4] To be sure, the refusal of an order can assume many forms, some of which are not entirely noticeable to the casual observer or even to those directly involved. Through the ages, members of the military have found unusual and inventive ways of disguising their disobedience. For instance, they malinger, execute the letter rather than the spirit of an order, and exact forms of revenge to "even the score" with leaders whose conduct they have found objectionable.[5] This brief list is not complete by any means![6] Yet, in other circumstances, the act of refusing to "carry-on" is unmistakable, clear, and obvious. When conditions are bad enough, when all other avenues of redress have been exhausted or when the situation is simply too important to leave without comment and action, soldiers, sailors, and air personnel, either as individuals or as groups, sometimes refuse to follow their superior's direction.

Within the Canadian military experience, acts of disobedience, large or small, have always accompanied honourable conduct in Canada's conflicts or overseas deployments. Such acts have also occurred in peacetime, but appear to be more prevalent when the risks to life are greater, when stress is more plentiful, when the conditions of military service are more austere and when the consequences of poor leadership are more profound. Drawing from the nineteenth and early twentieth centuries, this volume offers a number of case studies that clearly demonstrate that the "bad" has always accompanied the "good." Fortunately, the latter has been, and will surely continue to be, in greater abundance than the former.

This volume is the second in a "collection"[7] of works that seeks to understand the fundamental dynamics of disobedience in a Canadian context by first outlining the reasons that account for the occurrence of such behaviour and then by exploring a multitude of specific examples drawn from all three environments — Army, Navy, and Air Force — in which Canadian personnel have been anything but compliant and willing followers. The opening book in this collection, *The Unwilling and the Reluctant: Theoretical Perspectives on Disobedience in the Military*, published by the Canadian Defence Academy Press in 2006, explores disobedience from a multi-disciplinary perspective. The volume brings together learned studies from such diverse fields as psychology, anthropology, and history to offer a convincing exploration of the reasons why military personnel disobey their legal obligations.[8]

The third book offers historical case studies ranging in date from 1920 to the present and has been edited by Howard Coombs. In a similar manner to the present volume, a conscientious attempt has been made to offer analyses that cover land, sea, and air, and all of Canada's major military contributions throughout the mid to late twentieth century.

Taken together, these works encompass the better part of two centuries of Canadian military history. In the end, they will, in some small measure, provide a more complete and comprehensive understanding of the nation's experiences during its formative conflicts and later commitments.

For reasons of understanding and fluidity, this volume has been divided into two principal sections. The first deals with the nineteenth century and the second is devoted entirely to the First World War era. Given the magnitude of Canada's military contribution from 1914 to 1919, it is only fitting that the bulk of case studies has been drawn from these years. Aside from being organized chronologically, the second section, consisting of seven chapters in total, is also arranged geographically, thus demonstrating that disobedience occurred wherever Canadian soldiers were present, whether at home in Canada after being recruited, in France while engaged in the fighting (or immediately thereafter), or in England awaiting repatriation.

Many of the following chapters go beyond traditionally accepted explanations of certain events, such as those that account for the disturbances in the aftermath of the First World War. In this regard specifically, this volume offers fresh insight into events that have already received some attention from earlier historians and so, in a sense, can be considered somewhat "revisionist." Canadian historiography, with a few notable exceptions, has tended to overlook examples of mutiny and disobedience. As a consequence, many of the following chapters represent new and innovative contributions to the field of military history.[9] Many of these examples, it must be remembered, are being explored for the first time in a focused, concentrated, and academic manner. In this respect, then, this volume embodies a pioneering attempt to uncover and explain some of the lesser-known examples of misconduct.

It is fully expected that other scholars may take issue with certain interpretations offered here, and they are encouraged to do so, for only by examining the problem of disobedience with an eye to the finer nuances will we become more fluent with its origins, dynamics, solutions, and preventative measures. Because many of the following case studies have been attributed to failings in leadership, usually at the officer and senior noncommissioned officer (NCO) levels, those who engaged in illegal and inappropriate conduct have received a fairly sympathetic hearing by many of the volume's contributors. Such a result may have much to do with the manner in which each example has been studied, that is, from the perspective of the participants themselves or from the bottom up. In other instances, though, the blame for inappropriate conduct has been placed squarely and unmistakably on the protagonists.

This volume begins with an interesting analysis of how the mutinies of 1797 that engulfed certain elements of the Royal Navy at Spithead and the Nore had a profound and lasting impact on officer-man relationships that lasted well into the nineteenth century, particularly during the War of 1812. Using a case study approach, Martin Hubley and Thomas Malcomson discuss the dynamics of "promotion of interests" mutinies in which the participants reacted negatively to adverse conditions, such as the tyrannical conduct of their leaders or the all too frequent problems with rationing and pay. In addition, both authors suggest that the lack of stability, or alternatively, the frequent changes in the composition of ships both in terms of sailors and officers, played a role in the mutinies under discussion by disrupting the established system of discipline so crucial to success and, at the same time, by minimizing the opportunities for leaders and followers to interact with one another.

In the next chapter, James Paxton offers a probing examination of the experience of the Lincoln militia during the War of 1812. Although British commanders resented the unpredictability and fickleness of the militia, his discussion reveals that the farmers-cum-soldiers who deserted and returned to their farms were actually caught between the need to defend Upper Canada writ large and their homes and families. The militia would fight (and fight well and be brave), but when they believed that their duties unnecessarily compromised the welfare of their family, they returned to attend to their crops. For the most part, their loyalty was not so much in question, as was their willingness to allow their civil lives to suffer as a result of military obligations.

In Chapter 3, Howard Coombs, in his first of two contributions, discusses the experiences of the Leeds militia during the War of 1812. Forced to participate in the conflict, many militiamen deserted when they perceived their interests to be adversely affected by the war. Coombs argues that over the years, the inhabitants of Leeds and Lansdowne township had developed a shared awareness and a common understanding of their combined interests and resented any infringement, such as prolonged militia service, that jeopardized their success. In response to what they perceived as unnecessary intrusions into their daily lives, many resorted to desertion, while others failed to muster when called upon to do so. In some cases, they even refused to participate wholeheartedly in actions against the enemy.

In many respects, Coombs's and Paxton's chapters run parallel to one another. They point out that, in two areas situated at opposite ends of Lake Ontario, the needs of the government, it would seem, were secondary to those inhabitants who placed the welfare of themselves, their family and their community above all else.

Written by James McKillip, Chapter 4 serves as a bridge between the early and late nineteenth century. He argues convincingly that the less-than-professional behaviour of the Canadian militiamen who travelled west to quell the Métis rebellion in 1870 Manitoba might have encouraged the Métis to take up arms again in 1885 Saskatchewan. McKillip illustrates how Canadian soldiers assaulted the civilian population in and around Winnipeg and, for all intents and purposes, made a mockery of civil authorities, including the police. In accounting for their poor behaviour, he posits that the lack of strict discipline was much to blame, for when disciplinary standards were eventually enforced, though much too late to salvage relations between the militia and the Métis, the violence inflicted by the military on the civilian population abated significantly.

Chapter 5, by Carman Miller, examines the relationship between acts of disobedience and leadership in the context of the South African War. Officers who made few allowances for the cultural nuances of their force — e.g., failing to consider that their soldiers were volunteers, and that officers, NCOs, and men were frequently acquaintances or relatives in civilian life — quickly earned their men's resentment. Their leadership style, when combined with poor conditions of service, caused morale and discipline to wane, sometimes exceptionally.

The role of alcohol in dissolving the standards of discipline is highlighted as well. When used to counter the sapping influence of boredom or to make more enjoyable the imminent prospect of returning home, drink tended to impact negatively upon soldierly behaviour.

Interestingly, Miller takes his discussion of disobedience beyond the usual causes and reveals that nationalistic tensions also contributed to the misconduct of some. When the South African Constabulary was purged of its more rowdy and unsuitable elements, the bulk of the loss unfortunately fell on the Canadians who, on the whole, were not particularly well-suited to sedentary police work. In response, the behaviour of these soldiers-cum-constables left much to be desired as they confronted what they believed was a discriminatory institution dominated by the British who had little time for colonials.

Chapter 6 is the first chapter relating to the First World War era and the beginning of the second section of this book. P. Whitney Lackenbauer presents an interesting account of soldierly misbehaviour in

1916 Canada. The reasons for much of this disobedience stemmed from an overly developed patriotism and a hyper-xenophobia that viewed manifestations of "Germanism" as something to be reviled, and, in some cases, destroyed. Affronts to Canadian soldiers perpetuated by those considered to be "German" were met with swift, destructive, and often violent retribution.

In other instances the insidious effects of alcohol played an important role in the onset of misconduct by lessening inhibitions and providing a contentious issue over which a "dry" Canada could clash with a military culture that encouraged drinking. Although many of the case studies offered in this chapter focus on the inappropriate conduct of certain soldiers, one stellar example is offered wherein proactive leadership actually averted what was quickly promising to be another destructive riot by Canadian soldiers. In this regard specifically, the relationship between competent leadership and both the frequency and severity of disobedience is readily observable.

Chapter 7, my first offering, discusses a mutiny by 18 drivers of the Canadian Army Service Corps in England in November 1917. With so many participants, the reasons for their misconduct are many and diverse, but, by and large, their disobedience stemmed from significant failings in leadership. On the whole, the order that they were expected to follow was so poorly formulated and transmitted that many were completely unaware of the expectations of their superiors. Additionally, many believed that the treatment they were receiving from officers was entirely inappropriate, especially in light of their state of ill health and sacrifices made thus far. When their chain of command proved completely unwilling to hear, let alone act, on their many grievances, they disobeyed an entirely legal order so as to communicate their dissatisfaction.

Chapter 8, written by David Campbell, offers a comparative study of the number and type of disciplinary infractions committed within the many battalions of the 2nd Canadian Infantry Division during the First World War. He observes that the differences between them sometimes resulted from the fact that the soldiers were engaged in action and thus had no opportunity to commit such offences, while the lack of stability within the chain of command upset the smooth functioning of the disciplinary process in other instances, with the unfortunate result that the

20

number of offences tended to increase. In others still, the frequent influx of soldiers to replace casualties resulted in a heightened state of indiscipline as these new battalion members were unacquainted with the requirements of military service and obedience. Not surprisingly, alcohol is also given its due as a catalyst for disobedience. The main contention of this chapter, however, lies in the assertion that lapses in discipline were a failure on the part of leaders, especially officers, to act in a paternalistic manner, that is, in a manner that ensured that their men were cared for in all that affected their welfare. Contented soldiers were less likely to act inappropriately than those who had been neglected. Again in this discussion, the central role leadership plays in either avoiding or encouraging service offences is clearly apparent.

Chapter 9, my second contribution, discusses a small mutiny by soldiers of the 43rd Battalion who, incidentally, were already being punished for earlier breaches of military discipline. The analysis begins with a brief examination of "contractual relationships" through which soldiers believed that in return for their service, sacrifice, and if need be, their lives, their leaders were responsible for providing the necessities of life, for engaging in respectful relationships, and for protecting their welfare by ensuring that their comfort, as much as possible, was considered.

Essentially, First World War soldiers desired adequate leadership in all of its many manifestations, and when this was not forthcoming, the chances that an act of disobedience would occur increased significantly. Specifically, this group of soldiers had not received enough food in their opinion and, when they had the opportunity, they refused to parade until amends had been made. This example is unusual in the Canadian historical record as it is one of the few instances of mutiny that occurred during wartime in the field, although not in the presence of the enemy.

In Chapter 10, Ian McCulloch offers the first example of mutiny and disobedience in the aftermath of the First World War. Reprinted from the *Army Doctrine and Training Bulletin*, now *The Canadian Army Journal*,[10] his analysis contends that the mutiny in the 7th Canadian Infantry Brigade at Nivelles, Belgium, in December 1918, resulted not so much from the soldiers resentment at having to march with full packs, as is commonly asserted, but from their disgust in the quality of their leadership during their attack on Tilloy only a few months earlier.

The Apathetic and the Defiant

Saddled with a new brigade commander who discarded established and proven battle procedure, who failed to fully appreciate the relevant intelligence that he had at his disposal, and who could not, or would not, coordinate his infantry and artillery so that an effective attack might be made, the soldiers thought that their lives were being thrown away needlessly. In response, some later refused to parade when ordered to do so as a means of demonstrating their anger. McCulloch also notes, however, that the officers who should have been attending to the welfare of their men abandoned their subordinates in the post-Armistice period, opting instead to take extended periods of leave. Those who remained, often the inexperienced who had not had a chance to form the bonds necessary to encourage trust and obedience, insisted on peacetime ritual that greatly irritated their war-weary subordinates. By presenting the mutiny in this light, he contends that failings in leadership at many points throughout the brigade's entire command structure contributed to the outbreak of disobedience.

In his second contribution, Chapter 11, Coombs analyzes one of the most famous and well-known mutinies in Canadian history, Kinmel Park. Other interpretations of this episode have tended to focus on "material" causes such as poor food and poor accommodations. Although acknowledging the role played by these elements in encouraging the outbreak of disobedience, he moves beyond these reasons and asserts that the lack of effective communication between leaders and the led, specifically in regard to the reasons behind the repeated delays in repatriation, played an extremely significant role in hastening the onset of mutiny. More than anything else, poor leadership was at the root of the disturbance that cost the lives of a number of Canadian soldiers and resulted in the court-martial of many.

The final chapter, written by Nikolas Gardner, demonstrates that some of the disobedience that Canadian soldiers participated in after the cessation of hostilities while awaiting repatriation to Canada was not due solely to the frustration over repeated delays, as some historians have contended, but, at least in the case of the disturbances witnessed in Epsom, Surrey, from long-standing animosity between Canadian soldiers and the local populace.

The arrest of two Canadians in June 1919 caused this underlying tension to come explosively to the fore. In an attempt to free their incarcerated mates, Canadian soldiers attacked the local police station, thus causing the death of one police officer and the wounding of many more.

22

In recalling this episode, Gardner underscores the difficulties that can arise when the implicit contract binding soldiers to their command structure — in return for their service and adherence to disciplinary norms, subordinates expected to be well-led and properly cared for by those set over them — becomes null and void, as when wartime discipline seemed overly harsh and when soldiers were left with little guidance and purpose.

All in all, a number of important themes can be traced through this book that illuminate leadership's pivotal role in the genesis of disobedient acts. Many of these ideas, given in no particular order below, can be observed with a quick reading of these chapter summaries. The following discussion is not comprehensive by any means, but merely intended to whet the reader's appetite and to illuminate some of the book's most important concepts.

When communication failed, whether it was used to ensure that vital information was disseminated to all or that orders were understood completely, discontent usually resulted among those who would have benefited greatly from possessing the knowledge and clarity in the first place. Had certain soldiers understood *why* they were enduring certain conditions, it is arguable that the mutiny in which they eventually played a part would never have occurred at all.

Communication, however, was a "two-way street," insofar as the disaffected used a variety of means to inform their superiors that all was not well. In many of the examples in the following chapters, mutiny was the primary method of choice after they had attempted (and failed) to bring their complaints to the attention of their superiors through the formal chain of command, as they had been taught and encouraged. To be sure, a disobedient course was not blindly pursued in many of these cases, but embarked upon with the purpose of relating to those in superior positions that problems existed within the command over which they exercised authority. Only after appraising the situation in which they found themselves did many act illegally, and then only for precise reasons and in pursuit of precise objectives.

In addition, improper behaviour did not occur solely between military actors, for in many cases, soldiers terrorized the local civilian population by destroying property, damaging reputations, and in the extreme, taking lives.

Ironically, some soldiers fought directly with the communities they were sworn to protect. Either on their way to war or returning from it, some soldiers became social pariahs in certain Canadian cities or quaint English villages on account of their unruly and undisciplined conduct.

On the whole, the nature of the interaction between soldiers and nearby communities depended on time and place. While some deserted the military to assist their home communities in meeting the requirements of simple and basic survival, as was the case during the War of 1812, others, some 100 years later, assaulted local inhabitants out of spite.

As will be surmised, discipline usually suffered at the end of hostilities, especially when leaders abandoned their responsibilities towards their men. Rather than ensuring that their subordinates were well-looked after, both in terms of their physical well-being and their morale, many officers simply left them to their own devices. The unfortunate result was that the normal chain of command, which usually held all to a reasonable (and in some cases, excellent) standard of discipline, disappeared, with predictable results. In many instances, officers took leave of their men in order that they might enjoy the entertainment offered in nearby cities such as London or Paris.

Even in wartime, leaders who failed to act when confronted with disobedience, or who simply "looked the other way," inadvertently encouraged their soldiers to continue such conduct. However, when disciplinary standards were enforced and maintained, the frequency of such acts tended to subside. With rare exceptions, instances of disobedience and mutiny did not occur in the presence of the enemy; they occured in rear areas well away from the fighting.

The frequent changeover of both officers and men within an infantry battalion or aboard a naval vessel also created problems. On many occasions, the trust and respect that permeated the relationship between superior and subordinate was modified by new leaders who imposed their own personality and style on their command, thus upsetting arrangements that had served well in the past.

Through continuous service with their men, leaders set the disciplinary tone of their command and communicated to their subordinates, through deed or word, what they expected in terms of behaviour. The loss of a superior forced subordinates to begin afresh in building a relationship with their new leader. Additionally, new influxes of either sailors or soldiers, some of whom lacked a solid grounding in what was expected of them in terms of their behaviour, also accounted for an increase in the number of disobedient acts.

Not surprisingly, given the nature of their activities, the following studies reveal just how strong the intensity of the connection between soldiers, namely comradeship, truly was. Whether breaking their pals out of cells, "selectively remembering" only those details that would not incriminate their chums, or pursuing the path of mutiny and disobedience together, their collective actions demonstrate the negative effects of cohesion when such bonding is not directed towards reaching the legitimate goals of the military and government whom they served.[11] Because soldiers worked together, endured many of the same hardships and risks, and were subject to the same rules and regulations, it is not surprising to learn that they often acted improperly in concert as well.

And finally, soldiers expected many things from those set over them. Their wishes, as many authors suggest in the following pages, were both reasonable and justified. By desiring respectful treatment, adequate food, a responsive chain of command and competence on the battlefield, many took illegal action to protest when their leaders failed to deliver. It seems apt to suggest that many believed that they had entered into a form of "social contract" with the military, and that, in return for their service, they were somehow "entitled" to certain concessions, not the least of which was adequate leadership in all that that entails. And perhaps this fact is one of the most important lessons to be taken from this volume: those leaders who neglected their men in whatever manner and for whatever reason could usually expect a negative (and sometimes disobedient) reaction from those whom they affected. Conversely, those leaders who strove to treat their subordinates fairly, with respect, and who ensured their well-being generally received their trust, and more important, their obedience.

Once again, it is sincerely hoped that this volume will be of use to all who are interested in military leadership, but especially those who are actually charged with leading soldiers, sailors, and air personnel daily, in harm's way or not. The fact that this book offers historical accounts should not deter anyone from engaging in fruitful discussions about the topics raised here for many of the causes of past disobedience were the same as they are today, with a few notable exceptions of course.

The editor, along with the authors whose work appears in this volume, can only hope that this collective effort will in some small measure contribute to a greater understanding of our military past. Should this be the ultimate result, we will all be content and satisfied.

NOTES

1. First World War officer's commission, as cited in Desmond Morton, *When Your Number's Up: The Canadian Soldier in the First World War* (Toronto: Random House, 1993), 96.

2. In Canada, in accordance with the principle of civil control of the military, the chief of the defence staff takes direction from the prime minister, through the minister of national defence. Further to this point, "*The Constitution Act* of 1867 provides for establishing armed forces at the federal level. Their command, control and administration are set out in the NDA [National Defence Act], and the Government of Canada determines their mandate, mission and roles in the defence of Canada through legislation and Cabinet direction." See *Duty with Honour: The Profession of Arms in Canada* (Kingston: Canadian Defence Academy — Canadian Forces Leadership Institute, 2003), 13. For a brief legal description of this arrangement, see National Defence Act, Section 3 (Establishment of the Department), Section 4 (Minister) and Section 18 (Chief of the Defence Staff).

3. Military personnel are permitted, nay encouraged, to disobey those orders that are "manifestly unlawful," or in other words, illegal. As an aside, one of the principles contained within the "Statement of Defence Ethics" encourages members of both the Canadian Forces and the Department of National Defence to "Obey and Support *Lawful* Authority." (Italics added by editor for emphasis.)

4. Some of the more significant causes of disobedience are explained in detail in Craig Leslie Mantle, ed., *The Unwilling and the Reluctant: Theoretical Perspectives on Disobedience in the Military* (Kingston: CDA Press, 2006). A discussion of the relationship between elitism and disobedience can also be found in Colonel Bernd Horn, "The Dark Side to Elites: Elitism as a Catalyst for Disobedience," *The Canadian Army Journal*, Vol. 8.4 (Winter 2005), 65–79.

5. For a recent example of Canadian soldiers failing to conduct a patrol in Afghanistan as they had been ordered, in effect avoiding danger, see Adam Day, "Somalia Redux? The Yahoo Defence, Terminal Bullshit Syndrome and the Myth of the Isolated Incident," in Colonel Bernd Horn, ed., *From the Outside Looking In: Media and Defence Analyst Perspectives on Canadian Military Leadership* (Kingston: CDA Press, 2005), 149–51.

INTRODUCTION

6. See Richard Holmes, *Acts of War: The Behavior of Men in Battle* (New York: The Free Press, 1985), 316–31, for an interesting account of how soldiers of many ages in time have sought to disobey their orders.

7. These volumes, it must be noted, can be used independently and they can be read in any order without a loss in understanding. Since they discuss disobedience in one form or another, from a theoretical or historical perspective, these works naturally lend themselves to being grouped together as a related whole.

8. See Note 4.

9. Some authors who have already tackled the issues of mutiny and disobedience, and discipline in general, include Desmond Morton, "'Kicking and Complaining': Demobilization Riots in the Canadian Expeditionary Force, 1918–19," *Canadian Historical Review*, LXI, No. 3 (1980), 334–60; Desmond Morton, "The Supreme Penalty: Canadian Deaths by Firing Squad in the First World War," *Queen's Quarterly*, Vol. 79, No. 3 (1972), 345–52; P. Whitney Lackenbauer, "The Military and 'Mob Rule:' The CEF Riots in Calgary, February 1916," *Canadian Military History*, Vol. 10, No. 1 (2001), 31–43; P. Whitney Lackenbauer, "Under Siege: The CEF Attack on the RNWMP Barracks in Calgary, October 1916," *Alberta History*, Vol. 49, No. 3 (2001), 2–12; Christopher M. Bell and Bruce A. Elleman, eds., *Naval Mutinies of the Twentieth Century: An International Perspective* (London: Frank Cass, 2003); Andrew B. Godefroy, *For Freedom and Honour? The Story of the 25 Canadian Volunteers Executed in the First World War* (Nepean, ON: CEF Books, 1998); and Chris Madsen, *Another Kind of Justice: Canadian Military Law from Confederation to Somalia* (Vancouver: University of British Columbia Press, 1999).

10. For the original article, see Lieutenant-Colonel Ian McCulloch, "Crisis in Leadership: The Seventh Brigade & the Nivelles 'Mutiny,' 1918," *Army Doctrine and Training Bulletin*, Vol. 3, No. 2 (Summer 2000), 35–46.

11. Donna Winslow, for instance, has examined how an over-developed and inwardly-focused cohesion, where soldiers protected one another from those considered outside the group, impacted negatively upon discipline within the Canadian Airborne Regiment around the time of the torture-killing of a youth in Somalia. See, for instance, Donna Winslow, "Misplaced Loyalties: Military Culture and the Breakdown of Discipline in Two Peace Operations," in Carol McCann and Ross Pigeau, eds., *The Human in Command: Exploring the Modern Military Experience* (New York: Kluwer Academic/Plenum Publishers, 2000), 293–309, and Donna Winslow, *The Canadian Airborne Regiment in Somalia — A Socio-Cultural Inquiry* (Ottawa: Commission of Inquiry into the Deployment of Canadian Forces to Somalia, 1997).

Part One

The Nineteenth Century

1 ↣

"The People, from Being Tyrannically Treated, Would Rejoice in Being Captured by the Americans": Mutiny and the Royal Navy During the War of 1812[1]

MARTIN HUBLEY AND THOMAS MALCOMSON

The concept of naval mutiny has been well established in popular culture by the Hollywood image of the *Bounty* mutineers and their rebellion against a purportedly tyrannical Captain Bligh, and other bloody incidents involving large-scale, forcible takeover of a vessel by its crew. Yet, the reality of naval mutiny in the eighteenth century is quite different from this popular and largely inaccurate image. As several authors have shown, "seizure of power" mutinies, although not entirely unknown, were rare in the Royal Navy (RN) during this period. Mutiny was more likely to take the form of a labour stoppage over grievances affecting working conditions such as bad food, lack of or delays in pay, or harsh treatment by one or more officers, petty officers, or warrants. This type of "promotion of interests" mutiny has been defined as "a collective action to improve or maintain the position of the group with respect to its income or other work conditions."[2]

In the eighteenth century, RN officers used the word "mutiny" to describe individual acts of disobedience, collective resistance, and the rare, violent seizures of vessels in which officers were overthrown and killed. "Promotion of interest" mutinies, generally involving a minimum of violence, had a long history in the eighteenth century RN and were tied to a similar tradition of protest and mob action ashore at this time.[3] Yet, before the 1780s, large-scale violence was rare unless one side or the other violated informal "rules of mutiny."[4] Historian Brian Lavery estimates that between 1793 and 1815, 12 to 15 formal courts-martial for mutiny (of all types) occurred annually; this number rises to 1,000 incidents in total when the summary punishments that were imposed through the authority of an individual captain are included.[5]

Before and during the War of 1812, the "promotion of interests" mutiny was by far the most common variety in North American waters and it is with this form that this chapter is primarily concerned.[6] This discussion will: (1) briefly sketch the causes and after-effects of the 1797 Spithead and Nore mutinies on the RN; (2) examine how both the concepts of naval mutiny and the consequences of Spithead and the Nore were transferred to North American waters prior to the War of 1812; (3) assess the impact that they may have had on vessels during the war itself.

A case study approach will be used, with incidents on three vessels being examined.[7] Immediately after Spithead, HMS *Latona* (38 guns, henceforth only the number will appear) suffered a mutiny in St. John's, Newfoundland that almost spread throughout the other ships on that station. Two incidents during the War of 1812 itself, those on HMS *Epervier* (18) and HMS *Espiegle*, will shed light on how the collective resistance of seamen contributed to the loss of the *Epervier* to the enemy and to the dismissal of *Espiegle*'s "tyrannical" captain by court-martial after a number of unsavoury events, including a possible failure to engage the enemy.

SPITHEAD AND THE NORE

It is impossible to discuss mutiny in the RN during the War of 1812 without first outlining the importance of the great mutinies of Spithead and the Nore, as they set the precedent and context for discipline and resistance in the RN throughout the world in the following decades. There are many studies of the events of Spithead and the Nore, for these mutinies threatened not only the existence of the navy, but ultimately that of the British polity and empire itself, both of which rested upon the navy and its exercise of sea power.[8]

When the great wars against France began in 1793, the size of the RN quickly ballooned from 16,000 seamen and marines in 1792 to almost 86,000 in late 1794, and to over 130,000 by 1813. Although many of these men were volunteers, some were "encouraged" to volunteer, only when faced with the alternative of impressment, so as to receive the King's bounty. From

1795 onwards, a number of Quota Acts ensured that local authorities would raise fixed numbers of men for the service, all of whom were to be volunteers on paper. Most of the 30,000 men raised by this measure were young tradesmen from the countryside seeking employment, and not, as is often portrayed, highly educated, and literate political troublemakers.[9]

Others argue that although there may not have been obvious outside political influence on the mutineers in the form of a guiding hand, there were "men involved who were conscious of wider issues of freedom and tyranny." Such "issues" included the 1792 publication of Thomas Paine's *The Rights of Man* and the events of the French Revolution, as well as the political activities of the London Corresponding Societies. Actual radicals and revolutionaries on the lower deck were likely few in number and unable to dramatically influence the views and later demands of most of the seamen of the fleet.[10] Yet these new views, combined with the rapid growth in the size of the service and the influx of landsmen untrained in the way of the sea, meant that problems of morale and discipline in the navy grew in scope and difficulty.[11]

Throughout the months of February and March 1797, several anonymous petitions were received at the Admiralty and by Lord Howe, who was then in his last days as commander of the Channel Fleet, that asked for improvements in pay, which had not changed since 1652.[12] Neither Howe nor the Admiralty took the petitions seriously, so by 16 April, having waited weeks for a reply to their grievances, the seamen started a general mutiny at the fleet's base at Spithead, near Portsmouth, by collectively refusing to make sail. In the following days, elected delegates from each vessel negotiated with a series of senior officers, all the while proclaiming their loyalty to the monarch and their willingness to weigh anchor to fight the French should the enemy's main fleet at Brest sortie. The sailors also requested improvements in victualling and in medical treatment of wounded men, and began to take more note of officers who maltreated their men or used excessive punishment to maintain discipline. It would appear that another unstated grievance was the bounties paid under the Quota Acts to landsmen, who were often receiving far more than the seamen who had enlisted as volunteers before the Acts. Most of the demands were eventually met, and on 23 April, a royal pardon was proclaimed, thus ending the first mutiny.

Foot-dragging by Parliament in enacting the new measures, with the cost of improved wages and victuals estimated at some £536,000 per annum in the midst of a wartime fiscal crisis, resulted in the outbreak of a second mutiny on 7 May, this time with more violence.[13] Some 100 officers, including two admirals and 10 captains, almost one-fifth of those present, were sent ashore by the mutineers. The men also took effective control of the fleet.

The now-retired Lord Howe, using the high regard in which the men held him to his advantage, negotiated on behalf of the king to persuade the men that their grievances had been acknowledged and would be corrected. Parliament finally passed the Act to do so on 9 May. The mutiny was ended by 15 May when Howe additionally agreed to allow the removal of unpopular officers, without the permission of the Admiralty who were outraged at this action.

By now, another mutiny had occurred at the Nore anchorage near the mouth of the River Thames on 12 May. The Nore was not a fleet base like Spithead, but a recruiting nexus and an anchorage used by ships making passage to and from riverside dockyards like Chatham and Sheerness. The Nore mutineers desired the Spithead concessions (that, unbeknownst to them, the rest of the navy had already received), and changes to the *Articles of War,* regular pay, advanced wages for pressed sailors, additional leave rights, and a larger, more equitable share of prize money, as well as pardons for deserters and a veto on officer appointments. Given the absence of a permanent fleet at the Nore that was under the control of the mutineers, and the lack of public support after the Spithead compromises had been granted, the Admiralty refused to make any further concessions. By 27 May, the incident had become more threatening since the North Sea squadron off Yarmouth had mutinied and sailed to the Nore to join the vessels there.[14]

Reinforced, the mutineers posed a strategic threat with their attempts to blockade the Thames and the important London trade. The absent North Sea squadron increased the risk of an expedition by the Dutch fleet, which it was supposed to be blockading. This all contributed to a harder Admiralty line. Amid news of earlier concessions and argument among the ship's delegates, the mutiny eventually petered out because of a lack of supplies and support. Loyal seamen and vessels deserted the mutineers or persuaded their compatriots to do so, forcibly or otherwise. By 13 June, it was over.[15] No courts-martial were held on the royally pardoned mutineers of Spithead, although over 400 sailors were tried at the Nore. Sixty men were condemned to death, flogging, or imprisonment, but after royal pardons of mercy had been proclaimed, no more than two-dozen were actually hanged.[16]

The Spithead mutiny has often been portrayed as being led by some combination of political outsiders, Irish republicans or Quota men. In fact, the leaders were the flesh and blood of the navy, that is, able seamen and petty officers with years of service to their name, such as Valentine Joyce, a 26-year-old quartermaster's mate. It remains unclear who was behind the Nore mutiny, apart from its spokesman, Richard Parker, an educated Quota man. It is believed that, as in Spithead, long-serving petty officers and seamen likely comprised the main impetus and that there was little, if any, external influence. Yet, there were definite signs that within the ranks of the lower deck, "... time-honored traditions of patriotism and loyalty to the Crown were perforce making room for novel concepts of fundamental human rights."[17]

The great mutinies radically changed the attitudes of both seamen and officers in the RN and it is this legacy that would remain present in the fleet during the War of 1812. Historian N.A.M. Rodger has identified both short-term and long-term changes that flowed from the mutiny. He notes, "In the immediate aftermath of the mutinies, the men were disturbed and excited, and the officers were badly frightened. No Captain now knew where he stood.... The weaker Captains lost their nerve, and the tougher ones reacted with severity to the slightest sign of trouble."[18] Over the longer-term, the Admiralty realized that the concessions made at Spithead called into question the ability of officers to command as they desired, and although they were quick to claim that no further demands for dismissals of officers would be tolerated, seamen now believed that they had the right to make such requests. The Admiralty was determined to ensure that the new seamen's "rights" acquired at Spithead did not extend to questioning techniques of command or expelling officers. Lord St. Vincent quickly demonstrated a more strict approach to discipline in the Mediterranean squadron under his command, and a new policy of proferring Royal Marine enforcement of discipline on restive seamen became more prominent. New anonymous petitions were now treated as mutiny from the outset.[19]

Petty officers and long serving seamen were often the leaders of mutinies, as seamen would only follow those whom they respected and admired. Yet, they were also viewed as the "natural aristocracy" of the lower deck and key to its discipline, because they were the interface between officers and seamen. Allowing Marine landsmen to usurp the role of disciplinarian, undermined respect between sailors and their superiors, turned the naval world of the lower deck upside down, and eroded its long-term stability.[20] After the Nore, there were at least 15 other single-ship mutinies in the navy during 1797.[21] The *Latona* mutiny in St. John's, Newfoundland, provides an example of how this changing social world and the new reliance on the marines and brute force to maintain authority, in lieu of leadership and negotiation, was transferred to North America.

HMS *LATONA*

HMS *Latona*, a fifth-rate frigate with an official complement of 284 men, was built in 1781 and last commissioned in 1792. It was directly involved in the second mutiny at Spithead between 7 May and 15 May 1797, immediately before leaving for Newfoundland, but had missed the earlier mutiny between 16 April and 23 April as it had been refitting at Sheerness. The following summary of events is based on the surviving logs of its sea officers and master, and its muster books that shed new light on events in England and in Newfoundland.[22] Earlier accounts of the *Latona* mutiny, such as that by Captain A. Fisk, have generally focused on a purported passage from Spithead to the Nore during the mutiny at the latter anchorage near Sheerness and the disaffection of its crew. This unrest, moreover, was supposedly because the *Latona* had received pressed men and convicts to fill out its complement while at Sheerness. Yet, the logs and musters seem to cast doubt on the reasons for disaffection, the number of pressed men onboard, where they joined, and whether the *Latona* had even been present at the Nore during the mutiny there. An analysis of Admiralty correspondence also indicates that there may have been more widespread pay and victualling problems throughout the Newfoundland squadron.[23]

On 15 April 1797, one day before the start of the first Spithead mutiny, the *Latona's* captain, Arthur Kaye Legge, was given a new commission to take command of the *Cambrian* (40).[24] He had been the captain of the *Latona* for some years and was replaced on 26 April by John Bligh, a follower of William Waldegrave.[25] On 14 April 1797, 32 men of the *Latona*, more than two-thirds of them rated as able-bodied seamen and petty officers, were also discharged to the *Cambrian*. This represented some 16 percent of the 200 seamen borne for pay on the *Latona's* books at that date.

It was a fairly common practice at this time for officers to develop a following of men who moved with them from ship to ship. Legge undoubtedly wanted to take some experienced hands and familiar faces with him to the *Cambrian*. The 32 who transferred included his cook, clerk, ship's carpenter, ship's surgeon, three volunteer boys, and two midshipmen.[26]

The first mutiny at Spithead ended by 23 April, and on 27 April, the Honourable William Waldegrave, Vice-Admiral of the Blue, and his servant, came aboard in preparation for the upcoming voyage to Newfoundland. Waldegrave would soon take command of the Newfoundland station and act as governor of the colony. But by 8 May, the trouble had started anew at Spithead. That afternoon, the captain's log notes that the ship's company forced him to turn a boatswain and a master's mate out of the ship. Yet, even as the mutiny was underway, the logs show that cleaning and repairing the ship and rigging, loading stores, and other ship's business and duties proceeded normally.

The ship's company then twice insisted on the ship being taken to St. Helen's anchorage where the rest of the mutineers were mooring. On the first occasion, on 9 May, the captain "thought it prudent to comply" for the safety of the ship, but returned to Spithead the same day. On the afternoon of 11 May, the ship's company came aft to the quarterdeck, thus violating the sanctum of the captain and officers. When the captain and the ship's officers spoke against joining the mutiny, the men insisted, and sent the officers ashore, with Admiral Waldegrave perhaps among them, as the log records that his flag was struck that day.

Now commanded by the master, the *Latona* slipped out of Spithead and anchored again at nearby St. Helen's. That same day, at the height of the mutiny, Waldegrave was apparently occupied by changes in victualling, with his correspondence acknowledging receipt of a request from the Admiralty to authorize a 16-ounce (454.6-gram) cheese ration for all of his sailors.[27]

The next day, the crew again changed their mind and asked for the barge to be sent for the captain and officers so they could rejoin the ship. Once they had done so, *Latona* again returned to Spithead. Over the next few days, the various delegates of the ships met with Lord Howe, and by 16 May, the mutiny had ended.

On 25 May, 27 new men were transferred aboard the *Latona* from the *Royal William* to replace those who had left for the *Cambrian* and to fill other empty berths among the *Latona*'s crew. All the men were untrained landsmen. At least nine were Scots and five Irish.[28] On 26 May, Waldegrave returned to the *Latona* and re-hoisted his flag. Unfortunately, there seems to be no surviving record of his experiences or views on the mutineers.

On 27 May, only 12 days after the end of the second mutiny at Spithead, and while the events at the Nore were still in progress and the Yarmouth mutiny was just beginning, the *Latona* set sail from Spithead. In company with the *Adelphi* (18) and *Nereid* (36), it was to escort a convoy to St. John's and join the Newfoundland station, while the two other warships were to accompany it to St. John's, and then make their own way to Halifax to join the North American station.[29]

Its voyage would not be trouble free. After weighing anchor, the men who had been transferred from the *Royal William,* who were apparently volunteers, complained that they had not yet received their bounty.[30] They protested loudly enough that Waldegrave delayed his departure and allowed them to proceed to the dockyard where the commissioner, Charles Saxton, refused to pay them, it being a Sunday. Waldegrave was forced to anchor overnight so that arrangements could be made on the next day. The Admiralty later indicated that Saxton had acted incorrectly.[31]

The *Latona* finally set sail from England on 10 June, having been delayed both by the bounty issue and unfavourable winds.[32] Waldegrave was worried that any news of the proceedings at the Nore might incite his crew to rise up again. Although still in the English Channel, and dogged by bad weather, Waldegrave wrote to the secretary to the Board of Admiralty, Evan Nepean:

> it gives me much concern to inform their Lordships that from certain symptoms I discover'd in the Ships Company The Day we sail'd from Torbay, I am persuaded that had we once more anchored in any Port in

England that the People wou'd not have again put to Sea. Things at present are perfectly quiet, but the minds of the men seem to be in that state where the sight of an inflammatory Newspaper or any verbal account (no matter from whom) of the Seditious proceeding at Sheerness wou'd render them again wholly ungovernable.[33]

On 27 June, the *Latona* briefly anchored in St. Michael's Roads in the Azores, bringing news of the mutinies and Admiralty concessions to the ships of the Mediterranean Fleet that it found there. Its men wrote to the crew of the *Romulus* (36) frigate claiming, "… we are to have better Usage than we have had of late … nor a bad officer is allowed to stay in the ship." Furthermore, they asserted, sailors only had to put their complaints in writing, using precise terms, "and you May Depend on getting redress even from the captain to the Least officer in the ship." This prompted the men of the *Romulus* to mutiny, turning two forward guns aft at the quarterdeck, and demanding the expulsion of two officers. The captain, who promised no repercussions, quelled the affair.[34]

The *Latona* finally arrived in St. John's on 19 July (without the convoy, which had been lost sight of in thick fog some days earlier), finding the *Romney* (50), *Venus* (38), *Mercury* (28), and *Pluto* (14) already in port.[35] In terms of punishments, the voyage was relatively uneventful. Between the departure from England and arrival in Newfoundland, the logs record that only two men were punished, Jonathan Butler with 12 lashes for striking a superior and George Smith with 24 lashes for "Mutiny, Disobedience of Orders and Insolence to his Superior Officer."[36] Waldegrave almost immediately transferred his flag to the larger and more spacious *Romney*. On 22 July, Captain Frank Sotheron[37] came aboard the *Latona,* along with a new first lieutenant, Jason Slade, and relieved John Bligh of command of the ship. Their first act was to punish George Smith again with another 12 lashes for striking his superior.

On 22 July, Waldegrave wrote to London stating that the *Pluto* would soon return to England, as it was "in a bad state" and its crew had five years of pay in arrears.[38] The *Romney* sailed on 23 July and Waldegrave again hoisted his flag aboard the *Latona.* According to the logs, there was little warning of the events that were about to occur on the *Latona*. Between this date and the mutiny on 3 August, there were only two unusual incidents. On 28 July, William Courtney was punished with a dozen lashes "for Drunkenness and insolence to his superior Officer;" the same day, over 50 pounds of butter and 100 pounds of cheese were condemned as rotten.

On 25 July, the *Latona* discharged 39 men to the *Romney* upon the latter's return, some of whom it had been carrying as supernumeraries from England, and received in return some 30 men from that ship. It is of interest to examine the turnover of its crew as well as its ethnic composition at this point. The *Latona* only had a few foreign-born seamen, much lower than the figures of 10 to 14 percent, commonly accepted during this period, but a high percentage of non-English sailors, mainly Scottish and Irish.[39] Its muster for 30 July 1797, just before the mutiny in St. John's, shows that it had 43 landsmen, 42 ordinary seamen, and 94 able-bodied seamen. In this group of 179, of those whose place of birth was indicated, roughly 50 percent were English, 21 percent Scottish, 15 percent Irish, and three percent Welsh.[40] Among petty officers and seamen rated in other areas, such as mates and quarter-gunners, the picture is also varied. Of 53 men in this category, approximately 53 percent were English, nine percent Scottish, seven percent Welsh, six percent Irish, and four percent foreign-born.[41]

Between 1 January and 1 August 1797, some 81 men had joined the ship, or 36 percent of the number of men borne for pay on 30 July, while 91 men, or 40 percent, had been discharged. Another 10 men had been discharged to sick quarters in that same period and 14 men had taken the opportunity to desert from the vessel.[42] All in all, some 117 men, or 52 percent of the men borne for pay on the books, had been discharged for various reasons in a six-month period, with only 81 replacing them. Much of this turnover had resulted from the exchanges with the *Cambrian, Royal William*, and *Romney*. It would seem that the *Latona* was an unsettled vessel with regard to both composition and the stability of its crew, but not entirely for the reasons given in earlier accounts of the mutiny.

Exactly what transpired on 3 August may never be known, but Waldegrave's correspondence indicates that it was a more serious incident than what has been portrayed in subsequent accounts.[43] His letter to William Cavendish-Bentinck, the Duke of Portland, the home secretary, and secretary of state responsible for Newfoundland, is worth quoting at length:

As the very attrocious [*sic*] behaviour of the Latona's Ships Company at this place will no doubt be talked of in England, and the circumstances greatly exaggerated, I shall be obliged to enter into a more minute detail of the whole of the affair, than at first may appear as coming within your Grace's department.

On the 3rd Inst. The Foretopmen of the Latona refused to go aloft, and, in a body, desired to be put in Irons. On Captain Sotheron's proceeding to punish the Ring leader, the Men swore he should not be punished; however upon all the Officers drawing their Swords, and the Marines presenting their bayonets (on which some of the mutineers pricked themselves before they would retreat) the punishment was executed. The language afterwards of the Seamen when in their Hammocks was terrible. The Marines were threatened to be thrown overboard, and bloody work promised as soon as the Ship shou'd again be in blue water. The conduct of these wretches on shore has been no less wicked and daring — They have certainly endeavour'd to sow sedition within the Garrison, besides committing many outrages on divers occasions. On Sunday the 6th Inst. A Ship having the preceding day brought the joyful tidings of Parker's execution, and the Mutiny in the Fleet in consequence being quell'd in England, I thought it would be a proper opportunity to address a division of the Latona's Ship's Company previous to their entering the Church. This I did ... the Seamen at the time being surrounded by the Marines, Royal Artillery and Flank Companies of the Royal Newfoundland Regiment. My speech seemed not only to effect the Mutineers, but most of the bystanders, both Military and Civil. Upon the whole ... it was of much Service as will appear by the enclosed Addresses which speedily followed.

41

> All these Addresses, together with their answers, have been stuck up in the Latona, so that at this moment the Men appear totally … full of contrition: how far such appearance to be depended on, time will Shew.[44]

It is also worth examining the language used in the addresses made by Waldegrave to his seamen, their responses to him, and Waldegrave's subsequent reply. Specifically, the use of the terms "Englishmen" and "Briton," or "British," perhaps sheds some light on Waldegrave's views of the non-English seamen in his squadron. The address made on 3 August states:

> The Commander in Chief cannot help expressing his indignation on hearing the scandalous and mutinous behaviour of the Seamen of His Majesty's Ship Latona, and the more particularly after their most Solemn promise, at St. Michael's to ever behave themselves with obedience to their Officers. Until their Conduct is thoroughly alter and they can act like true Englishmen, they may rely upon every indulgence with held from them, and on being treated with that severity which their base proceedings so justly deserve. The Commander in Chief feels the highest satisfaction to learn that the Petty Officers, and some of the Seamen, and the whole of the Marines of the Latona, have behav'd with such exemplary conduct, and have proved themselves to be true and faithful Servants to their King and Country, and he returns them his thanks accordingly.[45]

As the mutiny appeared to worsen, Waldegrave upped the ante with his address to the marines and seamen as they went to church on 6 August. After first thanking his marines for their steady support, he noted the esteem felt by the inhabitants of St. John's for them, while pointing out that those same inhabitants viewed the *Latona*'s seamen with "horror and detestation … considering the infamy of their conduct both on Shore and a Float." The admiral went on to address the sailors:

In saying this you are not to suppose that I do not believe there is a single honest man and lover of his King and Country among you, on the contrary, I hope there are many; but if I am to judge from your conduct, I must think that the Majority of you are either Villains or Cowards. If the greater number of you are against your Officers and refuse to obey their lawful commands, I have a right to say that you are traitors to your King and Country; if there are only a few bad men among you, which you pretend to be the case, I maintain that you are a set of dastardly Cowards for suffering yourselves to be bullied by a few villains, who wish for nothing better than to see us become the Slaves of France … all the other Ships of the Squadron are belov'd and respect'd whilst Men, Women and Children here shun the Latona's mad dogs. Nay there is not a single Ship in the Squadron that will associate with you....[46]

Waldegrave informed the men that he had given directions to the local magistrates to imprison or flog any sailors who committed crimes ashore, and to only feed them a diet of bread and water as they had "forfeited the Title of British Seamen." Noting that they had been eager for news of their "Great Delegate Parker" and the Nore mutiny, the admiral sternly told them that Parker had been hanged, and although the men "look'd up to him as an example whilst he was in his Glory," they should now "look to his End as an example." He went on to argue that they could "reap some real advantage from contemplating the Condition of this vile incendiary." Emphasising that his address was targeted only at the "bad men" among the *Latona's* company, and that "true-born Englishmen" would not be deluded by such villains, "who are not Seamen, and can only maintain themselves by rapine and plunder," Waldegrave pleaded with the sailors to "come forth nobly as British Seamen" and retrieve their honour by turning in the mutineers.[47]

Waldegrave then warned that if the mutiny continued, its ringleaders would be put to death and that orders had been given to the artillery batteries in St. John's "to burn the Latona with red-hot Shot in case you drive me, by your mutinous behaviour, to an extremity." Recalling the "mutinous and traitorous" spectre of Spithead and the hypocrisy of the seamen's behaviour, Waldegrave noted that even when the mutineers had been in command of the *Latona,* discipline had been ruthlessly enforced, but:

> now that the King's Officers are once again restored to
> Command, you seem to think that all discipline should be
> at an end, and that you may get drunk, fly in the face of
> your Officers, disobey their Commands, stay on shore as
> long as you please, abuse and plunder the Inhabitants, and
> in short commit every enormity that merits the Gallows.

Finally, the admiral concluded his address with more appeals to the men to reflect upon their honour and loyalty and to " ... go into Church and pray to God to inspire you with such Sentiments as may acquire you the respect and love of your Countrymen in this World and eternal happiness in the next."[48]

As had occurred at Spithead and the Nore, the *Latona* mutiny further engendered a sense of suspicion and fear between officers and men and with the other military units stationed in St. John's. As the nineteenth century historian of Newfoundland, Charles Pedley, observed, "For a season men seemed not to know who to trust, and each one felt himself an object whom others regarded with distrust."[49] In light of this, Waldegrave received a series of sycophantic letters from his marine and petty officers, as well as from the various elements of the garrison ashore, pledging their loyalty to the King and country, with the Royal Newfoundland Regiment offering a reward of 20 guineas for any person who turned in a mutineer, followed by the artillery garrison offering a 30 guinea reward.

The admiral-cum-governor carefully replied to each of them in similar fashion, thanking them for their support and loyalty and ensuring them that it would be brought to the attention of his superiors in Britain.[50] Perhaps most important was his correspondence with the marines of the *Latona.* Sergeant John Williams wrote to Waldegrave thanking him for his address and noting that the marines:

> look with Horror and Indignation on every Symptom
> of Mutiny and disaffection, so are we determined to

support with our Lives, our Gracious Sovereign and
present glorious Constitution.

We know that every true-born Briton is indissolubly
attached to our happy Government, and that no individual except the most abandoned Wretch, the most diabolical Miscreant, can ever attempt to violate the present
sacred Order of Things.[51]

Waldegrave effusively acknowledged the "very Loyal and Manly
address" of the marines in a separate letter, no doubt well aware of their
crucial role in maintaining discipline on his ships and of what disaster
might occur should they ever side with the mutineers.[52]

The mutiny continued for several days. It is unclear what actions the
mutineers took while ashore, but it was obviously enough to turn the
townsfolk and other military forces against them. Another three able-
bodied seamen, all Irish, took the opportunity presented by the mutiny
to desert in St. John's on 12 August, while correspondence between the
two sides continued.[53] Astonished at Waldegrave's allegations, the men
protested their innocence and loyalty, while acknowledging that a minority had behaved in an unbecoming manner because of drunkenness, and
calling for "the severest Punishment that can be inflicted, tho humane"
for any disloyal man. They noted Waldegrave's positive reply to the
Newfoundland Regiment of Volunteers' offer of a reward of 20 guineas
for anyone who provided the names of mutineers. The seamen argued
that they were "as loyal as any Regiment or other set of Men whatsoever"
to King and Constitution, and to prove it, they offered a reward of 50
guineas to anyone who would submit names of men for punishment.[54]

Waldegrave was not impressed, noting that their conduct had seriously alarmed the inhabitants of St. John's. He acknowledged that
drunkenness had been a factor, hoping that the men were "heartily
ashamed and truly repentant." Yet he continued to question their claims
of loyalty, noting that:

from the first of the breaking out of the Mutiny in the
Fleet, you have been ever among the most seditious,

and since your arrival here, your insolence to your
Officers and your positive disobedience of their Orders
have merited Death.

Waldegrave told them that their "future conduct can alone convince
of your real repentance of your heretofore scandalous and rebellious
behaviour" and restore their loyalty. As to the question of a reward, the
admiral noted that their offer would be "highly meritorious" if it were not
for the fact that the men had "the power every day of your lives to bring
forward the Ring-leaders of your late diabolical proceeding." Until they
did so, Waldegrave's opinion would not alter, and he and his officers
would never have confidence in them, while the men could not:

> have one moments joy or comfort … Suspicious of
> each other, your guilty consciences will torment you
> day and night, till an untimely end shall relieve you
> from the Miseries of this world, to face that awful
> Tribunal, the justice of which neither the Monarch or
> the Beggar can escape.[55]

Yet, by 14 August, Waldegrave wrote from St. John's to London that
"everything here at present breathes the most perfect tranquility, and I have
the satisfaction to add that I have no sort of doubt of its continuance."
Waldegrave believed there were only 15 to 20 "real and designing Men" on
the *Latona*. This was based on the fact that on 12 August, Sergeant John
Dailey of the Royal Newfoundland Regiment had given himself up. Dailey
admitted having discussed the possibility of a more general mutiny (involving upwards of 500 soldiers from the garrison) with a few of the Latonas
ashore under a fish flake. When questioned, he claimed that he had been
drunk and was unsure of the details of the conversation. Waldegrave asked
the colonel of the regiment to reduce him to the ranks, and send him off
the Island, as he was "a man of bad character." He lamented not being able
to make a more severe example of him, but noted that he could not have,
even if it had been necessary for the "Saving of the Island." He complained
to Portland that as governor of Newfoundland, he did not have the power
to convene general courts-martial on non-naval personnel and would have

to send such offenders to Halifax for trial. Even if Dailey could have been brought to trial in St. John's, senior officers would also have had to remove themselves from their duties to appear as witnesses at a critical time when Waldegrave believed that he was "threatened with general mutiny both in the Squadron and in the Garrison."[56]

Of those 15 to 20 "designing" seamen whom Waldegrave believed were at the root of the problem, it appears that only five were actually punished, relatively lightly, despite his threats. The logs show that on 3 August, Archibald Gilles, a 24-year-old able-bodied seaman from Greenwich, was punished with an unrecorded number of lashes for mutiny, while another man was given a dozen strokes of the cat ("cat-o'-nine-tails," a whip used in flogging) for theft. Gilles was likely the ringleader of the original strike by the foretopmen who refused to go aloft. Later, on 7 August, one man was punished with six lashes for "Insolence to the Master at Arms," and another, Samuel Debett, a 26-year-old able-bodied seaman from Ireland, with three-dozen lashes for mutiny. Similarly, on 12 August, three more men were punished for "insolence and Mutinous expression," one receiving twelve lashes, and the others 15 lashes each.[57]

Waldegrave's threats of harsh punishment, followed by relatively light summary punishments being inflicted on a few men for such serious offences, illustrates what John Byrn has referred to as a "selective system of terror," where by its nature, naval law and punishment used similar methods of intimidation as the "bloody code" legal system ashore in Great Britian. Capital offences, despite being common in both civil and naval legal codes, were used relatively rarely to intimidate and set an example; summary punishment was much more common and often carried out in similar fashion. It is also possible that Waldegrave did not wish to call a naval court-martial, either because of a shortage of captains required for the court, or because the testimony brought forward might indicate more widespread discontent that would reflect poorly on him and his captains.[58]

The Admiralty was not impressed with Waldegrave's handling of events. In response to the admiral's missives, Nepean wrote expressing their concern, " … that such a disposition should have shown itself, and that from the circumstances you state you have not been enabled to bring the Offender to Punishment … ," while going on to express satisfaction at the conduct of the officers and marines in quelling it.[59]

It is obvious from the logs that the unrest on the *Latona* may have been settled, but it never entirely disappeared, and it was still by no means a happy ship.[60] Without asking the Admiralty for permission, Waldegrave had the *Latona* sail from St. John's to Madeira and then Lisbon with HMS *Surprize* (24) on 10 September 1797, there to pick up any ships bound for Britain and to escort them home. This was in complete violation of his orders and Waldegrave was severely reprimanded for it by London.[61] In his reply, Waldegrave hoped that the Admiralty would view his decision to send the *Latona* to cruise off Madeira and Portugal as an "error of judgement," made because of his wish to take the action "most conducive to the benefit of His Majesty's Service." Asking the Board to excuse his "wholly unintended" errors, he noted:

> from the hour I embark'd on board that ship till the one
> in which she left St. John's, the seeds of Mutiny had ever
> appear'd in her, more or less, and I really conceiv'd the
> best and indeed the only mode of taming them was by
> giving the Ship a very long Cruize….[62]

It is unclear whether Waldegrave believed that a change of climate was preferred for the health of his seamen, because fresh beef, lemon juice, and other provisions were in short supply in St. John's, or if his actions were simply the most practical way to remove a ship full of what he viewed as troublemakers from his station.

Three issues flowing from the grievances of his sailors dominated Waldegrave's correspondence with the Admiralty immediately following the mutiny. These included questions of provisioning, problems with coinage, and his legal and judicial powers as civil and military governor. In several letters he noted the need to provide better food for the men on the ships of the Newfoundland station, particularly sugar, fresh beef, and lemon juice. The latter was an anti-scorbutic, although reducing the amount of salt beef in the seamen's diets also helped to prevent scurvy.

He wrote on 18 October to inform them that the seamen of the *Pluto* had made a request to their captain to receive the same ration of lemon juice and sugar that the men of the *Romney* had been receiving since 1 May as local contractors had withheld fresh beef from the *Pluto* for three months over the summer. Waldegrave agreed to a retroactive supply back to 1 May, given "a desire to remove any sort of dissatisfaction from the Minds of the Crew of the said Sloop" and for the *Surprize* and the *Shark* (16) that had "been under similar circumstances." The Admiralty minute on the letter notes that although the Board concurred with issuing the ration, they did not approve of any retroactive issuance and would not allow "any charge of that description being brought [against] the public."[63]

The same month, Waldegrave wrote a series of letters that justified the letting of new contracts for the provisioning of pork and beef. These took account of the short period that the squadron was in port during its visits and the failings with the old contractors. He noted, "since I have assum'd Command on this station, the Ships have been necessarily kept much at Sea, and also, that the Seamen have, in part, been depriv'd the benefits of Lemon Juice and Sugar allow'd them ... the former Article being so extremely scarce in Newfoundland, as to be procured only with the greatest difficulty...."[64]

A specific examination into the state of provisions in St. John's was undertaken for both the garrison and the squadron with the aim that "... the provisions being served out to the men, with a view to their being furnished with what was good and wholesome, instead of such as a dog would refuse to eat ..." It revealed thousands of pounds of pork, flour, butter, beef, and peas in storage that were totally unfit for consumption. This examination was apparently only prompted by the events of the mutiny.[65]

Although writing to defend his actions during the mutiny, Waldegrave also explained that he was immediately sending HMS *Surprize* to Halifax to bring back money for the garrison, "their being none to be rais'd in the Island, and the Soldiers are much discontented (and I think with reason) with their usual mode of Payment, which is by giving them Bills upon Shops."[66] Pedley points out that the local merchants often used the lack of small denomination coinage to take advantage of soldiers, sailors, and other poor workers by pretending not to have change, forcing them to pay more than the price of an item, or giving them the balance of change in liquor. The paymaster of the garrison, also being short of money, gave out orders on local merchants for goods instead of pay, or bills for use with a merchant in England or Scotland that could only be cashed by paying a 10 percent commission. Waldegrave believed that if he had not taken the measure of sending the *Surprize* to Nova Scotia for more specie (money with intrinsic value, i.e., gold and silver coins), particularly small denominations, the mutiny could have spread throughout his local forces and become general.[67]

The fact that these concerns dominate his correspondence immediately following the events on the *Latona* indicate that Waldegrave likely believed that ameliorating the grievances of his seamen and the garrison ashore was the most positive way to prevent any future outbreaks of unrest. He also wanted to ensure that he had all the legal powers to punish any of the perpetrators, whether seaman, regular garrison soldier, or civilian volunteer, were such unrest to recur. In another long letter to the Duke of Portland, Waldegrave demanded that his duties not only include civil powers, but also military powers, as governor of Newfoundland. He pointed out that although he was practically exercising many military duties, he did not have the title or official powers to allow him to do so. He also corresponded at length with Prince Edward, then commander-in-chief of British Army forces in Nova Scotia and New Brunswick, on the issue of who had overall command of land forces in Newfoundland. These issues were eventually resolved in Waldegrave's favour.[68]

The topic of lemon juice, as odd as it can seem to us today, continued to remain prominent in the admiral's correspondence and highlights the importance of the health and victualling of the sailors as a possible cause of the mutiny. On 2 December, having returned with a convoy, Waldegrave was back in London writing to the Admiralty Board, convinced that his issue of juice to the *Pluto* and other vessels justified public expense, asking them to:

> take into consideration the temper of the times, and my own peculiar, delicate situation, which not only requir'd of me the nicest judgement to preserve my Squadron from breaking out with a determined open mutiny, but also demanded no less management and circumspection to prevent the Mutineers from increasing the apparent discontent of the Troops, forming a junction with them. In this critical situation the Pluto's Ship's Company applied to me for Lemon Juice and Sugar the same as had

been issued to the Latona and Romney ... being too sensible how little command I had over the Seamen of the Squadron, and being apprehensive that I should receive no real support from the Troops, I determin'd to make a virtue of necessity and comply with their request.... I could prove that this very measure kept the crew of the Pluto from joining in the mutinous proceedings ... which had it taken place, I am almost certain the Troops would have join'd in the league, the Pluto's people from their long residence in the county being closely connected with the whole of them.

It appears that Waldegrave's plea for reimbursement fell on deaf ears, as the Admiralty minute on the letter concludes "No directions of this nature in the order book."[69]

Although it is unclear what the exact trigger was for the *Latona* mutiny, it is probable that the fairly high turnover on the *Latona* immediately before the mutiny, seamen and officers alike (there were three captains in the span of three months) contributed to the unrest, along with the crew's grievances related to pay, victualling, and other matters. Concessions made at Spithead may have further emboldened the men.

The legacies of Spithead and the Nore would influence the RN's approach to mutiny, discipline, and resistance for decades to come. Although mutiny would remain essentially a collective action to obtain negotiated aims over grievances, discipline would be much more strict and responses to any disobedience more harsh in future. At the same time, attempts would be made to rectify any true grievances, without perhaps officially relating them to any unrest. It would be this two-sided carrot and stick approach that would provide the example to be followed by captains and senior officers in North America during the War of 1812.

HMS *EPERVIER*

Mutinous behaviour does not always involve the extreme actions that were observed in the first example in this chapter. The following two cases from the War of 1812 illustrate two other forms with two different outcomes. One involves a withdrawal from combat and the possible deliberate misaiming of weapons to avoid inflicting harm on the enemy. The other involves desertion, interpersonal conflict between officers, and an anonymous letter to the Admiralty. Both stories end with courts-martial yielding different decisions, yet upholding the same central tenet concerning authority.

Laid down in June 1812 and completed in January 1813, HM Sloop *Epervier*, built in the line of the *Cruizer*-class brig-sloop, carried 16 32-pounder carronades along the gun deck and two six-pounder long guns on the forecastle.[70] The brig-sloop design made the vessel suited to a wide range of purposes such as convoy escort, reconnaissance, and inshore work during landings and blockades. For Captain Richard Wales, this would be his second command, the last having been four years in the brig-sloop *Ferret* (14). Wales joined his new command on 11 January 1813, at Chatham, England, where the ship was receiving its rigging and stores.[71] On 14 January, 10 marines, a corporal, and Sergeant Charles Chapman came aboard from the Chatham Marine Regiment Barracks. Over the next few weeks, the remaining officers, seamen, boys, and marines came aboard.

On 12 March, the sloop sailed from England with a convoy destined for the North American station and the war in America. On the second day out, Captain Wales ordered the administration of six punishments. Five seamen were punished for drunkenness, one receiving 24 lashes and the others 12, while one marine received 12 for uncleanliness. The convoy sailed south past the Straits of Gibraltar and turned west headed for Madeira and the passage to the West Indies. The crew of HMS *Epervier* agreed to share prize money from any captures with the other RN ships, *Sceptre* (74), *Rifleman* (18), and *Forrester* (18) that were escorting the convoy westward. This agreement would remain in effect until they reached Barbados.

The convoy arrived at Carlisle Bay, Barbados, on 28 April 1813 where the *Epervier* began its role as an escort for convoys among the Leeward Islands. In early July, the *Epervier* headed north to Bermuda and then to Halifax where it joined the squadron blockading Boston and the Cape Cod area. On 12 November, *Epervier* was at anchor in Halifax harbour with the other ships and vessels of the squadron when a hurricane slammed into Nova Scotia. The storm mauled the squadron, although none of the larger ships were lost or irreparably damaged. *Epervier* was driven towards the shore, grounded, and sunk, with no loss of life. Ten days passed before efforts to raise the sloop were successful. The remainder of 1813 was devoted to repair work.

It is at this point in the record that the surviving captain's log ends. The next log was committed to the deep, along with signals and other important papers, when the *Epervier* was captured by the U.S. Sloop *Peacock*. It is necessary to pause at this point and consider some of the information contained in the available captain's log, as it will reflect on the story that develops from the account of the capture and the resulting court-martial.

During the War of 1812, captains had orders to record the occasions on which they practiced their crew at the great guns and small arms. Between leaving England and 6 November 1813, Richard Wales conducted great gun and/or small arms exercises 80 times. In most ships at this time, the movements would be a sham exercise without actually firing the gun, having the gun crews go through the motions in pantomime. Wales recorded holding only one exercise where the guns were actually fired at a mark (a cask). He did note exercising the marines at small arms with them firing at a mark on several occasions. In comparison with 26 other ships positioned during the War of 1812 on the North American and West Indies station, the *Epervier* held the second highest number of great gun and small arms exercises recorded in the captains's logs, well over the average number of exercises within the group of 27.[72]

Captains also recorded the number of incidents of corporal punishment that were administered aboard ship. Punishments aboard the sloop *Epervier* during the 357 days for which a log exists numbered 65. Twenty-one occurred before the vessel reached the West Indies; 21 took place in the West Indies; and 23 occurred when the sloop was with the Halifax squadron. There were no punishments after the hurricane of 12 November 1813. The average number of lashes that Wales applied to the backs of his men was 17.35 (Standard Deviation (SD) = 8.52), with a range from 6 to 36.

Twenty-nine punishments involved 12 lashes being administered for the crime, while 16 punishments brought 24 lashes to the guilty man. This is much lower than the average across the same 26 ships that were compared with the *Epervier* for conducting gunnery and small arms exercises. The average number of lashes from all 27 ships (26 plus the *Epervier*) was 23.80, (SD = 15.22), with a median of 24 and a range from 2 to 300.

The *Epervier* seems to have experienced a lower use of the cat-o'-nine-tails than the other vessels on the North American and West Indies station during the War of 1812.[73] Captain Wales's use of the lash conforms to the low number of lashes John Byrn's findings suggest for the Leeward Islands between 1784 and 1812. Byrn states, "… almost 60 per cent of the scourgings consisted of twelve blows or less."[74]

Markus Eder's study involving court-martial sentences found differences in the number of lashes assigned in sentencing as a function of station location. The courts based in the northern home waters assigned more lashes than those of the warmer climate, like the West Indies. Eder theorises that this was because of the negative impact on health of the warmer climate and that it took longer to recover from such punishments in such a climate.[75] Wales does not follow this line of thought. He punished 21 men in the West Indies with an average of 20.67 (SD = 9.69) lashes each; although sailing on the Halifax squadron, he punished 23 men with an average of 15.83 (SD = 6.74) strokes each. His lightest use of the lash came during the trans-Atlantic trip when the 19 men punished were given an average of 13.58 (SD = 6.27) lashes each. The crimes for which Wales administered corporal punishment included 23 for drunkenness, 21 for disobedient behaviour, eight for various combinations of contempt, insolence, disrespect, quarrelling, and disobedience, five for fighting, two for uncleanliness, two for desertion, and one each for theft and mutinous expression. Only three men experienced two punishments, the 62 others experienced the whip once.

Another important fact to consider is the number of people who ran from the ship, which is deduced from the muster table.[76] A total of 23 men deserted, comprising 21 seamen, one third-class marine, and one second-class boy. Of the 21 seamen, nine were ordinary seamen, and seven were rated as landsmen.[77] Only four had received punishment ranging from 12 to 36 lashes. The time between punishment and running ranged from 15 to 146 days, indicating that receiving punishment did not seem to greatly encourage men to run. Fifteen deserted in Halifax, five in the West Indies and three had left in England before the ship sailed. Twenty ran while on duty and three while on leave. Eight ran by themselves, while the others ran in groups from two to four in number.

Wales had a problem with his first lieutenant, Thomas Favell, whom he accused of having left the ship on 31 December 1813 without permission. A court-martial resolved that the lieutenant had not meant to wilfully disobey his superior, but did so only through ignorance of the service and misconception of his own duty. He was only penalized two years seniority as punishment.[78] Favell's time aboard *Epervier*, however, had come to an end and John Hackett superseded Favell on 13 January 1814.[79]

HMS *Epervier* was ready for sea duty in early January, sailing for Boston Bay where it captured the American privateer *Alfred* (16) on 23 February 1814. As he returned to Halifax with his prize, Captain Wales obtained information that the American prisoners onboard the *Epervier* were plotting to rise up with members of his own crew, seize both vessels and sail for an American port. Wales managed to retain control, in part because a storm struck that necessitated cooperation from everyone to ensure survival. Upon reaching Halifax, Wales wrote Vice-Admiral Sir John Borlase Warren of this near mutiny.[80] With the removal of the American prisoners, the matter seemed settled, and on 3 March, the *Epervier* sailed for the West Indies escorting a convoy.

Sailing from Havana on 25 April 1814 and carrying a cargo of U.S. $118,000 of specie bound for Halifax, HMS *Epervier* headed north convoying a merchant ship to Bermuda. At daylight on 29 April, a strange sail was sighted ahead. The stranger was identified by 0800 hours that morning as a square-rigged ship of war. At 0920, the *Epervier* cleared for action and stood to meet the stranger that was now bearing down on it. The unidentified vessel proved to be the United States Sloop *Peacock* that carried 20 32-pounder carronades and two long 18-pounders.[81]

The action commenced at about 0950 with the two sloops at a half gun shot distance from one another. Things began to go wrong from the first broadside that the *Epervier* fired. Three of the carronade slides on the starboard side of the quarterdeck unshipped upon firing. The bolts securing each slide to the deck were not properly fastened to the deck beam directly under the deck where the gun sat. The crews righted the guns, replaced the bolts and continued to fire. The working of the affected gun crews slowed dramatically with the effort necessary to reposition the carronade slide over the bolthole and in refastening the bolt after each discharge. The forward gun's effectiveness was also decreased by the loss of three men killed and five wounded. Meanwhile one gun drew the fighting bolt and another drew a breeching bolt which held the cables that restrained the recoil of the firing carronades, rendering them unserviceable. Several of the larboard guns also unshipped upon firing when their bolts came loose. Enemy fire disabled the remaining guns. At 1050, only one gun, on the larboard side, remained able to fire, but it faced away from the Americans. On top of these problems, several of the crew had refused to fight during the action, drawing away from the guns.

At the end of 50 minutes, the *Epervier* was a near wreck. Four and a half feet of water sat in its hold, the boom on the mizzen mast had fallen destroying the wheel, both the running and standing rigging had been shot to pieces and all the yards were damaged. Wales realized there was no hope of victory and with six dead and nine wounded in a crew of 114, he struck the British ensign and *Epervier* became another prize. The American *Peacock* had faired much better, with no shot in the hull and only minor damage to the rigging and fore yard.

The subsequent court-martial on Wales and his crew for the loss of the sloop focused on two issues: the gunnery exercise conducted by Wales and the men who had withdrawn from their stations during the action. The court asked each of the seven witnesses how Wales conducted the gunnery exercises, particularly whether the guns were ever fired before the action. All witnesses stated that the guns had never been fired since before the hurricane at Halifax. Captain Wales and Lieutenant Hackett testified that they had been too busy with resetting the rigging after they resumed sailing in January 1814 and had had no time for practices. In March, they could not practice with powder at a mark because the bowsprit and foremast were sprung and needed attention. Several witnesses noted that sham exercises occurred every evening weather permitting.[82] All those who testified agreed that the men knew how to fight the guns, but that they lacked actual live firing practice. Only one gun had been fired since November and that was to test the cross breeching tackle that had been repaired after the hurricane. Lieutenant Harvey reported that the breeching held. Lieutenants Hackett and Harvey told the court that less than 20 of the crew aboard had ever experienced an action. Quartermaster James Boyd testified that he had been "30 years at sea, 15 in the King's Service and never in action" before 29 April.

As to the men who had withdrawn during the action, Wales could only name four of them. He admitted to the court that he did not know the crew, for new recruits from England had replaced many of the ship's members in December 1813. Two members of the crew identified themselves as Americans and would not fight. After the battle, they entered the United States Navy. In the end, only eight men were specifically named as leaving their stations during the action. Not everyone in the captured crew returned from America to face court-martial and the exact number of returnees is unknown. Three of the men who withdrew from action were distributed into ships on the West Indies station when returned to Bermuda from the United States. Boatswain Joseph Dean was court-martialled separately from Wales and dismissed from the service for failing to show "that activity and example which an officer in his situation ought."[83] The court-martial of Wales found those officers and crew not identified as withdrawing during the action to be free of any misconduct in the loss of HM Sloop *Epervier* and so acquitted these individuals.[84]

During their testimony, the commissioned and warrant officers painted their crew as being very weak with such statements as, "a weak arm and not bred as Seamen," "not strong men and to appearance very unhealthy men," and "I never saw a worse crew in my Life in every respect." Master David Gorlan noted that the ship had been crewed at the Nore, as if invoking the image of the Nore mutineers of 1797 would add weight to his lowly assessment. Wales blamed the crew for being weak, old (James claimed two were 70), and made up of foreigners.[85]

The ship's muster does not support these statements. At the time of the action, the *Epervier* bore 83 seamen and officers, 16 volunteer boys, and 16 marines. Out of the 114 men aboard ship at the time of the battle, 105 had their ages recorded in the muster table. The average age was 26.04 (SD = 8.78) with a range from 13 to 53. This age agrees with the mean age stated in the literature for crews in the British and American navies during this period.[86] The men without ages given were commissioned and warrant officers, none of whom would have been 70.

The seamen of HMS *Epervier* were not older than any other ship's complement serving in the RN during the War of 1812. As for their place of origin, 71.34 percent of the complement was British, while 15.29 percent were from elsewhere, including America and Europe. Commissioned and warrant officers, all of whom were most likely British, account for the 11.46 percent of the entries that held no data about place of birth. The percentage of foreign-born seamen in the *Epervier* was the second highest among the 25 ships providing information in Thomas Malcomson's study of the means employed to establish authority's order within the RN during the War of 1812 and the behaviour that undermined that order.[87] *Epervier* had the highest count of people born in the West Indies (4.12 percent) and third highest percentage of American-born men (5.10 percent).[88] If the previously mentioned figure of 14 percent was the average in the period, then 15.29 percent was not that much larger, but if the average was closer to 10 percent, then Wales would have had a complement consisting of a larger than usual number of foreigners.

Wales also complained that the new men brought to the station had replaced a significant portion of his crew. He claimed he did not have the time to know the new seamen, but considered them weak. The muster reveals that 32 of the 114 aboard at the time of capture entered into the *Epervier* after 17 November 1813. Thus, 28.07 percent of Wales's crew were in fact new to the vessel and were possibly green enough to severely disrupt any discipline and expertise that Wales had structured before the hurricane. Wales blamed his failure to name all those who backed away during the action on not knowing many of the offenders, from the new group of 32, after being in command of them for four months. It seems odd that Wales and his lieutenants could not learn their names in that time.

Sir Edward Codrington, captain of the fleet on the North American station during the latter half of 1814, said of the loss of *Epervier*, "… the worst of the story is that our sloop was cut to pieces and the other scarcely scratched!" Writing to his wife, he noted that Wales was a nephew of Sir John Borlase Warren and lamented how the officers selected on "favouritism through influence" to command the navy's ships "should be dismissed [from] the Service." Codrington went further suggesting:

> It is said that butcher Corbett's people showed no spirit
> until he was wounded and carried below. Something of

that sort attaches to the name of Capt. Galpobi whose ship did not do so well as her reported discipline promised. This is the case with many of what are termed our crack ships where the people, from being tyrannically treated, would rejoice in being captured by the Americans from whom they would receive every encouragement.

Historian Robert Gardiner suggests that "Corbett" was a pseudonym for Wales and "Galpobi" for Captain J.S. Carden who lost the *Macedonian* to the *United States* on 25 October 1812.[89]

HMS *ESPIEGLE*

The story of HM *Cruizer*-class Brig-Sloop *Espiegle* and the revolt against its captain took a different path and was resolved with a different outcome.[90] The muster table of *Espiegle* reveals a largely British complement of 67.86 percent with a sizable percentage of foreign-born men at 19.64.[91] As in the *Epervier,* the places of birth of the officers, who as a group comprised 10.71

A painting by J.O. Davidson showing the United States *capturing the* Macedonian *in 1812. (Library and Archives Canada C-4847)*

percent of the names listed in the muster, are not recorded. Europeans formed 9.82 percent of the total crew, with people born in the United States accounting for 5.36 percent. The *Espiegle* carried more foreigners in its crew than did the *Epervier.* The mean age of those aboard the *Espiegle* was 24.20 (SD = 8.85), with a range of 11 to 52, being slightly lower than the *Epervier,* probably because it carried more young boys.[92]

Sailing from Spithead on 27 January 1813, the *Espiegle* accompanied a convoy to the West Indies and arrived at Demerara Roads on 22 February where Captain John Taylor found HM Sloop *Peacock* riding at anchor. Captain Taylor ordered First Lieutenant George Dougal, and Second Lieutenant George Dyer, to shift the topmasts and reset the standing rigging while he went ashore to discuss the defence of the harbour at Demerara with Governor Carmichael. *Peacock* sailed on 24 February and stumbled upon the U.S. Sloop *Hornet* that had been searching for the *Espiegle.* In the ensuing fight, the *Hornet* defeated the *Peacock* and in the process wounded 30 and killed its captain, William Peake, and seven others.

Lieutenant Dougal later stated at Captain Taylor's court-martial that on the day of the battle, he saw a strange sail standing out on a course to intercept the *Peacock,* but that the battle occurred out of their sight. Without his captain present and the ship's rigging taken apart and lying on the deck, there was nothing that the sloop could do to assist its comrades. Questioned why he did not send a boat to inform the captain, Dougal responded that while in Demerara Roads, the sloop was far away from the shore and the town to which the captain had gone.

Captain Taylor returned on the morning of 26 February with news from the governor of the destruction of the *Peacock.* In a state of agitation, he quickly put to sea in search of the *Hornet.* Finding nothing but wreckage from the destroyed sloop, he sailed back towards the coast of Surinam before heading to Barbados. At Barbados, Seaman Joseph Preston deserted while on shore duty. During the next visit to Barbados, Captain Taylor did not allow the bumboats (small boats used to sell goods to ships at anchor) to come out to the *Espiegle* because of his fear that more men would desert, something he had also done at Spithead before their departure. According to Lieutenant Dougal, the crew, upset by this refusal of what they believed to be one of the indulgences that they had a right to, began murmuring their discontent.[93]

The muster table reveals that only 10 men escaped the *Espiegle* by desertion, none of whom ran before its departure from England to the West Indies. Seven ran at St. Thomas, one at Barbados and two at Demerara. All the deserters were seamen.

Contradicting the muster, the captain's log reveals that more than 10 men ran and that some who escaped had made several attempts to leave. Nine other seamen appear in the log as running, but no "R" appears next to their names in the muster table, as would have been required when the muster was submitted after February 1814. The most startling missing "R" was for the master, John Smith, who ran on 19 June 1813 after being under arrest for an unknown offence since 28 May. The logbook lists 11 other men as deserting, all of whom were caught. Three of these men ran again. Seaman James Roach first deserted on 31 May 1813 at Demerara with Richard Finnis. Finnis escaped but Roach was returned on 21 September. Another man who returned the same day was James Griffin who had run on 27 August.

Griffin and four others who returned with Roach were punished the following day with 24 or 36 lashes, Roach for some unknown reason was not. Even with this reprieve, seamen James Roach departed for good on 15 October 1813 and Griffin managed to flee 1 December 1813. The other seaman who ran twice was James Cameron. Cameron first deserted on 15 August, was captured on 9 September and ran again 11 days later. August and September were the two months in which the majority of runnings or attempts at running took place. Although the muster table only reveals three men running at this time, the log names 13 others as running and two as attempting to desert.[94]

Reasons for this deluge of running appear in the exploration of punishment aboard the *Espiegle*. One of the charges that John Taylor stood accused of was "... exercising toward them [the seamen] continual acts of severity and cruelty such as starting the Sick [hitting them across the back with a stick], and flogging persons on the sick list." The court heard that seamen Francis Sturgess, Roger Preston, Thomas Wallis, and James Duncan were all on the sick list when they were started by one of two boatswain's mates, at Captain Taylor's orders, for various offences. Sturgess, Preston, and Duncan had ulcers on their legs or hands and were started for a variety of untold reasons, Duncan repeatedly. The case that caught the court's attention, though, was that of Thomas Wallis. Wallis was started at the captain's orders for smoking on the forward ladder leading from the lower deck to the forecastle. Taylor restricted his crew to smoking only in the forecastle. Boatswain's mate Richard Marchant testified that he gave Wallis 25 blows with a 2 1/2-inch line. Boatswain's mate John Foley relieved Marchant and delivered another 20. The court confirmed that Wallis's jacket was off at the time of the beating. The captain then accused Wallis of saying that he would smoke again off the forecastle. For that, Taylor had Wallis lashed at the gangway. The surgeon stopped the punishment after six lashes, saying that Wallis could not take it anymore. After this beating, Wallis's back appeared "all swelled up in large black whales" and "very black all over." He was eight more days on the sick list as a result of the punishments.

The court also heard how Taylor ordered punishments with the lash of men on the sick list. John Warm's rheumatism was keeping him off deck by order of the surgeon, yet Taylor punished him with 36 lashes because he did not believe seamen in their late twenties could have the disease. Similarly, John Roach, although a "little groggy," verbally abused Boatswain Francis Smith within hearing of Gunner William Checkley, who threatened to report Roach. Roach then turned his verbal tirade against Checkley, which the latter felt contained mutinous expressions. Checkley took an oar that was near by and smacked Roach in the head, causing a large contusion, and causing Roach to be put on the sick list. Three days later, while still on the sick list, Roach received punishment for his behaviour towards the gunner. When the surgeon objected, the captain told him "he didn't know how to make a pill" and that Taylor was going to punish the man. Roach received 24 lashes and a further three weeks on the sick list. As noted above, John Roach deserted the ship twice, the second time successfully.

There were 70 punishments handed down to 54 of the 139 men in *Espiegle*. Forty-six were punished once, six twice, one person three times and John Jones experienced seven punishments.[95] The average number of lashes handed out was 21.31 (SD = 8.76), with a range of 6 to 48. Thirty-seven percent of the punishments involved 24 lashes, while another 30 percent involved the offender receiving 12 lashes. Sixty-five of the 70 punishments were for one charge, one was for two charges together and four cases do not have information concerning the number of charges. Forty-seven of the punishments involved 18 to 48 lashes, while only 23 were for 6 or 12 lashes. Fifty of the corporal punishments occurred between June and October, a period when running was also at a peak. Taylor appears to have used the lash more frequently than Wales and more severely.

Another source of complaint for the seamen revolved around Captain Taylor's apparently obsessive concern over washing and cleaning aboard ship. The commissioned and warrant officers and the seamen testifying at the court-martial said that the seamen did not like the daily holystoning and washing of the decks, a ritual that began at 0400 hours and lasted for four hours, including a one-hour break for breakfast. Once a week, this ritual would last until 1130, even on the hottest of days in the West Indies.

Ship's work was performed well into the evening, which the seamen found gave them little time for rest. During the trip out to North America, when not on watch, the men had to stay on deck in the sun. They could not seek shade below. Taylor punished the last man to bring his hammock up in the morning by making him polish the ship's bell. This provoked the men into waking up early and preparing their hammocks in anticipation of the boatswain piping the hammocks up.

It was not only the seamen who experienced Taylor's oppressive behaviour, as the junior officers were also a target for his rage. Taylor had confrontations with lieutenants Dougal and Dyce, the surgeon, B.E. Omeara, the master, John Smith, Midshipman Henry Powell, and the carpenter. The incident with John Smith is unknown, but was serious enough for Smith to desert the ship after three weeks of confinement. The surgeon's interruptions of punishments and startings infuriated Taylor to the point where he had the surgeon removed from duty. *Espiegle's* surgeon Omeara traded places with Surgeon Hall in the *Goliath* (58) on 4 November 1813. Taylor also confined the carpenter to his quarters for returning to the ship drunk after working ashore in Demerara. Without permission to leave, except to go to the roundhouse, and with a sentry at the door to force compliance to confinement, the carpenter became delirious after three weeks. A straight jacket then had to be used to contain his raging. The court heard how this was not the only time that the carpenter had been delirious, it apparently being common when he had had too much alcohol.

Lieutenants Dougal and Dyer were also confined to their cabins and lost the use of their servants in the fall of 1813.[96] Dyer went to his cabin for directing scandalous language at Captain Taylor. He spent a week there until Taylor called him to the quarterdeck and returned him to service. Dougal's confinement lasted from 24 November 1813 to 1 February 1814 for failing to prevent the maintop men from dropping the top gallant studding sail boom. Taylor called Dougal an "ignorant Rascal" on the quarterdeck in front of the seamen and marines and confined him for arguing. As the ship neared Cork, Ireland, Taylor released Dougal and offered to shake hands and forget the incident. Taylor constantly insulted his officers in public, calling them names such as "an ignorant Son of a Bitch," "a stupid Whelp," and a "stinking scoundrel." Another charge brought against Captain Taylor concerned not exercising the seamen and marines at the great guns and small arms. Testimony revealed that in the entire voyage, he held only four practices, with one gun being fired twice. Although the men polished the guns daily, they did not practice the art of firing them.

An anonymous letter to the Admiralty brought the situation to their Lordship's attention, resulting in the convening of a court-martial in Portsmouth on 23 to 26 February 1814. Taylor delivered a statement of self-defence in which he first defended his honour on the point of not coming to the *Peacock*'s aid, accusing an unknown party of trying to ruin his character. In regard to the *Peacock,* he noted that he had been away on official business and reminded the court of the evidence given that the sloop was stripped down for repairs. He dismissed the other charges as vague and too many to properly defend himself against, stating that, "It is in Human Nature to be dissatisfied and to complain...." Taylor also testified that the seamen had been given leave at Surinam, eight seamen and two marines per day, for 20 hours. The bumboats were denied only twice, for fear of desertion.

He also claimed not to have started the sick, nor punished people on the sick list, although he admitted that he had no evidence, just his word. Of the seamen named to have been started frequently, Taylor said they were "very indolent Men and of every filthy and disgusting habits." He only punished the "the most indifferent or worst of Character." Taylor remarked that in the past five months, only those deserving of it had been started. To justify the excessive hours at cleaning, Taylor claimed that not one man had died of illness during the entire time away from England. With regard to his language, Taylor admitted it was rough, but called on the officers of the court to recognize that there were times when one was so frustrated with others or the situation that any captain would lose control of his temper. On the point of exercising the great guns, Taylor played the card that might have shaped the decision of the court. He said his experience as a captain allowed him to decide what needs doing and what could wait. Taylor reminded the court, "If a captain cannot make these decisions, then who has the power?"

Besides the above, the court heard evidence around the charge that Captain Taylor was frequently drunk. It appears that he would drink with his dinner and although not unable to perform his duty, as one witness testified, he was "different after dinner … more hasty and violent." The charges of drunkenness and those of not assisting the *Peacock* against the *Hornet* were disproved, the later labelled "scandalous and unfounded" by the court. They also found him not guilty of denying the crew "the usual Indulgence of the Service" while in harbour, and not guilty of treating the "Ship's Company so as to keep them in a state bordering on Mutiny." The court found Captain John Taylor guilty of "some Acts of Severity toward the Ship's Company, [and] that he had neglected to exercise the Sloops Company sufficiently at the great Guns."[97] The behaviours that appear to have resulted in Taylor's sentence, however, were the "Acts of Oppression towards some of the Officers," his "most scandalous Language" to Lieutenant George Dyer, and his overall conduct, which was deemed "unlike an Officer and Gentleman." The court dismissed Taylor from the service, with a recommendation of reinstatement.[98]

The decision of the court upheld the position of the junior officers that they had a right to fair and gentlemanly treatment by their captain, as they believed befitted their progress towards the status of gentlemen. The seamen were left with little acknowledgement of what they had endured under Captain Taylor's leadership. "Some acts of severity" minimizes the experience. Perhaps Taylor's question about "who has the power" left the court uneasy, for if the crew's complaints of the manner in which they were worked could lead to the disposal of the captain, then any ship's company could call for a court-martial to rid itself of a disliked officer. Possibly, in light of the previous experience at Spithead and the Nore, the court believed that the seamen's complaints could not be allowed to have such power. Such complaints had to be minimized to prevent a precedent from being set for future sailors to use. It is interesting to note that although forbidden in 1809, the common occurrence of starting the seamen aboard *Espiegle* failed to raise a remark by the gentlemen of the court.

Yet, the removal of a disliked officer is exactly what happened here. The anonymous note, most likely from Dougal, with the double level of complaint from the officers and the threat of a mutinous crew, brought about the court-martial. The overpowering case of acts of cruelty against his junior officers and the detailed description of punishment dealt out to sick men, with the shadow of drunkenness and a violent mean-spirited temper, were enough to have Taylor expelled from the navy. By the junior officers and seamen pulling together in the court-martial, they rose up and disposed of their disliked, and possibly tyrannical, captain by legitimate means. In a sense, this was a "mutiny by court-martial."

In the case of the *Epervier*, Captain Wales had the backing of his junior officers, who agreed that every measure possible to meet the enemy on advantageous terms had been taken. Not one of his junior officers suggested that the absence of live fire gunnery exercises was a significant factor in the loss. If Wales had conducted those exercises, though, the problems with the fighting bolts would have been found and remedied. The men's retreat from the guns indicates another significant problem with Wales's leadership. The full number of men withdrawing from the carronades in battle is unknown. During the engagement, not one round shot hit the hull of the American sloop, nor was a single American killed. This, coupled with the fact that many of the *Epervier*'s seamen stayed in the United States instead of returning to British control in prisoner exchanges, suggests a strong desire on the part of many in the gun crews not to fight. To escape their situation, elements of the crew of HM Sloop *Epervier* deliberately lost the battle and went to America as prisoners. Yet, in its conclusions, the court blamed the loss of the *Epervier* on faulty bolts, a more heavily armed enemy, and a weak crew.

It would seem that the court minimized the active role played by the crews in each scenario. In the case of the *Espiegle,* finding Taylor guilty of only "some acts of severity," and not of "repeated cruelty to the seamen," reduced the influence of the seamen's experience in the court's decision to remove Taylor from the service. In the case of the *Epervier,* the crew's portrayal as weak and sickly placed them in a passive stance, reducing their active involvement in the defeat. By denying agency to the seamen of both *Epervier* and *Espiegle,* the courts maintained the pretence that the officers were always in total command of the situation. Whether Codrington was referring to Wales and Carden in his letter or not, the point taken from his remark is that not everyone was deceived by the court's dismissal of the agency of the seamen and marines aboard His Majesty's Ships. The sentences passed by the courts also allowed the presiding officers to avoid using that most dreaded and feared word, "mutiny."

CONCLUSIONS

The experience of mutiny in the RN in North America was strongly based on experiences in home waters that were coloured by the events at Spithead and the Nore. The latter contributed to a change in the definition of discipline and led to a more heavy reliance on the marines to support authority onboard, overturning the previously accepted social and authority relationships that existed between senior petty officers and long-serving seamen and their officers. Yet the experience was also different because of the presence of an independent United States after 1783, its growing demand for skilled sailors to meet the needs of its trade, and the ability of men to run to a similar society, as well as an American naval service that offered better pay and more limited periods of service.

Frequent changes in leadership, or the break-up of the bonds and loyalties between members of a ship's company, such as occurred when captains changed ship and took their followers with them, could also contribute to such unrest, as can be seen by the cases of the *Latona* and the *Epervier.* The growing influx of landsmen in the navy, whether as volunteers or pressed men, was also a factor, although it should not be viewed out of proportion. Besides the problems posed in training and disciplining large numbers of men new to the service, some of these new sailors undoubtedly were more literate and educated. This allowed them to more easily make their complaints known to the Admiralty, organize among themselves, discuss their situation with warrant and other junior officers (as may have occurred on the *Espiegle*), or communicate in writing with other ships, such as when the *Latona* visited St. Michael's. It remains open to question whether involuntary military service helped create a sense of "Britishness" among such men, or if the ethnic mix below decks was more likely to contribute to unrest. Waldegrave's appeals to English honour likely did not resonate with his Scottish and Irish landsmen, just as pressed Americans onboard the *Espiegle* and *Epervier* felt no great desire to fight against their own countrymen for the British.[99]

Non-violent "promotion of interest" mutinies, following the unofficial and unwritten "rules" of such protests, were a common way in the eighteenth century for seamen to let off steam and for intelligent officers to reach a negotiated settlement over grievances before the pressure-cooker of the lower deck blew-up in a more violent and aggressive manner. When the "rules" began to change late in the century, and violence on both sides became more common, the navy often still tried to avoid using the term mutiny in its larger sense. Captains likely tried as many of these cases summarily as they could to avoid them having to be officially considered by a court-martial that could reflect badly on their own leadership. Men were regularly lashed for "mutinous expressions," "insolence to a superior officer," "striking a superior," "disobedience of orders" and other offences that could be used as a pseudonym for mutiny itself. As can be seen in the cases of the *Epervier* and *Espiegle,* even when such crimes were brought before a court-martial, the navy often avoided the use of the word to deny seamen agency, so that it would always appear that officers had remained in control. As Rodger argues, this also could lead to accusations that external influences were behind mutinies, when the reality was different, with the most experienced and capable petty officers and senior able-bodied seamen usually being the organizers, such as Archibald Gilles and the foretopmen on the *Latona.*

All these factors may have led to greater discipline on the North American station by individual captains trying to reduce desertion and maintain control of those ships with high turnover rates, which tended to contain large numbers of landsmen and pressed men of different ethnicities, some of whom were unfamiliar with the sea and the navy. As Markus Eder and John Byrn have shown, discipline in the navy tended to be more of the "bloody code" exemplar variety, meant to intimidate men into behaving by the existence in law of harsh penalties for capital offences such as mutiny and desertion, and their selective use for terror, rather than applying such punishments by the book in each and every case. Yet tyrannical captains could still apply excessive summary punishments in an effort to maintain control, while more judicious captains could also use summary punishment in a less extreme manner. Disciplinary efforts were often more detrimental than positive and required officers to walk a fine line that, if strayed from, could result in the generation of further unrest.

The main factor in preventing mutinies at the end of the day remained the leadership displayed by the captain, his empathy with his crew, and the balance between informal negotiation and authoritarian methods. The *Epervier* and *Espiegle* both required courts-martial to resolve disciplinary problems aboard ship. In Malcomson's ongoing doctoral study, it would appear that on ships where courts-martial were resorted to for this purpose, there was a higher frequency of summary corporal punishments, but a lower number of lashes per punishment than on ships that did not use courts-martial to solve shipboard problems. The latter punished summarily less often, but more severely. These cases also show how in courts-martial decisions, the Admiralty would generally have little hesitation in relieving an incompetent and/or tyrannical captain, particularly one with no political connections. Unfortunately for many seamen such action was often taken too late, and only after complaints and petitions had been ignored and a major incident had occurred.

NOTES

Editor's Note: Martin Hubley would like to acknowledge the assistance provided by a Social Science and Humanities Research Council of Canada doctoral fellowship that made research possible in England and by Keith Mercer of Dalhousie University for suggesting additional references concerning the *Latona* mutiny.

1.   The title of this chapter has been taken from a letter sent by Edward Codrington to his wife, while captain of the fleet on the North American station, remarking on the losses of HMS *Epervier* and *Macedonian*. See Library and Archives Canada [henceforth LAC], Sir Edward Codrington fonds, Manuscript Group [henceforth MG] 24–F131, letter from E. Codrington to J. Codrington, 7 June 1814.

2.   For the rarity of "seizure of power" mutinies, see A.N. Gilbert, "The Nature of Mutiny in the British Navy in the Eighteenth Century," in *Naval History: The Sixth Symposium of the U.S. Naval Academy*, D.M. Masterton, ed. (Wilmington: Scholarly Resources, 1987), 111–20; N.A.M. Rodger, *The Wooden World: An Anatomy of the Georgian Navy* (Glasgow: Fontana, 1988), 237–44; Leonard F. Guttridge, *Mutiny: A History of Naval Insurrection* (Maryland: Naval Institute Press, 1992), 5–11; and Lawrence James, *Mutiny in the British and Commonwealth Forces, 1797–1956* (London: Buchan & Enright, 1987), 12–3. For a typology, see Cornelis J. Lammers, "Mutiny in Comparative Perspective," *International Review of Social History*, Vol. 48, Part 3 (2003), 477.

3.   See Nicholas Rogers, *Crowds, Culture and Politics in Georgian Britain* (Oxford: Oxford University Press [henceforth OUP], 1998) for an excellent historiographical discussion of this field.

4.   As outlined by Rodger, who theorises three main guidelines: "1. No mutiny shall take place at sea, or in the presence of the enemy. 2. No personal violence may be employed (although a degree of tumult and shouting is permissible). 3. Mutinies shall be held in pursuit only of objectives sanctioned by the traditions of the Service." The "rules," and subsequent level of violence, were "rewritten" by events that occurred during the American Revolutionary War when such traditional mutinies began to be harshly suppressed by a navy desperate to keep ships in service. They would be rewritten again with the events of 1797. See Rodger, *Wooden World*, 237–39 and N.A.M. Rodger, *The Command of the Ocean: A Naval History of Britain 1649–1815* (London: Allen Lane, 2004), 403–04.

5.   The 1731 *Regulations and Instructions Relating to His Majesty's Service at Sea* and *The Articles of War* of 1749 were the legal basis of discipline at sea until 1806, when a revised version of the former was introduced. Among other changes, this gave more discretion to captains in allowing harsher summary punishment by removing the theoretical 12-lash limit for any one crime. The *Articles of War* recognized four types of mutiny. Article 19 dealt with "mutinous assembly" and "mutinous language," Article 20 with "concealment of mutinous designs" and Article 34 with the act of mutiny itself. Striking or attempting to strike an officer, covered by Article 22, was commonly viewed as equivalent to mutiny as well, although not codified as such. All the above were offences punishable by death or lesser sentences at court-martial, but were more often treated summarily. See Brian Lavery, *Nelson's Navy: The Ships, Men and Organisation, 1793–1815* (Annapolis: Naval Institute Press, 1989), 141–43, and John D. Byrn, *Crime and Punishment in the Royal Navy: Discipline on the Leeward Islands Station, 1784–1812* (Aldershot: Scolar Press, 1989), 17–8.

6.   Incidents of mass desertion before and during the war were generally less common than collective protests and lie outside the scope of this chapter. It is debatable whether these could be viewed as "seizure of power" mutinies *per se*, as the goal of the seamen involved was ultimately to remove themselves from the clutches of the RN, or at least, of the captain and officers of their current vessel. They are being investigated in doctoral research

underway by both authors, which will shed light on whether such events were more frequent in North American waters because of stricter discipline on that station, and the
desire and ability of deserters to essentially disappear in America if they ran from a ship.
This possibility seems to be hinted at in Jamieson's micro-study of three ships during the
American War of Independence. See A.G. Jamieson, "Tyranny of the Lash? Punishment
in the Royal Navy During the American War, 1776–1783," *The Northern Mariner,* Vol.
9, No. 1 (January 1999), 63–4.

7. The North American station was usually headquartered at Halifax, Nova Scotia, and
the command extended from Nova Scotia south to the waters off Florida. Ships of the
squadron often wintered in Bermuda from 1795, where a naval depot was established
in 1805. There was also a smaller Newfoundland station based in St. John's, with separate responsibilities for the protection of trade in those waters, particularly the fish-
eries and convoys to and from Britain. The admiral commanding was also responsible
for administering that colony. This chapter focuses on the experience of the "blue
water" navy in North America as a whole, including Newfoundland and the period
when the North American command was briefly combined with the West Indies station at Jamaica (and subsequently uncombined) during the War of 1812. Julian Gwyn,
*Frigates and Foremasts: The North American Squadron in Nova Scotia Waters,
1745–1815* (Vancouver: University of British Colombia Press, 2003), 95 and 100;
Markus Eder, *Crime and Punishment in the Royal Navy of the Seven Years War,
1755–1763* (Aldershot: Ashgate, 2004), 63–4 and footnote 1.

8. Excellent summaries of the events of the mutinies and additional works on them can
be found in Guttridge, *Mutiny,* 44–73; James, *Mutiny,* 33–75; and Rodger, *Command
of the Ocean,* 441–52, from which this account is primarily drawn. The best scholarly accounts are Conrad Gill, *The Naval Mutinies of 1797* (Manchester: Manchester
University Press, 1913) and James Dugan, *The Great Mutiny* (New York: G.P.
Putnam's Sons, 1965), but unfortunately the latter does not cite his sources in any
type of notes. The historiography is dominated by three categories of works: (1) those
that tend to have a Marxist viewpoint of Irish republicans and other radicals domi-
nating the organization of the mutinies, portraying striking seamen as a radicalised
proto-proletariat, such as Jonathan Neale, *The Cutlass and the Lash: Mutiny and
Discipline in Nelson's Navy* (London: Pluto Press, 1985); (2) those such as Gill and
Dugan who believe that although there was minimal radical influence, seamen were
aware of new concepts of human rights which influenced their actions; and (3) those
such as Rodger, who tend to see no radical involvement or notions of the rights of
man, but whose "rules" of mutiny are influenced by concepts such as "orderly disorder" and the moral economy of the crowd in English society in the eighteenth century, as expressed in such works as E.P. Thompson, *Customs in Common: Studies in
Traditional Popular Culture* (New York: The New Press, 1993), 16–96 and 185–351.
Guttridge and James tend to follow the middle path.

9. Rodger, *Command of the Ocean,* 442–44; and Christopher Lloyd, *The British Seaman
1200–1860: A Social Survey* (London: Collins, 1968), 263.

10. Gill, *Naval Mutinies,* viii–x and 355–58; James, *Mutiny,* 37–9; and Guttridge, *Mutiny,* 56.

11. For example, see Lavery, *Nelson's Navy,* 137–38, on problems with the integration of landsmen.

12. In addition, the army's pay scale had improved in 1795. This was, no doubt, also a source of resentment among sailors who expected, but did not receive, a similar increase. Some of the soon-to-be mutineers, writing to the Whig leader of the opposition in Parliament, Charles James Fox, noted that their patriotism was equal to that of the soldiers. See Guttridge, *Mutiny,* 46–7.

13. Gill, *Naval Mutinies,* 89–93 and 97–8; Guttridge, *Mutiny,* 47 and 53; and James, *Mutiny,* 57.

14. Their grievances included the monotony of blockade duty, arrears of pay, and tyrannical officers. See Guttridge, *Mutiny,* 61–4 and Rodger, *Command of the Ocean,* 447.

15. Rodger, *Command of the Ocean,* 447–48.

16. Guttridge, *Mutiny,* 70–2.

17. *Ibid.,* 56.

18. Rodger, *Command of the Ocean,* 450–53.

19. James, *Mutiny,* 63–5.

20. Rodger, *Command of the Ocean,* 450–53; and Gill, *Naval Mutinies,* 52. All of this contributed to the changing nature of discipline in the navy, which has subsequently been debated by many historians. In the eighteenth century navy, discipline generally meant only "the readiness of officers and men to fight and work the ship," in other words, their level of training or competence. By Spithead, and likely even earlier, this concept had evolved to include the enforcement of naval law on all ranks and "the working of an institution above and independent of the characters of particular men, and the maintenance of a standard of conduct in daily life." See David Hannay, *Naval Courts Martial* (Cambridge: Cambridge University Press, 1914), 39.

21. Lavery, *Nelson's Navy,* 143.

22. For musters, see The National Archives of the United Kingdom [henceforth TNA], ADM 36/12324, *Latona* Muster Books, March 1797 to January 1798. Logs used include: TNA, ADM 51/1245, Captain's Log of Arthur Kaye Legge, 31 July 1796 to 15 April 1797; TNA, ADM 51/1198, Captain's Log of John Bligh, 25 April to 21 July 1797; TNA, ADM 51/1227, Captain's Log of Frank Sotheron, 25 July 1797 to

December 1798; TNA, ADM 52/2636, Master's Log of John Davies, 21 September 1794 to 12 May 1797, and TNA, ADM 52/3153, Master's Log of John Davies, 12 May 1797 to 19 May 1802; and National Maritime Museum [henceforth NMM], ADM L/L/39, Lieutenant's Log of unnamed lieutenant from HMS *Latona*, 1796 to 1802. The interpretation of muster books throughout this chapter follows the guidelines outlined in N.A.M. Rodger, *Naval Records for Genealogists,* 3rd ed. (Kew, Surrey: Public Records Office Publications, 1998), 45–57.

23.   One of the most detailed, and perhaps best, accounts remains that of Rev. Charles Pedley, *The History of Newfoundland from the Earliest Times to the Year 1860* (London: Longman, Green, Longman, Roberts, and Green, 1863), 174–83, which is based primarily on Colonial Office records found in the Provincial Archives of Newfoundland and Labrador, GN 2/1/A series. Those relevant to naval matters seem to have been generally duplicated in the Admiralty correspondence of Waldegrave used in this account. Gerald S. Graham mentions the mutiny only in passing, avoiding a detailed account given the strategic focus of his work, and indicates that any anxiety created by the event was removed by the arrival of the news of the end of the Nore mutiny and the execution of Parker. See Gerald S. Graham, *Empire of the North Atlantic: The Maritime Struggle for North America* (London: OUP, 1950), 225–26. More recent works that discuss the *Latona* in somewhat more detail than Graham include: David A. Webber, *Skinner's Fencibles: The Royal Newfoundland Regiment, 1795–1802* (St. John's: Naval and Military Museum of Newfoundland, 1964); Captain A. Fisk, "Mutiny in Newfoundland, August 1797," *Canadian Defence Quarterly,* Vol. 16, No. 1 (Summer 1986), 58–62; Barry Judson Lohnes, "British Naval Problems at Halifax During the War of 1812," *Mariner's Mirror,* Vol. 59, No. 3 (1973), 317–33; Christopher English, "The Official Mind and Popular Protest in a Revolutionary Era: The Case of Newfoundland, 1789–1819," in *Canadian State Trials: Law, Politics and Security Measures, 1608–1837,* F. Murray Greenwood and Barry Wright, eds. (Toronto: University of Toronto Press [henceforth UTP], 1996), 296–322; and John Mannion, "'… Notoriously Disaffected to the Government …': British Allegations of Irish Disloyalty in Eighteenth-Century Newfoundland," *Newfoundland Studies,* Vol. 16, No. 1 (2000), 1–29. Webber discusses the mutiny in passing in his regimental history of the Royal Newfoundland Regiment. Fisk provides a succinct account based entirely on secondary sources (primarily Dugan and Webber) and focuses on the fears of a general mutiny among the St. John's garrison and the rather tenuous connections between the *Latona* and the later mutiny in the garrison at St. John's in 1800, which had a possible United Irishmen connection. His piece contains several minor points of contention that are discussed below. Lohnes only briefly mentions the incident, yet, among other geographical errors, manages to confuse St. John's, Newfoundland, with Saint John, New Brunswick. English relies primarily on Fisk and Webber and the CO 194 series of Waldegrave's correspondence (also largely duplicated in the ADM 1 records with regard to his squadron) for his account, and replicates some of Fisk's (and Dugan's) possible misconceptions, including the trip to the Nore and only one man being flogged for the mutiny. Mannion relies on Webber and the same correspondence used by Pedley. Both English and Mannion only discuss the *Latona* in a few paragraphs as one small part

within excellent articles that concentrate on the broader issues of popular protest, the legal system, and the perceived threat from the Irish presence in Newfoundland at this time. Paul O'Neill mentions the mutiny in passing and implies (without any real evidence) that the sailors had mutinied in sympathy with those at the Nore. He similarly asserts that the other ships in the squadron were supposed to follow the *Latona's* lead, but that this did not occur because of Waldegrave's prompt actions. See Paul O'Neill, *The Oldest City: The Story of St. John's Newfoundland* (St. John's: Boulder Publications, 2003), 63–4 and 497. The *Latona* incident is not mentioned by Jerry Bannister, *The Rule of the Admirals: Law, Custom and Naval Government in Newfoundland, 1699–1832* (Toronto: UTP, 2003), despite the legal issues raised regarding the prosecution of the army sergeant involved, perhaps because of its coverage in Mannion and English.

24. The Captain's Log states 15 April 1797, but the Muster Book shows him being discharged as of 13 April 1797. Legge was born on 25 October 1766, and by 1781, was serving as a midshipman on board the *Prince George* on the North American station under Rear-Admiral Digby. From 1791, he commanded the *Shark* sloop, was made post-captain on 6 February 1793, and given the *Niger* (32 guns), which along with the *Latona,* served at the Glorious First of June repeating Howe's signals. In spring 1795, he took command of the *Latona* until being appointed to the *Cambrian.* For his full career, see John Marshall, *Royal Navy Biography, or, Memoirs of the Services of All the Flag Officers* (London: Longman, Hurst, Rees, Orme, and Brown, 1823), Vol. 1, Part 1, 441–42.

25. No relation to William Bligh of the *Bounty* who, coincidentally, commanded the *Director* during the Nore mutiny. John Bligh was born in August 1771 and went to sea in 1782. After service in the West and East Indies to 1791, he was promoted lieutenant and saw service in the Mediterranean. As first lieutenant of the *Barfleur* (98), the flagship of then Rear-Admiral Waldegrave, he served for two years and took part in the Battle of Cape St. Vincent. He was promoted commander and given the *Kingfisher* (16) sloop and then made post-captain on 25 April 1797 in the *Latona.* In July 1797, he traded positions with Sotheron in the *Romney* and eventually moved to the command of the *Agincourt* (64), all of which were flagships of Vice-Admiral Waldegrave on the Newfoundland station. For full details of his career, see Marshall, *Royal Navy Biography,* Vol. 1, Part 1, 813–14.

26. TNA, ADM 36/12324, *Latona* Muster Table, 24 April 1797. See also, Rodger, *Wooden World,* 119–24 and 275–94, for more on the practice of followers.

27. TNA, ADM 1/473 f.366, William Waldegrave to Evan Nepean, *Latona,* Spithead, 11 May 1797. This may have been related to the common practice of pursers buying victuals using a 16-ounce pound and selling them to sailors using a 14-ounce pound. Neale, *Cutlass and the Lash,* 17; Rodger, *Wooden World,* 93–5; and Gill, *Naval Mutinies,* 12, 32 and 98.

28. TNA, ADM 36/12324, *Latona* Muster Table, 30 May 1797.

29. TNA, ADM 1/473 f.369, Waldegrave to Nepean, *Latona*, Spithead, 25 May 1797.

30. As these men were transferred from another ship, it is not recorded in the musters whether they were volunteers or pressed men, but Waldegrave refers to them as volunteers, and it is likely that they were Quota men. From 1790, the *Royal William*, a former 84 gun first-rate built in 1719, was a Portsmouth guardship, responsible for receiving new intakes of men and distributing them to other vessels.

31. TNA, ADM 1/473 f.374, Waldegrave to Nepean, *Latona*, Spithead, 28 May 1797.

32. It made brief stops at Yarmouth Roads on 31 May, from where it sailed, convoy in company, on 3 June, arriving at Torbay on 6 June. Dugan and James seem to think that the *Latona* was somehow involved in the mutiny at the Nore, but its surviving logs seem to indicate that it was not present there between the time it left Sheerness on 31 March, after refitting its copper, to arriving at Spithead on 4 April, and then leaving England in early June. It is possible that unrest occurred while at Yarmouth, as that squadron had mutinied earlier on 27 May, with some of its ships sailing for the Nore. It is unclear if the *Latona* was one of these ships, but it seems unlikely given its late arrival and lack of any obvious entry in the logs. See Dugan, *Great Mutiny*, 125 fn. There is no mention of the *Latona* being at the Nore in Gill, who notes its presence at Spithead in passing only. See Gill, *Naval Mutinies*, 97.

33. TNA, ADM 1/473 f.380–381, Waldegrave to Nepean, *Latona*, At Sea, 9 June 1797.

34. James, *Mutiny*, 61.

35. Both the *Romney* and the *Venus* had been in Spithead on 17 April during the first mutiny and had refused to sail with a convoy for Newfoundland. The seamen returned to duty and both vessels sailed on 20 April after receiving a letter from the delegates who had decided that the two ships should not join the mutiny, as any delay in the sailing of the convoy would injure British trade. Gill argues that this decision was made for the benefit of the Admiralty, and the public as a whole, to demonstrate the judgment and loyalty of the mutineers. See Gill, *Naval Mutinies*, 26. The authors have found no evidence of any similar agreement with regard to the sailing of the *Latona*'s convoy, which occurred after the second Spithead mutiny had ended and while the Nore was underway.

36. As this latter incident occurred on 29 June, it is possible that Smith, an able-bodied seaman from Devon, was involved in passing information to the *Romulus* at St. Michael's. Butler is not listed on the musters.

37. In 1783, Sotheron was assigned as a midshipman to the Newfoundland station, was then promoted lieutenant, and served on the frigates *Danae* (32) and *Aeolus* (32). He then saw service in the Mediterranean, including the *Romney* as first lieutenant, and in 1792, was given command of the *Fury* (14). Sotheron made post-captain on 11

December 1793, and in 1794, was given command of the *Monarch* (74), the flagship of Sir James Wallace. He moved with Wallace into the *Romney* when Wallace took up the appointment of commander-in-chief at Newfoundland. In 1797, he was given the *Latona,* in which he served for two years. For full details of his career see, Marshall, *Royal Navy Biography,* Vol. 1, Part 1, 501–03.

38. TNA, ADM 1/473 f393, Waldegrave to Nepean, *Romney,* at St. John's, 22 July 1797. When back in England and told that they would be returning to Newfoundland, the *Pluto's* crew petitioned the Admiralty to serve elsewhere. In the post-Spithead spirit of treating petitions as mutiny, several seamen were tried and one was hanged. The ship was sent back to St. John's. See "John Bryan, 14 July, Spithead" in TNA, ADM 12/24 ff.441–442, "Analysis and digest of court-martial convictions, arranged by offence: J-N 1755–1806"; *and* James, *Mutiny,* 65.

39. Excluding officers and warrants whose place of birth was shown on separate documents, only 26 seamen listed on the muster for 30 July 1797 have no place of birth indicated, so the percentages above are based on roughly 89 percent of seamen on the books. The *Latona's* figures for foreign-born sailors are lower than those postulated by Lewis. He estimates that 14 percent were foreigners, while noting that the *Victory* had eight percent foreign-born on its musters. The figures for the *Latona* are higher than Lewis's estimates for Scottish and Irish sailors. Lewis hypothesizes that the ethnic proportions of British seamen would be the same as for officers, which, using a sample of 1,500 officers, he determined were 68.3 percent English, 13.1 percent Scottish, 11.7 percent Irish, and 3 percent Welsh, for those who identified their birthplace. See Michael Lewis, *A Social History of the Navy, 1793–1815* (London: George Allen and Unwin, 1960), 60–82 and 129. Neale estimates that English sailors comprised only 50 percent of seamen in the fleet, with the Irish and the Scots the two next largest groups, for whom he does not provide an estimate. He believes that 10 percent of sailors would have been foreign-born. See Neale, *Cutlass and the Lash,* 13. Malcomson has shown that the navy's men on the Great Lakes in the War of 1812 were roughly 67.7 percent English, 13.5 percent Irish, 9.1 percent Scottish, and 3 percent Welsh, with 3.6 percent being foreign-born. See Thomas Malcomson, "Muster Table for the Royal Navy's Establishment on Lake Ontario During the War of 1812," *Northern Mariner,* Vol. 9, No. 2 (April 1999), 62–3. Fifty percent of the crew of the frigate from Jamieson's study that spent time on the North American station had a place of birth shown on the musters: 64 percent of them were English, 13.5 percent Irish, 11.8 percent Scots, 4 percent Welsh, and 6.7 percent foreign-born. See Jamieson, "Tyranny of the Lash?," 62.

40. Rounded to the nearest percent. The actual numbers are 90 English, 37 Scots, 27 Irish, five Welsh, one Newfoundlander, and 25 unknown. See TNA, ADM 36/12324, *Latona* weekly muster, 30 July 1797.

41. The actual numbers are 28 English, five Scots, four Welsh, three Irish, one Russian, one American, and 11 unknown. The average age of all seamen aboard, excluding

officers and volunteer boys, was 25.31, with a minimum age of 16 and a maximum of 44 (SD = 5.96), which falls within the normal range for this period. *Ibid.*

42. Most men ran at Sheerness or Portsmouth before the *Latona* left for Newfoundland, although one ran from a prize that had been taken on the voyage to St. John's on 1 August. Eight of these deserters were able-bodied seamen, two ordinary seamen, two landsmen, and two volunteer boys. In addition, another seven men (two landsmen, three ordinary and two able-bodied) had deserted in Portsmouth in August 1796. *Ibid.*

43. Fisk incorrectly has the *Latona* sailing from England under Captain Frank Sotheron, based on a rather vague reference in Dugan stating that the Latonas removed Captain John Bligh. The musters and logs seem to refute this entirely, as Bligh remained aboard until Sotheron took up his commission in Newfoundland. Lastly, Fisk claims that the *Latona* had a "significant number of malcontents among its crew," who "added to the dangerous atmosphere on board a ship which had already shown severe disciplinary problems." See Fisk, "Mutiny in Newfoundland," 58. As we shall see below, the disciplinary record of the *Latona* was by no means beyond the average for a RN vessel at this time, and if anything, may have been less harsh. See endnote 60 below. Fisk's evidence for this is Dugan's brief uncited and undated mention, which implies that the *Latona* had been present at the Nore where the Port Admiral had sent its pressed men to fill out its complement from the *Sandwich,* which was holding pressed men, convicts, and quota men for redistribution to the fleet. It is unclear whether Dugan believed this had occurred before or during the mutiny (See Dugan, *Great Mutiny,* 178–79). Dugan does list the *Latona* as being one of the ships under the control of the delegates at both "First Spithead" and the "Nore-Yarmouth" mutinies according to Admiralty records (See Dugan, *Great Mutiny,* 477). As Dugan does not cite his sources directly, it is difficult to use his account to verify the activities of the *Latona.* Its logs clearly show it was not involved in the first Spithead mutiny, only the second. Its musters show only two men ever being received from the *Sandwich* at the Nore, these on 31 March 1797, when *Latona* was refitting at Sheerness, some time before the mutiny there and shortly before it left for Spithead. The Yarmouth squadron mutinied on 27 May 1797, before the arrival of the *Latona* on 31 May. Based on these accounts and the tone of Waldegrave's correspondence before leaving England, it seems likely that there was unrest onboard at Yarmouth, but the *Latona*'s actual presence at the Nore when mutinies were underway seems circumstantial.

44. TNA, ADM 1/473 f.395–396, Waldegrave to the Duke of Portland, Fort Townshend, 14 August 1797. Underlined emphasis is in original. An almost identical letter was dispatched to Nepean at the Admiralty two days later. See TNA, ADM 1/473 f.398–399, Waldegrave to Nepean, Fort Townshend, 16 August 1797.

45. TNA, ADM 1/473 f.400, Waldegrave address, Fort Townshend, 3 August 1797.

46. TNA, ADM 1/473 f.401–402, Waldegrave address, Fort Townshend, 6 August 1797.

47. *Ibid.*

48. *Ibid.*

49. Pedley, *History of Newfoundland,* 178.

50. For examples of declarations of support and Waldegrave's replies, see TNA, ADM 1/473 f.403–404, Colonel Thomas Skinner, Royal Newfoundland Regiment, to The Governor, Fort William, 8 August 1797; TNA, ADM 1/473 f.405–406, Waldegrave to Skinner, Fort Townshend, 8 August 1797; TNA, ADM 1/473 f.406, Captain James Winters, Corps of Royal Newfoundland Volunteers *et al* to Waldegrave, St. John's, 8 August 1797; TNA, ADM 1/473 f.407, Waldegrave to Officers, NCOs and Privates of the Royal Newfoundland Volunteers, 8 August 1797; TNA, ADM 1/473 f.408–409, Sergeant-Major Robert Lomax to Major Charleton, Commanding Officer Royal Artillery, St. John's, 9 August 1797; TNA, ADM 1/473 f.409–410, Waldegrave to Charleton, 9 August 1797; and TNA, ADM 1/473 f.414–415, Waldegrave to Officers and Petty Officers of *Latona,* 11 August 1797.

51. TNA, ADM 1/473 f.410, Sergeant John Williams *et al* to Waldegrave, St. John's, undated.

52. TNA, ADM 1/473 f.411–412, Waldegrave to Marines, Fort Townshend, 8 August 1797.

53. Another English able-bodied seaman had run on 1 August. Overall, between 6 December 1796 and 31 January 1798, 27 men ran from the ship. Sixteen were able-bodied seamen, five ordinary seamen, four landsmen and two volunteer boys. Sixteen of the deserters were English, four Irish, three Scottish, one American and one from Smyrna. Twenty-three ran in Sheerness or Portsmouth before heading for Newfoundland, four in St. John's and four in Lisbon on the return to England. Two men ran within weeks of being punished for leaving their duty in England.

54. TNA, ADM 1/473 f.412–413, *Latona* Ship's Company to Waldegrave, St. John's, undated.

55. TNA, ADM 1/473 f.413–414, Waldegrave to *Latona* Ship's Company, Fort Townshend, 9 August 1797. English argues that disaffection, particularly pro-Irish disaffection, in the garrison was not widespread at this time, as it may have been by the time of the events of 1800, yet the "official mind" believed it was so. See English, "The Official Mind," 307–11. While disaffection in the *Latona* certainly included some Irish seamen, it also included Englishmen and others, and seems to have been more in response to local grievances and the events of Spithead and the Nore, rather than any Irish conspiracy.

56. TNA, ADM 1/473 f.395–396, Waldegrave to the Duke of Portland, Fort Townshend, 14 August 1797.

57. They included 30-year-old Walter Bourke, an able-bodied seaman from Limerick, Ireland, and two men who unfortunately do not appear on the ship's musters, Bryan Manning and Michael Burke.

58. Even when capital punishment was used, it was often counter-balanced by the royal prerogative of mercy. Byrn, *Crime and Punishment,* 10–11, and Eder, *Crime and Punishment,* 153–54.

59. TNA, ADM 1/473 f.27–28, Nepean to Waldegrave, Admiralty, 24 November 1797.

60. Between 25 August and 17 January 1798, when the *Latona* returned to Portsmouth, 11 more men were punished on the ship. In September, Christopher Chandler was given 24 lashes "for mutinous expressions and striking the Master at Arms" and Jason Smith seven for "mutinous expressions." Michael Farell received 12 blows for "insolence to his superior officer." Two other men were given a dozen lashes each for drunkenness and theft. In October, the unrest spread to the marines, with their sergeant being reprimanded for "Drunkenness and Neglect of Duty," while another marine, Jonathan Rose, was punished with 19 strokes of the cat for "mutinous expressions and insolence." Two other seamen, including Christopher Chandler from above, also received 12 lashes for insolence, and finally, in December, yet another marine was given 12 for "drunkenness and quarrelling." Overall, between March 1796 and January 1798, 32 men were punished summarily. For the 29 for which the logs record the number of lashes, the average was 14 (Min = 6, Max = 36, SD = 6.08). Seven men were punished for insolence, five for mutinous expressions, five for drunkenness, six for fighting or misbehaviour, three for leaving their duty, three for theft and two for striking their superior. Christopher Chandler and George Smith were the only men to be punished twice. It should be noted that this does not appear to be an abnormally high rate of punishment, either in terms of numbers of summary offences or lashes awarded, for this period.

61. TNA, ADM 2/930 f.29–31, Nepean to Waldegrave, Admiralty, 27 November 1797.

62. TNA, ADM 1/473 f.435–436, Waldegrave to Nepean, London, 28 November 1797.

63. See TNA, ADM 1/473 f.422, Waldegrave to Nepean, *Latona* at St. John's, August 1797; TNA, ADM 1/473 f.423, Waldegrave to Nepean, *Romney* at St. John's, 14 September 1797, complaining of the price of butter in Newfoundland and authorizing the issue of sugar to his seamen in lieu; TNA, ADM 2/930 f.28–29, Nepean to Waldegrave, Admiralty, 24 November 1797; TNA, ADM 2/930 f.32–33, Nepean to Waldegrave, Admiralty, 28 November 1797; and TNA, ADM 2/930 f.34, Nepean to Waldegrave, Admiralty, 2 December 1797.

64. TNA, ADM 1/473 f.424–425, Waldegrave to Nepean, *Romney* at St. John's, 2 October 1797. See also, TNA, ADM 1/473 f.426, Waldegrave to Nepean, *Romney* at St. John's, 15 October 1797.

65. Pedley, *History of Newfoundland,* 181.

66. TNA, ADM 1/473 f.398–399, Waldegrave to Nepean, Fort Townshend, 16 August 1797.

67. Pedley, *History of Newfoundland,* 182.

68. See TNA, CO 194/39 f.133–138, Waldegrave to the Duke of Portland, Fort Townshend, 25 October 1797; and TNA, ADM 1/473 f.437–457, Waldegrave to Nepean, London, 29 November 1797; enclosing copies of correspondence with Prince Edward and the Duke of Portland. See also, Pedley, *History of Newfoundland,* 183ff, on the overall command controversy. Edward would later be made Duke of Kent and commander-in-chief of land forces in British North America in 1799; the latter position was vacant in 1797.

69. TNA, ADM 1/473 f.462–464, Waldegrave to Nepean, London, 2 December 1797.

70. J.R. McCleary, "Lost by Two Navies: HMS Epervier, a Most Un-Fortunate Ship, Part One," *Nautical Research Journal,* Vol. 41, No. 2 (June 1996), 81–2, for details concerning *Epervier*'s construction.

71. Unless otherwise footnoted, the story of the *Epervier*'s experience is derived from TNA, ADM 51/2409, Captain's Log, 8 January 1813 to 31 December 1813; and TNA, ADM 1/5447, Court-martial of Richard Wales.

72. This comparison comes from the doctoral dissertation that Thomas Malcomson is now writing, dealing with control and resistance aboard ships of the RN on the North American and West Indies station during the War of 1812. The ship that exceeded the *Epervier* was the *Valiant* (74), with 111 exercises. The mean number of great gun and small arms exercises was 34.44 (SD = 26.42).

73. Indeed, the *Epervier* has the lowest mean lashes of the 27 ships (M = 16.76, SD = 7.96), with HMS *Shannon* (38) coming very close with 16.77 (SD = 8.77). The difference in the mean in this footnote and that in the body of the chapter derives from the fact that the data for Malcomson's comparative study does not include punishment administered before ships left port to head to the North American and West Indies station, therefore two punishments included in the present study (of 36 lashes each) were not included in the comparative study.

74. Byrn, *Crime and Punishment,* 75.

75. Eder, *Crime and Punishment,* 127.

76. TNA, ADM 37/4563, *Epervier* Muster Table, January 1813 to April 1814.

77. Of the remainder, one was an able seaman, two were in the carpenter's crew, one was captain of the foretop and the other a quarter gunner.

78. TNA, ADM 1/5440, Court-martial of Thomas Favell, 6 January 1814.

79. TNA, ADM 37/4563, *Epervier* Muster Table, 28 February 1814. John Harvey also superseded Second-Lieutenant William Lovett on 15 January 1814, thus Wales lost both of his lieutenants in the same week.

80. This almost mutinous episode comes from W.M. James, *The Naval History of Great Britain during the French Revolutionary and Napoleonic Wars, 1811–1827* (1837, repr., London: Conway Maritime Press, 2002), Vol. 6, 291. Warren held the overall command of the North American and West Indies station during the later part of 1812 and for all of 1813.

81. Captain Lewis Warrington commanded the *Peacock*.

82. Wales thus conducted more than the 80 practices noted in the available Captain's Log.

83. Quoted from McCleary, "Lost by Two Navies," 86, who references David J. Hepper, *British Warship Losses in the Age of Sail* (Rotherfield, East Sussex: Jean Boudriot Publications, 1994), 149.

84. Hackett had lost three fingers on his hand, had his left elbow shot off (necessitating the amputation of his arm) and suffered a large splinter through his hip. The court made special reference to his bravery in keeping the deck after receiving the first two wounds. Hackett received a pension and continued in the navy until 1838, retiring a commander. Lieutenant Harvey was appointed commander in 1819, retiring shortly after on half-pay. Wales was given the command of HMS *Childers* until 1817 when appointed a post-captain and relieved of duty, disappearing from our view. Most of the seamen and marines who returned to England for the court-martial probably returned to civilian life as a result of the post-war downsizing of the navy. See, TNA, ADM 1/5447, Court-martial of Richard Wales.

85. McCleary, "Lost by Two Navies," 83, and James, *Naval History*, Vol. 6, 294.

86. Malcomson, "Muster Table." Malcomson found a mean age of 404 seamen and officers to be 26.94 (SD = 5.93). Ira Dye reported the average age of American sailors in the War of 1812 was 27.12 with a median age of 25. See Ira Dye, "Physical and Social Profiles of Early American Seafarers, 1812–1815," in *Jack Tar in History: Essays in the History of Maritime Life and Labour,* Colin Howell and Richard Twomey, eds. (Fredericton: Acadiensis Press, 1991), 221. Robert Malcomson's charts produce an average age of the British seamen fighting at the Battle of Lake Erie as being 28.8 years. See Robert Malcomson, "The Crews of the British Squadrons at Put-in-Bay: A Composite Muster Role and Insights," *Inland Seas,* Vol. 51, No. 3 (Fall 1995), 43–56.

87. Of the 25 ships with place of birth listed in the muster tables, the mean percentage of foreign-born was 11.41 (SD = 3.31), with a median of 10.86.

88. These percentages translate into seven and eight people from the West Indies and America, respectively. See footnote 38 above regarding estimates of the percentage of foreign-born seamen at this time.

89. LAC, Sir Edward Codrington fonds, MG 24–F131, letter from E. Codrington to J. Codrington, 7 June 1814. This letter differs slightly from a similar passage quoted in Robert Gardiner, ed., *The Naval War of 1812* (London: Chatham Publishing, 1998), 91–2. Of most concern is the absence of the names Corbett and Galpobi, which are replaced in Gardiner's quotation with blanks, and the word "butcher" replaced by "fellow."

90. As with the *Epervier*, the story of Captain John Taylor and HM Sloop *Espiegle* is derived from TNA, ADM 51/2289, Captain's Log, 5 January 1813 to 8 February 1814; and TNA, ADM 1/5541, Court-martial of John Taylor, 23 to 26 February 1814.

91. TNA, ADM 37/4577, *Espiegle* Muster Table, 31 August 1814. The British percent breaks down as 50 percent of the entire crew born in England (also includes Wales), 12.5 percent in Scotland and 5.36 percent in Ireland. Of the 25 ships in Malcomson's Ph.D. study with place of birth available, *Espiegle* has the highest percentage of foreign-born among its crew and the second highest percentage of Americans and Europeans within its complement. These percentages translate into six and 11 people respectively.

92. The average age of the seamen (not including the one midshipman's age or the boys) was 25.97 (SD = 8.48). The boys mean age was 14.27 (SD = 1.83).

93. "Murmuring" was a common tactic of seamen, an informal method of letting officers know that the men were upset, by gathering in small groups and talking and then becoming quiet should an officer pass by. Neale, *Cutlass and the Lash*, 76.

94. Seven seamen managed to desert between 10 October 1813 and 1 January 1814 when the sloop headed for England. The log does not indicate other attempts at desertion during this time period. It is interesting to note that not one marine ran from the *Espiegle*.

95. John Jones received 138 lashes in total over the course of five months. His crimes were two events of being drunk, with 24 lashes each time, one act of neglect of duty receiving 12 lashes, an act of desertion for 24 lashes, two acts of insolence to a superior officer, each receiving 12 lashes, and one unstated charge that brought him 24 lashes. In all the 27 ships under analysis in Malcomson's doctoral study, only one other individual out of 1840 cases was lashed seven times. The overwhelming majority were lashed once.

96. The court seemed relieved to hear that the officers did not have to perform menial tasks like food preparation as the servants of the other people in the wardroom took care of them.

97. Commenting on this part of Taylor's sentence, James suggested that it "… seemed hard to punish the *Espiegle*'s commander for a piece of neglect which pervaded over two thirds of the British navy…." James laid part of the blame for a lack of live fire practice at the door of the Admiralty, who he felt did not give proper allowance of powder and shot for practicing at the great guns. James, *Naval History*, Vol. 6, 195.

98. His name was replaced on the Navy list in 1818, after which he remained on half-pay as "The Junior Commander." See Marshall, *Royal Navy Biography*, Vol. 4, Part 2, 536–38. George Dougal was appointed a commander 13 June 1815, but remained unemployed. See *Ibid.*, Vol. 4, Part 1, 364–67. Lieutenant Dyer's fate is unknown.

99. This may indicate that Linda Colley's concept of Britain's eighteenth century wars being crucial to the development of a superimposed British identity, a theory expanded upon by Stephen Conway to show the utility of naval and military service for building a sense of shared "Britishness" among the constituent populations of the United Kingdom, may not be applicable in every case, a possibility that is being investigated in doctoral research by Hubley. See Linda Colley, *Britons: Forging the Nation 1707–1837* (London: Yale University Press, 1992), 35–7; and Stephen Conway, *The British Isles and the War of American Independence* (Oxford: OUP, 2000), 165–68.

2

The Lincoln Militia's War of 1812

JAMES W. PAXTON

On 25 June 1812, word reached Major-General Isaac Brock at York that the United States had declared war on Great Britain. The general must have appreciated the irony in that he was now being called upon to defend a province that he disliked intensely. Located on the periphery of the empire, Upper Canada was too rustic, too "backwoodsy", and too far from the metropolis. He craved to be with the army in Europe, where his talents as a soldier could be put to better use against Napoleon. And the people of Upper Canada, Brock thought, were perfectly suited to their surroundings. The American-born majority were a jealous and petty people who held dangerous republican principles. Nevertheless, as he read the declaration of war, Brock realized that he had too few regulars to defend the province and he reluctantly called out the militia to bolster his force along the Niagara River.

Time and experience seemed to confirm the general's low opinion of these citizen-soldiers. A month later, Brock informed Sir George Prevost, his superior at Quebec, that "although I had no great confidence in the majority, [it] is worse than I expected to find it." He elaborated by observing that "the greater part [of the population] are either indifferent to what is passing or so completely American as to rejoice in the prospect of a change of government."[1]

Not surprisingly, Brock's assessment of the militia would not become part of the popular mythology surrounding the War of 1812. Much nineteenth- and early-twentieth-century writing on the conflict is suffused with the self-congratulatory glow of the militia myth, that is, the belief that Upper Canadians had united to repel the invader.

Beginning in the late 1950s, professional scholars began to challenge this longstanding interpretation. In two pioneering articles, historians C.P. Stacey and G.F.G. Stanley demolished the militia myth and demonstrated that British regulars, not militiamen, saved Upper Canada and did most of the actual fighting and dying in the process.[2] If Stacey's and Stanley's revisionism reduced the militia's role in the conflict, they did credit Upper Canadians for having capably played fewer glamorous, but necessary, supporting roles. Recently, historian George Sheppard has revised the revisionists and returned to Brock's more pessimistic view of the Upper Canadian militia. Looking at the high rates of absenteeism, profiteering, and hoarding, he has determined that a majority of the colony's inhabitants were too isolated, divided and self-interested to risk their lives to defend the province. Upper Canadians were not, as Brock feared, actively disloyal, so much as they were "unwilling participants." When militiamen did fight, they fought to protect their personal property.[3]

Despite the interpretive differences that separate Stacey and Stanley from Sheppard, together they all fail to situate the militia within a context that makes their actions understandable. Sheppard's rather flat and two-dimensional characterization of the colonials as atomized, individualistic and operating purely from the profit motive does not satisfactorily explain the range of behaviours that Upper Canadians exhibited. Militiamen did not disobey orders simply in reaction to incompetent officers and unpopular commands or because they were disloyal. To most observers, militiamen behaved in contradictory ways. They could impress regular soldiers by their discipline, coolness under fire, and bravery in battle, but they also drove their officers to distraction by refusing to submit to discipline, deserting in droves, and seeking paroles, that is, they surrendered and gave their word not to take up arms against the enemy until properly exchanged. In trying to make sense of this mixed record, it must be remembered that these men were not primarily soldiers, against whom they are too often judged, nor were they simply rational economic actors, as modern historians would have it; rather, they were, husbands, fathers, sons, and neighbours, entangled in dense webs of familial, social, and economic relations that profoundly influenced how they perceived the war and their role in it.

One cannot hope to understand these men as soldiers without first reconnecting them to the world that they inhabited. It is necessary, therefore, to examine the wartime service of Niagara militiamen within the context of the rural agricultural communities that produced them. Unlike regular soldiers, militiamen and their officers could not separate their duty to country and empire from their obligations as husbands and community members. With their families and farms in constant danger, colonists adopted flexible strategies — fighting one day, deserting the next — to negotiate the tensions between the homefront and the battlefield. The seemingly inconsistent behaviour of the militia ran directly

A portrait of Major-General Isaac Brock by John Wycliffe Lowes Forster. (Library and Archives Canada C-7760)

counter to the regular officers's sense of duty. Incompatible notions of warfare poisoned relations between regulars and militiamen, but, in time, forced senior British officers to reconsider the place of the militia in the larger struggle to defend Upper Canada.

NIAGARA BEFORE THE WAR

In 1812, the Niagara District, bounded on the north and south by Lakes Ontario and Erie and on the east and west by the Niagara River and Burlington Bay, was, like many North American frontier communities, overwhelmingly rural, agricultural, and local in orientation. Even though the region boasted three towns, Niagara, Queenston, and Chippawa, the largest of these (Niagara) sheltered only 500 to 800 residents. The large majority of the District's 13,000 or so residents lived and worked in the countryside.[4] The original settlers, the loyalists, and those whom historians have called the "late-loyalists," were joined later by thousands of immigrants from the United States, mostly from the northern states of New York, Pennsylvania, and New Jersey. On the eve of war, approximately 60 percent of the population was American-born.[5] Colonial administrators expressed misgivings about the newcomer's politics and loyalty, but there was no inherent conflict between the loyalists and these later immigrants. Both were an agrarian people who shared particular notions about the virtue of land and landownership that were rooted in what their contemporaries called "competence."

Most of Niagara's farm families strove to achieve competence, that is, the economic and material well being of the household. Competence was predicated on a man's possession of sufficient land to support a family, primarily with the labour of his wife and children.[6] Fathers also hoped to accumulate sufficient land and capital in their lifetime to ensure that their children, too, enjoyed competency. In this regard, at least, Upper Canada satisfied the ambitions of many settlers. Land, either through direct grants to the first settlers or through sales to immigrants, was distributed more widely and more equally in Upper Canada than in England. Widespread landholding allowed many families, after much hard labour, to attain the competency that was characteristic of middling farmers.

In 1795, one observer of colonial society marvelled at how few in number were the "Persons of great Property or consequence."[7] Lacking a significant landless lower class, labourers from Upper Canada commanded wages that only the wealthy could afford to pay.[8] Consequently, the self-working farm, where the landowner and his family provided most of the labour, became the norm. A Moravian missionary travelling through the province in 1798 noted the relationship between land and labour when he commented that a "well improved plantation bespeaks, not only an industrious, but hard-working owner."[9] Similarities in the daily lives and experiences of the province's upper and lower classes imparted to Upper Canada a roughly egalitarian, if not equalitarian, nature. This is not to say that Upper Canada was not a stratified society. Political power was vested in a small number of predominantly loyalist families, but as long as people came to the province primarily in search of land, as it seems that they did, agitation over inequalities in other aspects of life remained subdued.[10]

By necessity and choice, then, farming was a family affair. The household was the basic economic unit, where the father used the labour of his wife and children to raise the crops and livestock and to make the home manufactures that would sustain the family throughout the year. To ensure that the family's needs were met, men and women performed different, sometimes overlapping and complementary tasks.[11] Men grew flax and made the spinning wheels and looms that women used to turn flax into linen.

In this vein, in 1805, Robert Sutcliff, an English Quaker, described the domestic economy of a family of 12 who lived near Fort Erie. The family ate their meals in a room that doubled as a weaver's shop. Another room contained several spinning wheels, where the wife and daughters spun yarn. The daughters also made straw hats and bonnets for the family and presumably for sale in the nearby village. When not helping their father in the fields, the sons hunted and fished to supplement the family's diet. The division of household labour impressed Sutcliff for allowing the family to make a "living independently of the uncertainties of commerce."[12] Through their mutual efforts, wives, husbands, and children achieved competence.

Whatever Sutcliff's reservations about merchants and the market, competence should not be confused with self-sufficiency. No family could produce everything that they required, not even foodstuffs, nor was that their goal. Rather, households pursued flexible, but conservative strategies that combined production for home consumption, for local exchange, and for market. Wheat, for example, could be ground into flour for the family's use or sold to a merchant or the local garrison. Similarly, linen cloth could be turned into clothes, traded to a neighbour for barrel staves or shoes, used to pay off a labour debt, or taken into town and sold to a merchant for cash, tea, needles, and imported cloth. Men and women also bartered with their neighbours and friends for much of what they needed. John Smith of Forty Mile Creek (present day Grimsby), for example, kept an account book that documented a variety of exchanges with several neighbours. Over a period in 1796, Smith supplied his father-in-law with hay, beef, and wheat, and in return, received five quarts of salt and six shillings cash. How farm families disposed of their produce depended a great deal on personal circumstances, needs, market prices, and the degree of risk one was willing to incur in the pursuit of profit.[13]

Similarly, all farmers, no matter how many children they had, required extra labour at certain times of the year. In most cases, time-sensitive tasks like ploughing and harvesting and labour-intensive projects such as house- or barn-raising, could only be accomplished with the assistance of relatives and neighbours. Again, John Smith's account book is illustrative. In 1797, Smith charged Obadiah King £2 for borrowing his son, Benjamin, and a pair of oxen for six days. Although calculated in pounds, shillings, and pence, these debts were usually paid in kind.[14] Everyone benefited by participating in labour-sharing arrangements because one day they, too, would require their neighbours' help. Conversely, refusing to participate in communal activities courted social isolation and economic disaster. Many transactions involving small amounts of cloth, eggs, flour, meat, and labour drew individuals and households into a dense web of reciprocal obligations, weaving together the strands that formed competency. Interdependence, not independence, characterized these communities.[15]

The flexible economic strategies that made up competency precluded reliance on a single cash crop. To meet the needs of households and market, Niagara farmers grew a wide variety of cereals, vegetables, and fruits, a practice known as mixed agriculture. The rhythm of their lives followed closely that of the seasons and the agricultural calendar, leaving few idle periods.

The season began in May when farmers planted oats and potatoes. In June, they sowed barley and harvested hay. Cutting hay might continue into July when rye had to be planted. At the end of the month, wheat was harvested and stored indoors. Turnip planting followed the harvest. In September, farmers planted wheat and rye. Between October and November, families set to work digging potatoes and turnips. Throughout the year, farmers mowed grass, ploughed fields, and constructed and mended fences. The winter months were occupied with clearing land, splitting fence rails, and making barrel staves. On most farms, livestock were as important as crops. Pigs ran free most of the year and were brought in at the end of the summer to be fattened before slaughter. In the fall, farmers turned out cattle to browse in the woodland.[16] The routines of mixed agriculture employed all family members throughout the year, reinforcing patriarchal household structures and giving shape to an agrarian worldview that placed the welfare of the household above other considerations.

Few British officials in Upper Canada understood the values and ideals of the province's inhabitants. They believed that the predominantly American-born population was shot through with dangerous republican sentiments. For English-born imperial and colonial officials trying to transform the province into a "little Britain," the influx of American settlers was an ominous sign. One of these officials, who also won election to the colonial assembly, David W. Smith, complained that his fellow American-born legislators displayed "the most violent levelling principals" and decried the Assembly's habit of looking to the United States for "patterns & models."[17] A French traveller captured the anxiety of the time when he claimed that "the spirit of independence which prevails in the United States, has already gained ground" in Upper Canada.[18]

In the period before the War of 1812, there were no serious challenges to the colony's political system as most Upper Canadians were too busy clearing land and making farms. The anxieties of many imperial officials grew from their own firmly held principles that fit uncomfortably with the reality of life in Upper Canada. The men sent to administer and defend the colony were, almost without exception, born in Britain and had served in the army. Within the highly structured and hierarchical world of the British military, they developed an uncompromising and unambiguous loyalty to the crown and empire. In Upper Canada, these men served the interests of the mother country, not the colonists.[19] British leaders, naturally, understood the war in its imperial dimensions and viewed the province's inhabitants primarily as instruments in the empire's defence. Brigadier-General John Vincent, echoing the sentiments of many regular officers, relegated Upper Canadians to something less than full participants when he said, "it will not be supposed that [the militia's] attachment to *our* cause can be very steady."[20] Men like Vincent, David Smith, and Brock mistook localism for apathy or, worse, disloyalty. Pervasive distrust of the American-born colonials and a lack of empathy tainted relations between the British military and Upper Canadians throughout the war.

THE LINCOLN MILITIA IN PEACE AND WAR

If patriarchal and localized communities provided the context in which Niagara's farmers interpreted the war, the militia provided the vehicle by which they experienced it. Each county supported one or more militia regiments according to its population. In 1811, the Niagara District supported five regiments, called the Lincoln militia after the District's only county, with a total of 2,298 men on the rolls. The 5th Lincoln was the largest with 572 soldiers, while the 3rd was the smallest with 350 men.[21] Each regiment consisted of eight to 10 companies of between 20 and 50 privates. In theory, all able-bodied, adult men between the ages of 16 and 60 were obligated to serve in the militia. Certain professions, such as clergymen, millers, schoolteachers, ferrymen, surgeons, and public officials, received exemptions. All others were subject to a fine of 40 shillings for an officer and 10 shillings for other ranks for failing to appear on designated training days.

Militia service did not tax Upper Canadians heavily. All regiments mustered every 4 June in celebration of the King's birthday and an additional two to four days each year. Musters provided occasions for rudimentary military training, but for the men, they afforded opportunities to socialize and drink. For his troubles, a private received the relatively small sum of 6 pence a day. By contrast, a farmer contracted by the army to transport goods earned 20 shillings a day.[22]

Unlike professional armies that separated soldiers from society and created an unbridgeable chasm between officers and men, militia units represented the community in microcosm. Members served with their brothers, fathers, uncles, and neighbours. Officers were usually drawn from the upper strata of society and were distinguished by wealth, reputation, and political connections. Yet, the men who served as captains and colonels five days of the year were, for the remaining 360, the friends, relatives, and neighbours of the men whom they commanded. This fact greatly influenced their style of leadership. Officers who were drawn from the wealthiest segment of society had considerable influence in the neighbourhood, but the reciprocal nature of economic and social relations did not allow them to command their neighbours too strictly. Most officers found that persuasion and influence produced better results than did the enforcement of rigid discipline. In April 1812, Colonel John Warren deferred to his neighbours and mustered the 3rd Lincoln at two different locations so that his men would not have to walk 30 miles to the parade ground. Attendance increased when the men did not have to travel so far from their farms.[23] Still, some men felt uncomfortable exercising any kind of authority over their neighbours. Just before the war, a captain in the 5th Lincoln resigned his commission because "he does not like to get the ill will of his Neighbours by making them do their duties."[24] If officers like these are any indication, the militia embodied the values of the community more than it did those of the regular officers who sent them into battle.

To counteract democratic tendencies in the militia and to neutralize disloyal elements within the population, Brock sought to put the militia on a firmer footing. In February 1812, he persuaded the Assembly to amend the Militia Act of 1808 to subordinate militia officers to regular officers, to strengthen the penalties for disobedience to include trial by court-martial, to force officers to take an oath of allegiance and to make privates and non-commissioned officers liable to the same. The most important feature of the 1812 Militia Act was the creation of two flank companies within each regiment. The flank companies, which consisted of up to one-third of the regiment's strength, or 35 men each,[25] trained six days each month and received the most experienced and competent officers. Special provisions exempted flankers from arrest for civil matters and from performing statute labour or jury duty. It was expected that the most loyal inhabitants would volunteer to fill the ranks of these new companies, while men of dubious loyalty would remain in battalion companies that would be called out only in emergencies.[26]

By May, every regiment from Fort Erie to the Grand River and York had completed recruiting. The Lincoln regiments readily filled their quotas. How well the flank companies served their intended purpose is doubtful. Indeed, nearly every soldier in Colonel Thomas Clark's 2nd Lincoln volunteered for the new companies.[27] Many men likely enrolled to receive the perquisites of the new service, rather than from any sense of patriotic duty.

As the Lincoln men soon discovered, peacetime service did not prepare them for the demands of war. Compared with the Seven Years' War and the American Revolution, militia service during the War of 1812 weighed heavily on the citizenry. Increasingly, throughout the eighteenth century, militia units had acted like reserve battalions that raised and trained men to fill the spaces in the combat regiments. In the American colonies, the most marginal elements of society — landless young men, free blacks or aboriginals — filled the ranks as volunteers or as substitutes for wealthier individuals, for which they received generous bounties and better pay than regulars. In this way, poor men could accumulate some of the capital necessary to purchase land, while property holders either held officers' commissions or escaped military service altogether. Though patently unfair, such a system preserved stability at home by shifting the military burden to those most willing and able to perform it.[28]

While Brock's reforms went some way towards bringing the Upper Canadian militia into line with past practices, the militia system continued to place a greater military burden directly on the population and provided fewer rewards than had historically been the case.

The outbreak of war found Upper Canada woefully ill-prepared to resist an invasion. No one understood this better than Isaac Brock, the man entrusted with the defence of the province. In June 1812, only portions of the 41st Regiment of Foot and Brock's own 49th Regiment of Foot were available for service in Upper Canada; the militia flank companies were not yet fully trained. To bolster his force along the Niagara River, Brock called out the flank companies of the Lincoln and York militias. Within a few days, approximately 800 Lincolns had assembled at Fort George. The cheerfulness and alacrity with which the militiamen responded surprised and heartened the general.[29] Despite these auspicious beginnings, the militia's subsequent behaviour did nothing to raise their reputation in the estimation of their commander.

The Lincoln regiments took up positions along the Niagara River, stretching in a line from Fort George to Fort Erie. The raw volunteers settled into nearby homes and barns and became acquainted with military life. The first weeks passed quietly as the novelty of camp life and the urgency of the situation combined to hold men to their tasks. Regular officers noted with approval that the militia's discipline and skill "improved daily" and Brock took pains to publicly commend them on their "regular conduct" and willingness to learn.[30] One soldier, Charles Askin, believed American "regulars were not near so well disciplined as our flankers."[31] Worried American officers might have agreed as they watched the preparations being made on the far shore. American Major-General Amos Hall thought the Upper Canadian militia "well-disciplined and completely armed."[32]

By the middle of July, however, regular officers began reporting on a more worrisome development. The militia, Brock complained, "envince a degree of impatience under the present restraint that is far from inspiring."[33] When it became apparent that a battle was not in the offing, men used to the independence of civilian life soon began to grumble about having to perform monotonous guard and patrol duties. Many soldiers, free from the restraints of home, killed the boredom by turning to alcohol. Prohibiting the sale of alcohol to soldiers failed to remedy the problem and the Lincoln men continued to drink immoderately.[34] Before long, the militia gained a reputation for being an ill-disciplined and disorderly body of troops.

The Lincoln regiments arrived in camp poorly equipped for active campaigning. Soldiers provided their own uniform, that consisted of "a short coat of some dark-colored cloth ... pantaloons [and] a round hat," but the army was supposed to supply food, shelter, and other necessary equipment. Chronic shortages, however, forced officers to instruct their men to obtain their own "blankets and other necessaries."[35] Lacking proper clothing, footwear, tents, and cooking equipment, the militia was, in Brock's words, in a "wretched state."[36] Companies even carried different types of weapons, making it difficult to ensure that each received the proper ammunition.[37] In August, some men in the Lincoln regiments received "cast off clothing" from the 41st Regiment. The issue of worn-out scarlet tunics had more to do with fooling the Americans into thinking that Brock had more regulars, than with any sincere concern for the militia's comfort. In the absence of tents and bedding, militiamen began going home when the fall weather turned cool.[38] Many men simply could not stand such harsh living conditions. Fourteen men of Captain Daniel Servos's company of the 1st Lincoln received discharges because they were too old or infirm for such rugged service. Others simply went home without leave.[39] In November, Major-General Roger Sheaffe, Brock's successor, could still report that the militia "are in a very destitute state with respect to clothing, and all in what regards bedding and barracks comforts," although later that month, at least some of the Lincoln companies received jackets, pants, shirts and shoes.[40] The onset of cold winter weather brought a rise in desertion rates as ill-clad, poorly housed, and underfed soldiers returned home without permission.[41]

This anonymous portrait of Sir Roger Hale Sheaffe depicts the major-general who took command after Major-General Isaac Brock's death. (Library and Archives Canada C-111307)

The appearance of sickness among the troops turned the camps into vast hospitals, where men died daily. Unsanitary camps, densely packed with men who had little exposure to communicable illnesses, created an ideal disease environment. The shortage of proper clothing, equipment, and shelter contributed to the spread of illness. "We have lost a number of militia men by the Pleurisy," lamented Charles Askin in December 1812. "They are taken very sudden and very violently ill, and often die in eight or nine days." Sickness did not strike everyone equally. Disease-ravaged militiamen marvelled at the good health of the regulars. Askin attributed their better health to warmer clothing and more robust constitutions, and while this may have been part of the reason, the regulars had also survived the critical seasoning process and built up immunity to many diseases. Sickness and discharges drastically reduced the effective strength of many companies, placing a greater burden on those who remained. The optimistic young soldier, Askin, wrote his father that desertion had become "very common."[42]

Although militiamen chafed at the impositions of military life, the demands of the agricultural schedule may have played a more important role in determining the timing and number of desertions. Since all males over the age of 16 were liable to serve, militia duty removed most adult males from the workforce. With each passing week, more farm work went undone. After more than a month of active duty, militiamen became anxious to return to their farms and families. Not surprisingly, desertion rates soared at seeding and harvest time. The clamour to go home became so great that Brock grudgingly allowed one-half of each company to return to their homes. He gave "preference to those whose presence on the farms are most required to bring in their harvest." In rural Upper Canada, that was almost everyone![43] By bending to the will of the militiamen, Brock had set an example that all other British generals would follow for the rest of the war.

Hull's invasion of south-western Upper Canada in early July forced Brock to recall the flank companies a mere two weeks later. Soldiers unable to bring in their crops complained bitterly and many refused to return to duty at all. Magistrates and militia officers who refused to enforce the order enraged Brock more than did the absenteeism.[44]

Sympathetic officers understood perfectly the dilemmas that their men faced; they too had farms that needed attention and tended to look the other way when their men did not report for duty.[45] A month after Hull's invasion approximately one-third of the militia still had not returned to their posts.[46] In the army's view, if officers led with a firm hand, then their men would follow. Accordingly, militia officers became the targets of a campaign to combat chronic absenteeism. One circular reminded the commanders of militia regiments to familiarize themselves with "the militia laws of the land," to obey orders, to fill out their paperwork properly, especially in regards to absentee soldiers, and to bring deserters to justice.[47] In Upper Canada, where officers were first among equals, it was difficult to submit their men to harsh discipline or punishment. Pushing one's friends and neighbours too hard in the field could have negative economic and social consequences at home.

Regulars viewed desertion in stark terms and believed that the militia were indifferent to the war. Desertion not only drained the army of much needed manpower, but it also eroded its cohesiveness and morale. Brock despaired of ever raising a sufficient force to defend the province when so many of the people seemed to favour the United States.[48] In turn, militia officers accused British leaders, Brock excepted, of incompetence and bad management. They reserved their most caustic comments for the commissariat for its inability to supply even the most basic necessities, a failure that seemed to border on "criminal indifference."[49] Militiamen believed, not unreasonably, that the lack of vigorous leadership had left them destitute and inactive and had contributed to their wasting away in squalid camps. Some sympathetic British officers, who had witnessed the militia's privations first hand, agreed, attributing the lack of energy from above for the "drooping spirits of our once high-spirited militia."[50]

Like most volunteer soldiers, the Niagara militiamen served to protect their homes and families, and when their efforts bore no tangible results, they quickly became disillusioned with soldiering. Few were prepared for the inglorious routines of camp and garrison life. Many citizen-soldiers did not see the value in performing menial, and to them, meaningless tasks, while their families went uncared for and their farms lay unattended.[51] militiamen wanted a quick and aggressive war that took the fighting away from their homes and families. Upper Canadians liked that the energetic and combative Brock took the fight to the enemy. His death at Queenston Heights in October threw a pall over the militia.[52] In one breath, Colonel Robert Nichol of the 2nd Norfolk mourned their fallen leader, and in the next, denounced Brock's successors for "bad management and despondency."[53] After Queenston Heights, the war degenerated into a long, drawn-out defensive campaign that sat poorly with Niagara residents who found themselves living on the front lines.

THE FARMER'S WAR

Tensions between British officers and the militia rose throughout the winter and spring of 1813, until the disastrous campaigns of that year exhausted whatever goodwill may have existed between the two. An American army captured York in April and British forces at Niagara braced for an attack against Fort George. A few days before the battle, British Brigadier-General John Vincent, Sheaffe's replacement, complained that the militia were deserting in droves. "I can neither report favourably on their numbers nor their willing co-operation," Vincent wrote of the militia. "Desertion beyond all conception continues to mark their indifference to the important cause in which we are now engaged."[54] But when the rumble of cannon fire announced that the assault had begun, many deserters returned to defend the fort. "At the moment of attack," a British officer later reported, "instead of diminishing [the militia] actually increased to nearly double its numbers by the influx of its brave members who were within reach of the scene of action."[55]

Although militiamen proved willing to fight, by professional standards they made undependable soldiers. Regulars cast the militia's equivocations in the familiar terms of loyalty and disloyalty. Blinkered by such assumptions, generals could not predict with any accuracy when the militia would stand or desert. For many Niagara militiamen, the war blurred distinctions between their roles as soldiers and as the heads of households, all of which became apparent in their practice of serial desertion.[56] For most soldiers, desertion was not the final act of defiance. Men went back and forth between their homes and the front as the situation demanded. After-battle absenteeism was common among soldiers who sneaked away to tell their families that they had escaped unharmed, to give bad news to neighbours and friends, and to take care of neglected farms. Usually, men deserted during periods of inactivity when their presence at the front seemed unnecessary and returned again when battle was imminent. Serial desertion became easier and more common when the battlefield and the home front merged as it did at Niagara. Although absenteeism played havoc with British planning and logistics, unsanctioned leave allowed Niagara militiamen to defend and provide for their families. They likely saw nothing contradictory in these goals.

Following the capture of Fort George, Vincent ordered the British army to retreat up the Niagara peninsula towards Burlington. Although disheartened by the capture of the fort, many militiamen followed the army, believing it would regroup and make a stand at Forty Mile Creek. As the army retreated down the peninsula, a young officer of the Niagara Light Dragoons, Captain William Hamilton Merritt, was moved by the "distressing ... cries of the women" that lined the route. Rather than make a stand at Forty Mile Creek, Vincent dismissed the militia, an action that seemed to signal his intentions of abandoning the peninsula altogether. Merritt expressed his feelings in familiar familial language. "The thought of abandoning the country and leaving everything that was near and dear to me was distressing," he wrote, "still more so the unhappy situation of my family, who were left totally unprotected."[57] Vincent's withdrawal confirmed the suspicions of Niagara residents that the regulars were incompetent and timid. Most gave up hope that the British could or would protect them and returned home to await the American army.

During the American occupation of Niagara, U.S. soldiers plundered houses and either carried away or destroyed livestock, crops, and other valuables, thus leaving many families utterly destitute. Without knowing when or even if the British would return to Niagara, locals attempted to come to some sort of an accommodation with the enemy. The opportunity came at the end of May, when Lieutenant-Colonel James Preston, the American commandant of Fort Erie, while attempting to disarm a potentially hostile population, issued a proclamation offering to protect the families and property of anyone who would sign a parole agreeing not to take up arms against the United States.[58] Paroles provided a convenient way to deal with large numbers of men captured in battle, but they were not intended to lure unarmed men from the countryside. Neither Preston nor the area's farmers quibbled over legal niceties and hundreds of Niagara residents seized on the paroles as a way to protect their property and secure their livelihoods. And when British officers came by to recruit a work party, militiamen held out the little slips of paper and claimed exemption from such duties. When word of these abuses reached Quebec, Sir George Prevost threatened to treat anyone taking a parole as a traitor and proposed to banish them from the colony.[59]

Prevost need not have worried. When American officers proved either unwilling or unable to stop the destruction of private property, many Niagara residents once again took up arms.[60] In small parties, they used their knowledge of the terrain to ambush unwary patrols and to collect information for Vincent at Burlington. News of Vincent's victory over the American army at Stoney Creek on 6 June heartened many in Niagara, and as the British slowly reoccupied the peninsula, militiamen rose to attack the American rearguard.[61] "The whole population is against us," exclaimed Major MacFarland of the 23rd U.S. Infantry.[62] Some captured Upper Canadians had paroles in their pockets.[63] When competency was at stake, citizen-soldiers dispensed with the conventions of war.

British officers never truly understood what motivated the militia, but, when food supplies ran short, they learned to appreciate the dual role of Upper Canadians as soldiers and producers. Their American adversaries had learned to appreciate this fact early in the war. In the summer of 1812, an unidentified informant extolled the virtues of the British system to American Major-General Stephen Van Rensselaer who had problems with his own militia. From his vantage point, the implementation of the flank companies and agricultural furloughs seemed designed to raise a well-trained local defence force while keeping up the morale of the civilian-soldiers. The anonymous commentator believed that these measures "suit the circumstances of the people, and ... prevent them from feeling the burden of the war."[64] Van Rensselaer concurred, observing that the

> harvest has been got in tolerably well, and greater preparation is making for sowing grain then was ever made before. The militia duty is modified as much as possible to suit the circumstances of the people, and measures taken to prevent them from feeling the burden of the war. The women work in the fields, encouragement being given for that purpose.[65]

What looked from the outside like the result of a grand, well-rehearsed plan, was frequently the *ad hoc* response of British generals to unmanageable militiamen.

Compared to the situation in the United States, the British system for managing men and resources may have appeared to be the model of efficiency, but Van Rensselaer painted too rosy a picture of conditions in the Niagara District. Niagara was the breadbasket of Upper Canada, but by 1813, the war had taken a toll on the regions' farms and their ability to sustain both the inhabitants and the army. Abandoned land, war-ravaged fields, labour shortages, and hoarding combined to reduce farm output at a time when consumption increased.

Unlike modern militaries, nineteenth century armies obtained many of their supplies in the areas where they operated. Comparatively little came from outside the region because the long tenuous supply routes stretching across the Great Lakes, up the St. Lawrence and across the ocean to Great Britain and the West Indies, were unreliable, dependent upon weather conditions and susceptible to both interception and disruption. To acquire the tons of food that thousands of soldiers and their animals consumed each month, British officers fanned out across the countryside to buy corn, wheat, peas, beef, and any other consumables. Despite these Herculean efforts, several supply problems plagued the army throughout the war.[66]

Officials from the commissariat and quartermaster departments soon alienated local farmers. Their agents often paid less than the full value for the goods that they took or did not pay at all, leaving it up to the individual to seek compensation directly from the general-in-command. When, for example, Niagara farmer Isaac Vrooman's horse died after being requisitioned by the army, he was denied compensation.[67] For a middling farmer, a horse represented not only a substantial financial investment but, in the days before mechanized agriculture, it was also an important piece of equipment, without which a farm could not operate. Not surprisingly, farmers soon proved reluctant to surrender crops, livestock or horses to anyone in uniform.

The commissariat's voracious appetite was only part of the problem. For several reasons, Niagara farms yielded less during the war. Many American sympathizers left the province during the conflict, thus taking farmland out of production. Militia service took many of the men that remained away from their fields and orchards for extended periods of time, thereby lowering crop yields. One American officer posted in the recently captured town of Niagara informed his local paper that constant militia duty had left the fields uncultivated.[68] The destruction of Niagara by American forces in December 1813, and the sacking of St. Davids a year later, further stretched meagre resources by throwing refugees onto the charity of their neighbours. A growing propensity for farmers to hoard food indicates not just a reluctance to sell to the military, but also that surpluses were shrinking. Simply, when it came to food, farmers put the welfare of their families first.

The prolonged occupation of the Niagara region devastated the countryside and contributed to lower yields. Soldiers of both armies destroyed fences, trampled fields, stole food, and took wagons. Attacks against civilian property increased once the Americans established a foothold on the Niagara peninsula. From Fort George, American soldiers "plundered all the loyal inhabitants of their property" and burned Clark's and Street's mill, one of the few operating mills in the area.[69] When the British returned later in the summer, they found the area desolate. Gazing upon the ruins and blackened chimneys of the once-handsome village of Niagara, Lieutenant William MacEwan reported, "there is nothing to be got here for money."[70] Yet the soldiers still needed to be fed, and hungry men, who could get food in no other way, resorted to stealing. A York militiaman named Thomas Ridout, writing home from Forty Mile Creek near Niagara, regaled his father with stories about how he and his comrades "carry on an extensive robbing of peas, apples, onions, corn, carrots, etc.; for we can get nothing but by stealing, excepting milk which is carefully measured." "We burn rails, steal, pears and peaches at a great rate," Ridout boasted, before adding that the officer-in-command "thinks me the most innocent of the lot."[71]

The actions of hundreds of men like Ridout had serious consequences for Niagara residents. The British soldiers who occupied Richard Beasely's house, for instance, consumed all the rye in his barn and fields, burned his fences for firewood, and requisitioned, but did not return, a sleigh and harness to transport wounded men. Although Beasely's loss was comparatively small, it was personally and economically devastating. As his petition for compensation revealed, "the Farm on which he principally relied for the support of himself and family is rendered wholly useless to him."[72] In vain, generals tried to protect private property, but even threats of "drumhead court martial" could not deter ravenous and mischievous soldiers.[73] By 1814, the food shortage had become critical. There were 5,000 more troops in Niagara than anticipated and, for a period during the summer, the stores contained only enough food to last two weeks. Last year's crop had already been consumed and the current year's crop was still in the fields. The situation was made worse by the fact that many of the mills necessary to grind the wheat had been destroyed.[74]

The challenges of fielding and feeding an army under such conditions prompted British commanders to alter the way they employed the militia. The first of these changes arose from the less-than-satisfactory operation of the flank companies in 1812 and was embodied in the revised Militia Act of 1813. The Act did away with the flank companies and, instead, authorized the creation of a battalion of incorporated militia to be composed of volunteers who would train as regulars and who would serve for the duration of the war. The new militia organization was, according Sir George Prevost, intended to overcome "the difficulties of forming an efficient militia inseparable from a scanty population spread over an extensive surface."[75] More specifically, the crown recognized the "inconveniences" arising from keeping militiamen "from their families and their ordinary occupations" and sought to remedy the problem.[76] In proposing a permanent force of provincial volunteers from across the province, officials acknowledged the inadequacy of the current system and turned, or returned, to a system of raising men that more closely resembled strategies employed in previous colonial wars. The battalion, however, did not meet expectations. Attracting no more than 300 recruits, senior commanders resorted to a draft to raise a militia force.[77]

Before the 1814 campaigning season opened, Lieutenant-General Gordon Drummond, who had been appointed president of the colonial government and had assumed command of British forces in Upper Canada in August 1813, sought to solve both the manpower and supply problems. He asked the Assembly to draft three-fourteenths of the militia for one year, a smaller proportion of the militia than had been channelled into the flank companies. The small but stable militia envisioned by this plan would provide Drummond with a more dependable source of soldiers and would also free men to raise the crops that would feed the army. The Assembly, however, baulked at drafting such a large number of men and permitted the general to have one in every fourteen militiamen.[78] As a result, the Lincoln regiments were again pressed into service. Portions of the Lincoln militia participated in the major battles and skirmishes that raged throughout the summer of 1814. Two hundred men of the 2nd Lincoln fought tenaciously in the 5 July battle at Chippawa, losing over 20 percent of their strength and winning commendations from their commanders.[79] True to form, following the engagement, the men, without orders, dispersed and returned to their homes. Soldiers were not only anxious to see their families, but 16 Lincoln militiamen had been killed in the battle, thus leaving 11 widows and 35 children without fathers. Soldiers needed to take care of these families as well.[80]

On being informed of the latest rounds of desertions, Drummond fumed that "little reliance can be placed on the members of the militia."[81] Within a week, however, Drummond's subordinate, Major-General Phineas Riall, reported that the Lincoln militia was beginning to assemble at Twenty Mile Creek. Four days later, the Lincoln men skirmished with the enemy and won the praise of their commander for exhibiting "the most determined Spirit of Hostility to the Enemy."[82] After the skirmish, Riall anxiously awaited reinforcements that would allow him to strike the main American army. If the expected troops did not arrive, the opportunity would be lost. Citizen-soldiers would not serve long, because on their farms, the hay crop was "now receiving injury" and the "corn ripening fast." Drummond also weighed the benefits of keeping the militia on service, even though "the whole produce of the neighbouring county is in the greatest danger of being lost."[83]

As it turned out, the 1st, 2nd, 4th, and 5th Lincoln stayed long enough to participate in the battle of Lundy's Lane on 26 July and were released from service the next day.[84] Lundy's Lane was the Lincoln militia's last battle of the war.

The greater attention shown by Riall and Drummond to the militiamen's role as producers reflected the British officer corps' newfound desire to maximize both the military potential and productive energies of the militia. Systematic efforts to combat the chronic supply problems that plagued the army began in 1813 with attempts to bring more land under cultivation. The government adopted a policy whereby all farms abandoned by American sympathizers would be conveyed to loyal inhabitants.[85] Simply opening up more land, however, would not increase yields. Men had to be made available to work that land. Increasingly, officers became more conscious of the need to release farmers from militia duty to attend to their crops and made great efforts to retain as much of the fertile peninsula as possible. This policy was made possible by the arrival in Canada of several thousand British troops made available by the defeat of Napoleon in Europe.[86]

Collecting food from reluctant farmers remained the chief obstacle, however. As the commissariat was now held in disdain among local residents, the duty of securing wheat and cattle from the countryside fell increasingly to the men who knew the land and its people best, that is, the officers of the Lincoln regiments. Through July and August, militia officers received orders to procure provisions from their men. Company commanders were to obtain five to 12 bushels of wheat per soldier at a set rate of $2.50 per bushel and cattle at "a fair price." It was hoped that voluntary cooperation would "render coercion unnecessary."[87] Still, the army consumed more food than was available. In August, Drummond sent influential officers into the county to persuade farmers to begin threshing their grain early. Once the wheat was ready for processing, farmers were instructed to transport it to a nearby mill where officers would be waiting to purchase it.[88] Although such intrusions into the day-to-day operation of the farm rankled many, the army had shown itself open to innovation and was making adjustments to suit the demands of its citizen-soldiers.[89] Had the war in Niagara continued beyond 1814, one wonders how successful these reforms would have been.

RECKONING

By one historian's estimate, 75 Lincoln militiamen died as a direct result of the war. Twenty-one were killed in battle or died of wounds and another 54 fell victim to disease or accidents.[90] The number of wounded is unknown, but by applying the traditional ratio of three men wounded for every one killed, approximately 63 Lincoln militiamen received non-fatal wounds during the conflict. Many of these would have resulted in permanent disability given the near universal practice of amputating injured limbs. As many as six percent of the 2,298 men on the rolls of the Lincoln militia in 1811 were either killed or wounded. That rate would rise substantially after deducting from the rolls those men who absconded to the United States and the large number who proved too old or infirm for active duty. Compared with the large number of casualties sustained by regular regiments, the Lincoln militia escaped the war with relatively few losses. But these casualty rates were not inconsequential for rural neighbourhoods, where each man's labour was highly valued and the care of widows and orphans fell to family, friends, and neighbours.

In other ways, too, the war exacted an awful price. A traveller to the Niagara peninsula in 1815 remarked, "everywhere I saw devastation, homes in ashes, fields trampled and laid waste, forts demolished, forests burned and blackened, truly a pitiful sight."[91] It took years for the people of Niagara to rebuild and the region itself never recovered its pre-eminent position in the province. Areas that had not experienced fighting surpassed Niagara in population and prosperity.[92]

The end of the war also ended the association between the regulars and civilian-soldiers. For that, at least, everyone was thankful. The war had highlighted the divergent values and expectations of colonials and British

Burning the Don Bridge, York, 1813 *by Isaac Bellamy (artist) and Edward Scrope Shrapnel (engraver) gives a sense of the damage wrought during the War of 1812 to infrastructure and land, negatively impacting the civilian population. (Library and Archives Canada C-6147)*

officers who, when brought into prolonged contact. Officers charged with defending the empire appeared to be wholly indifferent to the needs and goals of farmer-soldiers, whose primary loyalty was with their families and neighbours, not some abstract entity called Upper Canada.

The Lincoln regiments would fight, as their service record demonstrates, but they did so on their own terms. British officers interpreted the militia's behaviour as apathy verging on disloyalty. But if neither party understood the other well, in time, militiamen, by their continued commitment to competency, forced British generals to grudgingly modify their expectations and utilization of civilian-soldiers. Regular officers did not do so out of any desire to ease the burdens of farmers. They did it in the face of the hard realities of trying to sustain an army in Upper Canada.

The Lincoln militia's war was not, then, about preserving Upper Canada for the empire or even about protecting the province from republican government. There is little evidence to suggest that either the loyalists' descendants or later immigrants cared much about such things.

This does not mean that the population of Niagara was indifferent or apathetic to the war. Their disobedience, also, did not spring from disloyalty or an aversion to military service. As a people living on the front lines,

Niagara's citizen-soldiers were most concerned about protecting their families and preserving the generation of hard work that had transformed the Upper Canadian wilderness into a world of small, but comfortable, farms. Bravely resisting American armies one day and deserting the next were different expressions of their overarching commitment to competence.

NOTES

Editor's Note: The author gratefully acknowledges the Social Sciences and Humanities Research Council and the Donald S. Rickerd Fellowship in Canadian-American Studies for funding the research from which this chapter is drawn. An earlier version of this discussion was presented at the Thirteenth Military History Colloquium held at Waterloo, Ontario, in 2002. I would also like to thank Jane Errington, Michel Beaulieu, Craig Mantle, and Richard Mayne for their insightful comments and criticisms.

1. Brock to Prevost, 12 July and 28 July 1812, in E.A. Cruikshank, ed., *Documentary History of the Campaign on the Niagara Frontier in 1812–1814* [henceforth *DH*] (Welland: Lundy's Lane Historical Society, 1896–1908), Vol. 3, 123 and 149.

2. C.P. Stacey, "The War of 1812 in Canadian History," *Ontario History,* Vol. 50, No. 3 (Summer 1958), 153–59; G.F.G. Stanley, "The Contribution of the Canadian Militia during the War," in Philip Mason, ed., *After Tippecanoe: Some Aspects of the War of 1812* (Toronto: Ryerson Press, 1963), 28–48.

3. George Sheppard, *Plunder, Profit, and Paroles: A Social History of the War of 1812 in Upper Canada* (Montreal and Kingston: McGill-Queen's University Press [henceforth MQUP], 1994), 3, 18–39, 83.

4. Janet Carnochan, *History of Niagara* (Toronto: William Briggs, 1914), 147. In calculating the population of the Niagara District, I have followed Douglas McCalla's formula of estimating the number of households from regimental muster rolls and multiplying this figure by six, which represents the average number of family members per household. In 1811, the rolls of the five Lincoln regiments listed 2,298 men, representing some 13,788 people. See Douglas McCalla, *Planting the Province: The Economic History of Upper Canada, 1784–1780* (Toronto: University of Toronto Press [henceforth UTP], 1993), 31.

5. Michael Smith, *A Geographical View of the Province of Upper Canada and Promiscuous Remarks on the Government* (Trenton: Moore and Lake, 1813), 61.

6. The following discussion of land, labour, and independence is informed by James A. Henretta, "Families and Farms: Mentalité in Pre-industrial America," *The Origins of American Capitalism: Collected Essays,* James A. Henretta, ed. (Boston: Northeastern University Press, 1991); Daniel Vickers, *Farmers and Fishermen: Two Centuries of Work in Essex County Massachusetts, 1630–1830* (Chapel Hill: University of North Carolina Press, 1994); and Richard L. Bushman, "Markets and Farms in Early America," *William and Mary Quarterly,* 3rd Series, Vol. 60, No. 3 (1998), 351–74.

7. Lieutenant-Governor Hope to Commissioners for American Claims, 29 January 1786, in E.A. Cruikshank, ed., *Records of Niagara: A Collection of Documents Relating to the First Settlement, 1784–1789* [henceforth *RN*] (Niagara-on-the-Lake: Niagara Historical Society, 1928), Vol. 39, 80.

8. La Rochefoucauld-Liancourt, William Renwick Riddell, ed., *La Rochefoucault-Liancourt's Travels in Canada, 1795,* in Alexander Fraser, ed., *Thirteenth Report* of the Bureau of Archives of the Province of Ontario (Toronto: A.T. Wilgress, 1916), 24.

9. Benjamin Mortimer, "From Pennsylvania to Upper Canada with Johns Heckewelder," in James Doyle, ed., *Yankees in Canada: A Collection of Nineteenth-Century Travel Narratives* (Downsview: ECW Press, 1980), 27.

10. Peter A. Russell, "Upper Canada: A Poor Man's Country? Some Statistical Evidence," in Donald H. Akenson, ed., *Canadian Papers in Rural History* (Gananoque: Langdale, 1982), Vol. 3, 129–47; Peter Marshall, "Americans in Upper Canada, 1791–1812: 'Late Loyalists' or Early Immigrants," in Barbara J. Messamore, ed., *Canadian Immigration Patterns from Britain and North America* (Ottawa: University of Ottawa, 2004), 33–44.

11. Elizabeth Jane Errington, *Wives and Mothers, School Mistresses and Scullery Maids: Working Women in Upper Canada, 1790–1840* (Montreal and Kingston: MQUP, 1995) xv, 81–4.

12. Cruikshank, Robert Sutcliff Journal, *RN,* Vol. 42, 2 December 1805, 22–3.

13. R. Janet Powell, ed., *Annals of the Forty, 1783–1818* (Grimsby Historical Society, 1955), Vol. 1, 29; McCalla, *Planting the Province,* 24–7.

14. Powell, *Annals of the Forty,* 29.

15. Catharine Anne Wilson, "Reciprocal Work Bees and the Meaning of Neighbourhood," *Canadian Historical Review,* Vol. 82, No. 3 (2001), 431–64.

16. George Hariot, *Travels through the Canadas* (London, 1807; reprint, Toronto: Coles Publishing, 1907), 154–55.

17. E.A. Cruikshank, ed., "Smith to Askin, 2 October 1792," *The Correspondence of Lieut. Governor John Graves Simcoe, With Allied Documents Relating to His Administration of the Government of Upper Canada* (Toronto: Ontario Historical Society, 1923–31), Vol. 1, 232. Jane Errington has shown that in constructing a distinctly Upper Canadian political ideology, elites did not uncritically embrace British institutions or reject out of hand all things American. In fact, Upper Canada's political leaders reached out to like-minded Federalists in New York and New England as allies in a struggle against the democratic excesses of the post-Revolutionary period. See Jane Errington, *The Lion and the Eagle in Upper Canada* (Montreal and Kingston: MQUP, 1988), 3–10. See also, Jane Errington and George Rawlyk, "The Loyalist-Federalist Alliance of Upper Canada," *American Review of Canadian Studies,* Vol. 14, No. 2 (1984), 157–76.

18. La Rochefoucauld-Liancourt, *Travels in Canada,* 30–1.

19. Errington, *The Lion and the Eagle,* 29.

20. Cruikshank, Vincent to Prevost, 28 May 1813, *DH,* Vol. 5, 252. Emphasis added by present author.

21. Cruikshank, *RN,* Vol. 42, 115.

22. Cruikshank, Militia Law, 1808, *DH,* Vol. 3, 3–7. William Gray provides an excellent overview of the Upper Canadian militia in William Gray, *Soldiers of the King: The Upper Canadian Militia, 1812–1815* (Erin: Boston Mills Press, 1995).

23. Cruikshank, Warren to Shaw, 12 April 1812, *RN,* Vol. 43, 22.

24. Library and Archives Canada [henceforth LAC], Record Group [henceforth RG] 5 A1, *Upper Canada Sundries* [henceforth *UCS*], Vol. 13, 5451–53, Bradt to the Adjutant-General of the Militia, 8 June 1811.

25. The Militia Act stipulated that flank companies should contain no more than 100 men per regiment, but Brock instructed regimental commanders to raise 35 man companies, exclusive of officers and sergeants. See Cruikshank, An Act to Amend the Militia Act, *DH,* Vol. 3, 5–11; *Ibid.,* Brock to Nichol, 8 April 1812, 51–2.

26. *Ibid.,* An Act to Amend the Militia Act, 5–11.

27. *Ibid.,* Brock to Prevost, 15 May 1812, 61–2; Cruikshank, Clark to Shaw, 3 April 1812, *RN,* Vol. 43, 21; *Ibid.,* Warren to Shaw, 12 April 1812, 22.

28. Fred Anderson, *A People's Army: Massachusetts Soldiers and Society in the Seven Years' War* (New York and London: W.W. Norton, 1984), 26–7; John Shy, *A People Numerous and Armed: Reflections on the Military Struggle for American Independence* (Ann Arbor: University of Michigan Press, 1990), 37–8, 173–74; and Charles

Royster, *A Revolutionary People at War: The Continental Army and American Character, 1775–1783* (New York: W.W. Norton, 1979), 65–6, 71.

29. Cruikshank, Brock to Prevost, 3 July 1812, *DH,* Vol. 3, 94.

30. *Ibid.,* 12 July 1812, 123.

31. *Ibid.,* Quartermaster-General to Clark, 3 July 1812, 95; Cruikshank, Askin to Father, 18 November 1812, *RN,* Vol. 43, 59.

32. Cruikshank, Hall to Tompkins, 28 June 1812, *DH,* Vol. 3, 79; *Ibid.,* Swift and Barton to Tompkins, 24 June 1812, 72.

33. *Ibid.,* Brock to Prevost, 12 July 1812, 123.

34. Cruikshank, District General Order, 20 October 1812, *DH,* Vol. 4, 141; *Ibid.,* District General Order, 9 November 1812, *ibid.,* 188.

35. Matilda Ridout Edgar, *Ten Years in Upper Canada in Peace and War, 1805–1815* (Toronto: William Briggs, 1890), 129; Cruikshank, General Order, 4 July 1812, *DH,* Vol. 3, 97.

36. Cruikshank, Brock to Prevost, 3 July 1812, *DH,* Vol. 4, 94; *Ibid.,* 12 July 1812, 123.

37. *Ibid.,* District General Orders, 21 October 1812, 153.

38. Cruikshank, Brock to Prevost, 28 September 1812, *DH,* Vol. 3, 199–200.

39. *Ibid.,* Brock to Evans, 17 August 1812, 186; Cruikshank, Roll of Males in the Limits of Captain John D. Servos's Company, 1st Regt., *RN,* Vol. 43, 34; Cruikshank, Brock to Prevost, 28 September 1812, *DH,* Vol. 3, 199–200.

40. Cruikshank, Askin to Father, 18 November 1812, *RN,* Vol. 43, 59–60; Cruikshank, *DH,* Vol. 4, 176.

41. Cruikshank, District General Orders, 4 December 1812, *DH,* Vol. 4, 277.

42. Cruikshank, Askin to Askin, 11 December 1812, *DH,* Vol. 3, 238–39.

43. *Ibid.,* Militia General Order, 10 July 1812, 119–20.

44. *Ibid.,* Brock to Prevost, 26 July 1812, *ibid.,* 145; *Ibid.,* 28 July 1812, *ibid.,* 149.

45. Cruikshank, Suggestions, 7 April 1813, *DH,* Vol. 5, 149–50.

46. Cruikshank, Myers to Prevost, 17 August 1812, *DH,* Vol. 3, 185–86.

47. Cruikshank, Suggestions, 7 April 1813, *DH,* Vol. 5, 149–50.

48. Cruikshank, Brock to Prevost, 11 October 1812, *DH,* Vol. 4, 64–5.

49. *Ibid.*, Nichol to Talbot, 18 December 1812, 327.

50. Cruikshank, J.B. Glegg to anonymous, 10 January 1813, *DH,* Vol. 5, 32–3; Cruikshank, Rottenburg to Prevost, 7 July 1813, *DH,* Vol. 6, 199–200.

51. American militiamen made similar complaints during the Revolution. See Royster, *A Revolutionary People at War,* 34, 59–63.

52. See, for example, Cruikshank, W. Chewett *and others* to anonymous, 8 May 1813, *DH,* Vol. 5, 200–02.

53. Cruikshank, Nichol to Talbot, 18 December 1812, *DH,* Vol. 4, 327; Cruikshank, W. Chewett *and others* to anonymous, 8 May 1813, *DH,* Vol. 5, 200–02.

54. *Ibid.*, Vincent to Prevost, 19 May 1813, 237.

55. *Ibid.*, Militia District General Orders, 4 June 1813, 301.

56. I have borrowed the concept of serial desertion from recent studies of the Confederate Army during the American Civil War. See Gary W. Gallagher, *The Confederate War* (Cambridge: Harvard University Press, 1997), 31–2; William Blair, *Virginia's Private War: Feeding Body and Soul in the Confederacy, 1861–1865* (New York: Oxford University Press, 1998), 66, 88–9.

57. Cruikshank, Notes by W.H. Merritt, [May 1813], *DH,* Vol. 5, 261–63.

58. *Ibid.*, Proclamation by Lieutenant-Colonel Preston, 30 May 1813, 73.

59. Niagarans were not alone in taking paroles. Men in the Home District also took paroles in large numbers after the capture of York. See Stanley, "Canadian Militia during the War," 39; Cruikshank, Bathurst to Prevost, 11 August 1813, *DH,* Vol. 7, 9.

60. Cruikshank, MacFarland to his wife, [1814], *DH,* Vol. 1, 73; Cruikshank, New York *Evening Post,* 30 May 1813, *DH,* Vol. 5, 272; Cruikshank, Notes by Captain W.H. Merritt, [June or July 1813], *DH,* Vol. 6, 209; *Ibid.*, New York *Evening Post,* 28 June 1813, 103.

61. Cruikshank describes a number of small actions that took place during the spring and summer of 1813. See "The Lincoln Militia," in E.A. Cruikshank, ed., *Records and*

Services of Canadian Regiments in the War of 1812 (n.p., n.d.), 17.

62. Cruikshank, MacFarland to his wife, [1814], *DH,* Vol. 1, 73.

63. Cruikshank, *Independent Chronicle,* 28 June 1813, *DH,* Vol. 6, 71.

64. Cruikshank, anonymous to Van Rensselaer, *DH,* Vol. 3, 16 September 1812, 268–69.

65. *Ibid.*

66. Sheppard, *Plunder, Profit, and Paroles,* 100–20.

67. LAC, RG 5 A1, *UCS,* Vol. 22, 9650, [Isaac Vrooman's Petition], 16 March 1815.

68. Cruikshank, Baltimore *Whig,* 14 June 1813, *DH,* Vol. 5, 275.

69. Edgar, *Ten Years in Upper Canada,* 228; Cruikshank, New York *Evening Post,* 28 June 1813, *DH,* Vol. 6, 103; *Ibid.,* Notes by Captain W.H. Merritt, [June or July 1813], *ibid.,* 209; Cruikshank, Prevost to Cochrane, 30 July 1814, *DH,* Vol. 1, 177.

70. Cruikshank, MacEwan to MacEwan, 31 March 1813, *DH,* Vol. 9, 266.

71. Edgar, *Ten Years in Upper Canada,* 212 and 225.

72. LAC, RG 5 A1, *UCS,* Vol. 19, 7977–78, Beasely to Drummond, 19 March 1814.

73. Cruikshank, District General Order, 29 July 1813, *DH,* Vol. 6, 291.

74. Cruikshank, Robinson to Prevost, 27 August 1814, *DH,* Vol. 1, 180–81.

75. Cruikshank, Prevost to Bathurst, 21 April 1813, *DH,* Vol. 5, 159.

76. Cruikshank, Bathurst to Sheaffe, 8 June 1813, *DH,* Vol. 6, 58.

77. Sheppard, *Plunder, Profit, and Paroles,* 70–6; Gray, *Soldiers of the King,* 31–4.

78. Cruikshank, Drummond to Prevost, 8 February 1814, *DH,* Vol. 9, 189–90; Cruikshank, Drummond to Prevost, 23 July 1814, *DH,* Vol. 1, 86.

79. Stanley, "Canadian Militia during the War," 42; Cruikshank, Riall to Drummond, 6 July 1814, *DH,* Vol. 1, 31–3; LAC, RG 5 A1, *UCS,* Vol. 20, 8644–50, Militia General Orders, 10 July 1814.

80. LAC, RG 5 A1, *UCS,* Vol. 20, 8602, A return of the Militiamen who were killed or wounded in the Sortie which Took Place on the 5th Instant, 6 July 1814.

81. Cruikshank, Drummond to Prevost, 16 July 1814, *DH,* Vol. 1, 54.

82. *Ibid.,* Riall to Drummond, 15 July 1814, 60; Riall to Drummond, 19 July 1814, in William Wood, ed., *Select British Documents of the Canadian War of 1812* (Toronto: The Champlain Society, 1923–1928), Vol. 3, Part 1, 138.

83. Cruikshank, Drummmond to Riall, 23 July 1814, *DH,* Vol. 1, 86.

84. *Ibid.,* Riall to Drummond, 17 July 1814, 71; Wood, *Select British Documents,* Vol. 3, Part 2, District General Order, 26 July 1814, 154; Cruikshank, "The Lincoln Militia," 23–4.

85. Cruikshank, Rottenburg to Prevost, 17 September 1813, *DH,* Vol. 7, 140; Cruikshank, District General Orders, 24 July 1813, *DH,* Vol. 6, 268–69; LAC, RG 5 A1, *UCS,* Vol. 16, 6662, Application of John Mann, 28 August 1813.

86. Louis L. Babcock, *The War of 1812 on the Niagara Frontier* (Buffalo: Buffalo Historical Society, 1927), 109; Cruikshank, Drummond to Prevost, 23 July 1814, *DH,* Vol. 1, 86.

87. *Ibid.,* Turquand to Secord, 8 July 1814, 58; *Ibid.,* Militia General Order, 25 August 1814, 187.

88. *Ibid.,* Drummond to Prevost, 24 August 1814, 186; *Ibid.,* Foster to Ball, n.d., 187.

89. Cruikshank, Rottenburg to Prevost, 17 September 1813, *DH,* Vol. 7, 140; Cruikshank, Drummond to Prevost, 24 August 1814, *DH,* Vol. 1, 186.

90. Cruikshank, "Lincoln Militia," 25–7. Cruikshank's estimates do not include six men reported killed at Chippawa. LAC, RG 5 A1, *UCS,* Vol. 20, 8602, A return of the militiamen who were killed or wounded in the Sortie which Took Place on the 5th Instant, 6 July 1814.

91. Thomas Verchères de Boucherville, "The Chronicles of Thomas Verchères de Boucherville," in *War on the Detroit,* M.M. Quaife, ed. (Chicago: Lakeside, 1940), as cited in Sheppard, *Plunder, Profit, and Paroles,* 172.

92. David Murray, *Colonial Justice: Justice, Morality, and Crime in the Niagara District, 1791–1849* (Toronto: UTP, 2002), 12–4.

3

Discontent in Upper Canada During the War of 1812: The 2nd Leeds Regiment of Gananoque

HOWARD G. COOMBS

The sense of Canadian nationality, which has radiated out from Upper Canada, or Ontario, through all the west and to some degree the Maritime provinces, dates from the War of 1812…. Upper Canada emerged from the War of 1812 a community, its people no longer Americans nor solely British subjects, but Upper Canadians. The essence of the War of 1812 is that it built the first storey of the Canadian national edifice.[1]
— Arthur R. M. Lower, *Colony to Nation: A History of Canada*

In his history of Canada, Professor Arthur Lower, a masterful historian with a profound grasp of the grand narrative, illustrates the mythic image of the War of 1812, a conflict that supposedly united the disparate groups that inhabited Upper Canada in the early nineteenth century. The reality of the popular sentiment that surrounds this conflict, however, is much more complex and, in this chapter, will be illustrated through the examination of an Upper Canadian militia unit, the 2nd Leeds Regiment, as described in the records of its commander, Colonel Joel Stone, and depicted in other primary and secondary sources.

Located between Kingston and Brockville, the township of Leeds and Lansdowne was surveyed in 1788, but did not receive a substantial influx of settlers until the 1790s.[2] The delay between initial mapping and settlement was in part because of early, erroneous reports of poor agricultural land in the region. As a result, the township was virtually ignored during the exodus of loyalists from the United States.[3] When it was discovered that there were sizable tracts of good farmland, the individuals who relocated to the area did so to better themselves financially.[4] One such settler was Joel Stone, whose correspondence records not only the viewpoint of the Upper Canadian administration, but also describes how the community expressed their dissatisfaction with their forced participation in the war. More important, these documents describe the willingness of local inhabitants to directly confront Stone to express their thoughts regarding participation in the War of 1812.

Tensions between the United States and Great Britain increased during the years before 1812. In August 1807, a British vessel sank the American ship *Chesapeake*. In the succeeding years, as a prelude to war, there existed a heightened degree of animosity between the two countries. The leaders of Upper Canada were concerned that most of the populace, who had recently immigrated, would not fight against their former countrymen. It was recognized that without the complete cooperation of all settlers, the likelihood of success in a war against the United States was minimal. Therefore, in the aftermath of the *Chesapeake* incident, the political leadership of Upper Canada actively encouraged loyalty to the Crown and extolled the virtues of the colony's link to Great Britain.[5]

The concerns of the authorities were justified. Ernest A. Cruikshank, in "A Study of Disaffection in Upper Canada in 1812–15," outlines many incidents that the authorities construed as disloyal and treasonous. He agrees that the underlying cause of this initial ambivalence, and later, active subversion, was the extensive immigration from the United States in the decades immediately before the war.[6] The trustworthiness of the Upper Canadian militia was of great concern to the governing elite and was the focus of much effort to ensure its obedience to the military imperatives of defence.[7] The government took steps to address seditious behaviour and to ensure the loyalty of the population through the enactment and enforcement of legislation designed to ensure compliance with the desires of the administration. Prominent loyalists, such as Stone, assisted with the implementation and enforcement of these laws.[8]

The organization for the defence of Leeds and Lansdowne had its origins in regulations from the Legislature of Upper Canada, that in 1793, decreed that all counties would have a sedentary militia that would be used only to repel an aggressor.[9] It was composed of all local men aged 16 to 60, whose officers were chosen from the area and selected according to property qualifications. Mustered annually, these militia units were structured as regiments, commanded by a colonel, who had a lieutenant-colonel and a major to assist him. Each regiment normally had five to 10 companies, each composed of 20 to 50 private soldiers and officered by a captain, lieutenant, and ensign.[10]

As a result of the increasing tensions immediately before the commencement of the war,[11] Brock issued a proclamation calling for the creation of flank companies for each militia unit. These companies were to be composed of volunteers who would train for six days per month. By enacting this legislation, Major-General Isaac Brock, the president of Upper Canada, hoped to create a nucleus around which the militia could be embodied in times of crisis.[12] Regrettably for the government of Upper Canada, these efforts were not successful and the militia, as a whole, demonstrated a marked reluctance to leave their local area or be used in a manner other than for regional protection. They were, for the most part, full-time farmers who reluctantly acquiesced to the need of being temporary soldiers in defence of home and hearth. Attempts to use them in a manner other than the role that they constructed for themselves were doomed to meet with failure.[13]

The county of Leeds had two militia regiments, the 1st Leeds, with Colonel James Breakenridge and Lieutenant-Colonel Livius Peter Sherwood, and the 2nd Leeds, led by Colonel Joel Stone and Lieutenant-Colonel Benoni Wiltsie.[14] Stone was a prominent United Empire Loyalist who had moved to the Gananoque region in 1792 or 1793, and during the war, in addition to his militia colonelcy, was a Justice of the Peace. He was also the postmaster and had been collector of customs since 1803. In February 1812, he was appointed as a commissioner for the district of Johnstown[15] to enforce anti-sedition legislation passed by Brock.[16] Stone was an important member of the community, with a vested interest in the preservation of British control of Upper Canada.[17] In *Soldiers of the King*, William Gray states that the 2nd Leeds in 1811 consisted of 418 soldiers or "rank and file," and that between July 1812 and late 1814, a total of 103 of these men deserted to the United States. Gray goes on to dryly suggest that the district of Johnstown "was not considered one of the more dependable."[18]

To explain this disaffection, Donald Akenson, in *The Irish in Ontario,* analysed the behaviour of those in the 2nd Leeds using a self-constructed paradigm of predicted behaviour. By utilizing the products of his considerable research in the district, he predicted that the general responses of the people to the war were non-ideological and rooted in self-interest. Any involvement with the war was viewed as a short-term commitment and the preponderance of the local populace drawn into the conflict expected to acquire material rewards from their participation. Concepts of patriotism and nationalism served to rationalize profiteering or seeking of post-war rewards.[19]

The economic networks of the region in combination with settlement patterns had created strong compacts across the border of Upper Canada and the United States that contributed to these pragmatic beliefs. As settlement developed on the American side of the border, the demand for Upper Canadian agricultural products and European manufactured goods from northern merchants increased. This situation created a local market for Upper Canadian farms and entrepreneurs on terms beneficial to the vendors. The alternative was to ship products to other regions for comparable prices, less the cost of shipping, handling and insurance.[20] Within these trade relationships, one can see the foundation of Akenson's theory of self-interest.

As will become apparent, Akenson's conclusions are supported by the actions of the 2nd Leeds themselves. The members of this militia regiment had constructed their world and, as such, possessed a common understanding of their perceived interests relative to those of the Upper Canadian administration. The English historian E.P. Thompson concludes when discussing class:

> And class happens when some men, as a result of common experiences (inherited or shared), feel and articulate the identity of their interests as between themselves and against other men whose interests are different from and usually opposed to theirs. The class experience is usually determined by the productive relations into which men are born — or enter involuntarily.[21]

It should be kept in mind that when delineating this articulation of shared awareness, Thompson viewed class as a "relationship not a thing."[22] Membership in a class is defined by the social role of the individual and history attempts to answer how this occurred. Class must be studied as a social and cultural process, defined by people, as they create their own history.[23]

The incidents of disaffection demonstrated by members of the 2nd Leeds can be viewed as an expression of the common interests outlined by Akenson. These common interests coalesced into collective action as a response to Upper Canadian participation in the War of 1812. Involvement in this protest was not derived from socio-economic status, but instead arose from an almost Thompsonian model of inherited and shared experiences and interests. The articulation of the mutual concerns of the people of Leeds against the actions of the governing elite evidenced itself in a number of forms. Desertion, refusing to muster, and the manner in which civil and military law was implemented to defend members of the community against the central government and military authorities were common manifestations of protest. As well, other indications of dissatisfaction were evidenced in how the 2nd Leeds performed during their engagement with American forces at Gananoque on 21 September 1812, and the theft perpetuated at Stone's farm where members of his regiment and others broke into his barn on 10 November 1814.

FORMS OF INDIVIDUAL PROTEST

Desertion is a form of protest traditionally used to demonstrate discontent, and during the War of 1812, many members of Upper Canadian militia units, including the 2nd Leeds, deserted from their regiments. Although desertion is not defined within the Militia Law of 1808, its usage in the context of the militia returns between 1812 and 1815 seems to indicate that it was mostly applied to those who fled the region during the war. These desertion rates demonstrate the willingness of individuals to undertake a form of action that was irreconcilable with the interests of the government and irrevocable once committed. Akenson suggests that in the absence of accurate opinion polls, desertion rates serve to provide an indication of popular sentiment regarding the war.[24] An examination of

Gray's 1811 figure of 418 soldiers in the 2nd Leeds and his 1814 reduction in numbers to 315 rank and file, would seem to indicate a decline in manpower between 1812 and 1814 of almost 25 percent. Akenson presents a similar picture of loss, using returns of deserters for three of the seven companies of the 2nd Leeds between 1812 and 1814.[25]

After examining the evidence presented by Akenson and Gray, there seems to be a discrepancy in the manner in which the figures were deduced. Akenson's figures are derived from the total of all ranks in each company; this calculation does not take into account the extremely small likelihood of the officers and non-commissioned officers (NCOs) leaving the community in such an absolute fashion. The Militia Laws provided that the governor, lieutenant-governor, or any person responsible for administering the province, was responsible for the selection and approval of officers and these officers, in turn, were to choose their NCOs. The likelihood of the government choosing officers and NCOs who did not support their objectives and who did not possess vested interests in their own communities is unlikely.[26] One can then reasonably assume that the probability of officers or NCOs deserting was negligible.

If this is the case, it may be of more utility to use Gray's method of calculation, derived solely from the number of soldiers, to gain a more precise perspective on desertion. Nonetheless, Akenson's figures are outlined in Table 3.1.[27]

Company Commander	Strength of Company (as of 4 June 1814)	Number of Deserters (from 1 July 1812)	Average Losses (%)
William Jones	41	6	14.6
Duncan Livingstone	46	14	30.4
Ira Schofield	38	11	28.9
Total	125	31	24.8

Table 3.1: Desertion Rates in the 2nd Leeds.

If the figures are changed, as in Table 3.2, so that the strengths reflect solely the rank and file, the desertion averages, using Akenson's method, increase.[28]

Company Commander	Strength of Company (as of 4 June 1814)	Number of Deserters (from 1 July 1812)	Average Losses (%)
William Jones	33	6	18.2
Duncan Livingstone	38	14	36.8
Ira Schofield	31	11	35.4
Total	102	31	30.4

Table 3.2: Amended Figures

Besides the three companies cited by Akenson, returns from a fourth company, that of Captain Joseph Wiltsee, reflect a much higher rate of loss. This return lists 28 men who "deserted to the enemy from the limits of Captain Joseph Wiltses Company since the first of July 1812," and, given a complement of 37 on 4 June 1814, would indicate a desertion rate of 75.7 percent.[29]

To gain a more accurate indicator of wartime attrition, it is more appropriate to use a quarterly return for 1812, after the commencement of the war, as a baseline measurement. The later return for 1814 can be utilized in conjunction with these figures to calculate percentages based on the rank and file, as well as the aggregate totals for the 2nd Leeds.[30] The results of these computations can be seen in Table 3.3 and demonstrate that the 2nd Leeds slightly increased in size during the war.

In the face of this seeming contradiction between the returns of deserters produced by the four companies and the unchanging wartime numbers in the 2nd Leeds, one can suppose that the greater portion of those who deserted did so during the summer of 1812. In many cases, these men left with their families, as Stone communicated to Colonel James Breakenridge of the 1st Leeds in July 1812:

A Mr. Wellor, a Blacksmith by trade, living near Joseph Haskins in Redaugh, who came with his family to Seman's, went off in a canoo — with Kinkcade one of the men who was in the Vessel that was burnt — as they said a fishing leaving their familys behind — they two were gone about three days — returned at Evening — and the next Morning about Ten o'clock there came a boat from the American shore with about fifteen armed men in it — who took off Wellor and two men Brothers name Kinkade with all their familys to the United States on the 14th July 1812.[31]

2nd Leeds Regiment	24 December 1812	4 June 1814	Difference (%)
Total Strength	365	378	+3.4
Rank and File	313	315	+0.6
Difference	52	63*	

*This increase was due almost exclusively to an increase in the number of officers.

Table 3.3: Comparison of Quarterly Returns of December 1812 and June 1814.

If this were the case, Gray's 1811 figure indicating a higher strength of 418 in the unit would support the conclusion offered immediately above. Consequently, by December of 1812, most of those who wished to leave had done so and those who remained with the 2nd Leeds employed other forms of dissent. An interesting postscript to this migration, however, is a list of deserters compiled by the 2nd Leeds in June 1816. It named 68 men who had returned to the Johnstown district after the conflict. This document included both pre-war American residents and native Upper Canadians.[32]

Another form of desertion was absenteeism from regimental parades. In the context of the 1808 legislation, it was an offence not to muster when so directed and the penalty was a large fine. If the offender was

This watercolour, Detachment of the 76th Regiment in Pursuit of Deserters, St. Andrew's, *by James Cumming Clarke is one of a series showing the regiment at work and play in and around the New Brunswick town. (Library and Archives Canada C-39748)*

unable to pay, he was to be imprisoned for six to 12 months.[33] The 1812 amendments to this legislation provided for a maximum sentence of death, although this penalty was avoided. Historian George Sheppard critiques Akenson and Shirley Spragge for not using attendance at regimental musters as an indicator of desertion. With the penalties that could be enforced, it would be a significant statement for an individual not to gather with the 2nd Leeds when directed to do so. Sheppard indicates that throughout the war, unit attendance was problematic and at times absences reached approximately 70 percent. One of the most severe incidents of refusing to muster occurred in October 1813.[34]

Stone reported to the President of the Province of Upper Canada, Major-General Gordon Drummond, in 1814: "Permit me to report to your honor the general state of the 2d Regt of Leeds Militia under my command since the month of June 1813 — At or about which time the 2d Militia appeared to be more negligent than usual."[35] Stone went on to describe how on 27 October 1813, he had received orders from Lieutenant-Colonel Thomas Pearson, the Inspecting Field Officer of Upper Canada,[36] on behalf of Major-General Francis de Rottenburg, "to order out the whole of my

[Stone's] militia." Most officers had mustered, but only 70 NCOs and soldiers had appeared. In response to this intransigence, Stone directed the bulk of his officers to go about the district and gather the remainder of the regiment. This endeavour met with little success and while the officers canvassed the area, the majority of the 70 who had initially attended returned to their homes. Stone immediately reported this situation to Colonel Nathaniel Coffin, the deputy adjutant-general of the Upper Canadian militia,[37] who ordered him, on 13 November 1813, to take such action as he "might deem most expedient for the good of His Majesty's service."[38]

Stone decided to use the provisions of the Militia Act to compel all local militia to muster, and on 2 December, he met with all of his militia officers to propose prosecuting the offenders under the existing laws. At this meeting, he and Lieutenant-Colonel Wiltsie, his second-in-command, had a falling out over this issue. According to Stone, Wiltsie "made use of such unbecoming words — as caused me to order him to retire."[39] On 27 December, Stone ordered courts-martial to be convened and directed a special session of the magistrates to charge people who were aiding these deserters.[40] Stone observed:

> ... we soon discovered to our full satisfaction — That many of the elderly persons in the county — suc[h] as Fathers — Mothers — and other heads of families had (by their bad examples and counsel) poisoned the minds of the youth — who at the commencement of the year promised to make good soldiers — and worthy members of society.[41]

Unfortunately for Stone, these attempts to enforce the law came to a halt when he tried to obtain the court costs of both the military and civil sessions from those whom he believed culpable. A James Breakenridge[42] and others, who threatened to "prosecute the said court of special session for extortion," caused the magistrates, who seemed to be reluctantly proceeding with these trials, to lose interest.[43] To be sure, the tacit approval of the community was the common thread that linked these actions of dissent.

This subversion of the laws and regulations of the government of Upper Canada is described by Stone as a reoccurring form of protest. In a letter to Drummond in March 1814, he notes that a tailor of his regiment had deserted to the enemy in 1812, leaving "his work and the King's cloth in confusion."[44] Stone recounts that this tailor was captured at Ogdensburg and was paroled. The tailor then sued Stone in the District Court at Brockville for £15. Even though Stone does not specify why the tailor sought this recompense, it seems as if it could have been for the work that he had been directed to complete on behalf of the 2nd Leeds two years previously. The judgment was levied against Stone and he was commanded to pay, despite his objections. He observed that the three magistrates who sat on this judgment included James Breakenridge.[45] Stone also made some succinct and poignant comments regarding the impact of what he viewed as an improper implementation of regulations:

> This singular use of Law — has Allarmed myself and other Commanding officers of Militia — who have ever considered it to be their Duty to give orders and to exert themselves to furnish every real necessary — to Accommodate the Said Militia when on Duty fully confident that the Government — will Soon provide against such unreasonable Litigation — The Decision as also appear to be a Signal — for all to come forward and Ruin — By the most perplexing Law suits those who were the most conspicuous in calling forth the strength of the Country — at a time when the exertions of the Militia was much required.[46]

Stone's concerns were justified, for in July 1813, Lieutenant-Colonel Wiltsie sent a letter to Stone stating that Breakenridge and others were assisting some individuals in attempting to prosecute Stone and Wiltsie through the courts for grievances that seemed to be connected to their enforcement of the Militia Act.[47] Regrettably, there seems to be no record concerning the final disposition of this matter; however, Stone does mention in a letter to the adjutant-general in 1818 that the prosecutions against him in the district had subsided, yet there were still attacks against him in the House of Assembly.[48]

In the final analysis, many members of the 2nd Leeds simply ignored any demands to parade if they thought it unreasonable to do so. This shared set of values went so far as to impede the implementation of the laws promulgated by the government and is a striking comment on the dialogue between the centralized authority of the period and the willingness of the people and local officials to disagree and take action. However, not everyone who disagreed with the government deserted or refused to parade; some petitioned for relief, others refused to obey orders, and many ignored the war and traded with the enemy or offered support to the United States.

Unfortunately, only two examples of petitions to Joel Stone requesting to be excused from duties with the 2nd Leeds can be cited. The first, dated in 1812 and signed by a "J" or "K" Breakenridge,[49] demanded to have another man excused from attendance with the militia: "Simon Gordon, in my humble opinon ougth to be excused from militia duty. I am told that you refused to speak of a certificate that I give him, but that I will not believe until you tell me so yourself."[50] The other petition, dated 13 October 1812, was from a Metty Doughlass who requested that her youngest son be permitted to absent himself from the 2nd Leeds. She already had three sons in the army and required the youngest for a "measure of peace to my mind and food and support to my tottering frame." Six male members of the community countersigned this appeal, unlike the first that only had the one signature.[51]

Examining these two requests, one can deduce that although a woman could claim voice, it was the men who provided her ability to be heard an acceptable form. Breakenridge's petition required no countersignatures, did not explain the necessity for Simon Gordon's exemption and was arrogant in tone; it was a discourse between equals. Metty Doughlass, whose husband was most likely either dead or absent, turned to male members of the community for support of her petition. From this limited sample, it seems evident that gender and status assisted in determining the accepted forms of disagreement.

Instead of petitions, some members of the 2nd Leeds made personal and direct representations to their colonel. A letter from Captain William Jones in July 1812 requested that if all companies were not required at the same time, that part be allowed to return home or there would "be a famine in the country if there are not some provisions made for the people to farm [?] their crops."[52] Lieutenant-Colonel Benoni Wiltsie, second-in-command of the regiment, in a letter dated 13 April 1813, also voiced his concern about the impact of militia duty on the local economy:

the due I owe to my fellow creatures and as a true Patriot to remind you of the certain calamity that must befall us if the Militia are there continually to be cawled from their families. If they are cawled one month or six weeks from their farms they can put no spring grain in the ground and the consequence will be that their families must suffer the famine that even threatens before the ensuing Harvest … what must be the feelings of a poor man driven from his plough when he sees that nothing but destruction and death for his wife and tender children….[53]

This tension between the demands of agriculture and those of the militia was a source of constant friction. Administrators of Upper Canada were aware of this reality and attempted to resolve the ongoing conflict between the exigencies of the land and military service diplomatically, but this was not always possible. Militiamen continued to experience demands from the military and civil spheres that were irreconcilable. When a choice had to be made by the government, the latter inevitably lost, thus forcing the settler into a disadvantageous personal position.[54]

For the advocates of local interests, such as Wiltsie, this must have been disappointing. As a prominent member of the community and the second-in-command of the 2nd Leeds, he had articulated his dissatisfaction in a manner acceptable within a military context, but would later realize that his concerns were not answered in a manner that he thought appropriate. Wiltsie's involvement in these protests indicates that the advocacy of the common interest was embedded in the shared norms and values of the region, as opposed to socio-economic status.

Further disagreement with the exigencies of military service is evident in several courts-martial conducted within the 2nd Leeds. On 14 July 1813, Stone ordered the court-martial of 10 men who had refused to obey his orders as "they considered them conterary to law and unjust." The court was presided over by Wiltsie and composed of Captain Ira Schofield, Lieutenant Levi Soper, and Ensign George Bates. As Bates was sick, Wiltsie ordered Ensign Nathan Hicock to take his place.[55] After conducting the proceedings, the determination of the court "was that no militia man above the age of fifty years … was liable to be cawled upon for any duty unless the whole of the militia whare cawled out." The accused were then dismissed without a fine.[56] Stone reported his dissatisfaction with Wiltsie's carrying out of his direction "to order a court martial and put the law into force." He felt that this "was so partially done that it did not produce the desired effect."[57] This action could be considered evidence of Wiltsie's mounting displeasure with the continuing disregard of the shared interests of the district.

Another court-martial that seems to have been conducted in a similar manner took place over six months later. In this instance, Schofield was the president of the court in which 14 members of the 2nd Leeds were tried for "desertion." No other details of these proceedings are available, but one can suppose that the desertion referred to was a refusal to muster. Schofield's report was extremely brief and noted that all were found guilty and fined the maximum of £20 that was immediately mitigated in all cases to lesser amounts.[58]

Open dissension erupted between Stone and Wiltsie in December 1813 and culminated in March 1814 with Stone petitioning Drummond for a court of inquiry to examine various complaints against Wiltsie:

> For treating my orders with Contempt — Issued by Order of Lt. Colonel Pearson — and approved by His Honor the late President — Dated 29th Oct 1813 at the time of General Alarm — And publicly making use of ward tending to Prevent — the men in my Regt — from Obeying the Said Orders — to go on Said Alarm — For giving Leave of Absence to one man at that time — without my knowledge or approbation and for making use of Unbecoming Language and improper conduct as an officer — to myself 27th December last — at which time I placed him in arrest....[59]

At the subsequent court-martial in Kingston on 15 April 1814, Wiltsie was found guilty, fined £50 and declared unfit to serve in the militia. He did not accept his sentence and declined to pay the penalty; as a result, he was imprisoned in Brockville.[60] Historian Shirley Spragge raises an excellent point when she opines, "the example of the Loyalist officer and advocate for the beleaguered militia man cum farmer could not have been lost on the populace."[61] In many ways, the conviction of Wiltsie would have sent a strong negative message to the inhabitants of the region concerning the lack of caring by the colonial administration regarding their welfare.

There are only a few documented examples of individuals within the district who voiced their discontent outside that recorded in the context of military or civilian prosecution. Some of these dissenters explicitly stated their disagreement with the war and their desire not to be involved. A warrant to take Johathon Stevens, for what was considered treasonable practices, was signed by Joel Stone on 6 August 1812 and illustrates one such incident:

> [he, Stevens] observed to Wilard Cleonkey that he was not indebted to the king for anything and that what property he had he brought with his money he had brought from the states and that Government had not given him one pence and said God Damn them-if he was amind to keep it and give it up to the States it was none of their business.[62]

Unfortunately, there is no record of the final disposition of this case.

There is also mention of other groups who articulated their active support for the United States. In January 1813, Joel Dunbar swore before Benjamin Simon a statement concerning such behaviour:

> David Kilborn of Witley said to him the said Dunbar that there was private meetings held amongst them, invited me to one that night, saying he believed it was to be held at Abner Chapins in Bastard. The said William further added, that there was a role of Mens names kept, so that when the United States come here they would know their friends.[63]

Again, regrettably, the results of this investigation are unknown.

Besides promises of support, some inhabitants of the Leeds district conducted cross-border trade with the United States throughout the conflict. Before the War of 1812, economic exchange with the United

States was an important facet of daily life in Upper Canada. As an entrepreneur, Stone participated in this trade. Among his papers is a receipt of purchase that allowed Joseph Cox "in a boat from the United States of America to unlode from onboard said eighteen barrels salt only, he having paid the duty thereon into His Majesty's Custom House at the Port of Kingston the Seventeenth day of September 1811."[64] Along with this regulated commerce, some residents were involved with smuggling, an activity that had provoked antagonism between the two countries prior to the conflict.[65]

Soon after the war commenced, the government of Upper Canada attempted to stop this illegal trade. A Garrison Book entry for Kingston in July 1812 directed that "All strange boats are in the future to land in the first instance at M.Walkers Wharf and to be immediately reported by the Centinal on duty to the Officer of the guard for the information of the Commanding Officer of the garrison."[66] However, various attempts by the authorities met with little success and this trade, sometimes officially condoned, continued to meet the requirements of life on the frontier.[67] Even Stone and his subordinates were involved with obtaining needed goods from the United States. In July 1813, he paid £9.16.0 prize money to Lieutenant Samuel Kelsey of the 2nd Leeds "on Account of Pine Spars Taken from the American Shore."[68]

Donald Akenson states that the amount of illegal trade conducted during the war is very difficult to identify. It was a well-established means of livelihood for many loyalist families that was not interrupted by the conflict.[69] The pragmatism of economic well-being took priority over other considerations. Together, these different forms of disagreement with the war formed a comprehensive articulation of protest that represented the sentiments of the populace. These sentiments also prompted larger-scale dissension such as that evidenced during the engagement with American forces at Gananoque on 21 September 1812.

THE ATTACK AT GANANOQUE

The American attack at Gananoque on 21 September 1812 is one of the few chronicled military actions in Leeds and Lansdowne during the War of 1812 and the documentation of this battle varies according to the source.[70] The Americans record it as a brilliant small-unit victory, focusing on the tactical action; the Canadian description promotes the incident as an example of American moral bankruptcy, emphasizing the insignificance of Gananoque and the unwarranted destruction that occurred. Benson J. Lossing, in *The Pictorial Field-Book of the War of 1812,* gives a description of the former:

> The vigilant [American] Captain Forsyth made a bold dash into Canada late in September ... They landed a short distance from the village of Gananoqui, only ninety-five strong, without opposition; but as they approached the town they were confronted by a party of sixty British regulars and fifty Canadian militia drawn up in battle order, who poured heavy volleys upon them. Forsyth dashed forward with his men without firing a shot until within a hundred yards of the enemy, when the latter fled pell-mell to the town, closely pursued by the invaders. There the fugitives rallied and renewed the engagement, when they were again compelled to flee, leaving ten of their number dead on the field, several wounded and four militiamen as prisoners. Forsyth lost only one man killed and one slightly wounded. For his own safety, he broke up the bridge over which he had pursued the enemy, and then returned to his boats, bearing away as the spoils of victory, the eight regulars, sixty stand of arms, two barrels of fixed ammunition comprising three thousand ball-cartridges, one barrel of gunpowder, one of flints, forty-one muskets, and some other public property. In the store-house were found one hundred and fifty barrels of provisions, but having no means of carrying them away, Captain Forsyth applied the torch and store-house and provisions were consumed.[71]

T.W.H Leavitt, in a *History of Leeds and Grenville, Ontario,* provides a Canadian counterpoint:

During the war, Captain Forsyth made a descent upon Gananoque ... They surrounded the residence of Colonel Stone, but failed to find him. Hearing some person moving upstairs, one of the soldiers fired in that direction. The ball took effect in the hip of Mrs. Stone, making a severe, but not dangerous, wound. Imagining that they had killed the Colonel, they immediately departed. Forsyth, in his report to the American authorities, gives a glowing account of the capture of Gananoque, and the destruction of the Government stores at the place. Mr. Hiel Sliter, of the Rear of Leeds, informs us that the stores consisted of half an ox, some old blankets and bed ticks, all of which were burned by the valiant Yankees.[72]

In both accounts, the 2nd Leeds is singularly missing.

To gain a fuller understanding of the events that transpired on 21 September, one can turn to the *Kingston Gazette,* a local newspaper. A report appearing on 26 September confirms that Forsyth attacked the militia, who numbered about 50, at Gananoque. American forces took and destroyed a small quantity of stores and took some prisoners, mostly militiamen. The article criticizes the behaviour of the American soldiery at Stone's House as being "truly disgraceful." It also criticized the manner in which the defence of Gananoque was conducted:

It unfortunately happened that Capt. Schofield and Lieut. Bradith with 12 men of the detachment at Gananoque were her[e, in Kingston] at the time, by which means that station was deprived of the assistance of these two excellent officers. But it is matter of astonunment that these two officers should have quitted their post to take the direction of so very small a party.[73]

A letter from Colonel Robert Lethbridge, then in command at Prescott, indicates similar concerns.[74] His letter was in response to a report of the affair by Stone, and although there is no surviving written record of that submission, it is unmistakable from the tone and structure of Lethbridge's response that he took issue with the information he had received:

> I cannot help in fearing from the terms of your letter that some omission of unnecessary vigilance must have occurred, and it is my particular desire that you will distinctly state what number of officers by name, non-commissioned officers and privates were present at this port when the attack on the part of the enemy [occurred].[75]

Lethbridge also acknowledges the injuries suffered by Mrs. Stone and offers his sympathies. One can see that the letter questions the effectiveness of the defence of Gananoque by the 2nd Leeds. Implicit in Lethbridge's demand to know the numbers of the 2nd Leeds who were present during the engagement and his comment on the strength of the flank companies are concerns about whether Stone had actually been able to muster his forces.

A post-war description of the action places Stone at the scene of the engagement. As it is a memorial requesting reimbursement, it provides little detailed information. Indeed, not surprisingly, it is slightly self-aggrandizing. Stone noted:

> That on the 21st September 1812 about 200 of the Enemy — under the late Colonel Forsyth, Attacked Gananoque — at a time when two detachments of the militia there had been sent away leaving Your Memorialist with 2 Subaltern [?] officers only — and not more than 40 efective militia men who — after our best endeavours to Defend the post — were obliged to retreat — and the Enemy proceded to Acts of cruelty and pillage — firing volleys of musketry into the private House of Your Memorialist without any provocation — Wounded Mrs. Stone — broke in and carried of[f] the contents of Several Trunks — burnt one new Store house — all the private property of your Memorialist — and carried away all the Arms and Ammunition left and burnt our provisions in Said Store house.[76]

Given the scanty evidence, one cannot deduce with authority the events of this evening. Nevertheless, it can be suggested that the ineffective reaction of the militia to the American force may have been a form of collective action, a refusal to participate.

J. Mackay Hitsman, in *The Incredible War of 1812,* has written that although the flank companies did muster at the alarm, "they fled after firing their muskets at the charging American regulars."[77] This was not the action of a determined force prepared to protect their homes; it was the action of a group of men who did not believe in their cause.

Incidents such as this led Lieutenant-Colonel Thomas Pearson[78] to provide his opinion of the militia of the Eastern and Johnstown districts to the adjutant-general at York in January 1813:

> From the experience which I had of the state of this portion of the militia *and the disposition of the major part of the inhabitants of those Districts,* I have no hesitation in asserting that this force in its present state will never be brought to meet the expectations of the country.[79]

One can interpret the reaction of the 2nd Leeds to the incursion of a small force of Americans at Gananoque on 21 September as illustrative of the disposition of the people. The prevailing community views of the war permitted elements of the 2nd Leeds to abandon Gananoque after mounting only the most perfunctory resistance. There is no evidence in the existing documentation of any further formal or informal punishment regarding this incident. It seems to have been quickly and conveniently forgotten by all concerned, except Stone.[80] He continued to vigorously enforce the laws of the state in a region where support for the conflict was lukewarm at best. In November 1814, some members of Stone's regiment, with others, expressed their dissatisfaction clearly.

INCIDENT AT THE STONE RESIDENCE

During the night of 10 November 1814, a number of individuals stole what seems to have been a considerable amount of property from Stone's barn.

Though there is almost no record of this incident, two letters addressed from Colonel Nathaniel Coffin to Stone allude to the occurrence.[81] In official correspondence, Coffin advised Stone that the President of Upper Canada, Lieutenant-General Sir Gordon Drummond, had been informed of the occurrence of 10 November, sent his regrets and directed that Stone could request troops at any time from the "Commanding Officer at Gananoque" to avert the reoccurrence of this event. Additionally, Coffin advised Stone that he would be reimbursed for any losses that he had incurred.[82] Coffin also wrote a personal letter to Stone and here he expressed a great deal of "regret and mortification at the Troops behaviour." He then encouraged him to continue with his work on behalf of the Crown:

> I [Coffin] represented to him [Drummond] that you could stand it no longer, that you would have to give up your property and go elsewhere as it was impossible for you to remain under existing circumstances at the Gananoque, pointed out the great loss it would be to the Public Service, your removal from Gananoque.

Coffin assured Stone that once he identified his requirements, he would be allocated a guard "to prevent any future occurrence of the kind."[83] Coffin also indicated that Sir George Prevost, the captain-general and governor-in-chief of the Canadas,[84] had ordered that the offenders be punished and the appropriate officers be made aware of their own personal shortcomings "for their sad neglect of their men."[85] This comment may, however, have resulted from a number of issues that involved the militiamen and their pay that are mentioned in various letters and documents.

From these communications, it is evident that both Prevost and Drummond believed that the episode at Stone's residence resulted from his official duties and that they were prepared to provide him protection and recompense and to punish the guilty militiamen. Coffin's references to Stone's letter of 14 November demonstrate that this event was significant to the latter. Not only were those who had participated in the incident his soldiers, but more important, they were part of his community. Stone had apparently pointed out that it might be necessary for him to leave the area and start anew, which could only be the result of what he viewed as strong community censure. It is reasonable to assume, then, that this incident was a form of collective action that expressed local interests, as Stone had not heeded other forms of grievance in the past.

The willingness of the community to directly confront Stone illustrates the escalating dialogue between the desires of the populace to remain uninvolved and the actions of the representatives of government in pursuing the aims of the war.[86]

CONCLUSION

Membership in the 2nd Leeds Regiment was compelled by law and included all men in the area who could reasonably have been expected to be physically able to participate in the struggle between the two nations. Because of the inclusiveness of the militia of the period and the records that are available for study, the 2nd Leeds provides an excellent vehicle to study the forms of disaffection in the Gananoque area. Donald Akenson has said the discontent of the local inhabitants with the War of 1812 arose from their non-ideological, self-interested perception of their relationships with their brethren across the St. Lawrence. There were social and economic accords among these settlers that were much stronger than the desires of an Upper Canadian administration that was acting as a proxy for a far distant king.

The forms of collective action varied over time. The initial form of protest entailed mass migration to the American side of the border by the disaffected and their families during the summer of 1812. There continued to be some desertion throughout the war, but never again on the scale of those first few months. The most prominent type of crowd action was in the form of a refusal to muster, with October 1813 attaining an almost complete refusal of the unit to gather when directed. Due to the manipulation of local magistrates and the militia itself, Colonel Joel Stone found it almost impossible to conduct legal proceedings against those involved. The community's management of the military and civil legal structures continued throughout the war, despite Stone's identification of the issue and appeals to the authorities. This systemic abrogation of legislated authority demonstrated the inability of the government to apply the rule of law in the face of mass disobedience.

Individuals also expressed their attitudes in acceptable forms such as letters and petitions. The structures of these requests were determined contextually by the gender and the status of the originator. Other people expressed their disapproval strongly, in words considered treasonable by representatives of the Crown. It is evident that support for the United States among the border inhabitants of Upper Canada was linked inextricably to the economic realties of the region. This pragmatic view of life and obtaining a living from the district also determined the reaction of agriculturists to involuntary service with the 2nd Leeds. As influential members of the community, officers of the unit recognized the need for the members of the regiment to maintain their farms and supported their right to do so. In the case of Lieutenant-Colonel Benoni Wiltsie, this recognition of shared interests crossed socio-economic barriers and led to the loss of his commission and eventual imprisonment.

Other indications of common opposition to the war were the ineffective and inadequate resistance mounted by the militia in the face of a limited American engagement at Ganonoque in September 1812 and the actions of the crowd at Stone's farm in November 1814. The reluctance of

Military Prison, Quebec, Shot Drill *illustrates one of many punishments imposed on military prisoners later in the nineteenth century.* (*W.O.C.,* Canadian Illustrated News, *1871, Library and Archives Canada C-56626*)

the militia to provide an effective defence of the settlement speaks volumes about the views of the local inhabitants regarding the war. Furthermore, the willingness to confront Stone, the theft of his property, his acknowledgement of his condemnation by the community and the lack of action taken against the offenders also reveals the overwhelming strength of local standards of acceptable behaviour.

It seems evident that in the Leeds area, the community felt the war violated a compact that had been established with the Upper Canadian administration before 1812 regarding the militia being used solely for the defence of the local district during crisis. The strength of the disaffection with this apparent breaking of faith led to a series of individual and collective actions that abrogated the authority of the state and permitted the community of settlers that formed this area to construct a world determined by their beliefs and values. The men of the 2nd Leeds may have been the King's soldiers in name, but the perceived realities of their existence determined their participation in the War of 1812, not the imperatives of an ineffectual and unheeded central authority.

NOTES

Editor's Note: In the many quotations offered above, a conscientious effort was made to avoid the use of "[*sic*]" to indicate a misspelled word in the original document. All quotations have been checked for accuracy and they appear herein exactly as they do in the sources from which they were taken. Given the lack of fluidity of some quotations and the poor grammar, punctuation, and spelling in many cases, it was thought best to make this general statement, rather than distract and interrupt the reader with an unending number of editorial remarks.

1. Arthur R.M. Lower, *Colony to Nation: A History of Canada,* 5th ed. (Toronto: McClelland and Stewart, 1981), 182.

2. Immigration increased greatly after 1791 when Lieutenant-Governor John Graves Simcoe invited potential colonists to move to Upper Canada and avail themselves of the free land and almost negligible taxes. See E. Jane Errington, "The 'Eagle,' the 'Lion' and Upper Canada: A Developing Colonial Ideology: The Colonial Elite's Views of the United States and Great Britain, 1784–1828," (Unpublished Ph.D. Thesis, Queen's University, 1984), 21.

3. Loyalists were those who had remained committed to the British during the American Revolution and, after it had ended, were unable or unwilling to remain in the newly

created United States. Taking advantage of available territory to the north, these supporters of the Crown made their way to the Canadas and attempted to restore their fortunes and families to a semblance of their previous normalcy. *Ibid.*

4. Donald Akenson states that the first loyalist settlers were forced to make choices about land allocations under political and military pressure, that is, in an atmosphere of haste and confusion. The settlement of Leeds and Lansdowne was conducted later, after these loyalists had established themselves. Akenson also notes that the townships formed a single municipal unit until 1850, thus the term "Leeds and Lansdowne" was used to refer to the general area. See Donald Harmon Akenson, *The Irish in Ontario: A Study in Rural History,* 2nd ed. (Montreal & Kingston: McGill-Queen's University Press [henceforth MQUP], 1999), 49–52.

5. Errington, "The 'Eagle,' the 'Lion' and Upper Canada," 149–52.

6. Regarding the extensive American immigration from the 1790s onwards, Errington concurs and suggests that before the War of 1812, of the 75,000 inhabitants of Upper Canada, only 20 percent were descended from the original Loyalists, while 60 percent were American. The remainder of the populace was comprised of British and other European immigrants. For these Americans, "Upper Canada was but a northern extension of the American frontier...." *Ibid.,* 21–2.

7. Brock had grave doubts as to the character and efficiency of the sedentary militia and, in February 1812, unsuccessfully attempted to introduce an amendment to the Militia Act that would compel its members to take an oath of loyalty to the Crown. He recorded his reaction, "The many doubtful characters in the militia made me anxious to introduce the oath of abjuration into the bill. There were twenty members present when this highly important measure was lost by the casting vote of the chairman. The great influence which the fear and number of settlers from the United States possess over the decisions of the Lower House is truly alarming and ought by every practical means to be diminished." See E.A. Cruikshank, "A Study of Disaffection in Upper Canada in 1812–15," in Morris Zaslov, ed., *Upper Canada and the War of 1812: The Defended Border* (Toronto: Macmillan, 1964), 207.

8. *Ibid.,* 205–23.

9. This legislation was incorporated into the Militia Law of 1808, which was an attempt "to explain, amend and reduce to one act of Parliament the several laws now in being, for the raising and training of the Militia of this Province." As cited in E.A. Cruikshank, *The Documentary History of the Campaign upon the Niagara Frontier in the Year 1812* (Welland: Lundy's Lane Historical Society, 1897), 1.

10. Shirley Campbell Spragge, "Organizing the Wilderness: A Study of Loyalist Settlement, Augusta Township, Grenville County, 1784–1820," (Unpublished Ph.D. Thesis, Queen's University, 1986), 170–71.

11. The declaration of war by the United States was proclaimed on 19 June 1812 with the information travelling to Canada in a circuitous manner. Two Montreal merchants who were involved with the fur trade and had associates in New York City learned on 24 June that war had been declared. They immediately forwarded the news to the capital of Lower Canada, Quebec City, where Lieutenant-General Sir George Prevost, the commander of British possessions in North America, commenced to implement plans for the defence of the Canadas. See J. Mackay Hitsman, *The Incredible War of 1812: A Military History* (Toronto: University of Toronto Press [henceforth UTP], 1965), 24 and 44–5.

12. "The chief object of the Flank Companies, is to have constantly in readiness, a force composed of Loyal, Brave, and Respectable Young Men, so far instructed as to enable the Government, on any emergency, to engraft such portions of the Militia as may be necessary, on a stock capable of giving aid in forming them for Military service." Brock, as cited in *Ibid.*, 36–7.

13. William M. Weekes, "Civil Authority and Martial Law in Upper Canada," in Morris Zaslov, ed., *Upper Canada and the War of 1812: The Defended Border* (Toronto: Macmillan, 1964), 193.

14. Spragge, "Organizing the Wilderness," 171. The 2nd Leeds was structured with a variable number of core companies, normally five, and one, later increased to two, flank companies. See Akenson, *The Irish in Ontario,* 118.

15. Akenson outlines the chronology of the boundary decisions pertaining to the township of Leeds and Lansdowne: In 1788, the four districts that later became Upper Canada were declared, with Leeds and Lansdowne being mostly in the Luneburg district; in 1791, Upper Canada was established; in 1792, the four districts of Upper Canada were renamed, with Leeds and Lansdowne being contained by Leeds County which ranged from the St. Lawrence to the Ottawa River; and in 1798, Leeds and Lansdowne townships became contained by the Johnstown District. *Ibid.*, 58.

16. Presidents of the Government of Upper Canada between 1812 and 1815 included: Major-General Isaac Brock (October 1811 to October 1812); Major-General Sir R.H. Sheaffe (October 1812 to June 1813); Major-General Francis Baron de Rottenburg (June 1813 to December 1813); and Lieutenant-General Sir Gordon Drummond (December 1813 to April 1815). See L. Homfray Irving, *Officers of the British Forces in Canada during the War of 1812* (Welland: Canadian Military Institute, 1908), 2.

17. H. William Hawke, "Joel Stone of Gananoque, 1749–1833: His Life and Letters," (Unpublished M.A. Thesis, Queen's University, 1966), 67–8.

18. William Gray, *Soldiers of the King: The Upper Canadian Militia 1812 — 1815: A Reference Guide* (Erin, ON: The Boston Mills Press), 41.

19. Akenson, *The Irish in Ontario,* 177–78.

20. Adam Shortt, "The Economic Effect of the War of 1812 on Upper Canada," in Morris Zaslov, ed., *Upper Canada and the War of 1812: The Defended Border* (Toronto: Macmillan, 1964), 298.

21. E.P. Thompson, *The Making Of The English Working Class* (London: Victor Gollancz, 1965), 9.

22. *Ibid.,* 11.

23. *Ibid.*

24. Akenson, *The Irish in Ontario,* 125.

25. These returns list men who left the area. *Ibid.,* 124. Spragge accepts Akenson's calculations with the proviso that they list "the three companies without explaining how many made up the Leeds regiment." She uses the same process as Akenson to calculate desertion rates for the 1st Leeds. See Spragge, "Organizing the Wilderness," 193.

26. Cruikshank, *Documentary History,* 1 and 7.

27. Moreover, Gray uses a pre-war baseline figure to obtain a rate of loss, while Akenson derives his calculations from the strength of these companies in 1814, not from pre-war numbers. In the present author's opinion, to gain an accurate idea of the percentage of desertion, it is necessary to use an earlier figure, before the desertions commenced, in the calculations. See Akenson, *The Irish in Ontario,* 124, and, Gray, *Soldiers of the King,* 41.

28. Library and Archives Canada [henceforth LAC], Record Group [henceforth RG] 9, I-B-7, Vol. 6, Document 284, Microfilm T-10381, "Return of the second Regement of Leeds Militia in the District of Johnston 4th June 1814."

29. Wiltsee's document is undated, but given the context of the return and its location on the microfilm reel, that is, among documents dated 1814, it is reasonable to assume it is a similar return. See *Ibid.,* Document 292, "Captain Joseph Wiltsees Deserters."

30. *Ibid.,* Document 281,"Quarterly Return of the 2d Regiment of Leeds Militia as it stood 24th December 1812."

31. LAC, Manuscript Group [henceforth MG] 24 — H II 1, McDonald Stone Papers, Vol. 1, Document 800, "Copy of a Letter from Colonel Joel Stone to Colonel James Breakenridge July 1812."

32. LAC, RG 9, I-B-7, Vol. 6, Document 296, Microfilm T-10381,"Return of the Names and Characters of Aliens together with the Names and Characters of Such as have Deserted in time of the Late War and Since Returned."

33. Section VIII of the Militia Law of 1808 specifies that if refusing to "repair to the place he is ordered to," commissioned officers would be fined £50, while non-commissioned officers and privates were required to remit £20, with imprisonment in the case of non-payment. See Cruikshank, *Documentary History,* 5–6.

34. George Sheppard, *Plunder, Profit, and Paroles: A Social History of the War of 1812 in Upper Canada* (Montreal & Kingston: MQUP, 1994), 89–91. Although, there is no supporting documentation, October is normally the harvest season and this could be a plausible reason for such widespread non-attendance.

35. LAC, McDonald Stone Papers, Vol. 1, undated, Document 70, "Copy of a Report from Colonel Joel Stone to President of the Province of Upper Canada."

36. Pearson was a British Army officer appointed to this office 28 February 1812. See Irving, *Officers of the British Forces,* 28.

37. Appointed 14 January 1813. *Ibid.,* 31.

38. LAC, McDonald Stone Papers, Vol. 1, undated, Document 70, "Copy of a Report from Colonel Joel Stone to President of the Province of Upper Canada."

39. *Ibid.*

40. There is no indication that these events ever transpired.

41. LAC, McDonald Stone Papers, Vol. 1, undated, Document 70, "Copy of a Report from Colonel Joel Stone to President of the Province of Upper Canada."

42. Although there is no confirmation, this may be Colonel James Breakenridge of the 1st Leeds. There appears to have been a degree of animosity between the two commanding officers. There are no details of Breakenridge or his life available in the *Dictionary of Canadian Biography* [henceforth *DCB*] (Toronto: UTP, 1966 onward).

43. LAC, McDonald Stone Papers, Vol. 1, undated, Documents 70–71, "Copy of a Report from Colonel Joel Stone to President of the Province of Upper Canada." Sheppard notes that of seven Upper Canadian courts-martial conducted between 8 March 1813 and 16 January 1815, all but one of the offenders came from the Midland, Johnstown, and Eastern districts. See Sheppard, *Plunder, Profit, and Paroles,* 90–1.

44. Queen's University Archives [henceforth QUA], Stone Papers, File 3077, "Copy of a Letter to General Drummond from Colonel Joel Stone March 13, 1814."

45. The other two were Samuel Wright and Henry Bogart, Esquire. *Ibid.*

46. *Ibid.*

47. *Ibid.*

48. These actions against Stone seem to have lost momentum by about 1820. LAC, McDonald Stone Papers, Vol. 2, Document 70, "Copy of Letter sent to the Adjutant General June 30, 1818."

49. This may be the same Breakenridge named by Stone concerning the resistance to the legal proceedings against members of the 2nd Leeds in 1814.

50. LAC, McDonald Stone Papers, Vol. 1, undated, Document 70, "Copy of a Report from Colonel Joel Stone to President of the Province of Upper Canada."

51. *Ibid.*, Vol. 2, Document 830, "Petition from Metty Doughlass to Joel Stone October 13, 1812."

52. *Ibid.*, Document 798, "Letter from Captain William Jones to Colonel Joel Stone July 14, 1812."

53. As cited in Spragge, "Organizing the Wilderness," 184.

54. Weekes, "Civil Authority and Martial Law," 192.

55. None of these men are mentioned in the *DCB*.

56. The names of these men were Lyman Judson, Rathal Judson, William Woolley, Derias Calmer, David S. Steel, Barnabus Chipman, John Gilbert, Daniel Patterson, Ezra Benedict, and Abel Smith. There is a mention of one Ireland, who was fined £5.13.0. LAC, McDonald Stone Papers, Vol. 2, Document 866, "Letter from Lieutenant-Colonel Wiltsie to Colonel Joel Stone dated July 19, 1813."

57. *Ibid.*, Vol. 1, undated, Document 70, "Copy of a Report from Colonel Joel Stone to the President of the Province of Upper Canada."

58. The particulars of those pronounced guilty and their fines are: David Curtis (£3.10.0); Dan Shnapp (£1.10.0); Baranbus Chipman (£5.10.0); Sergeant Benidict McCallum (£2.10.0); James Brickman (£3.0.0); James Hallada (?) (£0.10.0); Bob Boyc (?) (£0.10.0); David S. Steel (£0.10.0); John Slack (£0.10.0); Asabel Tryon (£0.10.0); Amos Griswald (£1.10.0); Case Brown (£4.10.0); Thad. Garoen (?) (£1.10.0); and Abrahem Tueby (£0.10.0), for a grand total of £26.10.0. See QUA, Stone Papers, "Unsigned Court Martial Report 4 February 1814."

59. *Ibid.*, "Copy of a Letter to General Drummond from Colonel Joel Stone March 13, 1814."

60. Regrettably, there are scant records of these proceedings and Wiltsie's subsequent refusal to conform to the penalty of the court, so a more comprehensive account cannot be provided. See Spragge, "Organizing the Wilderness," 187.

61. *Ibid.*

62. LAC, McDonald Stone Papers, Vol. 1, Documents 806–807, "Warrent to take Johathon Stevens signed by Joel Stone 6 August 1812."

63. *Ibid.*, "Oath respecting meetings in Witley January 18, 1813 by Joel Dunbar sworn before Benjamin Simon."

64. *Ibid.*, Vol. 2, Document 784, "5 October 1811 Customs Permit."

65. Errington, "The 'Eagle,' the 'Lion' and Upper Canada," 138–39.

66. LAC, MG 24–G 58, Vol. 1, Kingston Garrison Order Book for 4 July to 21 August 1812, "Kingston 28 July 1812."

67. Shorrt, "The Economic Effect of the War of 1812," 300.

68. QUA, Stone Papers, "Receipt signed by Samuel Kelsey, Lieutenant at Gananoque 8th July 1813."

69. Akenson, *The Irish in Ontario*, 130–31.

70. *Ibid.*, 118.

71. Benson J. Lossing, *The Pictorial Field-Book of the War of 1812* (New York: Harper and Brothers, 1868), 372–73.

72. T.W.H. Leavitt, *History of Leeds and Grenville Ontario, from 1749 to 1879 with Illustrations and Biographical Sketches of some of its Prominent Men and Pioneers* (Brockville: Recorder Press, 1879), 38–9. Italics in original.

73. "Communication," 26 September 1812, *Kingston Gazette*.

74. Hawke, "Joel Stone of Gananoque," 65.

75. LAC, McDonald Stone Papers, Vol. 2, Document 821, "Letter from Colonel Robert Lethbridge to Colonel Joel Stone 21 September 1812."

76. QUA, Stone Papers, "Copy of Undated [1815?] Memorial from Colonel Joel Stone to Major-General Sir Gordon Drummond."

77. Hitsman also notes that some of the militiamen were wearing red tunics discarded by the Kingston garrison, which led to the erroneous impression by the Americans that they had engaged British regulars. See Hitsman, *The Incredible War of 1812*, 96.

78. Inspecting Field Officer of Upper Canada, appointed 28 February 1812. See Irving, *Officers of the British Forces*, 28.

79. As cited in E.A. Cruikshank, *Record of the Services of Canadian Regiments in the War of 1812* (Toronto: Canadian Military Institute, 1915), 85. Italics added by present author.

80. In response to this incident, a blockhouse was later constructed to deter further incursions.

81. These public and private letters of 19 November were written in response to Stone's now-missing report of 14 November and provide the only indication to the events of that evening. QUA, Stone Papers, "Letters from Colonel Coffin to Colonel Stone 19 November 1814."

82. *Ibid.*, "'Public' Letter from Colonel Coffin to Colonel Stone 19 November 1814."

83. Coffin refers to General Robinson, who commanded British Army troops, as receiving this direction from Drummond, which indicates that the soldiers for Stone's protection would come from the British Army garrison at the Gananoque Block House. See *Ibid.*, "'Private' Letter from Colonel Coffin to Colonel Stone 19 November 1814." See also, Irving, *Officers of the British Forces*, 9.

84. *Ibid.*, 1.

85. QUA, Stone Papers, "'Private' Letter from Colonel Coffin to Colonel Stone 19 November 1814."

86. This protest made a lasting impression on Stone. An inkling of this can be glimpsed in a post-war draft to Drummond. "That the singular Local Situation of Your Memorialest, has exposed him to perculiar — as well as to the casual Losses and Deprodations and Damages…." See *Ibid.*, "Copy of Undated [1815?] Memorial from Colonel Joel Stone to Major-General Sir Gordon Drummond."

4

Emboldened by Bad Behaviour: The Conduct of the Canadian Army in the Northwest, 1870 to 1873

JIM MCKILLIP

In the early-morning hours of 24 August 1870, a small force of British and Canadian troops disembarked from boats at Point Douglas, two miles from the Red River settlement. As a torrent of rain fell on their heads, the troops deployed into battle formation and advanced towards the town. The march was slow as the soldiers struggled through thick black mud created by two days of rain. Finally, Fort Garry came into sight. No flag was flying from the fort, but the gates were shut tight and guns were visible in the bastions commanding the corners of the palisade. Everyone expected that the fight would soon begin.[1] But, to the disappointment of some and the relief of many, there was no battle.[2] The Métis who had been occupying the town left the area, and within a few hours, the place was in the hands of Colonel Garnet Wolseley.[3] Wolseley's little army had been dispatched to Manitoba by the new Government of Canada to end the insurrection that had broken-out the previous year.

Although there was, and remains, considerable debate around the causes of the rebellion,[4] by the spring of 1870, the Canadian Government had decided to exert its control over its new territory. Within the English-speaking community of the Red River settlement, there was nearly unanimous approval for the intervention and resulting military occupation of the new province.[5] The reaction of the French-speaking people of the area was considerably more circumspect but, for at least the period immediately following the arrival of the soldiers, the prevailing sentiments were of acceptance and guarded optimism.[6] Recognizing the military presence

Lord Wolseley, shown after the Red River Expedition, circa 1876 to 1880. (Notman & Sandham, Library and Archives Canada PA-138791)

may have been simply an acknowledgement of *force majeure*. But their guarded optimism was based on a degree of faith that the terms and conditions contained within the Manitoba Act, the Act of Parliament that established the new province, would be respected.[7]

By 1884, it was clear that at least a part of the population of the Canadian west was not content to be ruled by Ottawa.[8] Again, there was rebellion in the northwest. Again, the Government of Canada decided on the dispatch of a military force. But the arrival of Major-General Frederick Middleton's army in the West in 1885 did not end the rebellion. Instead of supervising an uncontested occupation of the territory, General Middleton found himself in the middle of a difficult operation punctuated by some bloody encounters, several of which, like the action at Cut Knife Hill, did not go at all as planned.[9] Additionally, instead of confronting only Métis, the Canadian force also found itself battling Native forces that had allied themselves with Louis Riel.[10] The rebellion was only quelled after the siege, bombardment, assault, and capture of the rebel headquarters and capital at Batoche and the dispersal of the Métis and Native army.[11]

In 1870, the Métis community of Manitoba was considerably larger and more homogenous than that of Saskatchewan in 1885 and the military potential of the group was considerable.[12] By contrast, the military force that was sent to quell the first rebellion was less than a third the size of that sent to deal with the rebellion of 1885.[13] Nevertheless, in spite of the greatly reduced capacity of the Saskatchewan Métis to resist the greatly increased force sent to subdue them, they chose to fight in 1885, though

An artistic re-creation of the Battle of Cut Knife Creek in 1885 in Saskatchewan by William Daniel Blatchly, Captain Robert William Rutherford, and Lieutenant R. Lyndhurst Wadmore. (Library and Archives Canada C-41472)

essentially the same people, under the same leadership, chose not to fight in 1870.[14] What had happened between the first and second rebellions that led to such a dramatically different choice in spite of the Métis's relative decline in power?

There is no simple, single answer to this question. Much had changed in the West in the decade-and-a-half between the two rebellions. The transfer of Rupert's Land from the Hudson's Bay Company (HBC) to Canada had been completed. Large numbers of Canadians had begun settling in the West and the Canadian Pacific Railway was nearing completion.[15] A series of treaties had been negotiated with Native groups in an effort to extinguish Native claims and lay the basis for further Canadian settlement.[16] The old Métis community of Red River had been transformed both demographically and economically, especially as a result of the decline of the fur trade.[17] In the opinion of Louis Riel and his Métis followers, this was all bad.

There was another factor. The Canadian government's decision to send a military expedition to the Red River area resulted in the community being effectively transformed into a garrison town. The troops inevitably came into daily contact with the various elements of the population of Canada's new northwest. From the perspective of the Métis, much of this contact was unpleasant and left a poor impression of military forces in general and Canadian militia forces in particular. This chapter suggests, therefore, that part of the decision to fight in 1885 may have resulted from the experience of the Métis with the military forces of Canada after the 1870 rebellion; that the Métis were emboldened to fight, at least in part, by the bad behaviour of the garrison forces of northwest Canada.

The proximate causes of the troubles in Red River were obvious enough, even if they seem to have come as a surprise and shock to even the most senior representatives of the Canadian Government.[18] By 1869, Canada had convinced the imperial government in London that the vast territory of Rupert's Land should be transferred from the authority of the HBC to Canadian jurisdiction.[19] In anticipation of this transfer, the Canadian government dispatched teams to the Red River area in July 1869 to conduct preliminary surveys.[20] The surveyors immediately inflamed local sensitivities by their conduct. In addition to an apparently undisguised contempt for the local population, the surveyors proceeded to lay out a plan that ignored existing land holdings and property conventions.[21] In particular, the teams were seen to be imposing the block survey system of Ontario onto the river lot system already in place.[22] Not only did this ignore the system that had been in use for generations, but the new survey threatened to undermine the legitimacy of individual holdings. By 11 October 1869, the local population had seen enough and, in what has become an iconic moment for the Métis, Louis Riel and a group of followers compelled the surveyors to stop their work.[23]

Even more provocative was the dispatch of a lieutenant-governor to the territory. In this, the Canadian government demonstrated both poor choice and poor timing. The lieutenant-governor designate, William McDougall, was a well-known member of the Ontario group that had been lobbying long and hard for the acquisition of Rupert's Land.[24] The aims of this group were unambiguous. They planned to fill the new territory with Canadian settlers and to transform the land into an integral part of the loyal Dominion.[25] Unsurprisingly, the existing Métis population at Red River expected the new governor to be an agent for their marginalization and displacement.[26]

To make matters worse, the governor was sent before the actual transfer of the territory had been finalized.[27] When he attempted to enter the territory and take-up his post on 30 October 1869, a Métis force intercepted him and denied him entry.[28] On 2 November, the Métis occupied Fort Garry, and on 24 November, they formed a provisional government. The "rebellion" had well and truly begun.[29]

The "land question" was not the only reason for discontent in the Red River area. In the view of some historians, it was not even the most important. One of the first to chronicle the times was George Stanley. Writing in the 1930s, he echoed the "frontier" model of F.J. Turner[30] and viewed the struggle as an inevitable clash of civilizations in which the "primitive" Métis were confronted with the advance of "civilization" from Canada.[31] In the 1940s, Marcel Giraud completed his massive study of the Métis and concluded, in a variation of the "civilizations" model, that the Métis had effectively fused elements of both primitive and advanced societies and had thrived as a consequence. In his view, however, this fusion was only superficial and was not able to survive the economic pressures that accompanied the end of the fur trade empire of the West.[32]

By the 1950s, W.L. Morton was prepared to challenge the notion that a clash of civilizations was at the heart of the Métis conflicts. Instead, he argued that the Métis were well along in the process of adapting to the changing circumstances of the Western economy and society in the 1860s. For Morton, Métis resistance was based on their justifiable fear of being culturally and religiously overwhelmed by a mass immigration of English Protestants in the wake of transition to Canadian rule.[33] The resistance in 1885 was a product of the failed resistance in 1869–70.

More recent writings have stressed a variety of "push" and "pull" factors in the dislocation and eventual dispersal of the Métis. Douglas Sprague and Thomas Flanagan offered sharply contrasting views on the question of land policies and their implementation. Sprague concluded that the Métis were the victims of a deliberate policy of manipulation by the Canadian Government that sought to remove them as obstacles to the settlement of the northwest. For Sprague, the 1885 rebellion was the direct result of these policies.[34] Flanagan's analysis of land claim policies and their implementation led him to conclude that the Métis had been treated fairly and that the real source of Métis activism in the 1880s was the appeal of Louis Riel's radicalism.[35]

All these studies tend to an analysis of the Métis based on an essentially two-dimensional picture of Métis economic life; nomadic bison hunting versus sedentary agriculture. The tensions and the "push" and "pull" factors remained focused on the hunt or the land. In the last decade, Frits Pannekoek expanded the essentially political discussion of the Métis by examining social and religious motivations within the Métis communities. His work suggested that much of the discontent within the Métis community of Red River was based on unresolved racial and sectarian conflict.[36] More recently, Gerhard Ens and Frank Tough have added to the understanding of the dislocation and dispersal of the Métis through their studies of aspects of the economic basis of Métis society.[37]

In all of this historiography, there is no specific analysis of the behaviour of Canadian military forces in the aftermath of the Red River Rebellion, nor is there any discussion of the Métis's reaction to this behaviour. However, given the scale and duration of the Canadian military presence in the northwest, it seems highly likely that there would have been a significant effect on Métis attitudes, for good or for bad.

The force mounted for the expedition consisted of one battalion of British regular troops and two battalions of Canadian militia. The former was a rifle battalion from the 60th Regiment that had been on garrison duty in Canada.[38] The latter had been raised specifically for this task and had only been together since early May.[39] The two Canadian battalions were formed along the same organizational lines as British battalions and mirrored the general structure of Canadian militia battalions. Organized into seven companies of 50 men, with the addition of officers, the battalions were approximately 375-strong.[40] It was originally intended that one of these battalions would be raised in Ontario and the other would come from Quebec; the units were thus designated the 1st Ontario and the 2nd Quebec Battalion of Rifles. However, as a result of recruiting problems in Quebec, many of the soldiers in the 2nd were actually from Ontario.[41] With the addition of artillery, engineers, and other support personnel, the total strength of the force was approximately 1,200.[42]

The men who made up the two battalions of militia that came to the Red River in 1870 were of a surprisingly consistent lot. No doubt many had enlisted for the adventure and challenge that often attracts young men to military expeditions. But many soldiers of the Red River Expeditionary

Force had enlisted in response to calls for vengeance against the French Catholic rebels who had been seen to oppose the Canadian takeover of Rupert's Land. Of special interest to many was retribution for the death of Thomas Scott, the obstreperous Orangeman who had provoked Louis Riel's wrath and had been executed by a Métis firing squad in March of 1870.[43] According to Lieutenant-Governor Adams Archibald, "Some of them [volunteers] openly stated that they had taken a vow before leaving home to pay off all scores by shooting down any Frenchman that was in any way connected with that event."[44] Another observer suggested that as many as 90 percent of the volunteers had enlisted, "… to avenge the death of Thomas Scott."[45]

Of the 1,000 volunteers, all of whom were men, approximately half were from Ontario and a third came from Quebec. The remainder came from the other provinces or from outside Canada. Although it was intended that half of the troops would be English and the other half French, the recruiting problems already referred to resulted in a predominantly English force dominated by Protestants.[46] Unsurprisingly, the troops were mostly young. While the oldest was 40, the youngest was only 17, and the average age was just 24. The vast majority of them were single.[47] Although Canada was predominantly rural in 1870, most of the men that joined the Red River expedition were either skilled or semi-skilled workers, professionals or urban labourers. Only 12 percent were farmers. The typical militiaman recruited to serve in the Red River Expeditionary Force of 1870 was a young, single, English-speaking, Protestant, urban worker.

The Canadian troops who eventually garrisoned the Red River area were part of a force that was widely hailed as having triumphed in the face of great adversity.[48] The journey of the Red River Expeditionary Force was perceived as an exploit of epic proportions and praise was heaped on Wolseley and his men for their accomplishments, all of this although the route used had been a fur-trade thoroughfare for more than a century-and-a-half.[49] The army began the trip in Toronto on 21 May 1870[50] and travelled more than 1,900 kilometres in just over three months by rail, steamship, canoe, boat, and foot.[51]

Colonel Wolseley's official report made much of the difficulties of the voyage. He described the physical obstacles that were overcome and commented that one of the most notable aspects of the deployment was that there had been no disciplinary problems among the troops.[52] This claim was repeated in several other accounts of the expedition.[53] Even the most optimistic observer with any experience of military forces would have found this claim to be almost incredible and it would indeed have been remarkable if it were true. Wolseley also claimed that his decision to impose a ban on alcohol during the trip contributed to the good conduct of his troops.[54] But a closer reading of personal accounts of the trek suggests that the soldiers were not the angels Wolseley had described. It is also clear that alcohol was readily available.

In fact, the force was having typical disciplinary problems early on in its deployment. Before the troops had even begun the arduous overland portion of the trip through what is now northwest Ontario and eastern Manitoba, some Canadian militiamen were caught spoiling rations. Soldiers were found to have drained some of the brine preserver out of barrels of salted pork to make them lighter and easier to carry.[55] As the force made its way into the depths of the forest and the maze of rivers and lakes, the workload increased and tempers frayed. On one occasion, a fistfight broke-out in one of the boats between two soldiers from the 2nd Quebec Rifles.[56] As the expedition neared its end, there were further instances of tampering with foodstuffs. On 10 August 1870, it was discovered that 24 of 31 barrels of pork had been "lightened" by soldiers from the 1st Ontario Rifles with the effect that the meat was completely spoiled. Although the incident did not find its way into the official report, Colonel Wolseley noted in his journal that he was "very angry" when he heard of this.[57] Additionally, although he made much of the fact that he had prohibited the consumption of alcohol, this was simply not true. Several observers noted the widespread use of alcohol[58] and the 60th Rifles went so far as to have "good wholesome beer" available in its regimental canteen.[59] None of these incidents are particularly noteworthy. What is significant is that either the incidents were not reported to the chain of command or the chain of command chose not to deal firmly with them. This did not bode well for the future.

Once the troops arrived in Fort Garry, all pretence of sober discipline vanished. Within hours of the uncontested occupation of Riel's headquarters, Colonel Wolseley released the troops from duty for the day. Accounts vary as to how much revelry ensued, but even the most conservative of the chroniclers noted that the troops had "… indulged rather freely in liquor."[60] Other observers were much less kind and described a "… wild scene of drunkenness and debauchery…."[61] Aggravating the situation was the fact that Wolseley's arrival had removed the only effective authority in the community. The Provisional Government had fled, the new lieutenant-governor had not yet arrived, the HBC was reluctant to govern and the army refused to assume responsibility for the civil administration.[62]

A photograph of Louis Riel made between 1879 and 1885. (Duffin and Company, Library and Archives Canada C-52177)

The force that arrived at Fort Garry on 24 August 1870 consisted almost exclusively of British regulars. Although the Expeditionary Force consisted of roughly one-third British and two-thirds Canadian troops, Colonel Wolseley decided to push his regular soldiers ahead of the militiamen.[63] There were no Canadian units in the line of battle that approached the Métis headquarters and the area had been completely secured by the time the first formed groups of militia began arriving on 27 August. The remainder of the troops came in over the next few days.[64] Almost as soon as the force had arrived, the 60th Rifles made ready to return to Ontario. The first detachment left Fort Garry on 29 August, and within five days, the entire contingent of regular troops had departed.[65] At the same time, some of the militiamen were already preparing to leave military service and enter the Red River community. By the time the lieutenant-governor arrived on 2 September, the garrison troops at his disposal were already reduced to less than two battalions of Canadian militia.[66]

It was not long before the tensions that had built-up in the community during the insurrection exploded in violence. On 1 September, a Catholic priest named Father Kavanaugh was shot at "presumably by volunteers."[67] On the same day, fences were torn down, private goods were stolen, lives were threatened, and a Métis by the name of Wabishka Morin was assaulted. On 6 September, a group of armed men broke into the home of the editor of a newspaper that had shown sympathy to the Métis cause. The editor, Thomas Spence, was beaten and whipped. After that the newspaper office was ransacked and the printing press was damaged. The gang was led by one of the leaders of the pro-Canadian faction known as the "Friends of Canada," a group that had attracted many new recruits from the ranks of the Canadian militia battalions.[68] On 13 September, Elzear Goulet was chased into the Red River by a mob and died of drowning or from blows to the head from thrown stones or from shots that were fired at him from the riverbank. Goulet's crime was that he had been a member of Riel's military organization. Although no one was held accountable for Goulet's death,[69] Canadian troops were widely assumed to have played a part in the incident.[70] At least one observer, a Canadian soldier himself, placed the blame squarely on other soldiers.[71]

More incidents followed. By the middle of September, the Toronto press had already picked-up on the lawlessness and reported on the "drunkenness, fights and assaults" in and around Winnipeg.[72] In October, another Riel sympathizer was killed when he was thrown from his horse after it had been deliberately frightened.[73] Meanwhile, on 18 October, officers from the Canadian militia organized the first Orange Lodge in Western Canada and began actively recruiting members from the battalions.[74] The members of the Orange Lodge, along with the Canada Firsters,[75] were among the most strident of those agitating on behalf of Canada. But these groups were not just pro-Canadian; they were also violently anti-Catholic and anti-French.[76] The anti-Métis elements in Red River were being greatly strengthened.

The violence in the community continued and spread. Beatings were commonplace and the house of one Métis was burned to the ground.[77] On 5 November, two Métis were attacked by a group of between 12 and 15 soldiers and were kicked, beaten, and dragged through the streets.[78] The inability or unwillingness of local authorities to maintain order was made plain when a group of soldiers tied a police constable to a cart, paraded him through Winnipeg, and then locked him in his own jail.[79] An American newspaper referred to the situation in Manitoba as a "reign of terror."[80] Lieutenant-Governor Archibald, anxious to re-establish control and fearing the worst from the aggressive Ontarians, decided to form a new constabulary.[81] Unfortunately, it proved difficult to recruit any of the local citizenry with the result that the new provincial police force was filled with recently discharged soldiers from the Expeditionary Force.[82] Unsurprisingly, the Métis watched these events with dismay. For many, it marked the beginning of "dark days."[83]

In December of 1870, events took another turn. Elections for seats in the new provincial legislative assembly were scheduled. These elections, like all of those in Canada at that time, were conducted in public meetings in an open vote. A group of approximately 100 soldiers, mainly from the 1st Ontario Rifles, put themselves at the disposal of the pro-Canadians and proceeded to methodically intimidate their political opponents.[84] In addition to smashing windows and other minor acts, the group went so far as to break into the houses of some of their victims.[85] Following the election, a group of soldiers broke into the local jail and released other soldiers who had been arrested for gambling.[86] James Taylor, the American consul in the area, wrote to his government, " … it would be an immense relief to the authorities if the Ontario Battalion was out of the country…."[87] In spite of this widespread violence and lawlessness, the army itself was doing little to enforce discipline. Throughout the period of the worst excesses, there was almost no serious effort to hold individual soldiers accountable for their actions. Investigations were typically inconclusive and when soldiers were convicted of offences, the punishments handed-out were routinely mild.[88]

Attacks on individuals continued in the following year. Soldiers beat two Métis on 4 January 1871,[89] and in March, one of the Métis who had served in the provisional government was killed after being struck on the head with a pistol.[90] Another Métis, Andre Neault, was attacked by a group of soldiers, bayoneted, and left for dead.[91] Particularly galling to devoutly Catholic Métis were the attacks on members of the Red River priesthood.[92] Nuns were insulted, Roman Catholic institutions were targeted for arson and there were even threats on the life of Bishop Alexandre-Antonin Taché.[93] The arrest and incarceration of a prominent Métis on charges of assisting Riel was clear evidence to many that they could not count on the protection of the civil authorities. Ontarians were seen to be able to commit violent acts with impunity, while even minor transgressions by Métis were harshly dealt with.[94]

In the spring of 1871, many of the troops that had been raised for the Canadian battalions were discharged from service at the end of their engagements.[95] The period just before these discharges was one of intense violence that culminated in a general mêlée in Winnipeg that involved more than 50 soldiers and Métis.[96] Although many of the soldiers returned to Ontario, many more chose to stay in the West.[97] These new citizens took-up a variety of occupations including farming, surveying, and prospecting. Some entered the business community while others joined the local police forces.[98] For the Métis, the settlement of the soldiers in the community was an unwelcome addition to the pressures that were already building as a result of increased immigration from Canada. According to members of the Roman Catholic clergy, the Métis were becoming despondent and were becoming more and more isolated within their own community.[99] One Métis commented, "our people cannot visit Winnipeg without being insulted, if not personally abused by the soldier mob."[100]

Late in 1871, the Canadian Government became aware of a possible attack on Manitoba by members of the Fenian Brotherhood.[101] On 3 October, the lieutenant-governor issued a proclamation that called on the citizens of the province to rally for the common defence of their territory.[102] The Métis realized that this external threat represented an opportunity to demonstrate their loyalty to the Government.[103] A body of approximately 1,000 troops was assembled from the remaining garrison and from the population at large. Many of troops were actually former members of the Red River Expeditionary Force.[104] The force was greatly strengthened when a group of 200 Métis presented themselves for service as a formed body of cavalry.[105]

In the event, the Fenians dispersed at the first sign of trouble and the episode ended almost as quickly as it had begun.[106] Unfortunately for the Métis, there was little appreciation on the part of the Canadian community for their offer of help. Although the officer charged with supervising the 50 Métis that were actually employed in a scouting role lavished praise on them for both their skill and conduct, little of this made its way into the general reports.[107] In fact, the lieutenant-governor was severely criticized for having accepted the Métis offer of assistance.[108] At the same time, the Canadian government had reacted to the threat from the Fenians by assembling a group of reinforcements for immediate dispatch to Manitoba.[109] By the time the incident had ended, the Métis realized that, not only had their cause not been advanced by their demonstrated loyalty,[110] the English-Protestant community had received a fresh infusion of strength in the form of the 200 men of the 2nd Red River Expeditionary Force.[111]

It was not long before the Métis were reminded of their plight. Although the lieutenant-governor had accepted their offer of help, even to the point of shaking the hand of Louis Riel, the leaders of the rebellion were still not able to re-enter the community.[112] By February of 1872, Riel and others were forced into exile in the United States with a bounty on their heads from the province of Ontario.[113] In the mean time, attacks continued on individuals in Manitoba.[114]

In 1872, the Canadian government extended the provisions of the Militia Act to Manitoba and reorganized the military forces there. The area was designated as Militia District 10 and the troops were consolidated into a unit designated the Provisional Battalion of Rifles (changed later to the Provisional Battalion of Infantry). Red River received a trickle of new troops when replacements filtered into Manitoba as other soldiers were demobilized.[115] The original Red River Expeditionary Force was slowly fading away. Also, by the end of 1872, there was a "tangible decrease in the direct violence against the Métis."[116]

The reasons for the decline in violence are not altogether clear, but there are at least three plausible explanations. The first explanation is that "assaults were continuing but not as many were being reported as doing so accomplished little … and … reporting violence … usually provoked more serious violence."[117] Another possibility is that many of the Métis had simply left the area in the aftermath of the rebellion and in frustration over the lack of resolution of land claims.[118] A third explanation is that the Government had finally become tired of all the violence and had decided to clamp down, especially after the riot that accompanied the Legislative Assembly elections of 1872.[119]

The army certainly decided to crack down. In spite of the relative quiet of 1873, the number of soldiers who were subjected to disciplinary action that year was dramatically higher than it had been at the height of the violence in 1871. Charges for being drunk and disorderly increased from 56 to 470; for disobedience, from 29 to 144; and for insolence, from 14 to 114. The charges for poor conduct went from a

Officers take part in a Winnipeg court-martial at the military school in 1891. (Henry Joseph Woodside, Library and Archives Canada PA-16026)

paltry 17 to 124, even though the number of troops in the area had shrunk by more than half.[120]

From September of 1870 until at least early 1873, the Métis of the Red River area were subject to widespread intimidation and violence, in large part at the hands of the militia soldiers of the Red River Expeditionary Force. Many of these militiamen came to Manitoba on an errand of revenge and the make-up of the force made linguistic, racial, political, and religious friction almost inevitable.[121] In the absence of tight discipline, this was an explosive combination and the result was, in many respects, unsurprising. Equally unsurprising would be the conclusion drawn by many Métis that the army was the embodiment of the ill-will, betrayal, and oppression that they had experienced in the aftermath of the Red River Rebellion. When the Métis were deciding on whether or not to oppose the force that was sent to Saskatchewan in 1885, the bad behaviour of the Canadian troops from 1870 to 1873 might well have been on their minds.

NOTES

1. Library and Archives Canada [henceforth LAC], Manuscript Group [henceforth MG] 29–E111, Irvine family fonds, Diary of Matthew Bell Irvine, "Journal of the Red River Rebellion," 23 August 1870, 115.

2. Roger Willock, "Green Jackets on the Red River," *Military Affairs,* Vol. 22, No. 1 (Spring 1958), 26–7.

3. There are several good accounts of the 1870 expedition. In particular, see Colonel Wolseley's official report, *Correspondence Relative to the Recent Expedition to the Red River Settlement; Journal of Operations,* which was presented to both Canadian Houses of Parliament in 1871; Colonel Wolseley also published a long account of the expedition in *Blackwoods Magazine* in December 1870; Directorate of History and Heritage [henceforth DHH], 83/309, "Narrative of the Red River Expedition: By an Officer of the Expeditionary Force," 1870; Captain G.L. Huyshe, *The Red River Expedition* (London: MacMillan and Co., 1871); LAC, MG 29–E111, "Journal of the Red River Rebellion."

4. A sample of the range of views can be found in George F.G. Stanley, *Louis Riel* (Toronto: Ryerson Press, 1963); J.M. Bumsted, *The Red River Rebellion* (Winnipeg: Watson and Dwyer Publishing, 1996); and, D.N. Sprague, *Canada and the Métis: 1869–1885* (Waterloo: Wilfrid Laurier University Press, 1989).

5. Stanley, *Louis Riel,* 160.

6. Marcel Giraud, *The Métis in the Canadian West,* two volumes (1945; reprint, Edmonton: University of Alberta Press [henceforth UAP], 1986), 370–74.

7. Canada, Parliament, Journals of the House of Commons, 1874, Vol. 8, Appendix 6, *Report of the Select Committee on the Causes of the Difficulties in the North-West Territory in 1869–70,* "Petition of Rev. N.J. Ritchot and Alfred H. Scott to Queen Victoria, February 8, 1872," 84.

8. Sprague, *Canada and the Métis,* 174.

9. For a first-rate discussion of this action, see Robert H. Caldwell, "'We're Making History, Eh?' An Inquiry into the Events That Occurred Near Cut Knife Hill, North West Territories, 1–2 May 1885," in Donald E. Graves, ed., *More Fighting for Canada: Five Battles, 1760–1944* (Toronto: Robin Brass Studio, 2004), 73–144. See also, Stanley, *Louis Riel,* 324–25.

10. Thomas Flanagan, *Riel and the Rebellion* (Saskatoon: Western Producer Prairie Books, 1983), 8.

11. Bob Beal and Rod Macleod, *Prairie Fire: The 1885 North-West Rebellion* (Toronto: McClelland and Stewart, 1984), 256–90.

12. R.E. Lamb, *Thunder in the North: Conflict over the Riel Risings, 1870–1885* (New York: Pageant Press, 1957), 128–29. See also, William R. Morrison, *The Sixth Regiment of Foot at Lower Fort Garry*, Occasional Papers in Archaeology and History, No. 4 (Ottawa: Department of Indian Affairs and Northern Development, 1970), 168.

13. The strength of the 1870 Red River Expedition was 1,163 military and 256 civilian personnel. See DHH, 693.003 (D3), "Regimental Chronicle of the 60th (King's Royal Rifle Corps)." By contrast, nearly 8,000 men were mobilized in response to the 1885 Rebellion. See George F.G. Stanley, *The Birth of Western Canada: A History of the Riel Rebellions* (1936; reprint, Toronto: University of Toronto Press [henceforth UTP], 1960), 352.

14. Stanley, *The Birth of Western Canada*, 316.

15. Gerhard Ens, *Homeland to Hinterland: The Changing Worlds of the Red River Métis in the Nineteenth Century* (Toronto: UTP, 1996), 145.

16. Alexander Morris, *The Treaties of Canada with the Indians of Manitoba and the North-West Territories* (1880; reprint, Toronto: Prospero Books, 2000). See also, Frank Tough, *As Their Natural Resources Fail: Native Peoples and the Economic History of Northern Manitoba, 1870–1930* (Vancouver: University of British Columbia Press, 1996), 78–91.

17. Harold A. Innis, *The Fur Trade in Canada: An Introduction to Canadian Economic History* (1930; reprint, Toronto: UTP, 1956), 341–44.

18. This extended even to the governor general. On 22 June 1869, at the prorogation of the second session of the first parliament, the governor general commented favourably on the arrangements for the transfer of Rupert's Land to Canada, noting that, "… in reference to the North West Territories, that wide expanse will, I hope, ere long be opened to settlement, and become the abode of myriads of thriving and industrious immigrants." There was no hint of trouble. See Canada, House of Commons Debates, *Governor General's Address to Parliament*, Prorogation of 1st Parliament 2nd Session, 22 June 1869. However, when the governor general opened the next session of parliament on 15 February 1870, his address was full of foreboding. He noted, "I have watched, with much anxiety, the course of events in the North West Territories. Unfortunate misapprehensions of the intentions with which the country was sought to be acquired by Canada have led to complications of a grave character." *Ibid.*, *Governor General's Address to Parliament*, Opening of 1st Parliament 3rd Session, 15 February 1870.

19. By 1869, the Hudson's Bay Company (HBC) had more or less accepted that Rupert's Land would be transferred to Canada and the negotiations were really a discussion of

the terms of transfer. The "Deed of Surrender" stipulated that Rupert's Land would pass to Canada in exchange for the sum of £300,000. The HBC also kept possession of all of its 120 forts, approximately 45,000 acres of land around its forts, a grant of territory that eventually amounted to 7 million acres, and it retained the right to trade in the area. There was no mention of the Métis or any of the other members of the Red River population. See J. Arthur Lower, *Western Canada: An Outline History* (Toronto: Douglas and McIntyre, 1983), 88–9. There was some later reflection on whether or not it would have been better to consult the local population; this came too late to influence events. See Paul Knapland, "Gladstone on the Red River Rebellion — 1870," *The Mississippi Valley Historical Review*, Vol. 21, No. 1 (June 1934), 76–7.

20. The survey party was led by Colonel John Stoughton Dennis and was sent to the Red River on the authority of the Canadian minister for Public Works, William McDougall. Both of these men were known to be strong supporters of the "Canadian party" that advocated annexation of the territory and its rapid settlement by Canadians. See D. Bruce Sealey and Antoine S. Lussier, *The Métis: Canada's Forgotten People* (Winnipeg: Manitoba Métis Federation Press, 1975), 76–8.

21. A-H. de Tremaudan, Elizabeth Maguet, trans., *Hold High Your Heads: History of the Métis Nation in Western Canada* (Winnipeg: Pemmican Publications, 1982), 58.

22. Thomas D. Rambaut, "The Hudson's Bay Half-Breeds and Louis Riel's Rebellions," *Political Science Quarterly*, Vol. 2, No. 1 (March 1887), 145. See also, Giraud, *The Métis in the Canadian West*, 269.

23. Don McLean, *Home From the Hill: A History of the Métis in Western Canada* (Regina: Gabriel Dumont Institute, 1987), 82–3.

24. Bumsted, *The Red River Rebellion*, 11–12.

25. G.M. Hougham, "Canada First: A Minor Party in Microcosm," *The Canadian Journal of Economics and Political Science*, Vol. 19, No. 2 (May 1953), 175.

26. DHH, "Narrative of the Red River Expedition," 711–12.

27. Rambaut, "The Hudson's Bay Half-Breeds," 147–48.

28. The curt note denying him entry read, in its entirety, «Monsieur: Le Comité National des Métis de la Rivière Rouge intime à Monsieur McDougall l'ordre de ne pas entrer sur le Territoire des Nords-Ouest sans une permission spéciale de ce comité. Par ordre du président. John Bruce. Louis Riel, Secretaire. Daté a St. Norbert, Rivière Rouge ce 21e jour d'octobre, 1869.» See Sealey and Lussier, *The Métis*, 78.

29. "Declaration of the People of Rupert's Land and the North-West," *Canada Sessional Papers* [henceforth *CSP*], Vol. 5, No. 12, 1870.

30. Frederick Jackson Turner, *The Frontier in American History* (New York: Holt, Rinehart and Winston, 1998), ix.

31. Stanley, *The Birth of Western Canada,* vii-ix.

32. Although it is dated, this is still the only work that attempts a comprehensive analysis of the Métis. See Giraud, *The Métis in the Canadian West,* 488–524. See also, M. Giraud, "A Note on the Half-Breed Problem in Manitoba (in Notes and Memoranda)," *The Canadian Journal of Economics and Political Science,* Vol. 3, No. 4 (November 1937), 541–42.

33. W.L. Morton, ed., *Alexander Begg's Red River Journal and Other Papers Relative to the Red River Resistance of 1869–1870* (Toronto: The Champlain Society, 1956), 2–6.

34. Sprague, *Canada and the Métis,* 184.

35. Flanagan, *Riel and the Rebellion,* 51–3.

36. Frits Pannekoek, *A Snug Little Flock: The Social Origins of the Riel Resistance, 1869–70* (Winnipeg: Watson and Dwyer Publishing, 1991), 11.

37. Ens, *Homeland to Hinterland;* and Tough, *As Their Natural Resources Fail.*

38. DHH, "Regimental Chronicle of the 60th (King's Royal Rifle Corps)."

39. Stanley, *Toil and Trouble,* 94.

40. DHH, Militia Reports, *Annual Report on the State of the Militia for 1870,* 3–4. See also, Frederick John Shore, "The Canadians and the Métis: The Re-Creation of Manitoba, 1858–1872," (Unpublished Ph.D. Thesis, University of Manitoba, 1991), Appendix II.

41. Stanley, *Toil and Trouble,* 92.

42. Huyshe, *The Red River Expedition,* Appendix D.

43. Erwin E. Kreutzweiser, *The Red River Insurrection: Its Causes and Events* (Gardenvale, QC: The Garden City Press, 1936), 134.

44. *Report of the Select Committee,* Lieutenant-Governor Archibald's evidence, 139–40.

45. Roderick G. MacBeth, *The Romance of Western Canada* (Toronto: William Briggs, 1918), 163.

46. The actual ratios were 85.2 percent English and 14.8 percent French. The data for this section was compiled from a number of sources. Of particular note is the work

of Frederick Shore who compiled more or less comprehensive lists of all the personnel in the Red River Expeditionary Force. See Shore, "The Canadians and the Métis," Appendices 2 and 3.

47. Ninety-two percent single, 7 percent married and 1 percent widowed, plus one priest.

48. Major Boulton, *Reminiscences of the North-West Rebellions* (Toronto: Grip Printing and Publishing Co., 1886), 145.

49. At least one observer was not nearly so impressed. See Simon J. Dawson, *Report on the Red River Expedition* (Ottawa: n.p., 1871), 219.

50. Huyshe, *The Red River Expedition,* 37.

51. Some of the lines of communication troops had left earlier. The first ship to leave Collingwood departed on 3 May 1870. See Stanley, *Toil and Trouble,* 92.

52. DHH, "Narrative of the Red River Expedition."

53. "Another unique aspect of the Expedition was the total 'absence of crime' at least during the three month period of the advance [...] and there were no reported instances of malingering or discontent." See Willock, "Green Jackets on the Red River," 28. This is also the position taken by Huyshe in *The Red River Expedition,* 186–97.

54. Stanley, *Toil and Trouble,* 255.

55. Matthew Bell Irvine, *Report on the Red River Expedition of 1870* (London: n.p., 1871), 5.

56. John Tennant, *Rough Times: 1870–1920* (Winnipeg: n.p., 1920), as cited in Stanley, *Toil and Trouble,* 142.

57. Wolseley, *Journal of Operations,* 9 August 1870, 87.

58. LAC, MG 29 — E34, John Andrew Kerr fonds, Diary of John Andrew Kerr, "Journey of Coy #7, Ontario Rifles, Red River Expedition." See also the private correspondence in note 46 of Stanley, *Toil and Trouble,* 46.

59. Huyshe, *The Red River Expedition,* 64.

60. Alexander Begg, *The Creation of Manitoba: A History of the Red River Troubles* (Toronto: n.p., 1871), 391.

61. William Butler, *The Great Lone Land: A Narrative of Travel and Adventure in the Northwest of America* (London: n.p., 1873), 192.

62. Stanley, *Toil and Trouble*, 184–85.

63. There seem to be two possible explanations for this. The standard explanation is that Wolseley had received intelligence from Fort Garry that suggested that a quick attack might result in the capture of the rebels during a period of weakness. The other explanation is that Colonel Wolseley wanted to ensure that British regular troops would get the glory in any battle with the "rebels" and had deliberately left the Canadians behind to keep them out of any action. See Stanley, *Toil and Trouble*, 170.

64. Huyshe, *The Red River Expedition*, 64.

65. Stanley, *The Birth of Western Canada*, 143.

66. Stanley, *Toil and Trouble*, 184–87.

67. Shore, "The Canadians and the Métis," 230.

68. Stanley, *Louis Riel*, 159.

69. *CSP*, Vol. 5, No. 20, 1871.

70. Bumsted, *The Red River Rebellion*, 222.

71. Tennant, *Rough Times*, 66–7.

72. Editorial, *Telegraph*, 16 September 1870.

73. Editorial, *The Manitoban*, 10 December 1870.

74. Bumsted, *The Red River Rebellion*, 223.

75. Canada First was a nationalist movement founded in 1868 by Ontarians who sought to promote a sense of national purpose and to lay the intellectual foundations for Canadian nationality. The group was stridently anti-French and anti-Catholic.

76. Shore, "The Canadians and the Métis," 240.

77. Editorial, *Le Nouveau Monde*, 15 October 1870.

78. The Métis involved were Landry and Romain Neault. Three days later, a Métis named Rivard received similar treatment. See *Daily Pioneer*, 8 November 1870.

79. Bumsted, *The Red River Rebellion*, 222.

80. *Daily Pioneer*, 6 October 1870, as cited in Shore, "The Canadians and the Métis," 230.

81. Lieutenant-Governor Archibald warned Prime Minister Macdonald that some of the Canadians believed that "… the French half-breeds should be wiped off the face of the globe." See Stanley, *Louis Riel*, 159–61.

82. Stanley, *Toil and Trouble*, 194–95.

83. Giraud, *The Métis in the Canadian West*, 377.

84. Bumsted, *The Red River Rebellion*, 223.

85. Archives de l'Archevêché, St. Boniface, Manitoba, Archives Deschâtelets [henceforth AD], J. Tissot to Monsigneur Taché, 10 December 1871. The attacks extended to anyone who was "French, Catholic, of native background or … thought to be sympathetic to the Provisional Government." See Ruth Ellen Swan, "Ethnicity and the Canadianization of Red River Politics," (Unpublished Ph.D. Thesis, University of Manitoba, 1991), 47.

86. Bumsted, *The Red River Rebellion*, 223. Astonishingly, only two soldiers were punished as a result of this incident of mutiny. Only two soldiers were punished for the breakout. LAC, RG 9, II-B-2, Vol. 33, Return of Defaulters, Red River Force, 1870–73.

87. DHH, Report No. 2, *Canadian-American Defence Relations, 1867–1914*, August 1965.

88. LAC, RG 9, II-B-2, Vol. 33, Adjutant-General's Office, Subject Files, Red River Force, 1870–73.

89. The two Métis were Toussaint Voudrie and Joseph McDougall. *Ibid.*

90. *Daily Pioneer*, 7 March 1871, as cited in Shore, "The Canadians and the Métis," 242.

91. *Ibid.*, 247.

92. Editorial, *Telegraph*, 4 October 1870. The relationship between the Métis and the priests and nuns of their church was very strong. See Raymond J.A. Huel, *Proclaiming the Gospel to the Indians and the Métis* (Edmonton: UAP, 1996), xviii.

93. Archives de l'Archevêché, AD, J. Royal to Monsigneur Taché, 23 February 1871.

94. *Ibid.*, J. Dubuc to Monsigneur Taché, 2 December 1871.

95. Individuals had been engaged under a variety of terms of service ranging from six to 12 months. See Militia General Orders, 12 May 1870.

96. Shore, "The Canadians and the Métis," 251. This period also saw the public whipping of a Métis named Bourassa and the rape of Marie Riviere. LAC, RG 9, II-B-2, Vol. 33, Return of Defaulters, Red River Force, 1870–73.

97. LAC, RG 15, Vol. 3170, Military Bounty Land Warrants, Department of the Interior, Land Patents Branch, 27 February 1926, Military and NWMP Warrants.

98. Stanley, *Toil and Trouble*, 200–01. See also, Bumsted, *The Red River Rebellion*, 224.

99. Archives de l'Archevêché, AD, G. Dugas to Monsigneur Taché, 18 October 1873.

100. *Daily Pioneer*, 14 March 1871, as cited in Shore, "The Canadians and the Métis," 247.

101. McLean, *Home From the Hill*, 75.

102. Editorial, *Le Métis*, 3 October 1871.

103. Stanley, *Louis Riel*, 172.

104. Stanley, *Toil and Trouble*, 207.

105. Stanley, *Louis Riel*, 174.

106. Editorial, *Le Métis*, 19 October 1871.

107. DHH, Militia Reports, 1870–71, "Capt. Royal's Report," 17 October 1871, 80.

108. Stanley, *Louis Riel*, 175.

109. C.P. Stacey, "The Second Red River Expedition: 1871," *Canadian Defence Quarterly*, Vol. 8, No. 2 (January 1931), 3.

110. During the crisis, editorials in the French-language press were clearly optimistic that their loyalty would be recognized. See, for instance, *Le Métis*, 12 and 19 October 1871.

111. *CSP*, Vol. 7, No. 26, 1872.

112. John Peter Turner, *The North-West Mounted Police: 1873–93* (Ottawa: King's Printer and Controller of Stationery, 1950), 76–8.

113. Stanley, *Louis Riel*, 181.

114. Editorial, *Le Métis*, 1 and 15 May 1872.

115. LAC, MG26–A, Sir John A. Macdonald fonds, Letterbook 16, Vol. 519, 342, Macdonald to J.J. Burrows, 17 August 1871. See also, LAC, RG 9, II-B-1, Vol. 519, Letterbook, August 1872 to April 1873.

116. Shore, "The Canadians and the Métis," 281.

117. *Ibid.*, 272.

118. Sprague, *Canada and the Métis,* 139.

119. *CSP*, Vol. 5, No. 1, 1873.

120. Shore, "The Canadians and the Métis," 287.

121. Although it is beyond the scope of this chapter, an important element in militia/Métis relations was the role of Military Bounty Land Warrants. Each soldier of the expeditionary force was awarded a bounty for his military service. These grants were for 160 acres of land in the same territory as the land that was to be granted to the Métis as a result of the stipulations of the Manitoba Act. Since the Military Bounty Land Grants were transferable, and because the grants were awarded at the time of discharge, the militia soldiers would have been in a position to profit from their awards almost immediately, whereas the Métis were forced to wait years for the resolution of their grants. The total grants for the Red River Expeditionary Force would have constituted almost a quarter of a million acres of land in direct competition with the 1.4 million acres that was reserved for the Métis. See LAC, RG 15, Vol. 3170, Land Patents Branch, Military Bounty Land Warrants, 27 February 1926, "160 acres of land open to ordinary homestead entry...." See also LAC, RG 15, Vol. 227, Dominion Lands, "Grants of Land Under Manitoba Act, and Militia Bounty Land Orders-in-Council."

5 ⊱

Bringing Our Heroes Home: Resistance, Disorder, Riot, and "Mutiny" Among Canada's South African Warriors

CARMAN MILLER

Managing a collection of socially and culturally diverse, hastily recruited, untrained citizen-soldiers, and moulding them into a coherent, effective fighting force, requires leadership and good fortune. Demobilizing these men and returning them to civil society, after months of constraint, stress, and deprivation, can prove equally challenging.[1] Although individual soldiers responded to the strains of warfare in various ways — fighting, drinking, stealing, being absent without leave, and refusing to obey orders[2] — this chapter will focus primarily on collective acts of resistance by Canada's South African warriors.

The Canadian government's decision to recruit citizen-soldiers for service in the South African War (October 1899 to May 1902) brought a flood of eager applicants; there were far more volunteers than places.[3] Before the war came to its bitter end on 31 May 1902, at least 7,368 young Canadians had served with the British Army in South Africa.[4] Organized into 11 different units, only seven (the 2nd Battalion, Royal Canadian Regiment of Infantry (RCRI), the Royal Canadian Field Artillery (RCFA), the Royal Canadian Dragoons (RCD), the 1st Battalion, Canadian Mounted Rifles (CMR), the Strathcona's Horse, the 2nd Battalion, CMR, and a consignment of 1,200 Canadian constables in Major-General Robert Baden-Powell's South African Constabulary (SAC)) engaged in active warfare. The rest (the 3rd, 4th, 5th, and 6th Battalions, CMR), about 2,000 men in all, arrived in South Africa too late to participate in the fighting against the Boers, though not for fighting among themselves.[5]

In battles at Paardeberg, Zand River, Mafeking, Liliefontein, Lydenburg, Harts River and elsewhere, Canada's citizen-soldiers fought with tenacity, stamina, skill, and courage; feats that their compatriots followed with pride, identifying with their success. During the course of the conflict, four Canadian volunteers won the coveted Victoria Cross (VC), 19 received the Distinguished Service Order (DSO), and 17 were awarded the Distinguished Conduct Medal (DCM). One hundred and seventeen Canadians were mentioned-in-despatches.

In selecting volunteers for these units, Canadian recruiters sought males between the ages of 22 and 40, with a minimum height of five feet, six inches (two inches taller than that required by the British Army) who could pass a standard medical examination. Recruiters preferred men with military or police experience, if ever so recent or rudimentary.[6] In some instances, character, sobriety, and moral antecedents were considerations, if not requirements.[7] Except for the Canadian constables in the SAC who signed a three-year service contract, all other Canadian volunteers agreed to serve for six months to one-year or until the war's end, whichever came first.

Canadian recruiters did not always get what they sought. Men lied about their age; many were younger than 22, the youngest was 15 (who at the end of his service with his first unit, re-enlisted in another) and a few were older than 40. Sympathetic, careless, or corrupt doctors turned a blind eye to physical disabilities. Although a number of volunteers possessed previous military and North-West Mounted Police (NWMP) experience, a large majority could claim little or no military experience at all. Sobriety and moral rectitude were not always the volunteer's most conspicuous characteristics. Moreover, political and military favouritism found places for friends and relations.

Nor were the volunteers a mirror image of Canadian society, even of Canadian male society. Canada's South African War contingents were disproportionately young, anglophone (only three percent were French Canadians), British-born, urban workers who were drawn from the low-paid, white-collar, blue-collar, and service sectors of the population; more than a few were clerks, blacksmiths, carpenters, plumbers, and electricians. A contingent's social composition reflected the time and region of recruitment. Those raised in central and eastern Canada possessed a number of university students, teachers, lawyers, engineers, and sons of notables.

Those from Western Canada contained large numbers of cowboys, ranch-
ers, farm labourers, packers, prospectors, and policemen, many of them
British-born. These restless sons of the empire, who were in search of
adventure, also included a smattering of "well bred" sons of British gentry,
such as the 12th Earl of Dundonald's son.

The volunteer's motives for seeking service were mixed and multiple:
personal, ideological, and material. Although the recruiters were not so
hard pressed for suitable volunteers that they filled the ranks with "useless
ruffians, the lame, halt and the blind," as one highly placed observer care-
lessly complained,[8] neither were the recruits the "pick of the nation's sinew
and brain," the "representatives of ideal Canadian manhood," nor were
they "pure as the air of the sunlit North," as their medical and defaulters
files demonstrate.[9] All the contingents contained "rovers and adventurers
of no fixed occupation who always turn up when there are heads to be broken."[10] Some were men who, in Rudyard Kipling's words, were "out on
active service rubbing something off their slate," while a few enlisted
under a false name, were deserters from a regular unit or, in one case, a
fugitive from justice.[11]

Managing these raw, inexperienced, and undisciplined citizen-soldiers
required skilled, responsive leadership, a quality that was in short supply
in a few units. Nowhere was leadership tested more severely than in
Canada's first contingent, the 2nd Battalion, RCRI. It was commanded by
Lieutenant-Colonel William Dillon Otter, a conscientious, diligent, 56-
year-old professional soldier who became the lightening-rod for his battalion's grievances, rivalries, tensions, and discontent. A career officer who
viewed war service as a means of personal advancement, within the British
Army if possible, Otter made little allowance for his battalion's civilian,
voluntary, and Canadian character. In his citizen force where personal and
family friendships transcended rank, and where no social distinction separated commissioned officers from non-commissioned officers (NCOs),
Otter's insistence on the rigid separation of men and officers and the strict
deference to rank and distinction seemed exaggerated, irksome, and insen-
sitive, especially in the distribution of favours, food, and accommodations.

Conscious of his "colonial" status and anxious to appear professional
and to create a favourable impression upon his British superiors, Otter
adhered uncritically, and often needlessly, to British military regulations.

His obsession for copying "all the wrinkles of the British"[12] irritated many of his junior officers and men. They resented his "petty edicts," such as his insistence upon saluting aboard ship, an order that required men lying or sitting to come to attention every time an officer appeared; they later learned with relish that saluting was normally dispensed with aboard British troopships. The "Old Woman,"[13] the men's unflattering sobriquet for their commanding officer (CO), captured their resentment of his obsession with protocol and ceaseless fussing over form and appearance, impressions of Otter that remained with some veterans for life.[14]

The Royal Canadians's untimely arrival in Cape Town, 10 days before the British Army's disastrous defeats of "Black Week" (10 to 15 December 1899), sorely tested Otter's leadership during his unit's first two months in South Africa. This situation later repeated itself at Belmont during a five-week wait while the army of the newly appointed commander-in-chief of British forces in South Africa, Field-Marshal Frederick Roberts, re-organized and prepared for their "final" march to Pretoria. The paralysing confusion, uncertainty, and jockeying for position that the Royal Canadians observed after Black Week as the British changed command and strategy, and re-organized, re-mounted, and re-armed, unsettled Otter's restless, underemployed officers and men; at Belmont, disease compounded their discontent.

Anxious for action, Otter's officers and men became irritable, bored, and quarrelsome. With their morale sapped by disease, the plague of sedentary troops, they blamed Otter for their lack of active service, their poor campsite and food, and accused him of favouritism and indifference to their plight; they expressed their dissatisfaction through insubordination, looting, fighting, drinking, and by neglecting their duties. Otter's only solution to their discontent seemed to be to lecture, drill, and punish, sentences that the men often considered excessive and degrading. Relations between Otter and his subordinates deteriorated further as their complaints found their way into the Canadian press.

A better desk officer than a field commander, Otter was a methodical administrator who reported fully and promptly, in clear concise language, to his superiors at home and in the field. An inveterate letter writer, he maintained a broad network of correspondence with useful friends, family, and supporters. Conscious of his professional career's dependence upon political favour and public approval, he scoured the Toronto newspapers for criticism of his command and became increasingly angered by what he read. He blamed his "conniving" officers and men for their unprofessional communication with the press, but he made certain that his own friends and supporters answered the unfavourable publicity.

Contrary to the men's impressions, Otter cared about his battalion's welfare. He worried and fretted over their health and material depravations, but he refrained from seeking better for fear of being considered "amateurish" or unprofessional by his British superiors. Above all, he failed to communicate to his officers and men his genuine concern for their welfare. Increasingly isolated from his officers and men, a hostage of the few whom he trusted, Otter effectively lost control of his battalion towards the end of his command, an estrangement that his battalion's consignment to line of communication duty during their last months of service only exacerbated. Posted in five separate locations some distance from one another, away from the watchful eye of their CO, company solidarity grew at the expense of regimental unity. Otter "will get roasted when the Boys get a chance," Private Albert Perkins perceptively predicted as early as January 1900.[15]

Controversy over the contingent's return provided an occasion to turn up the heat. The British military's need to respond in kind to the Boers' guerrilla tactics following the British occupation of Pretoria in June 1900 put a premium on mounted soldiers without diminishing the need for infantry to protect the lines of supply and communication, and to hold what they had taken. Consequently, when Otter, conscious of the approaching expiry of his battalion's year of service, sought instruction on arrangements for his battalion's return to Canada, the British commander, Field-Marshal Roberts made a personal request that the Royal Canadians prolong their service, confident of the war's imminent termination, and to serve as an example to the other colonial contingents whose time was about to expire as well. After consulting a few of the officers at his station, Otter immediately agreed to the request from Roberts and published his decision in a regimental order.

The companies at the other stations were furious. Tired and disillusioned with the war, and worried about their civilian employment at home, the officers at these stations informed Otter that their men had refused to extend their service; moreover, they resented his failure to consult them before complying with Roberts's request and issuing his

The return of the Canadian Contingent from South Africa. (Library and Archives Canada C-7978)

regimental order. Otter wrote immediately to Roberts regretting his misjudgment, explaining that most of his men and officers could not "with justice to themselves or families re-engage."[16] Undeterred by Otter's communication, Roberts attempted to reverse the decision, asking Otter to re-canvass the men, reassuring them that the war would soon end, and informing them of his wish that they participate in the formal annexation ceremonies. As an additional incentive, he promised that the Queen herself would "honour with her presence" those who complied with his request. Otter relayed this message to all stations, asking them to respond immediately; the former had not long to wait.

All the stations responded within two days. The result was worse than Otter had expected. Deeply embarrassed, he informed Roberts that only 300 men would remain. The rest wanted immediate passage to Canada, a response that Otter correctly interpreted as a want of confidence in his command. Although Otter had assured Roberts that 300 men would remain, in the end, only 262 agreed to stay, whereas 462 left. The majority of those who remained had little choice, since they were from the Permanent Force or reinforcements whose time had not yet expired.

Moreover, of those who remained, few were happy with their decision. As soon as Roberts received Otter's second report, he ordered his staff to arrange for the immediate return of dissenting Canadians. Eight days later, they left their stations for Pretoria where Roberts graciously thanked them for their service. The men then boarded a train for Cape Town where the SS *Idaho* waited to transport them to a hero's welcome in Halifax.

Meanwhile, things deteriorated back in South Africa. The remnant envied their departing comrades. "It's like the last link with home broken," one man confided enviously to his diary.[17] Many of those who remained regretted their decision and sought every opportunity to reverse it. When Roberts's second-in-command and successor, Lord Kitchener, attempted to renegotiate the terms of the extended service of the Royal Canadians, the remnant adamantly refused his proposal; they would not even consider a three-month extension. Two or three weeks were all that they would countenance. Otter's attempt to negotiate a compromise with Kitchener failed as well. Once again, Otter gave his men two days to make up their mind. The men responded in half that time: not one man would remain. Embarrassed by their response, Otter again had to report his failure to his superior.

The folly of retaining the men became painfully obvious daily. Morale plummeted, men quarrelled, and drinking, theft, and insubordination increased. The situation got out of hand. Although Otter lectured, paraded, and punished, nothing seemed to work, except the news of their release from service. Six days after the annexation ceremonies in Pretoria, the remnant of Otter's Royal Canadians left by rail for Cape Town where they boarded a comfortable, well-stocked vessel bound for England. Then, after an exhausting 13-day schedule of entertainment in England that included an inspection by Queen Victoria, one of her last official public appearances, they left Liverpool for a rousing welcome in Halifax.[18]

Otter was not the only CO who encountered difficulties while managing the return of Canadian troops. All three units of Canada's second contingent (the RCFA, the RCD, and the 1st Battalion, CMR), in addition to Strathcona's Horse, created disturbances. The cause, occasion, and object of their high-jinks, however, contrasted sharply with those faced by Otter's battalion.

Leadership was not a problem in the units of the second contingent or the Strathcona's Horse, at least not for long. The RCFA's CO, Lieutenant-Colonel

Charles W. Drury, was the popular, competent "father" of the Canadian artillery. Similarly, the diligent, skilful, 39-year-old CO of the RCD, Lieutenant-Colonel François Lessard, possessed the respect of his men, officers, and British superiors. Leadership, however, plagued Lessard's brother unit, the 1st Battalion, CMR. After three months under the turbulent command of Lieutenant-Colonel Laurence Herchmer, the harsh, 59-year-old British-born former commissioner of the NWMP, the CMR came under the command of Major Thomas Dixon Evans, Lessard's 41-year-old second-in-command, whom many of the British higher command considered to be one of their most dependable Canadian field commanders. The British were no less impressed by the CO of Strathcona's Horse, Lieutenant-Colonel Samuel B. Steele, the 51-year-old legendary superintendent of the NWMP, who was an energetic, shrewd manager of men and his own best publicist, but who had little time for the stupidities of barrack square drill. Sobriety, however, was not one of his virtues.

Drink is a potent dissolvent of discipline, especially among sedentary and celebratory troops. Perhaps significantly, the bottle claimed Canada's first South African War casualty. During the departure of Canada's first contingent from Quebec, Private Teddy Deslauriers, the popular 28-year-old Ottawa grocery clerk who was a strong cross-country rider, bon vivant, and corporal in the Princess Louise Dragoon Guards, died aboard ship four days out from "delirium tremens" induced by his excessive drinking during his last night in Quebec City.

Containing the celebration of the troop's disengagement proved even more difficult. For example, in October 1900, rumours of a premature release from service touched off a dangerous round of drunken celebrations among the officers and men of Strathcona's Horse. Although Steele's battalion of mounted scouts had been recruited in early January 1900, it had seen no real action until early June. During the succeeding five months, however, Strathcona's Horse had been fully engaged, first with General Sir Redvers Buller's Natal Field Force as it fought its way towards an intersection with Roberts's forces at Belfast-Bergendal, and then with Buller as he moved north to Lydenburg to quell the guerrilla resistance there.[19]

Soon after his occupation of Lydenburg on 2 October 1900, Buller disbanded his column, thanked his men, and left for Pretoria, confident that his mission had been accomplished. Three days later, Lord

Dundonald's Brigade disbanded (in which Strathcona's Horse had served) and Steele and his staff began to prepare an inventory of their stores and equipment, convinced that their service had terminated and they, like the Royal Canadians, were to be ordered home. Meanwhile, Steele commanded his battalion to return to the railway at Machadodorp to await transport to Pretoria where he had gone to arrange their passage home and to receive further orders.

Relaxed and in a celebratory mood, the men remained for three days at Machadodorp, camped on either side of the rail, unprotected from the incessant rain, thunder, and lightening. Officers had difficulty maintaining order among the restless, rowdy men and some made no effort to do so, especially after Steele's departure. Damp, cold, bored, and anticipating their immediate release from service, many of the men wanted alcohol. Resorting to a familiar ruse, the more enterprising of the lot marched to the quartermaster's store and forged the signature of Steele's second-in-command, Major Robert Belcher, to procure drink.

Very shortly, the men became drunk, noisy and disorderly, shouting and firing their revolvers in the air. The British Provost-Marshal (PM), a major, with a couple of mounted policemen in tow, came to investigate. As the PM stooped to examine a crude, suspicious looking "bivouac with a light in it and in which a sergeant and a corporal were making merry with a bottle full of rum," one of the Canadians came up behind him and "fired his revolver close to each side of his head."[20]

The shaken PM ordered several companies of British infantry to surround the Canadians and to parade the merrymakers for several hours until they sobered up. The authorities investigated the affair the next day but, surprisingly, took no action since they were "irregular troops and our Colonel was away."[21] Steele's political skills, Buller's broad tolerance and Lord Strathcona's reputation may also have weighed in the balance. Whatever the cause of their indulgence, the incident received no publicity in Canada, nor did it tarnish the battalion's image or prevent Steele from later obtaining a more important command in Baden-Powell's SAC.

Two months later, drink and disorder embroiled all three units of Canada's second contingent in a more serious disturbance in Cape Town. By November 1900, almost a year after they had been recruited, most of the men were more than ready to return home, especially those who had been consigned to more sedentary service. Canada's gunners, generally considered the country's "best arm," who were represented in South Africa by three batteries of the RCFA, had had little opportunity to prove their worth during their year of service. Divided, dispersed, and under-utilized, two of the three batteries spent most of the war posted along the railway guarding rails, telegraph lines, and supply lines, and fighting both disease and boredom. It was a claustrophobic routine that was broken only occasionally by futile, poorly led, rebel-chasing adventures. The exception was "C" Battery that claimed Mafeking and Liliefontein among its battle honours.

The second contingent's two mounted infantry battalions, the RCD, and the 1st Battalion, CMR, were more fortunate, fighting their way to Pretoria and engaging in battles to clear its environs and to protect rail and supply routes. Even when they were consigned to line of communication duty and deployed in small autonomous groups along the rail line, mounted men possessed a degree of personal freedom and the possibility of personal adventures that was all but denied to foot soldiers. Absences, looting or liaisons with civilians could be explained in terms of losing one's way or taking a wrong turn! Whatever their experience, by November 1900, most of the men of Canada's second contingent greeted the news of their release and imminent return to Canada with relief.

Celebrations began soon after the Dragoons, Mounted Rifles, and gunners left Pretoria on 2 December. At Kroonstad, while their officers enjoyed a champagne dinner, the men "commandeered a carload of beer which they proceeded to drink up ... in short order." They soon became disorderly and insubordinate, despite the threats of their officers and civil authorities.[22] Diverted briefly to Worcester to intimidate a Boer sympathizers' convention that the British feared might precipitate a revolt in the Cape Colony, the men arrived in Cape Town on 11 December where they were billeted at Maitland Camp with about 500 returning Australian troops.

The next day, as the Canadians were loading their baggage aboard the *Roslin Castle* in preparation for their return voyage, they heard rumours of celebrations that were being planned for their last evening in Cape Town. Immediately, they sought permission to go into town. When it was refused, they decided to go nonetheless, aided and abetted by their Australian comrades. Sore "as hell," the Canadians and Australians walked out of camp determined "to have a good time before they sailed."[23] When officers and sentries tried to stop them, one group hijacked a horse cab. One of their number mounted the horse (they were horsemen after all), another took the reins on the box, and the rest crowded in behind. Gathering up speed, the Canadians approached the sentries at a gallop. The Canadians' "cavalry charge" overcame the British guards and the British were "obliged to make way for the cab and its load."[24] The men headed straight for the bars on Adderly Street.

Some of the Canadians had just entered their first bar when a military order arrived forbidding the bar to sell alcoholic drinks to any of the soldiers. When the bar's manager failed to convince the men that he could sell them no drinks, the men took things into their own hands and shot up the bar in Wild West fashion. "Pistol bullets shattered the chandeliers. Men tried to shoot their monograms into the big plate glass mirror … others vaulted the bar and worked as volunteer barmen."[25] As soon as they had exhausted that bar's supply, they moved on to the Grand Hotel where the manager was more legalistic and shrewd than his counterpart in the previous bar. Although military orders forbade the manager of the Grand Hotel's bar from selling alcoholic drinks to the soldiers, no order prevented him from giving them away, so long as the men did not wreck the bar. Not only did the men leave his bar intact, they collected "three big Canadian felt hats full of golden sovereigns," and presented them to the manager. According to Canadian gunner Jack Randall, news of the free drinks at the Grand brought a crowd of thirsty customers who were packed solid for two city blocks about the hotel. "Traffic was stopped. The Military Police saw they couldn't do a thing with that mob, so they didn't even try."[26]

But this was not only a Canadian riot. The Australians were on their way home, too, and they had scores to settle with a "Dutch paper" that had called them "descendants of convicts." The Australians visited their accusers, "wrecked the plant and were now marching about the town looking for trouble in general." Incapable of containing the disturbance, the city police called out the military authorities. About 30 Cape Mounted Rifles:

> supported by infantry patrols with fixed bayonets formed
> in line and drew their swords, then chose the most solid
> looking body of rioters, and advanced at a walk, broke

into a trot and finally a gallop. They used the flats and
the backs of their swords and cracked many heads.[27]

A show of force was all that was required. The mob dispersed and the
men found their way back to camp, carrying their casualties of the sword
and the bar.

Official reports were singularly silent on the Cape Town riot. The
British military authorities' response to the disturbance was strikingly
indulgent. They initiated no extensive investigation and made no effort to
single out and punish the offenders or reprimand their leaders. Men who
were "absent without leave" received a mere seven days detention, a somewhat meaningless sentence given the number of men involved and the fact
that they were aboard ship. According to the Canadian VC winner
Captain Richard Turner, they "paid for their spree like real men," perhaps
by a voluntary fine or a collection to cover the property damages.

Turner's light-hearted reference suggests that the British authorities
had dismissed the riot as youthful high spirits, and since the rioters were
colonial citizen-soldiers, it would have been unwise to pursue them, especially since the British were seeking more colonial recruits. Neither did the
riot appear to dampen the cordiality of the official departure ceremonies
for the Canadian and Australian troops the next day, nor the warmth that
Cape Town's cheering spectators showed towards the previous evening's
happy rioters as they marched peacefully through their streets to the waiting vessels. Perhaps the spectators were simply relieved to see them leave!
According to one of the gunners, fear that the departure of Strathcona's
Horse would be even more turbulent, as "they are worse than the CMR's,"
led the British authorities to embark troops the day the Strathcona's Horse
"arrived from the front."[28]

Although British authorities were frequently indulgent towards colonials, relationships between Canadian and British troops were not always
friendly.[29] Tensions took various forms ranging from recreational competi-
tions and verbal sparring to barroom brawls and more serious group confrontations. Some Canadian senior officers may even have encouraged
these rivalries as a means to build morale and group solidarity. For example, men in the Strathcona's Horse believed that their CO was proud of
them when they got the better of their imperial comrades in a barroom

brawl ... and they often did.[30] Tensions were not confined to the ranks alone. Many Canadian officers felt snubbed by British officers who made them feel "that they were members of the mess by sufferance."[31] On occasion, conflict between colonial and imperial officers reached such unpleasant levels that both Lord Roberts and his successor, Lord Kitchener, issued confidential orders regretting the "unfriendly spirit of regimental officers to members of H.M. colonial forces."[32]

The most spectacular example of conflict between Canadian and imperial soldiers entailed two Canadian troops of Baden-Powell's SAC.[33] Recruited between October 1900 and June 1901, the constabulary was the suggestion of Lord Milner, the dynamic British High Commissioner to South Africa. What Milner proposed was a permanent local police force under civilian command, designed to maintain law, order and public security in the recently occupied Boer territory. More than that, he wanted a force that would help to "civilise," pacify, resettle, and reconstruct South Africa along British lines. Consequently, recruits were required to sign a three-year contract, renewable for two years, as opposed to the one-year contract signed by all other units recruited in Canada. At the end of his

Back from South Africa, the Canadian Contingent arrives in Ottawa in 1900. (Library and Archives Canada C-7977)

service, each recruit was offered a land grant as an incentive to settle in South Africa, thereby becoming a reserve militia and the backbone of a reconstructed "British" South Africa.

Milner originally envisaged a force of 6,000 strong-armed, dependable recruits of good character, who were loyal, courageous, and sporting, and whose character and behaviour exemplified the hierarchical, manly, and genteel ideals of his new imperialism. The British War Office (WO) endorsed his plan immediately on the condition that Milner increase the proposed force to 10,000 and place it under military command until the war's end. For that the WO would pay the extra expense.

The constabulary's CO, Major-General Robert S.S. Baden-Powell, the ingenious, self-advertising, 44-year-old hero of Mafeking, was convinced that he could raise at least 1,200 of his 10,000 constables in Canada. He immediately sought the services of Lieutenant-Colonel Sam Steele, a man whom he admired greatly, to raise the men and command one of the constabulary's four geographic divisions. The hybrid police/soldier character of the new force, however, attracted men who were interested in the fighting, but who had no desire or aptitude for police work or any intention of settling in South Africa. Organized into 12 regionally defined 100-man troops, the 1,200 Canadian constables were far from the well-bred skilled horsemen and land-hungry settlers that Baden-Powell and Milner sought. About half of the Canadian constables were raised in central or eastern Canada, largely from among restless, urban, blue-collar workers, "unaccustomed to horses and [who] made poor horse-masters."[34] Many were wild, reckless, and rowdy men with no interest in settling into the sedate, sedentary life of a country constable in a quiet Afrikaner town.

Although Baden-Powell was initially impressed with his Canadian constables' "splendid" physique and excellent quality, and predicted that they would be a valuable addition to his force,[35] he soon recognized the social difference between the Canadian constables and some of the gentrified recruits from the British Isles. He acknowledged that the Canadian constables were hard-working and "brave to foolhardy in the field," an assessment confirmed by other officers, their performance in the field, and their casualty count, but he regretted their obvious resistance to sedentary, blockhouse consignments and feared that they would prove unsuitable for police work once the war ceased and the opportunity for action ended.[36]

Baden-Powell's worries were well founded. Once the war ended and the constabulary was confined to isolated, sedentary civilian employment, a serious crisis developed. The difficulty was precipitated by the WO's withdrawal of its funding and the consequent necessity of reducing the force by 40 percent to its proposed original strength of 6,000. Determined to reconstitute the civilian force along the lines originally envisaged by Milner, the constabulary was ordered to rid the force of "the rotters," retaining only the steady, able, educated men who would give no offence to the Boer population so "easily offended by the slightest impropriety in language, and demeanour."[37] The Canadian constables felt themselves specially targeted by the ensuing purge and they reacted strongly, framing their protest in nationalist terms.

Misunderstanding and conflict with the British authorities had plagued the Canadian constables from the beginning. The constables volunteered on the understanding that they would be kept together as a Canadian unit under Steele's command. Upon their arrival, however, Baden-Powell distributed the Canadian constables among the four divisions and only Steele's intervention prevented him from going further and breaking up the troops themselves and distributing the men among the other units. Discipline, moreover, was never the Canadians' strongest suit, nor was it reinforced by Baden-Powell's nebulous objectives and unorthodox and imprecise training instructions, including his desire to reject army methods in order to mould his force into "one happy family." Soon after the Canadian constables arrived in South Africa, relations in one of the troops became so tense that one constable predicted that there was "a danger of an uprising."[38]

Immediately following the war's end, the conflict came to a head in two of the Canadian troops, numbers 14 and 17, which had been recruited in Saint John, New Brunswick, and Montreal, Quebec, respectively. During a rigorous tour of inspection, an imperial officer reported to his superior that the interior economy of these two troops was especially unsatisfactory. Discipline was lax and the men displayed no deference to rank and hierarchy. Men were insubordinate, ignorant of rules and regulations, lacked initiative, and were mutinous, dishonest, and drunken. Upon receipt of this devastating report, the divisional officer commanding reprimanded the Canadian captains commanding these two troops, F.W.L.

Moore and A.H. Powell, and ordered them to restore order to their troops at once. When the Canadian captains failed to comply with these orders, they were informed that they would be transferred to other units and that British officers would replace them.

The Canadian constables responded immediately and mutinously to this edict. They first petitioned their divisional commander, denouncing the threatened transfer of their captains, making clear that they would serve only under Canadian officers who "understand the Canadian disposition."[39] When the divisional commander refused the constables' petition, all the troops' NCOs demanded permission to revert to the ranks. When this tactic proved no more successful, on the day set for their troops' change of command, the constables simply left their posts without orders and went into town leaving "the district without police" and obliging the sub-divisional commander to replace them temporarily with constables from other districts.[40]

The personal intervention of the sub-divisional commander only exacerbated the situation. His visit to one of the posts and his attempts to address the men during dinner ended in confusion. The men's behaviour became threatening. They refused his order to fall in for rifle inspection and as he was leaving the post, warning "shots were fired in the air." Similarly, when the sub-divisional commander sent an experienced superintendent to another post to restore order, the defiant Canadian constables greeted him at the railway station, hooted at him, and subsequently shot a government Cape cart "into matchwood" to reinforce their message.[41]

Immediately, the sub-divisional commander ordered the arrest of nine of the constables' leaders and constituted a board of officers to try them in Bloemfontein. The board met but it was unable to secure sufficient evidence of individual guilt to lay charges since none would implicate the other in this tightly knit group. Although the board failed to press charges, the nine leaders and 24 other constables were discharged, most with no entry on their defaulters sheet and some whose official record ironically described their conduct as "very good."

They and over 100 other discontented Canadian constables angrily returned to Canada. They claimed publicly that they had been victims of national discrimination and that they had been singled out by imperial officers, being the object of arbitrary and petty regulations simply because they were Canadian. Their complaints generally received a sympathetic hearing in the Canadian press. "Canadians are not, nor does the public opinion of this country demand that Canadians become the lackeys of English officers," wrote one irate correspondent. "A Canadian trooper is a fighting man; he is not a soldier."[42] When the issue was raised in the House of Commons, the Minister of Militia and Defence, Sir Frederick Borden, requested the British military authorities to investigate the complaints; the investigation predictably cleared the British officers of all blame.[43] Many of the constables' complaints, however, were real and legitimate, but were the result more of social than national bias.

While these collective acts of resistance are the most conspicuous and overt examples among Canada's South African War soldiers, others exist as well,[44] such as the organized system of looting, ignored and often condoned by commissioned officers and NCOs.[45] Major-General E.T.H. Hutton, the former general officer commanding the Canadian militia, who now commanded the 1st Mounted Infantry Brigade in South Africa, described the Canadians as the "biggest thieves in the Army,"[46] a distinction challenged by other claimants; he was annoyed because the Canadians had liberated his horse! A question that requires more attention is the complicity of junior officers in collective resistance, a complicity not confined to sanctioning organized looting, but implied in all the incidents described above.

The trials of bringing the nation's heroes home were many. Aboard their homeward bound vessels, men neglected and were careless of their duties, drank, fought, broke into stores, and refused orders.[47] Their arrival in Canada and their reversion to civilian status provided an opportunity to settle old scores, that is, to tell an officer what they really thought of him — assessments accompanied by threats.[48] Drunkenness turned civic receptions for the heroes into a source of public embarrassment; local organizers soon learned to pour the men onto trains as soon as possible and to send them to their next destination. Even so, their grossly exaggerated reputation sometimes preceded them.

Steele had wisely disarmed his men soon after they had left Cape Town; other COs had not. Consequently, tales circulated of trigger-happy veterans' "shooting up of some peaceful eastern town and of bloody battles with the police." Local police occasionally forbade them to leave the trains until their officers disarmed them to avoid further incidents.[49] As the trains crawled across the country with their happy and at times riotous troops, men left the trains at the station stops closest to their various centres of concentration. The men then scattered to the cities, towns, villages, settlements, or farms from which they came, for a time local heroes, acclaimed and feted by their families and communities.

NOTES

1. See Desmond Morton, "'Kicking and Complaining': Demobilization Riots in the Canadian Expeditionary Force, 1918–19," *Canadian Historical Review*, Vol. 61, No. 3 (September 1980), 334–60, and, R.L. Kellock, *Report on the Halifax Disorders, May 7th–8th, 1945* (Ottawa: King's Printer, 1945).

2. Although many acts remained unpunished, there are several conspicuous examples. For instance, two members of the Royal Canadian Dragoons, Private John Alexander Hopkins and Private William Pearce, were court-martialled for robbing prisoners and selling them back their guns; they were sentenced to 10 years penal servitude for "assisting the enemy with arms." See Carman Miller, *Painting the Map Red: Canada and the South African War, 1899–1902* (Montreal and Kingston: Canadian War Museum and McGill-Queen's University Press, 1993 and 1998), 238–39. Sometimes even officers crossed the line of acceptable behaviour. Captain W.T. Lawless was cashiered from the South African Constabulary for what he dismissed as a "fit of horseplay" when he shot out the lights "in a beastly little Dutch club in Krugersdorp." Baden-Powell saw things differently. Library and Archives Canada [henceforth LAC], Manuscript Group [henceforth MG] 27–IIB1, Gilbert John Elliot-Murray-Kynynmound, 4th Earl of Minto fonds, W.T. Lawless to Minto, 8 June 1902. Such examples could be multiplied.

3. For an account of the war's causes and Canada's decision to participate in this conflict, see Miller, *Painting the Map Red*, 3–48.

4. This aggregate figure of the strength of all units recruited in Canada may be misleading, since many men re-enlisted in subsequent units, and it does not include the 300 or more Canadians who joined British irregular units such as Howard's Canadian Scouts.

5. For more detail see Miller, *Painting the Map Red*, 422, or, Carman Miller, *Canada's Little War: Fighting For The British Empire in Southern Africa — 1899–1902* (Toronto: James Lorimer, 2003).

6. To qualify, some men joined a militia unit literally days before they volunteered for overseas service.

7. Bill Rawling, *Death Their Enemy: Canadian Medical Practitioners and War* (Quebec: AGMV Marquis, 2001), 47.

8. National Library of Scotland, Minto Papers, Gerald Kitson to J.H.C. Graham, 22 March 1900.

9. Miller, *Canada's Little War,* 27–9.

10. LAC, MG29–E20, T.E. Howell fonds, "Reminiscences," 1.

11. Miller, *Painting the Map Red,* 396.

12. W. Hart McHarq, *From Quebec to Pretoria with the Royal Canadian Regiment* (Toronto: W. Briggs, 1902), 196.

13. Lucien Valle to father, 10 April 1900, Valle collection, Private collection.

14. "Patriots, Scalawags and Saturday Night Soldiers," Canadian Broadcasting Corporation *Ideas,* Part II, November 1991, 10.

15. LAC, MG29–E93, Albert Perkins fonds, Albert to mother, 2 January 1900.

16. Canada, Sessional Paper 35a (1901), Report A, 28–9.

17. LAC, MG30–E219, E.F. Pullen fonds, Diary entry for 15 October 1900.

18. For greater detail on Otter's difficulties, see Miller, *Painting the Map Red,* Chapter 11.

19. For a more complete account of their activities, see *Ibid.*, 288–367.

20. LAC, MG30–E357, R.P. Rooke fonds, "A Record From Memory," 26 April 1908.

21. *Ibid.*

22. W.A. Griesbach, *I Remember* (Toronto: Ryerson Press, 1946), 311.

23. Jack Randall, *I'm Alone* (Indianapolis: Bobbs-Merrill, 1930), 68.

24. Griesbach, *I Remember,* 312.

25. Randall, *I'm Alone,* 51–3.

26. *Ibid.*

27. Griesbach, *I Remember,* 312.

28. LAC, MG29–E91, Muncey family fonds, Muncey to father, n.d.

29. See Carman Miller, "The Crucible of War: Canadian and British Troops during the Boer War," in Peter Dennis and Jeffrey Grey, eds., *The Boer War: Army, Nation and Empire* (Canberra: Army History Unit, 2000), 84–98.

30. See Miller, *Painting the Map Red,* 306–07.

31. "British Press Comments," 8, 7 April 1902, *Globe.*

32. The National Archives of the United Kingdom [henceforth TNA], War Office 108/117, General Order 1329, 10 March 1902.

33. See Carman Miller, "The Unhappy Warriors: Conflict and Nationality Among Canadian Troops During the South African War," *The Journal of Imperial and Commonwealth History,* Vol. 23, No. 1 (January 1995), 77–104.

34. TNA, Colonial Office [henceforth CO] 526/3/24, Captain Charles Beer to Assistant Deputy Sub-Divisional Officer [henceforth ADSO], E Division, 30 June 1903.

35. LAC, Minto fonds, Baden-Powell to Minto, 1 June 1901.

36. *Ibid.*

37. TNA, CO 526/3/24, Colonel Pilkington to Chief Staff Officer, SAC, 24 July 1903.

38. 7 July 1901, *Nelson Daily News.*

39. TNA, CO 526/3/24, Petition to Colonel Pilkington, n.d. In 1884, the Nile Voyageurs had difficulties with English officers and refused to extend their service. See Charles Lewis Shaw, "Random Reminiscences of a Nile Voyageur," 23 December 1893, *Saturday Night Magazine.*

40. TNA, CO 526/3/24, Captain Charles Beer to ADSO, E Division, 30 June 1903.

41. *Ibid.*

42. 11 April 1903, *Mail and Empire.*

43. Canada, House of Commons, *Debates,* 16 April 1903, 1027.

44. Miller, *Painting the Map Red,* 422.

45. *Ibid.,* 231–32, and A.E. Hilder, A.G. Morris, ed., *A Canadian Mounted Rifleman At War, 1899–1902: The Reminiscences of A.E. Hilder,* Second Series, No. 31 (Cape Town: Van Riebeeck Society, 2000), 31, 36–7. One veteran recalled that their captain, Maynard Rogers, called his company together after one of his men, Private Arthur Boylea, had been sentenced to 56 days of field imprisonment for stealing a chicken, a decision that attracted broad public criticism in Canada. He informed them that Boylea had not been punished for stealing a chicken, but for getting caught, "so watch yourself." See "Patriots, Scalawags and Saturday Night Soldiers," 11.

46. LAC, MG30–E242, W.D. Otter fonds, Otter to Molly, 2 June 1900.

47. LAC, MG29–E101, J.W. Jeffrey fonds, Diary entries for 12, 18, and 24 October 1900.

48. Miller, *Painting the Map Red,* 287.

49. Griesbach, *I Remember,* 314–15.

Part Two

❧

The First World War

6

Soldiers Behaving Badly: CEF Soldier "Rioting" in Canada During the First World War

P. WHITNEY LACKENBAUER

"There have been several instances of riots in which soldiers have taken part," Sir Wilfrid Laurier informed the House of Commons on 5 April 1916. "Everybody recognizes that the majority of these soldiers are young men, and we can forgive them a great deal; but they must be taught that the first duty of a soldier is to maintain discipline."

In response, Acting Minister of Militia and Defence A.E. Kemp, downplayed the seriousness of the "alleged riots" and Prime Minister Robert Borden stressed that individuals found culpable had been handed over to civil authorities for prosecution. "I think the military authorities should impress upon the soldier that his first duty is to obey the law," Laurier replied. "We know that these young men like to have a lark sometimes, and nobody will be severe on them for that; but they must be taught the necessity of discipline."[1] After all, obedience and discipline were critical soldierly traits. But the military had different priorities and refused to take collective responsibility for the destructive hooliganism perpetrated by its recruits. "The government is in no way responsible for acts of lawlessness committed by soldiers not on duty, whether individually or collectively," was the judge advocate-general's (JAG's) common refrain.[2] Although subjected to courts of inquiry and treated as soldiers therein, riotous soldiers were seen, in legal terms, as civilians in uniform.

Nineteen hundred and sixteen was a year of uncertainty. From Perth, New Brunswick, to Calgary, Alberta, ill-disciplined soldiers of the Canadian Expeditionary Force (CEF) took to the streets and battled with local authorities on "various patriotic pretexts," to borrow historian Desmond Morton's apt characterization.[3] Canadian soldiers used collective action to stand up to pernicious "enemy alien" or anti-military currents, perceived civilian encroachment on military jurisdiction, and sundry injustices that upset their rudimentary understanding of their soldierly mission and roles. Ethnic intolerance and patriotism were obvious motivations, but so too were alcohol, over-zealous camaraderie, and weak leadership at the non-commissioned officer (NCO) and officer levels. Although the domestic "riots" varied in severity, the sheer number of episodes and men involved revealed a serious problem. Most of the rioting soldiers were new recruits who had not yet embraced the strict discipline and hierarchical control demanded by military life. As citizen-soldiers-in-the-making, they were unable to disengage from their civilian referents and misapplied their unique role as the "social guardians" of society, as well as their primary group loyalties to their uniformed mates.

Drawing upon existing literature on this period, this chapter probes deeper to ponder the underlying causes of riotous military behaviour and how it reflects on military management.[4] First, the actual events need to be described in the context of the time. What did disaffected soldiers hope to achieve through their disobedience? What means did they adopt and who were their targets? What civil-military interactions took place? What steps, if any, were taken to dissuade the soldiers from unsanctioned and unlawful behaviour? Second, how did military authorities perceive the events and allocate responsibility? What action was taken to punish the battalions or soldiers involved in the riotous activity? Finally, how and why did the military evade responsibility for the riots? Testimony collected by courts of inquiry [5] provide insight into the soldiers' rationales for riotous activities, the official response from the government and military, as well as the social/structural distinctions between the other ranks (ORs), NCOs, officers, and civil authorities. Not only did the responses of the soldiers who appeared before the courts indicate specific patterns that explain the context in which the riots erupted, they also showed the shortcomings of the military system in punishing and deterring criminal activity.

The *Oxford Dictionary* defines a "riot" as a "tumult, disorder, disturbance of the peace by a crowd; loud revelry." It is an act of collective disobedience, often resulting in wanton destruction and violence. Rather than undertaking a definitional exercise to distinguish between so-called "riots" and other forms of military disobedience, I will limit my narrative and analysis to those cases identified by Edwin Pye in his unpublished sketch of domestic disturbances in which soldiers played a part. His 1946 report, while limited, distinguished between significant cases and "trivial" incidents that the press sometimes mislabelled as "riots." These unpublished notes helped frame the ensuing narrative overview that draws mainly upon the archival record.[6] Rather than lining up the cases in chronological format, they are grouped according to the dominant pretext used to justify the disorderly behaviour. Two broad categories suffice: (1) riots related to alleged "enemy alien" activities; and (2) riots related to alcohol. A few riots do not fit tidily into either category and are thus discussed separately.

BACKGROUND

When the Great War broke out in August 1914, Canada was ill prepared. Minister of Militia and Defence, Sir Sam Hughes, was a fanatical proponent of the "militia myth," holding the "citizen soldier" ideal above a professional, permanent force. In Hughes's vision, the regulars existed to train the militia; the real Canadian fighting spirit was in the broad populous who had rallied to the cause in 1812 and thwarted American manifest destiny. Citizen soldiers made better soldiers and better citizens, he believed, and military socialization could transform a boy (in the words of his contemporary Maurice Hutton) "from a hooligan into a self-contained, restrained, and self-respecting person." Mass mobilization would bolster "muscular masculinity," instill discipline, and benefit society as a whole. To achieve this end, Hughes refused to abide by pre-war mobilization plans and instead concocted his own. Newly formed numbered battalions were sent directly to a new campsite being constructed at Valcartier, Quebec, rather than concentrating near their place of mobilization and moving on to Petawawa, Ontario, as the 1911 mobilization plans recommended.[7] Hughes has been sharply criticized for the considerable confusion, even the chaos that surrounded mobilization in the summer and fall of 1914. Given the shortage of training space in various regions, however, there is no certainty that local mobilization would have proven more coherent.

Canada's early war was voluntary. To be "attested," enlistees agreed to serve with the CEF, swore their allegiance to the King and committed to "observe and obey all orders of His Majesty, His Heirs and Successor and all of the Generals and Officers set over me." A private soldier was then kitted out in khaki — cap, tunic, breeches, greatcoat, boots, and puttees — and was expected to wear his uniform at all times. But a new soldier still had to learn how to behave like a man befitting the dress. "His new comrades expected a man to drink, smoke, swear and gamble," Desmond Morton explained. NCOs, most of whom had little exposure to war, were responsible for forging the recruits into fighting men.[8] They had to inculcate a spirit of *esprit de corps*, as the 1914 British infantry training manual outlined:

> The objects in view in developing a soldierly spirit are to help the soldier bear fatigue, privation and danger cheerfully; to imbue him with a sense of honour; to give him confidence in his superiors and comrades; to increase his power of initiative, of self-confidence and of self-restraint; to train him to obey orders, or to act in the absence of orders for the advantage of his regiment under all conditions; to produce such a high degree of courage and disregard of self that in the stress of battle he will use his brains and his weapons coolly and to the best advantage; to impress upon him that, so long as he is physically capable of fighting, surrendering to the enemy is a disgraceful act; and finally to teach him how to act in combination with his comrades to defeat the enemy.[9]

By the end of 1915, it was apparent that any thoughts of a short war were merely delusions. It would be a long and costly road to victory, and more men would be needed. In September 1915, a small Canadian Corps was formed and the government's manpower commitment grew accordingly: from 150,000, to 250,000, to 500,000 men on 1 January 1916. Chief of the General Staff Willoughby Gwatkin had argued from the war's onset that centrally located depots were needed to gather and train unbrigaded recruits. Accordingly, Hughes reversed the government's policy in the fall of 1916. Prominent men in local communities were granted the rank of lieutenant-colonel and authorized to recruit full battalions from their local areas, assisted by citizen recruiting leagues and committees. Over the winter, recruits were billeted locally. Soldiers averaged eight months between enlistment and departure from Canada, and days of physical training, drill, and route marches became dry and onerous. This made the ranks increasingly restless. Canada had gone to war in August 1914 because Britain went to war. By late 1915, however, the conflict had become a national crusade: It was not only about defeating the Hun, but also about winning international recognition. Patriotic organizations sprung up to encourage enlistments, to collect donations for war-related charities, and to knit socks for the boys at the front. Social reformers saw an opportunity to leverage this context to encourage sweeping social change. If war productivity was the highest priority, then it only made sense to prohibit the "demon drink."[10] The war became a crusade that cut to the core of what Canadian society did — and hoped to — represent.

As the dream of a short war died on the Western Front, so too did tolerance for ethnic minorities at home. "The Great War ... marked an end to the age of innocence for Canada's Germans," historian Ken McLaughlin explained. "From being a much favoured people within the nation, overnight they were vilified as the enemy. This was a war not just against Germany, but against 'Germanness,' and it was no longer possible to be both a German and a Canadian."[11] The loyalty of German, Austro-Hungarian, and Ukranian peoples came under serious suspicion and anti-"enemy alien" hysteria swept through Anglo-Canadian society. Propaganda circulated macabre tales of atrocities committed by the barbarous "Huns:" Unleashing poison gas against the Canadians at the Second Battle of Ypres; torpedoing civilian vessels; murdering babies; raping women; and crucifying soldiers. Canadians became convinced that they were no longer participating in the war out of obligation to Britain: They were defending civilization itself.[12] In mid-January 1916, Senator James A. Lougheed spoke of Germany's lust for territorial conquest, thereby feeding the paranoia:

> For years Germany has been conscious of the advantages
> Canada would afford for German expansion. Germany,

199

through its system of espionage, has a more thorough knowledge of Canada in the pigeon-holes of its foreign office than would be found in the departments of our own Government.... The manifest duty of Canada at the moment is to help our Allies to prosecute this war to the end. There is no alternative except we become passive and are prepared to accept the subjugation by Germany of our country and our race. The fight must be made with the same intensity and seriousness as if the enemy were [*sic*] thundering for admission at our gates.[13]

Conspiracy-minded Canadians blamed the burning of the Parliament Buildings in February 1916 on Germans, compounding existing anxiety.

ANTI-"ENEMY ALIEN" SENTIMENTS

The first group of riots are fraught with this public spirit of ethnic intolerance. Anti-immigrant discrimination "became the rule rather than the exception," served as a pretext for enlistment, and filled aspiring soldiers with a sense of duty and purpose.[14] In wartime, Paul Jackson recently explained, "many men who had been jobless, transient and unwanted were catapulted into the role of saviours of the nation."[15] Even before they crossed the Atlantic, some saw opportunities to root out enemy enclaves at home. "I think I should be excused from putting my weight on the side of anything unBritish," Sergeant-Major Granville P. Blood of the 118th Battalion argued in self-defence after leading a riot in Berlin, Ontario. "I want you to judge me as having been brought up since the war broke out to destroy everything that is German. I have been trained to destroy everything of military advantage to the enemy."[16] This bastardized interpretation of the soldiers' responsibilities at home came to impact several properties owned by alleged "enemy aliens" in Canada.

Calgary, Alberta

Western Canada proved to be the CEF's best recruiting ground in the early years of the war. During the last three months of 1915 alone, 23 new battalions raised 21,897 men. Winter conditions dashed enlistees' expectations of excitement and serious training; indoor physical drills and disturbing news from overseas heightened feelings of restlessness. In Calgary, home to the largest urban German population in Alberta, speakers like Senator James Lougheed inflamed passions among the recruits stationed in the city. Accordingly, some decided to take matters into their own hands. The local White Lunch restaurant had purportedly fired a British veteran and had replaced him with an enemy alien. The rumour quickly circulated around the military camp. Consequently, on the evening of 10 February 1916, several hundred soldiers marched through downtown Calgary and destroyed the White Lunch restaurant, while an excited crowd of more than a thousand watched. A "second division" of soldiers converged simultaneously on another White Lunch location and destroyed the restaurant in one rush. Within a few minutes, the *Albertan* observed, the place "looked as though it were situated 'somewhere in Ypres,' and that a howitzer shell had exploded." The district commander, Brigadier-General E.A. Cruikshank, proceeded to the scene and ordered the soldiers to return to their quarters. They quickly complied. By midnight all was quiet again, but the gaping fronts of the wrecked buildings and the littered debris of smashed furniture and fittings on the street bore witness to the night's destructive events.[17]

Cruikshank addressed all the units under his command at their various quarters the following afternoon and pointed out the penalties that such outrages warranted. The officers of the battalions optimistically estimated that no further riots would follow, but they were wrong. That evening, a group of 500 soldiers and civilians proceeded to the Riverside Hotel on another anti-German pretext, absorbing soldiers and civilians as it moved along. Upon their arrival, the mob quickly overwhelmed the few police and military officers on the ground and "for two hours a veritable reign of terror prevailed." Little was left of the hotel when the mob was finished. The piquets (also spelled *pickets*) ordered by Cruikshank that afternoon failed to arrive in time to arrest the destruction. The mob, satisfied that its work was done at the hotel, confidently strode back over the bridge and dispersed uptown.

In the wake of the riots, military authorities imposed stringent restrictions on the soldiers, and the local battalions were sent on long marches to walk off "a whole lot of effervescent animal spirits." City Council, succumbing to the rioters' demands, immediately dismissed all civic employees of alien nationality. Resolutions such as this, coupled with media and public sentiment that condemned the unruly activities, but upheld the motivations of the rioters, meant that the new recruits had indeed achieved a measure of success.

Cruikshank did not believe that the military was responsible: He was "very strongly of the opinion that these disturbances were largely due to inflammatory letters and articles which appeared in certain newspapers, and the injudicious remarks made by civilians."[18] As a result, the adjutant-general did not feel that the military authorities had to take any further action, but local reporters and police officers remained unconvinced. Calgary Police Chief Alfred Cuddy criticized local military officials: Their inaction in preventing disorder made them culpable for the damage. The subsequent courts of inquiry uncovered the roles of camaraderie and liquor in inspiring participation and relieving inhibitions. The "mob" mentality was provoked by anti-alien sentiments, but the individuals often participated because of the more sanguine inducements of comradeship and curiosity. In a show of group solidarity, the witnesses withheld individual names (both of fellow soldiers involved in the riots and civilian

A 1916 riot at the Riverside Hotel in Calgary resulted in extensive damage. (W.J. Oliver, Glenbow Museum NA-2365-16)

As this photograph shows, the 1916 riot in Calgary's Riverside Hotel caused considerable destruction. (Glenbow Museum NA-3965-11)

"friends" who procured liquor) to preserve anonymity. The soldiers stuck together and it appeared that they could "stonewall" the authorities and get away with just about anything. Furthermore, the city's subsequent decision to fire all civic employees of "enemy alien" descent and to offer their jobs to returned soldiers seemed to validate the mob's actions. The recalcitrant soldiers had indeed succeeded in affecting the desired change.[19]

"The strong public sentiment in Calgary against the employment and employers of alien enemies and the presence in the city of a considerable number of troops fresh from civil life and fully sharing the prejudices of the community and as yet only partially accustomed to military discipline, furnished the underlying conditions which made possible what followed." These apt observations, made by a civilian lawyer lobbying for compensation after the war, revealed prescient insight into the February 1916 disturbances.[20] For new citizen-soldiers still possessing the biases and concerns of civilian society and only beginning their transition into a new soldierly role, boredom, curiosity, inactivity, and indiscipline in the Calgary camp contributed to a volatile environment.

In a closed society, like a military camp, anti-ethnic rumours easily became truths and generated outrage. Fledgling soldiers, full of anticipation and anxious to take it to the Huns, banded together in a common "mob mentality." Alcohol, the urging of civilian onlookers and the anonymity of large crowds whipped the riotous mob into a fevered pitch. The failure of military authorities to take meaningful action or to read the riot act to troops hardly convinced the restless ranks to stand down. The local commander did not establish sizable and timely piquets after the first episode and the Riverside Hotel suffered as a result. It was a sorry state of affairs.

Berlin (Kitchener), Ontario

The story of the riotous 118th Battalion in Berlin, Ontario, has assumed mythical proportions as the quintessential example of anti-German intolerance during the war. Local historian Patricia McKegney characterized the 118th as little more than a "vengeful mob" often inspired to "drunken rampages;" playwright William Chadwick likened the battalion to an "outlaw gang."[21] Historian Nikolas Gardner has more carefully situated these events in the context of the broader Canadian war effort. Although the confluence of ethnic intolerance and ill discipline spelled disaster, Gardner argues that the real culprit for the strife was "the often ill-advised and inconsistent decisions and regulations of the Department of Militia and Defence,"[22] a verdict that stands in sharp contrast to the conclusions of the 1916 court of inquiry.

Berlin was the major "German" city in Canada when war broke out and consequently became a focal point for conflict. Before men of the first contingent left for overseas in 1914, they had removed a bust of Kaiser Wilhelm I from its pedestal in Victoria Park and threw it into the lake — it was recovered and deposited at the Concordia Club (belonging to a German musical association) for storage. The 118th, assembled in Waterloo County during 1915, was plagued with undisciplined, raw recruits who realized that they would never get to go overseas unless they filled their ranks. Frustrated by sluggish local responses, the soldiers embarked on self-appointed — and increasingly bellicose — missions to encourage area enlistments in early 1916. "The men in uniform were out in force and adopted the strong-arm system of canvassing," the Berlin *News Record* reported on 24 January, "hustling in the civilians by force if they did not accompany the soldiers willingly." Battalion officers sent mixed messages: Lieutenant-Colonel W.M.O. Lochead assured his men that "horseplay" would not be tolerated, while Captain R.E. McNeel derided the selfish, "pampered pets" who had not enlisted "while their brother Canadians (real men) are enduring discomfort, bleeding and even dying." After various fights between local civilians and men in uniform, Lochead implemented vague "Street Recruiting Regulations," but local voices continued to criticize the soldiers for their over-zealous tactics.[23] Compounded by anti-German hysteria and local controversy over Berlin's name, members of the battalion eventually took direct action to demonstrate their patriotism.

At about 2000 hours on 15 February 1916, soldiers from the machine gun section (recently transferred from Toronto and hardly attuned to Berlin's German culture) marched to the Concordia Hall, removed the bust of the Kaiser, and marched it back to their barracks. It was fittingly detained in the detention room. Lieutenant-Colonel Lochead then spoke to about 30 ORs and NCOs on the parade grounds and told them "not to do anything in any way destructive, and to be soldiers, and we promised him we would." They assured him that they were going out to have a recruiting parade. An hour later, about 50 soldiers, parading down the main street and singing patriotic songs, came across men from the earlier group and learned that the hall was decorated with German flags, bunting and pictures. They decided to take matters into their own hands and marched to the Concordia. Aided and abetted by several dozen civilians, soldiers entered the hall and found a picture of King George V draped with German flags. There was "no dust on the glasses" and ample alcohol on site, evidence that the Hall had been used as a club despite the Concordia Singing Society's public assurances, following the sinking of the *Lusitania,* that it would remain closed until the end of the war. As a consequence, the enraged mob proceeded to ransack and burn the contents of the building (including a piano) in a huge bonfire while the helpless police watched.

The provost acknowledged that they could not have intervened or "they would have been killed." Indeed, "no civilian, police officer or municipal or other official interfered or attempted to interfere at any time" and no one notified battalion headquarters until the disturbance was nearly over. When the officer commanding and other officers — who had been out skating — finally received an NCO's report, they went to the scene and ordered all the soldiers back to barracks. Most complied immediately.[24]

The 118th's destructive activities elicited national attention. "We never dreamed that the lads would take the law into their own hands in the manner they did," Lieutenant-Colonel Lochead told reporters. He convened a court of inquiry that concluded that the attack was not premeditated and that the primary causes were threefold:

> 1. The spirit of pro-Germanism rampant in certain circles of this city and the general belief that this spirit is founded largely in the Concordia Society which occupies the said Hall.

> 2. The general knowledge that the bust of Kaiser Wilhelm I was contained in said Hall.

> 3. The desperation of the men at the slowness of recruiting, which they attributed to an unchecked anti-British sentiment, well knowing that the membership of said Society includes a great number of young men.[25]

None of these causes seemed particularly disconcerting; in fact, the soldiers seemed patriotic through and through. "We wear the King's uniform and we intend to stand by the King all the way," the machine gun section explained during their collective appearance before the inquiry.[26] Consequently, the military court placed the blame on the civilians and municipal authorities who had allowed intolerable conditions to prevail in the region "that loyal British citizens found impossible to tolerate…." In the court's final verdict, "the Concordia Club, supposed to be a singing organization, was in reality a strong German club with a large membership of young men and everything we found in connection with the club went to such that it was an organization to foster and maintain a strong German spirit and love for the fatherland."[27]

The soldiers believed that they had done their duty. "If we have got to fight them in Berlin," Private Williamson heard Sergeant-Major Blood tell the mob, "we might as well fight them here and in Germany too."[28] The first stage of the battle had been won, without any casualties to the 118th, because the court could not fix individual responsibility for the destruction on anyone in particular. The matter was duly laid to rest.

Less than three weeks later, members of the battalion were at it again. First they smashed the windows of A. Hanni's tailor shop because, according to the local newspaper, "the name didn't sound British enough to suit them." Then they visited various German-owned businesses and removed pictures of a "German nature," smashing one over a restaurant patron's head when he objected. Finally, they homed in on C.R. Tappert, an American citizen and a controversial Lutheran pastor living in Berlin.

Earlier in the war, Tappert had been arrested for seditious utterances when he publicly disputed atrocity stories circulated by the press, but the charges were dropped. Members of the 118th harboured no love for him: Tappert's denunciations of the war went against all that they represented; he allegedly declared his continued loyalty to Germany; and his son had threatened a sergeant's boy. As early as February, Captain S.N. Dancey had told a meeting of officers and NCOs that "Tappert ought to be tarred and feathered." When Tappert gave *Toronto Star* interviews explaining the local German community's perspective, threats poured in. The pastor told his congregation and the mayor that he would leave the city by 1 March. He did not.

On 5 March, about 50 soldiers confronted him at his Alma Street home, paraded him around the town and then dragged him to the barracks. By the time officers of the 118th rescued him, he had lost a tooth and gained a black eye. An annoyed Lochead had "no apologies for Tappert's conduct but I regret the outbreak of the men and the effect it must have upon discipline." He finally took decisive steps to prevent further disobedience and posted local piquets to patrol the streets.[29]

A few days later, Lochead explained to the adjutant-general in Ottawa that Tappert had been "most indiscreet in his language and attitude towards soldiers" and that if he had been polite he would not have been assaulted. Lochead had "sternly warned" his battalion on "different occasions not to approach Tappert or his house." While Lochead was absent, however, they had disobeyed his orders and he promised to help the civil authorities in every possible way "to see that proper punishment is awarded."[30]

His readiness to turn responsibility over to civilian authorities conformed to general practices at the time. "Soldiers in uniform lose none of their rights or responsibilities as citizens, and therefore are entitled to all privileges of the law, but are also subject to its penalties," Minister Hughes explained in Parliament. He also stressed that the government had treated "alien enemies … in a most tolerant and lenient manner; but utterances and conduct that even indirectly encouraged sedition, treason or disloyalty, will not be tolerated," an implicit confirmation that the disobedient soldiers had justifiable cause.[31]

The two ringleaders identified by the court of inquiry in Berlin (Sergeant-Major Blood and Private E. Schaefer) were tried by civilian authorities and convicted of assault. A sympathetic judge gave them a severe reprimand and a stern lecture "that no doubt they and all others will remember." The men were allowed to go on suspended sentence and both promised that they would not "misconduct themselves" again. Lochead immediately convened a joint dinner for officers and ranks and gave a talk on discipline "which was attentively listened to and which will no doubt be productive of good results."[32] A relative calm prevailed for the next two months, indicating that the local commander had finally established some control over his men.[33]

Frustrated members of the under-strength 118th were still itchy to travel overseas, but struggled to reach adequate numbers. Emotions ran high. To thunderous applause, Sergeant-Major Blood pledged on 2 May that any pro-German people or institution would be "wiped out" and "smashed." Following a recruiting rally held in Waterloo's market square three days later, 10 soldiers with the 118th removed a bronze bust of the German Emperor Wilhelm I from the Acadian Club in Waterloo. Later that evening, soldiers seemed to make good on Blood's promise. Between 30 and 40 soldiers from the battalion returned in a "sharp night raid" and demolished the club's furnishings. It was essentially a repeat of the Concordia episode. This time, the logic seemed less certain: the Acadian Club was hardly a pro-German hotbed, as 28 of its members had already enlisted. "The suddenness and swiftness with which the operation was carried out made it impossible to find the guilty persons," historian E. Pye later concluded, based on the subsequent court of inquiry's inability to incriminate any individuals. The battalion was clearly responsible and the club asked for $529.75 in damages, but no payment was made, lest "further ill-feeling might be engendered."[34]

Once more, the soldiers achieved their objectives outside of the authorized structures of command and control. Soon thereafter, Berlin's name was changed to Kitchener, a symbolic move that reaffirmed imperial loyalties and superseded the city's German heritage. The soldiers had won their local battles and now readied to fight the Hun in Europe. On 20 May, thousands of local citizens turned out to send the soldiers off to Camp Borden, thus ending their tumultuous sojourn in Waterloo County.

Based on a sober appraisal of the evidence, Gardner concludes that the 118th had faced particularly acute recruiting and discipline problems by trying to raise a full battalion in a predominantly German district. Local apathy and resistance ensured that officers' "appeals to duty and pro-British patriotism provoked only a limited response:"

> As recruiting efforts floundered, the soldiers realized that their failure would cast aspersions on the loyalty of the district, as well as delay their departure overseas. The frustration of the men thus increased. Seeking to suppress the "pro-Germanism" which apparently hindered their efforts, the soldiers, often led by the Toronto-bred machine-gun section, provoked numerous confrontations with local citizens.[35]

When ideas of duty, patriotism, and loyalty failed to generate sufficient local enthusiasm, which was construed as evidence of disloyalty, those who had already enlisted took direct action to show their commitment to the war effort. "From what I can gather the citizens as well as soldiers did what they considered to be their duty in cleaning up some of the German element of the city," Sergeant Bowden had told the court of inquiry in Berlin. "From what civilians said it was a job that should have been undertaken by the Government."[36]

Windsor, Nova Scotia

Riotous actions of the 239th Railway Construction Battalion in Windsor, Nova Scotia, were more organized and truncated than the disturbances in either Berlin or Calgary. The trouble began with civilian remarks against the proprietor of the Windsor Garage Company. Canadian-born E.C. Muller's grandfather had immigrated to Canada with his family when his father was four. "There is no clear evidence that there is any reason for the ill-feeling against Mr. Muller except that he is of German descent," the district commander, Major-General T. Benson, noted. The mayor testified, however, that when the Red Cross had canvassed for funds in Windsor, Muller had refused to donate and had allegedly sneered at the representatives. This caused "a great deal of adverse comments by the citizens of the town," and likely stirred up the animosity of the soldiers as well. In the barracks and pool halls, the soldiers formulated a plan to raid his garage in late fall. On the evening of 14 November 1916, upwards of 150 men from the 239th marched in groups of four down to his garage, broke in the doors and systematically destroyed his tools and records. They seriously damaged three automobiles and ran them out of the building, overturning one on the street and sending another into the Avon River. After 10 minutes, the soldiers had destroyed all the stock in the garage, which was by this point on fire. Most of the soldiers then promptly formed up on the street and marched for several blocks before dispersing into groups and mixing with other people, making it impossible for the orderly corporal, who went to investigate, to determine who was involved.[37]

The court of inquiry left no doubt that battalion members were responsible and that they had foreknowledge of the attack. Given that "the damage was done very quickly and in a fairly orderly manner and was not accompanied by any rioting either before or after the occurrence and have been quite orderly since," the convening officers determined that "the outbreak was largely patriotic, and there were no signs of mutinous conduct." It was a strange conclusion, particularly given the comment that there was no evidence substantiating popular ill will towards Muller. "As it is impossible to fire the guilt on the right men and since practically all the men had previous knowledge and were in sympathy with those who participated," the court recommended that the owner should be compensated by deducting pay from all the officers, NCOs, and men of the unit. Local military officials made promises to Muller and his lawyer that he would be duly compensated.[38]

The adjutant-general did not concur. "The Court of Enquiry does not seem to have investigated this case as thoroughly as it might," he observed. "In fact no attempt seems to have been made to follow up the possible sources of evidence." The district commander disagreed and explained that the court had proven that "the damage was done entirely by men of the 239th Battalion." It would take weeks to obtain "direct evidence against the 150 men who did the work" and he felt it "would be better to place the responsibility on the Battalion and leave the further investigation and disciplinary action in the hands of the Officer Commanding." The adjutant-general reiterated his opposition, this time in policy terms:

> It has always been the policy of this Department not to recognize any liability for damage done by soldiers in a community. If they damage property they are in the same position as any *other civilian* [italics added] who does likewise, and it is for the injured parties to take action in the usual course. I would have suggested, however, that the question of compensation should have been submitted to the Battalion to settle for the sake of their own reputation, but as this Battalion has now been ordered overseas it is probably too late for that method.

He found it hard to believe that "a riot of such an extensive scale could take place without its [*sic*] being possible to obtain the name of one single individual responsible therefor [*sic*]." Regardless, the bureaucracy had defeated Muller and his lawyer. They had not undertaken civil action only because the local military authorities had assured them that they would receive payment for damages. Once they learned that this was not forthcoming, "it was then too late" since the battalion, and the culprits, were already overseas and beyond the reach of civil law.[39]

Regina, Saskatchewan

The simmering anti-"enemy" frustrations in Regina were similar to Calgary, Berlin and Windsor, but the outcome of the disturbance that broke out in its "foreign quarter" was unique. In the weeks before the attack, Lieutenant-Colonel J.H. Hearn, the officer commanding the 214th Battalion explained that his men had "been more or less insulted and aggravated by the Austrian and German element in several places of amusement and bad feeling exsisted [*sic*] between these people and the soldiers." Private George Tomsha attended a dance at the Roumanian Hall and encountered a group of Austrians. They exchanged harsh words and engaged in fisticuffs and Tomsha told an exaggerated version of the affair to his friends in uniform. Rumours grew among the soldiers stationed in the city. The *Regina Leader* published a misleading story that a member of the 214th who had been abused at a dance was in the hospital and that there had been no redress. Another report circulated that a man had been killed at the hall because a uniform had been found in the city cemetery, but no one really knew whether the man was dead or a deserter. It was perhaps irrelevant, as local soldiers believed that they had sufficient pretext to raid the hall on 22 November.[40]

The manager of the poolroom owned by Cornelius Rink (a Boer who had fought against the British Empire in South Africa) insulted several soldiers when they went in to ask for directions to the Roumanian Hall. The men in khaki, now numbering between 300 and 400, held a brief meeting out front and decided to "clean the place up." Projectiles went through the windows, billiard tables were thrown over, and cues were smashed and thrown. Local officers took action as soon as they learned of developments and four from the 214th drove to the scene. "On arrival there they found from forty to sixty men in possession of the place and in the act of demolishing the furniture, windows, etc." The men told the officers that the owner, who they claimed was a German, had insulted them and they "intended to wreck the place in consequence." The officers commanded them to stop and disperse, which they did. Lieutenant-Colonel Hearn later claimed, "the men were at no time beyond the officers, but obeyed their request promptly."[41] The swath of destruction in their wake suggested otherwise.

The district commander, Major N.S. Edgar, established a court of inquiry to investigate. Proceedings were delayed because the battalions were quarantined for diphtheria, and in the end, yielded little substantive information. The court was "unable to localize any blame for the disturbance and resulting damages to any particular unit" and simply concluded that as men from the 214th and 217th Battalions and the 77th Battery had been present, they would have to be held collectively accountable. "It is regretted that a riot of such an extensive nature could take place without its [*sic*] being possible to obtain the name of one single individual responsible therefore," Major-General W.E.S. Hodgins, the acting adjutant-general, noted once more in Ottawa. "The evidence given before the Court of Inquiry gives rise to the impression that no very real attempt was made to obtain the names of any persons responsible." Nonetheless, he reiterated that the Department would assume no liability for damages and suggested "that the question of compensation should be submitted to the Battalions implicated to settle for the sake of their own reputation." In this case, they agreed to do so. Cornelius Rink received $140.20 in damages and quit his claim accordingly.[42]

LIQUOR

If anti-"enemy alien" sentiment served as an obvious catalyst for disobedience, alcohol served a two-fold role in the soldier riots of 1916. First, alcohol suppressed inhibitions and encouraged soldiers to get involved in illicit behaviour. Second, the wartime crusade against alcohol — in the form of prohibition and temperance — was cast in patriotic terms and enjoyed a sudden surge in support. By the end of 1916, every provincial government except Quebec had created regulatory regimes to abolish the sale of liquor. This new "dry" culture clashed with a military culture that had always included heavy drinking. Indeed, historian Tim Cook has shown how "demon rum" was an important source of morale and courage and played a crucial social function during the Great War. [43] When soldiers broke drinking laws and were imprisoned, their comrades felt a compulsion to "rescue" them from the civilian authorities. The "all for one, one for all" spirit inculcated during basic training, used to recondition citizens into cohesive military units, was twisted to include not letting down your mates when they were "unfairly" subjected to civilian rules. Several major domestic disturbances thus arose from alcohol infractions.[44]

Saint John, New Brunswick

The send off of a local unit was cause for celebration in 1916 and local spirits — patriotic and alcoholic — flowed freely. On 31 March, the 4th Canadian Siege Battery was departing Saint John, New Brunswick, for overseas and thousands of civilians gathered at the train station to give the men a warm send-off. A few hundred members of the 69th, 115th, and 140th Battalions joined in to show the colours. When these units were dismissed from the parade, the soldiers mingled with civilians crowded onto King and Charlotte Streets and remained there through the evening. The excited throng numbered between 2,000 and 3,000 people. Several soldiers, who had just been paid and thus had ample funds to buy liquor with, began to get out of hand. Small fights broke out between uniformed men and civilians rushed to watch the fighting that seemed to divide along regimental lines. The 69th, in particular, seemed ready to jump in and help the men "on their own side." Zealous citizens were accused of fanning the emotional flames, calling the 115th "farmers" and the 69th "frogs:" An obvious reference to the sizable French-Canadian representation in the latter battalion. The city police tried to keep the crowds moving and broke up more than a dozen fights, but the sheer volume of people made their task particularly daunting.[45]

Apparently, the police had stopped the public brawling until the piquet from the 69th arrived on the scene. When a Military Policeman (MP) from the 140th tried to move along 10 intoxicated members from the 69th, the "ringleader" thought it would be fun to knock off his hat and cajole him. The MP responded with his fist and other members of the 69th came to their comrade's assistance. Civil Police Sergeant Joseph Scott recounted that the fighting resumed because the MPs from the 69th arrived and provoked even more trouble. "The Sergeant in charge of the Military Police lacked judgment," Scott noted. "He seemed to be excited and got fighting with the military police of the other battalions." Police Inspector W.C. Wickham added that this NCO acted as if he was intoxicated and clearly did not have control over his men. Feelings ran high as a result. Men from the other battalions approached Wickham and told him, "If these Frenchman are looking for trouble we will give them all they want." He wisely ordered them back and they complied. "The men in general behaved themselves very well," the Inspector concluded, "and only a few roughnecks among the soldiers gave me trouble." He ordered his police officers to focus on civilians and let the MPs "handle their own men." Eventually, officers with the various local battalions ordered the men in uniform still loitering to return to barracks. Most cleared the streets in short order, thus ending the night's festivities.[46]

In the end, there were "many black eyes and bloody noses," but no property had been damaged. Local commanders concluded that the disturbance did not leave any bad blood between battalions or with the local citizenry and a court of inquiry determined that the disturbance was "not in any way prearranged or premeditated but was simply due to the fact that a few soldiers became more or less intoxicated and started to fight amongst themselves." The concentration of civilians and soldiers on the street hindered any civil and military police efforts to quell the boisterous crowd, the officers concluded, and civilians had to shoulder much of the blame. "The evidence shows that a number of Civilians at last gathered and were egging the soldiers on to fight by telling the men of one Battn. that the men of another Battn. were out to do them up." These untruths fed a scenario that produced "very little fighting but a good deal of noise." The real culprit, the court suggested, was the "liquor of a vile quality illicitly sold to [the intoxicated soldiers] by 'Boot-leggers.'"[47] Civilians, it seemed, were relentless in trying to provoke soldier unrest through inflammatory rhetoric and the bottle.

Winnipeg, Manitoba

On 1–2 April 1916, soldiers and civilians clashed with police on the streets of Manitoba's capital. The ostensible cause was an arrest by civilian police officers of an intoxicated soldier lying outside the Imperial Hotel. A second soldier, who had been helping the drunken man, began to berate the police. "Don't let those cock sucking bastards take him," he called to the crowd of soldiers who had quickly gathered around. When the police tried to arrest the second soldier, the mob "rescued" him from their custody.

The crowd soon swelled to several hundred and became increasingly agitated. Several more soldiers were arrested. "A running fight kept up between the police and the mob," Lieutenant-Colonel H.N. Ruttan, the district officer commanding (DOC) at Winnipeg explained, smashing streetcar windows, throwing ice, and threatening to beat up the police. The soldiers followed the police up Alexander Street shouting, "We will get them out." The crowd, now "surging backward and forward," approached the police station. The police drew a cordon across the street but were unable to disperse people through peaceful urgings. They took out their batons and "without a moment's notice or warning" charged, causing several injuries.

The situation quickly spun out of control. In subsequent actions, the police mistakenly charged the provost-marshal's piquet sent to help restore order. Members of the crowd went to a woodpile and armed themselves with cordwood sticks to meet the police on a more level playing field. Finally, the 100th Winnipeg Grenadiers arrived on the scene and cleared the crowd before more serious violence transpired.[48]

The following morning, a crowd of soldiers (allegedly members of the 108th who had already imbibed whisky) assembled in front of the police station and demanded the release of the "soldier-prisoners." When their calls were refused, they bombarded it with bricks and smashed the windows. The police took immediate action. Forty policemen wielding batons fanned out in two lines and charged to break the crowd. One civilian described the scene as follows:

> All at once the garage doors opened and out came the police who began hitting right and left. They came very quickly and cleared the street following the people our way…. They struck one soldier who went down on his hands and knees and one of the policemen got his baton up and struck him…. I saw them hit a chinaman [*sic*], but they were hitting soldiers right and left giving them no chance in the world…. I never saw such a brain storm of hysteria in my life as those police were in.

The DOC ordered about 1,000 soldiers to fix bayonets and restore control over the central section of the city. Thousands of people continued to line the streets into the evening, but the trouble had ceased by mid-afternoon. Piquets from the 90th, 144th, and 179th Battalions, as well as from the Lord Strathcona's Horse, effectively restored the peace. There would not be a recurrence: Off-duty men were confined to barracks, all bar rooms were placed out of bounds and the DOC promptly convened a court of inquiry.[49]

The court revealed a myriad of causes in addition to the superficial pretext provided by the initial arrest of a drunken solider. The officers concluded that there was "considerable drunkenness" among the troops, despite military testimony to the contrary. It was payday for the troops and the soldier population had swelled that weekend thanks to 500 men from the 108th Battalion who had come into town from Selkirk where all the bars were closed.

Testimony suggested that the first and foremost cause of the deep-seated animosity were rumours of police ill-treatment of and brutality towards the soldiers. Military officers blamed the police for charging the soldiers without provocation — it was "just a curious crowd." Garrison police testified that the civilian police had used their batons in an indiscriminate, "unnecessary and violent manner." Indeed, several claimed that the police "lost their heads entirely" and that their overzealous charges added "fuel to the fire." A senior city police officer suggested that there was confusion about lines of authority: Soldiers did not all think that they were subject to civil law and thus felt persecuted by the civic police. The court concurred that part of the catalyst was "ignorance on part of soldiers and civilians as to the powers of the civic police and garrison police and consequent resentment against the Civic police arresting soldiers." Nevertheless, it found no conflict between the roles of the civilian authorities and Garrison Duty Police in making arrests. Finally, it typically blamed civilians for adding to the difficulties by refusing to disperse, but applauded the battalions for providing piquets that "materially assisted in restoring order."[50]

Calgary, Alberta[51]

Liquor laws in Alberta became much less forgiving when the provincial Temperance Act came into force on Dominion Day, 1916. Soldiers stationed in Calgary soon perceived themselves to be an easy and unfair target. At 1100 hours on 11 October, the Police Magistrate of Calgary convicted five men of the 211th Battalion[52] for offences under the Liquor Act. Their punishment was the minimum allowed (a $50 fine or 30 days in jail), but the fines exceeded the soldiers' meagre wages and the city police handed the prisoners over to the Royal North-West Mounted Police (RNWMP) to serve their prison terms. At about 1930 that evening, more than 200 soldiers descended upon City Police Headquarters. They shouted and booed and sung and cheered, interspersing their clamour with threats and demands that the five men sentenced that morning be released. Was this any way to treat men in uniform? The mob broke some windows before learning that the men they sought were at the RNWMP Barracks.[53]

Falling into "rough formation with bugles blowing," 300 members of the 211th, 218th, and 233rd Battalions marched towards their new destination. About 200 civilians, gathered in front of the barracks, joined the mob. Several NCOs demanded the prisoners' release, amid shouts of "We want justice" and "Our comrades are inside." The local RNWMP inspector promised to contact a local judge, but the soldiers charged the east door, forced an entrance and began to smash police equipment and windows. The best efforts of officers with the 211th, as well as the few police constables on hand, failed to quiet the men. Soldiers flooded into the building and continued to destroy its contents, but they were unable to find the main entrance to the guardroom. In a concurrent attack through the prisoners' yard, Private Julio Pelegrino of the 211th made his way up a fire escape towards the barred guardroom window. He found four RNWMP men watching over the prisoners. When the police warned that they would shoot, the soldiers retorted, "we can shoot too and we would sooner die here than in the trenches." One of the constables duly shot Pelegrino in the shoulder. The main crowd carried the casualty out into the street and no one attempted any further offensives, but an unfortunate constable (who happened to return to the barracks at that time) elicited the mob's wrath. "He shot him, get a club and kill him," someone mistakenly proclaimed. Soldiers yelled "mob him; mob him." They chased and tripped him to the ground, "piled on top," and pounded him with sticks. A cry of "We've got him; we've got rope; lynch him," thankfully went unanswered and the inspector pulled him into a car.[54] Both casualties recovered in hospital.

Brigadier E.A. Cruikshank eventually arrived and assured the mob "that in the event the men who were incarcerated had any just grievance or had been unfairly treated, [he] would make every effort to see that justice was done to them." He persuaded the soldiers to withdraw, but

the concourse of civilians standing around the barracks made the task
of dispersing the soldiers much more difficult. Lieutenant-Colonel May
stated that civilians "failed to see the point that it would help us if they
would move off and go home and the majority just stood and leered at
us."[55] By 2230 hours, the mob had dispersed, a strong military piquet
had arrived from Sarcee Camp and the prisoners were shipped out of
Calgary as soon as possible.

Political and military officials worried about aftershocks. The prime
minister himself was sufficiently concerned to ask the minister of militia
and defence for an official inquiry:

> As this is the second serious disturbance which has taken
> place in Calgary and as this incident seems graver than
> anything that has yet occurred insomuch as it was a direct
> attack upon those responsible for the maintenance of law
> and order I must ask that a thorough and rigid inquiry ...
> be made into the affair and that any who may be found
> guilty shall receive adequate punishment. Any other
> course would certainly tend to bring about a repetition of
> such disturbances which must be sternly suppressed.

The subsequent court of inquiry lasted seven days. The police convinced the officers that the soldiers had had no grounds for complaint
because the cases against them were morally and legally sound. As a result
of the investigation, 22 men were handed over to the civil authorities for
prosecution. Five men were found not guilty, in two cases the charges were
withdrawn and two prisoners successfully escaped from the east guardroom at Sarcee Camp. The remainder were found guilty and fined.[56]

Who was to blame? Characteristically, the "foreigner" became a target
of official criticism. The RNWMP found it "most humiliating ... that the
ringleaders were all foreigners" with "a big Russian, or German, who could
hardly speak English, leading the attack." Others confirmed that the men
"that were doing all the bad damage were foreigners who spoke broken
English." Appeals to public nativist sentiments deflected responsibility
away from the military, but RNWMP officials were directly critical. Given
the number of soldiers at Calgary and their past history, military officers

should have had a piquet patrolling the downtown every evening. The local RNWMP commander lamented that "there is not a strong arm at the helm in charge of the men at Sarcee Camp as, had there been, all this trouble with the soldiers would certainly have never occurred."[57]

MISCELLANEOUS

London, Ontario

The catalyst of a "slight disturbance of the public peace" in London, Ontario, on 11 March 1916, stemmed from a different pretext. At about 1500 hours, Peter Smerlies, the owner of the National Poolroom, questioned four uniformed soldiers about their ages: a municipal by-law barred minors from such establishments. The soldiers had used the poolroom on previous occasions and had never been asked their ages, but that day their inexperience at billiards (they took longer than more seasoned players to finish their games) caused a problem because the tables were in strong demand. When the proprietor asked them to leave, they assumed that this had little to do with regulations and took it personally. About 50 soldiers showed their solidarity by dropping their cues, falling in, and leaving the pool hall collectively. The story soon mutated to a conspiracy against all men in khaki. Shortly afterwards, the soldiers posted signs on the windows along Dundas Street (courtesy of a local printer who "thought he was doing the boys a favour") proclaiming "Soldiers Barred from the National Poolroom." The building also included a bowling alley, barber's shop, bathhouse, and cigar store, all of which were guilty only by geographic association.[58]

News of the incident spread through the ranks in London, as well as the city more generally. A crowd began to gather in front of the building, including between 75 and 100 soldiers from No. 2 Field Ambulance Depot, the 70th, 135th, and 142nd Battalions, and "a greater number of civilians." Many soldiers assumed that the people in charge of the poolroom had posted the signs, not the soldiers, and took exception accordingly. The ringleaders did not disabuse them of their misunderstanding. When the cigar store manager scraped one of the posters off of his window, an officer approached him and asked, "Do you want to raise a riot in this town?" Ralph Benenati replied that the city police were not giving him any protection. Indeed they were not, and tempers boiled over at around 1730 hours. The mob began to throw stones and bricks smashing several plate glass windows and using passing cars as a screen to conceal their identities. Even the hurried placement of a Union Jack in one of the cigar store windows did not save the pane — "the boys cheered and right after a brick came and broke the window." Only the arrival of Major E.M. McLean, the Field Officer of the Day, and other officers, dispersed the crowd. About 1830, Smerlies asked a local policeman to ban soldiers from the establishment but he refused, saying, "I can't help it, Mr. Smerlies, [I'd] lose my life to do it that way." The mob reformed at about 1900. On their own authority, the civilian police closed Dundas Street to civilian traffic and the soldiers stopped their boisterous behaviour as soon as military piquets arrived. Peace and order was restored by 2100.[59]

Troops were confined to barracks and a court of inquiry was appointed to investigate. Typically, the court yielded inconclusive evidence: Only five privates were identified by name as being active in the disturbance, but they could not be held personally accountable for the actual destruction. The court recommended that they be "punished severely by their Officers Commanding," but there is no evidence that this occurred. Instead, "owing to the apparent avarice of the proprietor and improper use of the toilet room in the poolroom for the consumption of liquor," the court recommended that the poolroom be placed out of bounds to all soldiers in the 1st Division Area. When local businesses filed for damages, the local officers recommended that the battalions should pay $1,068.45 on a *per capita* basis. Colonel L.W. Shannon, the officer administering the division, promptly put the establishment "out of bounds," but he did not agree that the battalions should pay storekeepers for damages and lost revenues. He felt that it was the police, not the military, who had acted inappropriately in closing the street to civilians, thereby causing business-owners to lose income.[60] Fingers were pointed elsewhere and the soldier-rioters were never held accountable.

Winnipeg, Manitoba

Friction between soldiers and civilian police plagued relationships in

Winnipeg in the spring of 1916. At about 1700 hours on 22 March, a piquet composed of Sergeant D.J. Walker and six men of the 144th Battalion (familiarly known as the "Little Black Devils") went to a boarding house at 49 Austin Street in search of a deserter. Such searches were a fairly regular practice within the battalion. Walker placed "guards" at the front and rear of the building and went in to check for the deserter with about 30 soldiers. Inside they found "some waiters and some foreigners" working in a restaurant and ordered them about.

When the Garrison Military Police (GMP) arrived, they questioned the soldiers' authority to be there. Sergeant Walker "acted stubbornly" and refused to fall in with the other soldiers present at the scene, who threatened to clear out the house. Indeed, an obstinate Walker refused to move off unless arrested and claimed that "they were not my men and I had no authority" to order them off. The provost-sergeant promptly arrested him, as well as a private, and he marched them down to the Immigration Hall.

A couple of hours later, a crowd reassembled, this time consisting of between 200 and 300 members of the 144th and other battalions who were "looking for trouble." The soldiers threw bottles and chunks of ice at the windows, breaking several. The house was filled "to the door" with soldiers, who apparently stole $27 from the restaurant's till. When Captain E.H. Goddard, the assistant provost-marshal, arrived at the scene, he "found Austin Street very full of Civilians and Soldiers, a shouting, howling mob." He immediately ordered the soldiers to fall in and dismissed them. "The order was instantly obeyed and I think within two minutes of my arrival there was not a soldier in the street." Once they left, the civilians followed. There were no further disturbances that evening.[61]

Quebec City, Quebec

Soldiers and the GMP also clashed in Quebec City on 6 November 1916. Relations between the 8th and 9th Regiments, both home guard units, and the 171st Battalion had been tumultuous in the preceding weeks, with various soldiers citing assaults, threats, and general bad blood between the units. At about 1830 hours, a piquet from the GMP approached members of the 171st Battalion who were standing around the YMCA auditorium and told them to move along. Members of other regiments (including the 8th and 9th) were not ordered away, so several "Russians" in uniform refused. When the MPs tried to place several soldiers from the 171st under arrest, "they took off their belts and started to beat the police," Rifleman George Billingsly of the 8th Regiment recounted. "The Russians whistled with the result that crowds of their comrades came running from all directions swinging their belts and crying out 'we are the Russians.'" A "free fight" followed. When district headquarters learned of the riot and the few hundred soldiers involved, it recognized that the outbreak could "assume perilous proportions" and immediately sent officers and piquets to the scene. Lieutenant H.A. Sewell of the 171st drove his car through the mob and ordered the soldiers to fall in, bringing the general melee to an end. Military and civilian onlookers jeered the men, causing them to break ranks and chase after the crowd, still wielding their waist belts as weapons. When the piquets arrived, they secured control of the rioters and Lieutenant Sewell managed to collect the men and march them back to barracks. Piquets remained at the scene until late in the night.[62]

The district commander, Brigadier-General A.O. Fages, blamed the "slight fracas" on bad feelings and "jealousy" between units. Local officers immediately convened a court of inquiry. The testimony was general and no names were demanded or given, so the court did not find out which individual(s) actually started the fight. The original outbreak seemed premeditated between "Russians" in the 171st and the GMP, but both sides cast the other in the role of instigator.

Many men claimed that they had been jumped by soldiers from other battalions and revealed their injuries from fists, belts, and bayonets. Everybody claimed to be a victim. The court concluded that the 171st, "a new unit where discipline has not, as yet, become second nature," had probably prearranged the disturbance. After all, its members formed into groups and rushed at the sound of a whistle. The GMP, however, had anticipated trouble and should "have shown more tact in the handling of the men." Given the absence of any subsequent clashes, the local officers were prepared to let the matter drop. But the adjutant-general in Ottawa was unimpressed with the court's findings. The GMP's lack of tact and the 171st's ill discipline hardly justified disobedient behaviour and Brigadier Fages was ordered to meet with the officers of the home guard units to "impress upon them their responsibility" and to inform them that any recurrence would lead to their removal from command. They were paraded accordingly and nothing further arose.[63]

ANALYSIS

Testimony before the various military courts of inquiry established to investigate the riots provide further insight into the reasoning behind these unlawful actions. The courts, that made official reports and recommendations to Ottawa, generally interpreted evidence in a manner sympathetic to the soldiers and comparatively hostile to civil authorities and civilians. Nonetheless, the transcripts of these proceedings serve as particularly rich sources to analyze motivations for riotous behaviour, civil-military relations, and command and control. The role of historian (as opposed to social theorist) is to use evidence to understand past events, with a careful eye to historical context. The following theoretical considerations are not intended to be comprehensive, nor do they offer a generalized theory of military disobedience. They are meant as critical reflections with which to ponder the riots of 1916, particularly as they bear on command and leadership in a domestic setting.[64]

Historian Robert Rutherdale observes, "conceptually, the central issue of collective behaviour within crowds is concerned with volition. A vast literature has become preoccupied with debates over the extent to which crowds are guided either by irrational, unconscious, and emotional impulses or by objectives that are consciously understood and generally shared." Predicating their perspectives on "law and order," the "classical" theorists saw collective behaviour as irrational, irresponsible, and destructive.[65] There is an obvious application to these case studies. Descriptions in newspapers and courts of inquiry suggest that the riotous crowds developed their own pulse as they marched towards their destination, gathering strength. When the anonymous mass struck their targets, they did so blinded by adrenaline, hyper-patriotic fervour and misplaced loyalty to disobedient comrades. Enthusiastic, frenzied scenes followed. In Berlin, when Sergeant P. Hayward saw German paraphernalia coming out of the Concordia Club, he later confessed, "I could not hold my temper any longer." Sergeant Deal was also present, as was his wife who shouted from the street: "Albert don't get so excited." He testified: "That was the state I was in. It was merely a state of excitement."[66] In most cases, the privates who appeared before the courts of inquiry simply fell in behind their chums and followed processions or crowds. They claimed that the riots were spur-of-the-moment actions, not premeditated assaults.

Revisionist interpretations, falling under the banner of "new social history," consider collective actions like riots as "instrumental and purposeful," replacing the old paradigm with a "politico-rational" explanation that sees crowd behaviour as democratic, creative, and rational.[67] Given prevailing political and social expectations, did the soldiers creatively manipulate and apply their rudimentary understanding of soldierly roles and responsibilities to disturbing local circumstances? If soldiers believed that they were a distinct sub-culture, and civil authorities were not suited to judge their behaviour, then collective action seemed an appropriate means of "springing" comrades from the clutches of civil society. Rather than explaining away soldiers' instigation and participation in anti-"enemy alien" riots as anti-ethnic hysteria, they might be seen as a form of populist uprising designed to accomplish what civil authorities were loathe to attempt: Ensuring that society was safe and symbolically united behind the British-Canadian cause. Although offensive from today's vantage point, were they not reflective of their society's beliefs and values at the time? Officers often stressed how "orderly," even "gentlemanly," soldiers behaved during various destructive episodes (unless they were intoxicated, of course).[68] Can the soldiers be summarily dismissed as "irrational" actors? After all, when piquets arrived at the scenes and officers issued direct orders for soldiers to disperse, did they not fall in and march back to barracks?

"Soldier participants," Edwin Pye discovered when he reviewed the documents in 1946, "were invariably new recruits of the battalions being raised and, therefore, had not yet absorbed the rudiments of discipline."[69] The riotous soldiers had not been fully assimilated into military culture and their limited understanding of hierarchical authority and control helps to explain their disobedience. This observation warrants further critical reflection on why newly recruited soldiers rioted. In a previous paper with Gardner, I have suggested that they were in the midst of a "liminal" — or transitional — phase.[70] Recruits, only recently drawn from the civilian population and undergoing the process of transformation into soldiers, were given uniforms and billeted in barracks, thus they were symbolically detached from their earlier roles in civil society. But the decision to train recruits near their places of origin may have exacerbated problems by not allowing for a cleaner break from societal prejudices and pressures. The physical proximity to the region from which they had been drawn mitigated their detachment from civilian life and influences during basic training. During this pivotal phase of soldier formation, recruits are forced to reflect upon their allegiance to the Crown and the state, and the explicit need to preserve and protect the "democratic" powers that sustain them and their society. They must be prepared to sacrifice their lives to this end. Perceived threats could be connected to national and formative military identities — the need to defend the empire, the country, their units, and their comrades were highlighted in basic training. They found ample opportunities to act in this direction before heading overseas.

The role of rumours was central to establishing pretexts for riotous behaviour. Loyalty to country was, of course, a primary catalyst. If wartime serves as a litmus test of society's values, then Great War Canada was indisputably "nativist"[71] and soldiers felt a duty to keep Canada staunchly British. "I heard remarks amongst the boys that they did not intend to leave that bust of Kaiser Wilhelm I in town," Company Sergeant-Major Blood of the 118th explained to the Berlin court of inquiry. "They didn't intend to leave it, as it had no place in a British city, in a British empire." The men had become restless, "intensified by the prolongation of the war, and due to the fact that the people of this city have refrained from joining." Asked whether he tried to stop the boys from smashing the Concordia Hall, Blood replied: "No sir, not to get the pictures. I had no desire to stop them from getting those pictures." He and Corporal Brennan seized the opportunity of appearing before a huge crowd of civilians to give recruiting speeches amid the commotion, a strange spectacle indeed.[72]

In Calgary, soldiers embraced rumours that various establishments employed enemy aliens or allowed them to gather and contemplate disloyal activities.[73] Officers considered the destruction of Muller's garage in Windsor to be "patriotic," even though the grounds for his alleged disloyalty were sketchy. Similarly, the perceived affront to soldiers by the "Boer" who owned the poolroom in Regina constituted equally sketchy grounds for destruction, but their heightened emotions over alleged soldier beatings at the hands of Romanians set a volatile context. Soldiers probably believed that they represented social good and saw their crusades as a way to perform their soldierly roles on the home front: they would contest "enemy aliens" for control of public space.[74]

Loyalty to comrades and one's unit was the other primary inducement for collective action. Primary group loyalty is a positive state in the military, Donna Winslow explains, but highly intense unit cohesion can be disruptive.[75] When soldiers heard rumours that their mates were being mistreated, they took action. Alleged police brutality against soldiers in Winnipeg precipitated their challenge against the civil authorities and their demands to release prisoners. This reflected an evident mistrust between the soldiers as an emerging "in-group" and civil authorities as an "out-group."

Similarly, the riot against the RNWMP in Calgary stemmed from discontent with prohibition regulations that led to the incarceration of soldiers. It seemed inappropriate to allow men who were willing to fight overseas to be taken captive by civil authorities for minor alcohol infractions.

In London, how was it fair that young men, who had signed-up for the army and would eventually put their lives on the line for their country, should be denied access to pool tables because of their age? For the soldiers who joined together to wreck the National Poolroom on 11 March, this was nonsense.

Inter-unit rivalries produced the fracas in Saint John, New Brunswick, the mêlée between the 144th and the garrison police in Winnipeg and the 171st and the GMP in Quebec City. These exaggerated and distorted expressions of unit pride and group cohesion reveal that soldiers held respect for members and officers of their own unit, but resented outsiders. Winslow's insights seem appropriate: "What is clearly an effective and necessary attitude for the battlefield can … become an exaggerated force that undermines good order and discipline."[76]

For other soldiers, the more sanguine inducements of curiosity and peer pressure help to explain their presence at the various disturbances. In Calgary, several soldiers testified that they only learned about the raids when they arrived downtown and ventured to their favourite spots (such as the pool rooms, skating rink, or hotels), or when they saw a throng of their uniformed mates moving past.[77] Most cited peer pressure as the reason they joined the crowd — they were simply told to "fall in" and they did, often unaware of where they were heading.[78] This obedience was, after all, part of what they had been taught in training. What was missing was the crucial understanding that proper orders to "fall in" were only to be obeyed when they came from a superior with sanctioned authority. Curiosity was the other driving force for participation. In Winnipeg, for example, testimony suggested that most of the soldiers were on the streets out of idle curiosity; they did not intend to fight the police.[79]

At the same time, several of the riots bore clear trademarks of ritual. In Berlin, the throng of soldiers marched towards the Concordia Club led by a Union Jack and singing "Rule Britannia." After they had captured the bust of the Kaiser, it was marched through the streets and carried back to the barracks as a trophy, just as they later tried to do with a bloodied Reverend Tappert.[80] These bonding experiences were more exciting than drill or route marches, yet bore characteristics of loyalty, courage, discipline (in an informal, bastardized sense), camaraderie, and teamwork.

Crowd behaviour is buoyed by the relative anonymity of operating in large groups, which reduces the risk of direct accountability and responsibility for one's actions. The soldiers carried this spirit of anonymity into the courts of inquiry, where a vast majority displayed a common reluctance to disclose any names. Very few ORs and NCOs were willing to incriminate their comrades. Even officers were wary to share the names of men from their units. In Regina, for example, Major J.C. de Balinhard "recognized my own men by badges and faces but individually I did not recognize any of them." Captain John Child was also present but testified that he had not recognized anyone there from his company and had not heard of anyone who was there.[81] In Winnipeg, an evasive soldier was asked directly if he was "trying to shield anybody" with his deliberately vague recollection of who was involved.[82] Similarly, after the Berlin riots in February, the NCOs who had been at the scene (and in several cases directly involved) refused to give any specific names, even though they were well-acquainted with all the troops. Questioning a sergeant, one officer remarked during the Berlin inquiry, "I can't understand … how you can walk with all these men down there and not recognize any, not even their faces." He continued, "You have been with them four months, right from London till down here." This NCO did not provide any further insight. As one witness put it, the soldiers were "all strangers" in the midst of the fracas.[83] So it was in nearly every case. This mass amnesia could be partly attributed to the excitement, the free flow of alcohol or the sheer number of people present, but senior officials in Ottawa were unimpressed. They, like the soldiers appearing before the inquiries, knew that the anonymity precluded prosecutions in civil courts and chastised local officers for failing to elicit more substantive testimony to identify those culpable.

Efforts to "stone-wall" authorities through the construction of "walls of silence" are a common phenomenon among soldiers subjected to official inquiries. Donna Winslow observed that soldiers are reticent to offer names of fellow soldiers accused of improprieties and that perceived "whistleblowing" is equated with "blasphemy" against one's regiment.[84] The numbered battalions to which the recruits belonged were void of regimental tradition and history, but soldiers quickly bonded to them all the same. A recruit's primary loyalty and identification rested with his company and battalion, where strong bonds would hopefully carry the men into battle for one another. These group loyalties, however, impeded attempts to identify rioters. When probed about their mates, soldiers suffered temporary amnesia that reinforced their solidarity with the troops of their own unit. Private P. Quinn's testimony to the court of inquiry in Berlin was particularly evasive:

> *Question:* Tell us in a few words as to your whereabouts last night?
> *Answer:* I don't know any of the fellows here at all.
> *Q:* You helped carry the bust down, didn't you?
> *A:* No sir.
> *Q:* Did you see the bust?
> *A:* I saw the bust coming down the street and I followed the procession.
> *Q:* What men out of D Company were carrying it?
> *A:* I don't think any were, sir.
> *Q:* Who were the B Company men?
> *A:* I don't know any of their names.

Q: You ought to know the names of B Company?

A: We all go by "Buddy."

Q: Were you drunk last night?

A: I had a few drinks, sir.

Q: What other men helped to break up the chairs and tables?

A: I don't know. I knew them as "Buddy."[85]

Recruits were team players, simply "buddies" to one other. In contrast to the individualism of civil society, this testimony suggests that individual names were subsumed by a common military identity. In theory, this should have made the group responsible for each "buddy's" behaviour. But officers and soldiers were disposed to shield their battalions from blame. In Saint John, Major R.H.K. Williams of the 69th denied seeing drunken soldiers on the streets, although nearly every other observer noted a striking state of intoxication among them. Lieutenant McKinley Millman of the 135th knew several of the soldiers from his regiment at the scene of the London disturbance, but "there were none of ours acting disorderly at all."[86] Everyone displayed an implicit awareness that you were expected to cover up for "teammates" and even defend inappropriate behaviour if this protected unit cohesion.

Anonymity was further preserved when soldiers participating in several raids removed their badges before engaging in destructive behaviour. In Calgary, Corporal L.E. Grace saw some of the soldiers take off their badges before leaving for the White Lunch. "I might have recognized a few of the boys," A.D. MacLennan, the owner of the destroyed Dance Academy, noted, "but they took good care to take off their badges."[87] Similarly, the absence of identifying badges made it very difficult for Major Butler of the 70th to separate rioting men from the various units in London accordingly. He had to ask the men their affiliation in order to "exercise command," and even then could not be sure that they were being truthful.[88] This pattern was commonly repeated from Windsor to Winnipeg.[89]

Military uniforms served a symbolic purpose, and in one case, forcing a soldier to remove his set off a ruckus. The Magistrate's Court in Winnipeg had a peculiar custom that obliged all military prisoners to exchange their uniform for civilian clothing before entering civil court.

Although local military authorities were aware of this procedure, the soldier-prisoners were not. Private R.L. Larson of the 90th Battalion was arrested during the April disturbance and protested when asked to don mufti. He told the court of inquiry:

> I would not take my uniform off the next day without the permission of my officer. Two of the military police appeared and [Private Fred] Fieldhouse [of the 90th Battalion] was one of them. They told me to take it off and I would not do it without the officers' permission, without authority. The police said 'How about if we stripped it off you' and I said I would not put it on again and the [civilian] police said: 'You skunk you are no good anyway.' I was sore and said to the policeman: 'You son of a bitch why don't you put on a uniform, you have cold feet.' Two of them got hold of me and punched my head against the wall and were going to take my uniform off; Fieldhouse said 'Go easy' and the police told him to keep his mouth closed or the same thing would happen to him. They took my coat off and were going to take my pants off too but they put civilian pants over them.[90]

It was a strange but revealing situation. Larson refused to take off his uniform without explicit officer approval, yet he had participated in the riot without direct military orders. The uniform served as a status identifier, without which his behaviour could be construed as mere hooliganism.

Although the courts of inquiry were military by nature, the role of civilians in the riots was a subject of intense discussion. In most cases, civilians were blamed for inciting the soldiers to action and for preventing military piquets from clearing the streets immediately. In Winnipeg, Deputy Chief Constable C.H.C. Newton of the city police noted, "soldiers look more prominent but there was a large number of civilians there. I should say the civilians made more trouble — the type of man arrested were men well known to the Department, most of them, men likely to egg on the soldiers against the police."

Peculiarly, most soldiers testified that the crowd was almost entirely military and at most one-third civilian.[91] "Had the civilians supported the soldiers and kept away we would have had no trouble," an officer suggested to the court of inquiry in London.[92] In Berlin, officers tried to pin the destruction of the Concordia Club on civilian agitators, even though it was clearly the product of military initiative.[93] After the Calgary riots, most soldiers blamed civilians, even though civil law authorities saw only soldiers taking part in the actual attack. Military authorities held the onlookers culpable for cheering the soldiers and urging them on. In the case of the Riverside Hotel riot, Lieutenant Sidney DeBarathy of the 56th said that a civilian threw the first projectile and Sergeant Robert Lawry offered his opinion that "the civilians were more to blame than the soldiers."[94] At Quebec, the internecine battle between soldiers was blamed on civilian cajoling and name-calling, despite the history of tense relations between the 171st and the GMP. The situation was similar in Saint John. "In my opinion," Major R.H.K. Williams of the 69th concluded:

> The alleged disturbance was caused by the large number of civilians who followed every bunch of soldiers egging them on to fight between themselves. In the 69th Battalion there is a very bitter feeling among French and English Canadians against the rougher element of the Civil population of St. John, as they declare they were freely insulted on the night in question.[95]

The soldiers may have done the rioting, but were the civilians responsible for the destruction? Major Williams also blamed alcohol, especially the "doctored poison" obtained from illegal bootleggers that "taken, even in small quantities, sends them crazy and probably caused a certain amount of the excitement that night" in Saint John.[96]

The destruction of the National Poolroom in London was partially deflected by claims that civilians had sold liquor to soldiers in the washrooms and that the owners of the establishment must have known that this was transpiring. Indeed, officers identified alcohol as a common culprit for the disturbances, twisting the minds of soldiers and intoxicating the mobs with malicious energy. In the midst of a ruckus, alcohol offered liquid courage and boosted morale. When one police constable grabbed a large jar from around the neck of one soldier in Calgary, he pleaded, "For God's sake let me go, I'm the wet canteen!" The majority of testimony at the Berlin inquiry stated that alcohol was not a factor, but one private conceded that the soldiers had tapped a keg of beer on the spot and just let it run continuously during the fracas. The "Russian" ringleaders who allegedly started the Quebec City riot were accused of being "under the influence of liquor." "I had a few drinks but was not drunk" was a familiar refrain from soldiers testifying in Winnipeg and across the country.[97]

For those soldiers identified at the crime scenes, drunkenness appeared to be an acceptable means of denying participation and of evading some responsibility for one's actions. Soldiers evidently did not see alcohol infractions as a serious offence. For example, intoxication was a common defence voiced at the Riverside Hotel inquiry in Calgary. Private H.H. Thompson of the 82nd Battalion was caught with a box of cigars that were obviously stolen from the hotel; he claimed that a soldier gave these to him while he was "under the influence of liquor" and thus he knew little about their origins. Private Thomas Howarth of the 56th had followed soldiers down to the Riverside after having half-a-dozen drinks at the Alberta Hotel and was arrested for being drunk and disorderly; like others who drank before the riot, he conveniently remembered little of the evening's subsequent events.[98] After the London riot, Privates R. Roberts and William Russell of the 142nd admitted to purchasing alcohol from civilians, but explicitly refused to name anyone and conveniently forgot how much whisky they had consumed that day. For his part, Russell denied any direct involvement in the destruction of the National Poolroom, but admitted to being so drunk that he did not remember what he was doing and "might have" thrown a brick through a window. His drunken haze prevented him from being certain "either way."[99] Of course, drunken disorderliness was still an offence and some soldiers were convicted of crimes committed while under the influence. Alcohol-induced boisterous behaviour, followed by amnesia, was not an adequate defence to get a soldier absolved of all responsibility ... just most of it.

Everyone tried to avoid blame. Officers pointed at unruly ORs or civilians, and NCOs and privates denied participation. The code of shared responsibility and accountability that is theoretically enshrined in a military ethos was nowhere to be found. All men in uniform were prepared to justify the pretext for collective action, but few were willing to take responsibility. As Lieutenant-Colonel K.W.J. Wenek recently noted, the assurance of "anonymity through norms of group loyalty" can serve to facilitate acts of subversion and defiance.[100] Fierce loyalties meant that authorities could not determine who was responsible, reinforcing the notion that inappropriate norms could be entrenched without incrimination.

LEADERSHIP

To paraphrase John Keegan, obedient and law-abiding armies are a mark of civilization. Armies of this quality are not established or maintained without effective leadership. It is the leaders who ensure that the values of society are both protected and respected by its armed forces. It is the leaders, too, who foster the values and norms unique to the military. In Canada, navigation through the complexities of these responsibilities is assisted by one of the central values of Canadian society — the rule of law.[101]

To be certain, the riots reflect shortcomings in leadership and training. Military leaders have several critical functions: to seek and accept responsibility; to socialize new members into military values and conduct; to exemplify and reinforce the military ethos; to maintain order and discipline; and to uphold professional norms.[102] CEF leadership (officers and NCOs) faced an uphill battle in trying to instill a military ethos before their units went overseas. By 1916, recruiting had become "a mass enterprise, involving men and women across Canada," Desmond Morton observed. "Making soldiers out of recruits was a more specialized business, left to officers and NCOs who had little or no experience of war." Climate made outdoor training difficult in winter and summer, and billeting soldiers in local detachments made training (and the enforcement of orders) particularly difficult.[103] Recruits were supposed to be acculturated with core military values such as obedience, discipline, loyalty, truth, duty, valour, and sacrifice. Obviously, participants in the various riots were imperfectly invested with the first two values. Most argued that their activism was an expression of loyalty and perceived duty, however distorted and misplaced their interpretation of these concepts. Their confusion reflected the competing pressures that they faced in familiar social surroundings.

The recruits were not isolated from civil society as in most basic training scenarios and were not stripped of their normal referents. In this context, the military ethos only partially supplanted their previous system of understanding and exaggerated loyalties to British-Canadian society, their units and their comrades-in-arms led to dysfunctional and disobedient behaviour. The moral responsibilities with which they should have been inculcated through training were corrupted accordingly.[104]

NCOs are responsible for the daily conduct of their men, and particularly, for advising officers on matters of discipline and morale. Anthropologist Anne Irwin explains that "cohesive, cooperative team-work" between officers and NCOs is "the critical factor in the cohesion and proper functioning" of military units:

> This team of the officer and NCO is the ideal working relationship at every level of the organization. The officer/NCO relationship is the nexus between the officers and the men and as such, the quality of the relationship determines, in the sense of setting limits to, the success of the hierarchy generally. If the officer and NCO can work together to produce an impression to the men and to those higher up in the hierarchy, there is much less stress on the structure of the Battalion.[105]

NCOs are essential and thus their insubordination placed critical stress on the military hierarchy. The frequent participation of NCOs in the riots suggests a serious problem with army socialization in 1916; testimony before the courts of inquiry further demonstrates that the military hierarchy was not functioning properly. In Calgary, for example, NCOs were supposed to be responsible for instilling and enforcing discipline in the ranks, but instead led the procession to the police and RNWMP Barracks. Sergeant Campbell testified that he had taken no part in the attack, but that he had spurred the excited crowd to action by announcing the location of the prisoners. Lance-Corporal Webster was seen leading a "sort of organized mob" to the barracks and the RNWMP identified Sergeant Cohen of the 218th as the "chief agitator." All three were sent to civilian trial because they were "particularly blameworthy," given their rank. Despite NCO involvement, the military stressed that the attack was not premeditated but spontaneous, and therefore the officers had little control over the actions of the NCOs and men who happened to be in uniform.[106] This lack of control, however, was the most damning indictment against the local officer corps. The testimony before the inquiry made it apparent that the necessary "cohesive, cooperative teamwork" between officer and NCO had broken down.

Various courts of inquiry revealed a "we" and "they" mentality between officers and NCOs and ORs. This reflects a socio-cultural distinction built into the military system to ensure that combat orders are followed, but this cleavage also upset the chain of command when NCOs cut off the flow of information to officers, thereby precluding preventive or punitive action. During the February proceedings in Calgary, for example, there was a discernible difference in the testimony of NCOs and officers. NCOs tended not to incriminate the soldiers who had been involved in the riotous acts, while some officers would name and incriminate a few individuals that they saw at the riots.[107] In a Canadian infantry battalion, historian David Bercuson has said, "the onus for leadership falls mainly on the officers [who issue commands], while the responsibility for management [and the implementation of commands] falls mainly on the NCOs." Officers bear the responsibility for the "overall good conduct and discipline of their men," while "NCOs are responsible for their daily conduct."[108] This vertical division of labour meant that the NCOs were responsible for the maintenance of discipline on the ground, and accordingly, were less disposed to turn in individuals for whom they were directly responsible.

Of course, the shortcomings of NCOs in these cases do not absolve the officers of responsibility. Given their managerial function, officers were responsible for overall good conduct and for producing training plans that would indoctrinate recruits with the proper military attributes. If they were not blameworthy for the immediate causes and activities, they were accountable for their subordinates' disobedience in a more general sense. "Leadership is a product of today's actions and yesterday's groundwork," and many officers displayed woeful situational awareness.[109] They were either out of touch with morale, discipline, and the well-being of the ORs and NCOs, or they simply ignored the violent and brazen proclivities of their subordinates. The officers should have recognized that the socialization process was failing to develop sufficient judgment and capacity for self-regulation, and thus, external regulation and control were required.[110] In most cases, the throngs of NCOs and ORs dispersed when battalion piquets arrived on the scene, demonstrating some level of obedience and discipline. The officers' failure to anticipate developments forced them to react to situations that never should have arisen. The necessity of direct intervention revealed that the officers lacked indirect influence over their subordinates. This suggests definite shortcomings in their development of healthy units armed with clarity of purpose.

Language is fundamental to leadership and is central to the ability to command. Greg Dening observed in his brilliant *Mr. Bligh's Bad Language,* "Bligh's bad language was the ambiguous language of command. It was bad, not so much because it was intemperate or abusive, but because it was ambiguous, because men could not read in it a right relationship to authority."[111] On several levels, this helps to explain why commanders lacked control over their men in 1916. The arduous experiences of Lieutenant-Colonel Lochead in Berlin are illustrative. In January, already facing civic embarrassment and humiliation over meager enlistments, he issued vague street recruiting regulations to his men after the local press and citizens complained of the 118th's pressure tactics. He asked his men to be "firm and persuasive in your endeavours to induce men to enter recruiting rooms," and to "not resort to force unless circumstances absolutely warrant[ed]." He set an example by openly engaging civilian critics, ferreting out local men and charging them with sedition and publicly berating the local Trades and Labour Council for being "un-British." He clearly focused on the value dimension of loyalty and he repeatedly expressed with fury that "pro-Germanism" lay behind all of his battalion's troubles.

This singular obsession with a particular dimension of his command (recruiting his battalion to full strength by overcoming perceived disloyal elements in Waterloo region) sent a distorted message to his subordinates.[112] Indeed, his statements before the courts of inquiry suggest that his command was indeed marked by a chronic ambiguity. The soldiers ignored his orders not to attack various German clubs and individuals on several occasions, but may have believed that they had "unofficial" approval to do so. After all, when members of his battalion trashed the Concordia in February, Lochead told the court that the Club "had been a great source of annoyance to local citizens."

Articulating defences like this seemed to rationalize and legitimize the soldiers' behaviour, thereby furnishing a broader moral authority for such actions. As a consequence, though Lochead had not officially sanctioned the attacks on various local establishments, his rhetoric encouraged immediate action and left the impression that the soldiers were operating in a permissive atmosphere.

Lochead's leadership and command obviously lacked meaningful influence over his subordinates. Before the Concordia raid, he had reminded Sergeant-Major Blood of his role as an NCO: "If you are up town with these men any time see that they moderate themselves and don't let their enthusiasm run away with their better judgment."[113] Blood did not understand (or chose to ignore) this direction:

> *Captain Fraser:* Didn't you think that you should have used your influence to try and stop this … ?
>
> *Sergeant-Major Blood:* No sir. I do not believe that any such thing has any place in the British Empire…. I don't think that it should be necessary for the boys to have to clean up these things.
>
> *Fraser:* Anybody thinks that.
>
> *Blood:* I think there should be sufficient legislation in the Dominion of Canada to keep it clean.
>
> *Fraser:* You think it is all due to pro-German sentiment? You think it is due to feeling?
>
> *Blood:* Insulting remarks of civilians. The night before last we met some boys on the street and we said, would you like to be in khaki, and a German looked around with a sneer at us. That is what we have to take when we ask them to join the army.
>
> *Fraser:* What definite object was there in going to Concordia Hall in the first place?
>
> *Blood:* To get the bust of the pro-German organization which is working against recruiting.

In the ensuing weeks, Lochead told his men that they had an obligation to "be soldiers" and not to do anything rowdy and destructive, but they persisted in disregarding his warnings despite his threats of severe punishment and dismissal. When Blood and others confronted Tappert in early March, Lochead was disappointed, but stressed to his superiors that Tappert's "defiant attitude" led to the altercation.[114] Rather than focusing on how misguided loyalties had prejudiced good order and discipline, he sent ambiguous signals about which soldierly values were most central and what conduct might be appropriate to "defend" societal and military honour.

Whether intentional or not, Lochead sent his battalion the message that excessive emotionalism, poor judgment, and action without command authority were *pardonable* offences, so long as one's loyalty to empire remained unimpeachable. He had repeatedly described the role of an NCO to Blood, but forgave him when "his enthusiasm for the British cause ... drown[ed] out his good judgment and sense of proper self-control." Lochead failed to appreciate that the fatal aspect of his command lay in his inability to transform civilians into disciplined soldiers by teaching them obedience. "You will appreciate that I am in no way condoning the action of the soldiers in respect of this or any other outbreak," he pleaded to the divisional commander in London, "because I fully realize that any leniency on my part would be fatal to discipline." He asserted that maintaining discipline was his foremost priority (which he claimed to establish by supporting civil authorities who prosecuted those responsible), but the impact was marginal. For their "disgraceful" behaviour, Blood and a private were given slaps on the wrist in civil court and faced no further punishment from their commanding officer (CO).[115] In short, Lochead was not prepared to reprimand them as soldiers. If he wanted to instill high standards of discipline and obedience (and a proper military ethos more generally), he should have modelled behaviour through more transparent statements of intent and by directly exercising his authority. Instead, as a commander, he was ineffective in language and in action. He failed to reinforce an ethos of discipline and self-control and failed to balance the strong "in-group" identity held by the local soldiers with a respect for authority and the rule of law.[116] His battalion's boisterous behaviour was the unfortunate outcome of his weak leadership.

Although the military maintained that the various units that rioted were under control, testimony given by the media and police indicated that officers demonstrated a chronic inability to enforce discipline. In Calgary, for example, the chief of police's assessment of the situation was critical of local military officials whom, he felt, were guilty of inaction. Officers belonging to the same battalions as the men that were destroying local properties made no effort whatsoever to stop them. Furthermore, it was "common talk amongst the citizens and the soldiers who took part in the rioting or who were then in camp" that Brigadier Cruikshank bore at least partial responsibility. Had he taken ordinary preventive measures and "asserted his authority in a more vigorous manner," rather than simply addressing the men ("a sign of weakness" according to Chief Cuddy's sources), the attack on the Riverside Hotel would never have taken place. Cuddy's sympathy was with the proprietor who, "through no fault of his own and as a result of the failure of the military authorities to control the situation," had lost everything that he owned.[117] Such opinions eroded the military's credibility in the eyes of civil society.

Other local commanders were quick to downplay the severity of the various disturbances, despite their unnerving implications for public order and stability. Colonel L.W. Shannon reported the London riots as a "slight disturbance of the public peace." The general officer commanding in Quebec called the riot there "a slight fracas last night in town between a few soldiers … and some Military Police." There was never an acknowledgement that things were completely out of control. In Winnipeg, the district commander alleged that the police had stopped the disturbance "at once" and it had been "exaggerated by news papers into [a] riot." "The men were at no time beyond the officers," Lieutenant-Colonel J.H. Hearn reported from Regina, where the officers seemed to applaud the soldiers for their restraint. "I might say that I personally know that with the exception of the time when they cleaned up the Pool Room of C. Rink, they were perfectly orderly and systematic in their endeavours," Colonel N.S. Edgar, the district commander, reassured his superiors in Ottawa.[118] These reports sought to reduce worries that command and control had waned. Officers sent proactive letters to dissuade their superiors from becoming alarmed, an anticipatory strategy that, unfortunately, had been absent before the riots themselves.

A Positive Example: Edmonton, Alberta

There is always a tendency to fixate on the negative at the expense of the positive. The case of Edmonton serves as an example of how prompt action by local leadership could pre-empt the outbreak of a riot. An *Edmonton Bulletin* editorial that appeared on 9 and 10 February 1916 contained the following passage:

> The dog is a very useful and estimable animal in his own place. And this place is a large one. But the street of a city is not part of that place. Child life in this community would be safer and parental life freed of a great deal of worry if the hides of about three battalions of good-for-nothing mongrels were nailed to the fence.

The editorial, in estimating the number of canines in military terms, did not go over well with the soldiers serving in the local CEF battalions who believed that the newspaper was calling the 51st, 63rd, and 66th Battalions "mongrels." On 11 February 1916, soldiers gathered on the streets of the Alberta capital to take action, presumably as their cohorts had done in Calgary just a few days before. Their first objective was purportedly the *Bulletin* office. Their second was the Macdonald Hotel as rumours had identified enemy alien employees there.[119] When troops began to gather, the chief of police immediately telephoned the COs of the three battalions to apprise them of developments. He knew that the city police would be powerless without military support. The officers took immediate action:

> Lieut.-Colonel McKinery, of the 66th, immediately jumped into his auto, leaving Major Durrand in charge of the men at the grounds. The colonel upon reaching the danger zone put officers in charge of all the soldiers on leave, with instructions to prevent disturbance. At the same time the men at barracks, under Major Durrand, were marched into the city, and upon arriving at [the corner of] Jasper and Fraser, cleared the street of all soldiers not on duty, at the same time ordering civilians to disperse.
>
> The other battalions responded with promptitude, pickets [*sic*] being sent from each, and stationed at ... the four points of vantage. Their arrival was not a moment

too soon, a crowd of khakied men already having assumed a threatening attitude. They formed, of course, but a small proportion of the total number of soldiers in the city, but their number was sufficiently large to provide considerable excitement for the time being.[120]

Rather than fanning the flames, the officers' actions allowed cooler, rational minds to prevail. The CO of the 63rd arranged for the *Bulletin*'s manager to address the soldiers in front of his building. He carefully explained that the editorial intended no reference to the actual battalions and was only about the local dog problem, plain and simple. Satisfied, "the soldiers then dispersed with cheers for the colonel."[121] Military piquets remained on duty for several hours after the incident, and with the help of city police, ensured that the soldiers did not get out of hand. Indeed, backed by the military authorities, the police made a number of arrests "while the excitement was at its height." Disaster was successfully averted. In the House of Commons, the member of parliament for Edmonton, Frank Oliver, applauded the "promptitude and action energy with which the officers of these battalions handled the situation. Their action certainly left nothing to be desired."[122]

In short, a competent and decisive leadership cadre, not unduly maligned towards civilians and civil authority, could exercise direct influence, change the collective direction of a crowd of soldiers, and act as an effective interlocutor between the civilian and military worlds. In Edmonton, the officers provided a context whereby the would-be rioters realized they were mistaken and misguided (rather than simply blaming the newspapers and civilian onlookers). This undermined the irrational basis for collective action and brought the soldiers firmly into line behind their officers.

RESPONSIBILITY

Senior officials in Ottawa refused to concede that the military was responsible for the destruction that rioting soldiers wrought on private property. Its common refrain: The government was "in no way responsible for the acts of lawlessness committed by soldiers not on duty, whether individual-ly or collectively."[123] The Department of Militia and Defence followed the minister of justice's opinion in the case of the Acadian Club: "In accor-dance with the considerations which he had given other claims ... arising out of unauthorized wrongful acts on the part of undisciplined soldiers impelled by motives of private malice, has the honour to report that there is no legal responsibility on the part of the Crown."[124] In the Calgary case, the judge advocate-general explained, "the persons who did the injury in question were rioters, answerable to the law as criminals, and answerable to the injured for the damage done; but the public are not answerable for such conduct." When a law firm demanded compensation for its client, a more substantive defensive was issued:

> The evidence shows that the destruction complained of was done by a mob composed for the greater part of men in military uniform, with some civilians. The men in uni-form, however, were not there as soldiers, were not under orders or on duty as a military body, were not acting as servants or agents of the Crown, but proceeded merely as individual citizens subject to the Criminal Law of the land, and amenable to civil tribunals. Indeed, ... the Magistrate convicted 5 of them of the offence in ques-tion, and fined them in sums varying from $50.00 to $20.00 with alternative terms of imprisonment.
>
> It must then be plain to you, as it is to the Officials of this Department, that much as the outrage in question is to be deplored, much as your clients are entitled to sympathy, and much as the rioters are deserving of the severest punishment, yet the public as represented by the Government at Ottawa are not answerable for the depre-dations in question.[125]

The problem, of course, was that guilty parties had to be identified before civil action. The soldiers' unwillingness to implicate their mates, their tendency to remove their badges and the inability of officers and courts of inquiry to expose those responsible made this difficult.[126]

To those directly affected, the military's position seemed untenable, irresponsible, and unjust. Lawyer E.P. Allison, representing the man whose garage had been destroyed by soldiers in Windsor, is worth quoting at length:

> Whatever force there may be in this contention so far as any of the common soldiers — if any such there were — who took no part whatever in the destruction of my client's property are concerned, it seems quite irrelevant when taken to refer to the Officers in command…. Public opinion — and I should suppose military law as well — holds regimental officers responsible for the good conduct of the soldiers under them, so far at least as taking all proper precautions to prevent the possibility of riotous aggression on the property of civilians, and especially by searching out and subjecting to proper discipline and punishment those who actually perpetrate it. On neither score would it appear that the Officers of these malicious destroyers of property did their duty aright. It is incredible that a body of troops wearing the King's uniform should march in regular order and in the most above board manner to the commission of such a deed of violence … without a most serious and culpable laches on the part of their Commanding Officers. Equally inexplicable is it to me that no attempt whatever seems to have been made by the latter to bring the perpetrators of the outrage to justice. Having taken no steps to either prevent or avenge the wrong, I fail to see that those responsible for the maintenance of order within the scope of their command should not be called on to make good my client's loss.[127]

His argument could speak for the other cases equally well. The military refused to pay compensation for damages in all but one case: The attack on the RNWMP Barracks in Calgary.[128]

To establish and ensure social order, the rule of law provides stable and consistent guidelines applicable to all members of a society. Riotous CEF soldiers failed to appreciate that everyone is subject to common laws, even men in uniform. But if the aim of military justice was to uphold discipline, the transfer of responsibility to civil authorities embodied the military's evasion of responsibility for the soldier riots themselves. In the House of Commons, Wilfrid Laurier asserted, "it might have been better for the military authorities to deal with these cases. I think they could inculcate the necessity of maintaining discipline better than the civil authorities."[129] He was calling for a display of strategic leadership to create institutional and environmental conditions more conducive to formal control.[130] Indeed, the military's denial of responsibility for riots and their transfer of responsibility for "soldiers" who participated to civilian authorities perpetuated the sense that these men remained "betwixt and between" military and civilian society ... and were accountable to neither.

CONCLUSIONS

All told, 1916 proved a disastrous year for the Allies. Verdun and the Somme had brought crippling losses and exposed the operational and tactical impotence of allied offensive doctrine. The British abandoned Gallipoli, quashing any hopes of winning the war through the "soft underbelly of Europe." The collapse of Russian armies in the east meant that Germany would soon be able to focus its attention on the Western Front. For the Canadians, who were transferred out of the Somme in the fall of 1916, there would be respite from major operations over the winter so that they could train, recuperate, and strengthen the defences on a 10-mile sector north of Arras. On paper, the Canadian Army had grown to more than 250 overseas battalions by the end of 1916. Sir Sam Hughes proved unable to cope with the administrative demands of the war and his amateurish approach became increasingly estranged from the growing professionalism of the Corps overseas. The meat-grinder of the Western Front was far less forgiving to ill discipline, intolerance, and marginal leadership than authorities had been at home. And looming before the Canadian Corps was the daunting Vimy Ridge, a seemingly impregnable German position that had already claimed the lives of thousands upon thousands of French and British troops.

"The First World War was a calamity," historian John English has recently written, and produced various common effects: "decrease in rationality, increased emotionality, and a focus on the calamity that paradoxically makes choices about dealing with it more difficult."[131] In 1916, soldiers made poor choices in dealing with the stresses that they faced on a local level. The training of newly recruited (or recruiting) battalions in their places of origin created a liminal space for soldiers. They recognized their familiar surroundings, but through the eyes of a neophyte citizen-soldier being inculcated with a budding military ethos of loyalty, teamwork, and bold action. "If we have got to fight them in Berlin," Sergeant-Major Blood told the mob in Berlin, "we might as well fight them here and in Germany too." Such proclamations were telling: The men craved action to test their mettle, to support their mates and to help end the war. While undergoing formative basic training, these men had ample access to civil society that confused the process of shedding their civilian world for a new military system of meaning and behaviour.

If a soldier is progressively stripped of his civilian identity while "deprived of any alternative sources of meaning," L.B. Lewis explains, "The trainee almost invariably adopts the frame of reference defined by his social context." Once the recruit's normal referents are removed, military regimen provides a "new system of meaning that restores shape and coherence to the world."[132] The military's failure to isolate the soldiers from civil society, coupled with an insufficient discipline, control, and leadership, led to breakdowns in military command and social control in 1916. Donna Winslow has critically elucidated how intense primary group bonding, while necessary for combat, is a "double-edged sword:"

> Misplaced loyalty can lead to stonewalling, preventing the proper investigation of criminal activities. Group bonding also prevents individuals from speaking out against inappropriate behaviour, which can therefore continue unchecked. The Chain of Command thus becomes short circuited by strong affective ties which it itself encourages. Strong affective ties, which are encouraged by combat norms, create highly cohesive units that can actually impede the good functioning of the overall organisation.

One way to control this tendency is through formal authority that encourages primary group loyalty "in an environment of strong leadership and discipline." She stressed that small-unit-level leadership, particularly by NCOs, is vital to hierarchical cohesion and control.[133] Extending this argument, Anne Irwin says that the successful operation of a battalion depends on the "quality of the relationships between officers and NCOs at the points where the two chains of command are connected."[134] Obviously the chain of command had not functioned effectively before the riots or they would not have occurred. Nor did it function with maximum effectiveness during courts of inquiry, given the chronic unwillingness of NCOs and soldiers to "name names" and the ineffectiveness of officers in holding units and individuals responsible and accountable.

Particularly in periods of transition, when civilians are being retooled as soldiers, values-based discipline and leadership must be consciously and rigorously fostered with a clear emphasis on the rule of law and obedience to command authority.[135] When obedience cannot be ensured through willing compliance, commanders must be prepared to apply coercive disciplinary measures. The unwillingness of officers to use coercive powers, both formal and informal, in a rigorous and unequivocal manner opened the door for misinterpretation and disobedience.

Before, during, and after most riots, officers chose to blame civil society for the disorder rather than working cooperatively with civilians and civilian authorities to prevent disturbances. They frequently pointed fingers at civilians who seemed to encourage disobedient behaviour by treating soldiers improperly, by harbouring disloyal ideas, or by watching, cheering, cajoling, and even participating alongside the riotous soldiers. By failing to appreciate the necessary constraints on soldierly behaviour, did civilians provide recruits with the mistaken impression that their behaviour was acceptable, even expected? Were the soldiers' "conduct values"[136] confused through this interaction with civilians who did not appreciate the necessary constraints on soldierly behaviour? Regardless of the answers, the soldiers and their officers should not be exonerated for these reasons. The purpose of military command and control is to ensure that discipline and obedience overrides passion. When this discipline breaks down, it demonstrates a failure of military socialization that must be partly attributable to commanders.

Hughes's predecessor, Sir Frederick Borden, claimed in 1909 that "the principal object" of having a national defence force was "perhaps the upholding of the Civil power in the different parts of the Dominion."[137] The behaviour of CEF battalions seven years later made such an assertion appear strange indeed. The riotous disturbances in 1916 showed that soldiers could be a source of domestic disorder. The failure of senior officers to take responsibility for recalcitrant soldierly behaviour, and the military's refusal to acknowledge their soldierly identities, undermined the military ethos of collective responsibility. Distributed leadership should have meant shared responsibility and accountability. Instead, the department's denial of liability on the grounds that disobedience stemmed from "private malice" should not conceal that these riots were collective actions undertaken by men in CEF uniforms. "The acts complained of were not done by soldiers, as soldiers, but by citizens who chanced at the time to be enrolled as soldiers," the JAG asserted in September 1916.[138] This peculiar logic reflected a failure on all levels of the military as recruits took the law into their hands, their officers failed to hold them sufficiently accountable as soldiers and the department denied any legal implication whatsoever. In 1916 Canada, William Chadwick noted, the image of the military as an "outlaw gang terrorizing the streets of a Wild West town while the sheriff cowers in his office was not so very far from the truth."[139]

NOTES

1. *Hansard,* 5 April 1916, 2548.

2. See, for example, Library and Archives Canada [henceforth LAC], Record Group [henceforth RG] 24, Vol. 1257, File 593–1-110, Deputy Minister [henceforth DM] of Militia and Defence to E.P. Allison, 4 April 1917.

3. Desmond Morton, "'No More Disagreeable or Onerous Duty': Canadians and the Military Aid of the Civil Power, Past, Present, Future," in D.B. Dewitt and D. Leyton-Brown, eds., *Canada's International Security Policy* (Scarborough, ON: Prentice-Hall, 1995), 135.

4. See, for example, Nikolas Gardner, "The Great War and Waterloo County: The Travails of the 118th Overseas Battalion," *Ontario History,* Vol. 89, No. 3 (Fall 1997), 219–36;

P.W. Lackenbauer, "The Military and 'Mob Rule': The CEF Riots in Calgary, February 1916," *Canadian Military History*, Vol. 10, No. 1 (Winter 2001), 31–42; P.W. Lackenbauer, "Under Siege: The CEF Attack on the RNWMP Barracks in Calgary, October 1916," *Alberta History*, Vol. 49, No. 3 (Summer 2001), 2–12; and P.W. Lackenbauer and N. Gardner, "Soldiers as Liminaries: The CEF Soldier Riots of 1916 Reassessed," in Yves Tremblay, ed., *Canadian Military History Since the 17th Century* (Ottawa: Department of National Defence [henceforth DND], 2001), 164–74.

5. Courts of inquiry are not judicial bodies. They are intended to gather information and are established pursuant to military regulations, at the discretion of the convening officer, "to collect evidence or assist him in arriving at a correct conclusion on any subject on which it may be expedient for him to be thoroughly informed. With this object in view, such Court may be directed to investigate and report upon any matters that may be brought before it, or give an opinion on any point, but when an inquiry affects the character of an officer or soldier, full opportunity should be given such officer or soldier of being present throughout the inquiry, and of making any statement he may wish to make, and of cross-examining any witness whose evidence, in his opinion, affects his character, and producing any witnesses in defence of his character." See Major-General Sir William D. Otter, *The Guide: A Manual for the Canadian Militia (Infantry)*, 9th ed. (Toronto: Copp, Clark, 1914), 150–51. See also Militia Act, s.98–99.

6. Directorate of History and Heritage [henceforth DHH], E. Pye Papers, Folder H, 74/672, "Disturbances in Canada in 1916 — in which Canadian Soldiers were Involved," 2. For a justification of the case study approach when an investigator desires to: (1) define topics broadly and not narrowly; (2) cover contextual conditions and not just the phenomenon of the study; and (3) rely on multiple and not singular sources of evidence, see R.K. Yin, *Case Study Research: Designs and Methods,* revised ed. (London: Sage, 1989).

7. Mike O'Brien, "Manhood and the Militia Myth: Masculinity, Class and Militarism in Ontario, 1902–1914," *Labour/Le Travail,* Vol. 42 (1998), 115–41. Ronald Haycock called the creation of Valcartier Camp, the Minister's "greatest achievement in the mobilization process." See Ronald Haycock, *Sam Hughes: The Public Career of a Controversial Canadian, 1885–1916* (Waterloo: Wilfrid Laurier University Press [henceforth WLUP], 1986), 177–97. For a critical appraisal of Hughes's mobilization decisions, see Stephen Harris, *Canadian Brass: The Making of a Professional Army* (Toronto: University of Toronto Press [henceforth UTP], 1988), 94–7.

8. Desmond Morton, *When Your Number's Up: The Canadian Soldier in the First World War* (Toronto: Random House, 1993), 72–4.

9. As quoted in *Ibid.*, 79–80.

10. G.W.L. Nicholson, *Canadian Expeditionary Force 1914–1919* (Ottawa: Queen's Printer, 1964), electronic version available through DHH website, 191–92; R.C.

Brown and R. Cook, *Canada 1896–1921: A Nation Transformed* (Toronto: McClelland and Stewart, 1974).

11. K.M. McLaughlin, *The Germans in Canada*, Canada's Ethnic Groups booklet, No. 11 (Ottawa: Canadian Historical Association, 1985), 12.

12. H. Palmer, *Patterns of Prejudice: A History of Nativism in Alberta* (Toronto: McClelland and Stewart, 1982); Paul Maroney, "The Great Adventure: The Context and Ideology of Recruiting in Ontario, 1914–1917," *Canadian Historical Review* [henceforth *CHR*], Vol. 77, No. 1 (1996), 62–79. On propaganda, see also, Jeffrey A. Keshen, *Propaganda and Censorship during Canada's Great War* (Edmonton: University of Alberta Press, 1996).

13. Canada, *Senate,* 18 January 1916, 14–5.

14. John Herd Thompson, *Harvests of War* (Toronto: McClelland and Stewart, 1978), 73.

15. Paul Jackson, *One of the Boys: Homosexuality in the Military during World War II* (Montreal and Kingston: McGill-Queen's University Press, 2004), 8.

16. LAC, RG 24, Vol. 1256, File 593–1-87, Proceedings, Court of Inquiry, Berlin, 16 February 1916, 8. Blood, a resident of Berlin, was born in Shepshed, Leicestershire, England. See LAC, RG 24, Vol. 1255, Accession 1992–93/166, Box 825, File 38, Attestation Paper, "Blood, Granville Poyser."

17. For a fuller treatment and detailed references, see Lackenbauer, "Military and 'Mob Rule,'" 31–42, and P.W. Lackenbauer, "'The Government is in no way responsible for the wrong-doing of its soldiers:' Disciplinary and Legal Dimensions of the Canadian Expeditionary Force Riots in Calgary," in C. Bullock and J. Dowding, eds., *Perspectives on War: Essays on Security, Society & the State* (Calgary: Society for Military and Strategic Studies, 2001), 75–91.

18. LAC, RG 24, Vol. 1255, File 593–1-86, General Officer Commanding [henceforth GOC], Military District [henceforth MD] 13 to Secretary, Militia Council, 13 March 1916.

19. Lackenbauer and Gardner, "Soldiers as Liminaries," 164–74.

20. LAC, RG 24, Vol. 1255, File 593–1-86, "Memorandum, William C. Dennis, Washington, D.C., re: claim of Thomas and Neil M. Sorenson for damage to and destruction of their property and business in Calgary, Canada," [July 1916].

21. Patricia McKegney, *The Kaiser's Bust* (Wellesley: Bamberg Press, 1991), 156; William Chadwick, *The Battle for Berlin* (Waterloo: WLUP, 1992), 177; Gardner, "Great War and Waterloo County," 219.

22. Gardner, "Great War and Waterloo County," 220–21.

23. Gardner, "Raising the 118th Battalion CEF," (Unpublished M.A. cognate essay, Wilfrid Laurier University, 1994), 30–3; Untitled article, 1, 24 January 1916, *News Record;* LAC, RG 24, Vol. 1256, File 593–1-87, Proceedings, Court of Enquiry, Camp Borden, 25–26 June 1916, 1–2; Chadwick, *Battle for Berlin,* 47; D. Morton and J.L. Granatstein, *Marching to Armageddon: Canadians and the Great War 1914–1919* (Toronto: Lester & Orpen Dennys, 1989), 26; and Adam Crerar, "Ontario and the Great War," in D. Mackenzie, ed., *Canada and the First World War* (Toronto: UTP, 2005), 256, are mistaken in their chronology and description.

24. LAC, RG 24, Vol. 1256, File 593–1-87, Proceedings, Court of Inquiry, Berlin, 16 February 1916; Pye, "Disturbances," 3; Gardner, "Great War and Waterloo County," 224; A.S. Forbes, "Volunteer Recruiting in Waterloo County during the Great War, 1914–1918," (Unpublished M.A. thesis, University of Waterloo, 1977), 140. In the days ahead, Lochead assigned sentries to patrol the streets of downtown Berlin to ensure that the local soldiers behaved more appropriately.

25. Proceedings, Berlin, 16 February 1916.

26. *Ibid.*, 24.

27. As quoted in John English and Ken McLaughlin, *Kitchener: An Illustrated History* (Waterloo: WLUP, 1983), 116, and Barbara Wilson, *Ontario and the First World War* (Toronto: Champlain Society, 1977), 80–1, from the original transcripts held in LAC, RG 24, Vol. 1256, File 593–1-87. The proceedings concluded, "Most of the ... destruction was done by civilians who were actually selling on the street souvenirs of the occasion, such as piano keys, etc." This ignored several contradictory testimonies before the court of inquiry.

28. Proceedings, Berlin, 16 February 1916, 23.

29. Gardner, "Great War and Waterloo County," 225; Proceedings, Berlin, 16 February 1916, 16; "Berlin Pastor is Roughly Handled," 1, 6 March 1916, *Ottawa Free Press;* LAC, RG 24, Vol. 1256, File HQ 593–1-87, Carter to Colonel A.P. Sherwood, 5 March 1916. A lively overview can be found in Chadwick, *Battle for Berlin,* 76–85. Dancey's initials are presumed based upon the Officers Declaration Paper from LAC, RG 150, Vol. 1256, Accession 1992–93/166, File 14, Box 2283, "Dancey, Stanley Nelson."

30. LAC, RG 24, Vol. 1256, File HQ 593–1-87, Lochead to Hodgins, 6 March 1916. He finished with, "You will do well to suggest to the American Consul General that Tappert be advised to leave Canada as soon as possible because he and his family being Prussian at heart are taking advantage of their American citizenship to make themselves most offensive to Canadian soldiers and Canadian citizens generally."

31. Gardner, "Raising the 118th Battalion," 39–40.

32. LAC, RG 24, Vol. 1256, File HQ 593–1-87, Officer Commanding [henceforth OC], 118th Battalion to Officer Administering [henceforth OA], 1st Division, 6 March 1916. "Tappert has left, and therefore there is little more to be feared. He will of course continue to cooperate with the authorities and will if necessary place a body of military police on the streets ... to make sure law and order are maintained."

33. Gardner, "Great War and Waterloo County," 225.

34. Pye, "Disturbances," 6; Chadwick, *Battle for Berlin,* 121–23.

35. Gardner, "Raising the 118th Battalion," 57–8.

36. Proceedings, Berlin, 16 February 1916, 16.

37. LAC, RG 24, Vol. 1257, File 593–1-110, GOC, MD 6, to Secretary, Militia Council, 20 November 1916; *Ibid.*, Proceedings, Court of Inquiry, Windsor, 17 November 1916.

38. Proceedings, Windsor, 17 November 1916. Military authorities had promised Muller's lawyer, E.P. Allison, that they would notify him when the court was assembled and he could attend accordingly. They did not do so, much to his, and Muller's, chagrin. After encountering much military reticence, Allison eventually secured a copy of the court's recommendations through his Member of Parliament.

39. LAC, RG 24, Vol. 1257, File 593–1-110, Adjutant-General to GOC, MD 6, 24 November 1916 and 15 December 1916; *Ibid.*, GOC, MD 6, to Secretary, Militia Council, 28 November 1916 and 1 February 1917; *Ibid.*, Allison to A.E. Kempt [*sic*], 13 March 1917. The GOC sent a cable to the OC, 239th Battalion, in February 1917 requesting voluntary payment for the damages, but the men refused to do so.

40. LAC, RG 24, Vol. 1671, File 683–340–6, Lieutenant-Colonel J.H. Hearn, OC, 214th Battalion to District Officer Commanding [henceforth DOC], MD 12, 1 December 1916; *Ibid.*, DOC, MD 12, to Secretary, Militia Council, 1 December 1916.

41. LAC, RG 24, Vol. 1256, File 683–340–6, Lieutenant-Colonel J.H. Hearn, OC, 214th Battalion, to DOC, MD 12, 1 December 1916; *Ibid.*, DOC, MD 12, to Secretary, Militia Council, 1 December 1916; *Ibid.*, C. Rink, testimony to Court of Inquiry, Regina, 8 January 1917, 13.

42. LAC, RG 24, Vol. 1671, File 683–340–6, Acting Adjutant-General to DOC, MD 12, 17 January 1917; *Ibid.*, C. Rink to MD 12, 8 March 1917. Major N.S. Edgar was appointed temporary colonel while DOC from 1916 to 1917.

43. Tim Cook, "'More a medicine than a beverage': 'Demon Rum' and the Canadian Trench Soldier of the First World War," *Canadian Military History,* Vol. 9, No. 1 (Winter 2000), 6–22. On drinking and army culture, see also, Donna Winslow, *The Canadian Airborne in Somalia: A Socio-cultural Inquiry* (Ottawa: Minister of Public Works and Government Services, 1997).

44. A more tangential case occurred in Perth, New Brunswick, on 12 May 1916, when 75 members of "D" Company, 140th Battalion, wrecked the Dew Drop Inn restaurant. The owner repeatedly refused to serve meals or sell tobacco to soldiers, and allegedly heaped abusive language on potential patrons in uniform. The Court of Inquiry discovered that he was "carrying on an illegal business in the sale of liquor and he was afraid that if a soldier got drunk it would be charged that he had sold the liquor, if soldiers were allowed to frequent his restaurant." See Pye, "Disturbances," 7.

45. LAC, RG 24, Vol. 4550, File 123–1-17, Testimony of Sergeant Joseph Scott, Sergeant Charles H. Rankine, Police Constable George H. Seely and Sergeant G. Pickup to Court of Inquiry, Saint John, New Brunswick, 4 April 1916.

46. *Ibid.,* Testimony of Joseph Scott, Harry Donohue, W.C. Wickham and Major Hubert Stethen to *Ibid.*

47. *Ibid.,* Testimony of Nicholas Jacobsen, Captain G.C. Clark and Stethen to *Ibid.* Finding, 5 April 1916.

48. DOC, MD 10, to Secretary, Militia Council, 4 April 1916, reproduced in *Hansard,* 5 April 1916, 2548; LAC, RG 24, Vol. 1256, File HQ 593–1-95, Proceedings, Court of Enquiry, Winnipeg, 12–15 April 1916.

49. *Ibid.,* Proceedings, Winnipeg, 12–15 April 1916, 29, 50, 62, 63; *Ibid.,* DOC, MD 10, to Adjutant-General, 2 April 1916 and 4 April 1916.

50. *Ibid.,* Proceedings, Winnipeg, 12–15 April 1916, 14, 16, 20, 20a, 28, 35, 36, 38–41, 43, 46, 51, 62, and Findings.

51. For a more detailed overview, see Lackenbauer, "Under Siege."

52. The 211th Battalion was one of five American Legion battalions raised in Canada to recruit Americans anxious to join the war effort. Discipline in these battalions was a problem from the onset and continuous deployment delays and high desertion rates "led to low morale and frequent incidents of alcohol abuse and fist fights." See Clive M. Law, "Colonel Bullock's American Legion of the Canadian Expeditionary Force," *Military Collector and Historian,* Vol. 51, No. 4 (1999), 150, 153–55; Ronald G. Haycock, "The American Legion in the Canadian Expeditionary Force, 1914–1917: A Study in Failure," *Military Affairs,* Vol. 43, No. 3 (October 1979), 115–19.

53. LAC, RG 18, Vol. 3274, File 1915-HQ-1184–15–1, Commissioner to Comptroller, Royal North West Mounted Police [henceforth RNWMP], 25 October 1916.

54. LAC, RG 24, Vol. 1255, File HQ 593–1-86, pt. 1, Testimony, Constable Dan Finlayson and Staff-Sergeant S.R. Waugh, RNWMP, Proceedings, Court of Enquiry, re: Attack on Calgary Police Headquarters and RNWMP Barracks, 11 October 1916; LAC, RG 18, Vol. 3274, File 1915-HQ-1184–15–1, Superintendent Commanding "D" Division to Commissioner, RNWMP, Regina, 16 October 1916; *Ibid.*, Newson to OC, RNWMP, 13 October 1916.

55. Proceedings, Calgary, 11 October 1916.

56. LAC, RG 24, Vol. 1257, File HQ 593–1-108, pt. 1, Borden to Hughes, 13 October 1916; *Ibid.*, Cruikshank to Secretary, Militia Council, 3 November 1916; Lackenbauer, "Under Siege," 10. Private Pelegrino, who had been shot by the RNWMP, was released on suspended sentence because of his wounds.

57. LAC, RG 18, Vol. 3274, File 1915-HQ-1184–15–1, Superintendent Commanding "D" Division to Commissioner, RNWMP, 11 October 1916.

58. LAC, RG 24, Vol. 1256, File 593–1-91, Proceedings, Court of Inquiry, London, 13 March 1916.

59. Proceedings, London, 13 March 1916, 2; *Ibid.*, OA, 1st Divisional Area to Secretary, Militia Council, 16 March 1916.

60. Findings of the Proceedings, London, 13 March 1916; *Ibid.*, OA, 1st Divisional Area to Secretary, Militia Council, 16 March 1916.

61. LAC, RG 24, Vol. 1256, File HQ 593–1-95, Proceedings, Court of Inquiry, Winnipeg, 28 and 30 March 1916, 1–4, 7, 23, 27, 52.

62. LAC, RG 24, Vol. 1256, File 593–1-101, Proceedings, Quebec City, 7 November 1916, Testimony of Lieutenant H.A. Sewell, Sergeant D.R. Rennie, Private L.R. Plante, Private M. Shami, Private Zubowich, Bugler Redners McCaul, Private N. Stace (171st Battalion); Rifleman George Billingsly, Private A. Campbell (8th Regiment); Private G. Vezina (9th Regiment, Garrison Military Police).

63. Proceedings, Quebec City, 7 November 1916; *Ibid.*, Adjutant-General to GOC, MD 5, 22 November 1916; *Ibid.*, GOC, MD 5, to Secretary, Militia Council, 30 December 1916.

64. Not all theories or considerations are pertinent to each case, nor do they add up to a tidy, totalizing whole. To enforce conformity to a predetermined theoretical template would distort the historical picture.

65. Robert Rutherdale, "Canada's August Festival: Communitas, Liminality, and Social Memory," *CHR*, Vol. 77, No. 2 (June 1996), 221–23. See his detailed footnotes for lists of relevant sources on crowds and collective behaviour.

66. Proceedings, Berlin, 16 February 1916, 11, 13.

67. Rutherdale, "Canada's August Festival," 221–23.

68. For example, the men of the 69th Battalion carried sidearms but never drew them, nor used belts or bayonets, and swore "very little" during the disturbance at Saint John. See LAC, RG 24, Vol. 4550, File 123–1-17, Proceedings, Saint John.

69. DHH, Pye Papers, Folder H, 74/672, Draft text of Chapter VII-10.

70. See Lackenbauer and Gardner, "Soldiers as Liminaries," for an overview of theories about liminality.

71. By "nativism," the author refers to a prevalent attitude in a society of rejecting alien persons or culture.

72. Proceedings, Berlin, 16 February 1916, 3, 5, 7.

73. Proceedings, Calgary, 12–24 February 1916.

74. On the other hand, once hysteria set in and the mob was worked into a fevered pitch, patriotic symbols were not sufficient to stem an orgy of destruction that spilled over onto property not implicated in the ostensible "purpose" of the riots. The dance hall in Calgary was a clear example. A thoughtful manager also hung a Union Jack in a cigar store window during the London riot, but the window was nonetheless smashed 15 minutes later.

75. Donna Winslow, "Misplaced Loyalties: The Role of Military Culture in the Breakdown of Discipline in Two Peace Operations," *Journal of Military and Strategic Studies,* Vol. 6, No. 3 (Spring 2004), 2–3.

76. *Ibid.*, 8.

77. Proceedings, Calgary, 12–24 February 1916, Testimony of Private A. Kerss (56th Battalion), Private Jack McLeod (56th Battalion), Private Charles Wren (89th Battalion), Private Henry Havelock Thompson (82nd Battalion), and Private Robert Grierson (56th Battalion).

78. *Ibid.*, Testimony of Private Stanley Albert Rossier (137th Battalion) and Private Harold William Kennedy (137th Battalion).

79. Proceedings, Winnipeg, 28 and 30 March 1916, 42.

80. Proceedings, Berlin, 16 February 1916.

81. Proceedings, Regina, 8 January 1917, 3, 7. See also, 10. Initials based upon LAC, RG 150, Accession 1992–93/166, File 37, Box 2398, Attestation Paper, "De Balinhard, John Carnegy," and LAC, RG 150, Accession 1992–93/166, File 21, Box 1678, Attestation Paper, "Child, John Waller Laurence."

82. Proceedings, Winnipeg, 28 and 30 March 1916, 49.

83. Proceedings, Berlin, 16 February 1916, 2, 9, 13, 14, 20–1, 22.

84. Winslow, *The Canadian Airborne in Somalia,* 72.

85. Proceedings, Berlin, 16 February 1916, 19, also quoted in Chadwick, *Battle for Berlin,* 67.

86. Proceedings, London, 13 March 1916, 18.

87. Proceedings, Calgary, 1916, 12th witness, Riverside Hotel; 28th and 73rd witnesses, White Lunch.

88. Proceedings, London, 13 March 1916, 9, 30.

89. Proceedings, Windsor, 17 November 1916, Roach testimony; Proceedings, Winnipeg, 12–15 April 1916, 28.

90. LAC, RG 24, Vol. 1256, File HQ 593–1-95, Proceedings, Winnipeg, 28th witness, R.L. Larson (90th Battalion).

91. Proceedings, Winnipeg, 12–15 April 1916, 9, 62.

92. Proceedings, London, 13 March 1916, 13.

93. Proceedings, Berlin, 16 February 1916.

94. Proceedings, Calgary, 12–24 February 1916.

95. Testimony of Major Williams to Court of Inquiry, Saint John, 4 April 1916.

96. *Ibid.* Rather than dealing with the substantive issue of indiscipline and disobedience, he boasted that his regiment's record that night — only five drunks arrested and about 20 absentees on a pay night — was impressive "for this or any other regiment."

97. LAC, RG 24, Vol. 1256, File 593–1-91, Proceedings, Quebec City, 7 November 1916, Captain L. Bouchard (9th Regiment, Voltigeurs de Quebec); Proceedings, Winnipeg, 12–15 April 1916, 22, 23, 26, 453.

98. Proceedings, Calgary, 12–24 February 1916.

99. Proceedings, London, 13 March 1916, 31–38, 41.

100. Lieutenant-Colonel K.W.J. Wenek, "Behavioural and Psychological Dimensions of Recent Peacekeeping Missions," *Forum: Journal of the Conference of Defence Associations Institute,* Vol. 8, No. 5 (1993), 20.

101. Canada, DND, *Leadership in the Canadian Forces: Conceptual Foundations* (Kingston: Canadian Defence Academy — Canadian Forces Leadership Institute, 2005), 44.

102. DND, *Leadership in the Canadian Forces,* 49.

103. Morton, *When Your Number's Up,* 74, 79.

104. Winslow, *The Canadian Airborne in Somalia,* 64–5. Basic training demands that soldiers get along with their comrades and meet the expectations of their superiors. This socialization process is achieved by applying maximum pressure to ensure that everyone conforms to military norms, and by making the group responsible for every member's behaviour. Officers and non-commissioned officers (NCOs) play a vital role in imposing and enforcing the rules and regulations of the system. Soldiers and officers are expected to respect values and interests that reflect a foremost loyalty to country, then to the group, and then to the chain of command before thinking of themselves. Effective leadership, then, is about creating and upholding civil, legal, ethical, and military values using direct and indirect influence. See Winslow, "Misplaced Loyalties," 3–4. *Direct influence* refers to "face-to-face influence on others which has an immediate effect on their ability, motivation, behaviour, performance, attitudes, or related psychological states, or which progressively modifies the slow-growth attributes of individuals and groups." *Indirect influence,* by contrast, refers to "influence on others mediated by purposeful alterations in the task, group, system, institutional, or environmental conditions that affect behaviour and performance." See DND, *Leadership in the Canadian Forces,* 6.

105. Anne Irwin, "Canadian Infantry Platoon Commanders and the Emergence of Leadership" (Unpublished M.A. thesis, University of Calgary, 1993), 186–87.

106. LAC, RG 24, Vol. 1257, File HQ 593/1/108, pt.1, Report from Court of Inquiry, 26 October 1916; *Ibid.,* Proceedings of Enquiry, Witnesses Constable Thomas Ward, City Police; *Ibid.,* Waugh, RNWMP; *Ibid.,* Sergeant Campbell, 211th Battalion; and *Ibid.,* Lieutenant-Colonel Robinson, 17 October 1916. The soldiers at Sarcee Camp did not represent a united front. Other battalions were apparently furious with the

211th for what had happened, and there were rumours that the 211th was going to attack the 187th "for their derogatory utterances" against the former. *Ibid.*, Superintendent. Commanding "E" Division to Commissioner, RNWMP, 11 October 1916.

107. See, for example, Proceedings, Calgary, 12–24 February 1916, Lieutenant R.J.J. Quinlan (89th Battalion); Lieutenant Thomas Dick (56th Battalion); Lieutenant William F. Armstrong (56th Battalion); Lieutenant Sidney Alex. DeBarathy (56th Battalion); and Lieutenant Frederick Bertram Cooper (56th Battalion).

108. David Bercuson, *Significant Incident: Canada's Army, the Airborne, and the Murder in Somalia* (Toronto: McClelland and Stewart, 1996), 111–12.

109. DND, *Leadership in the Canadian Forces*, 77.

110. External regulation and control are required when people: (1) do not fully understand what is required of them, either with respect to performance outcomes or standards of behaviour; (2) lack knowledge or skill concerning how to proceed; (3) are unwilling to comply with directions and rules; or (4) are unwilling to furnish the effort necessary to fulfil their responsibilities. See DND, *Leadership in the Canadian Forces*, 18.

111. Greg Dening, *Mr. Bligh's Bad Language: Passion, Power and Theatre in the Bounty* (Cambridge: Cambridge University Press, 1992), 61, quoted in John English, "Political Leadership in the First World War," in D. Mackenzie, ed., *Canada and the First World War* (Toronto: UTP, 2005), 89.

112. McKegney, *Kaiser's Bust*, 154–58; Chadwick, *Battle for Berlin*, 27, 47, 49–52, 64. The recently released *Leadership in the Canadian Forces: Conceptual Foundations* explains that military leaders must be careful not to "over-emphasiz[e] one value dimension at the expense of the others, or ignor[e] any value dimension," without repercussions. See DND, *Leadership in the Canadian Forces*, 31.

113. Proceedings, Berlin, 16 February 1916, 7–8; Proceedings, Camp Borden, 25–26 July 1916. Blood had already served in the Royal Navy before the war and was thus appointed senior NCO of "A" Company, 118th Battalion. "He was a fearless and fearsome leader of men," William Chadwick characterized, "and also rabidly patriotic, though one source alleges that it was his wife, Agnes, who was the real power behind this particular throne and that it was she who pushed him into some of his more outrageous exploits." See Chadwick, *Battle for Berlin*, 33.

114. "Berlin Pastor is Roughly Handled," 6 March 1916, 1, *Ottawa Free Press;* Proceedings, Camp Borden, 25–26 July 1916.

115. LAC, RG 24, Vol. 1256, File HQ 593–1-87, Lochead to OA, 1st Division, 6 March 1916. The magistrate told them that he would impose the suspended sentence ($100

fine and/or six months in prison) in the case of any future offence by Sergeant-Major Blood or Private E. Schaefer. See McKegney, *Kaiser's Bust,* 160. Lochead also assured civilians after the Concordia Raid that he would invoke strict measures to prevent a recurrence in the future and promised that offenders would be punished. His efforts failed on both counts.

116. Later in 1916, Colonel L.W. Shannon described the battalion as "just fair, its chief weakness being lack of strict enforcement of discipline which is accounted for by the fact that the officer commanding had no previous military training." Lochead was a "good character, keen on his work; knew nothing of it prior to this command; is not regarded as a good disciplinarian." Quoted in McKegney, *Kaiser's Bust,* 169.

117. LAC, RG 24, Vol. 1255, File HQ 593–1-86, pt. 1, Chief Cuddy to Messrs. Lent, Jones, Mackay & Mann, Barristers, etc., Calgary, Alberta, 8 May 1916.

118. LAC, RG 24, Vol. 1256, File HQ 593–1-91, Shannon to Secretary, Militia Council, 16 March 1916; *Ibid.,* File HQ 593–1-101, GOC, MD 5, to Secretary, Militia Council, 7 November 1916; *Ibid.,* File HQ 593–1-95, DOC, MD 10, to Adjutant-General, 24 March 1916; *Ibid.,* Vol. 1671, File 683–340–6, Colonel Edgar to Secretary, Militia Council, 1 December 1916.

119. *Edmonton Bulletin,* as quoted in Pye, "Disturbances," 2.

120. *Edmonton Bulletin,* 12 February 1916, quoted in *Hansard,* 17 February 1916, 929–30.

121. *Ibid.*

122. *Hansard,* 17 February 1916, 929–30.

123. LAC, RG 24, Vol. 1257, File 593–1-110, Major-General Eugene Fiset, DM, Militia and Defence, to George C. Boyce, Halifax, 1 October 1919.

124, Quoted in Pye, "Disturbances," 10.

125. LAC, RG 24, Vol. 1255, File HQ 593–1-86, pt. 1, Judge Advocate-General [henceforth JAG] to Assistant Adjutant-General, 10 April 1916; *Ibid.,* DM, Militia and Defence, to Messrs. Foster, Martin & Co., Montreal, re: White Lunch Limited — Calgary, 14 April 1916.

126. In garrison towns, the military handed over soldiers who were guilty of contravening civil law to the civil authorities for punishment. After the February riots in Calgary, 13 soldiers were tried in civilian court, with five being convicted and two being discharged from the military. These individuals were never forced to pay damages to the property owners.

127. LAC, RG 24, Vol. 1257, File 593–1-110, Allison to A.E. Kempt [*sic*], 13 March 1917.

128. The Department of Justice reported that "as the loss is an incident to the war it might very well be repaired out of the war vote, but whatever disposition be made of the matter I do not think it can affect cases like that of the Canadian Club at Waterloo in which a private concern is preferring a claim against the Government." LAC, RG 13, A-2, Vol. 208, File 1917–37, DM, Militia and Defence, to DM, Justice, 2 January 1917, and reply, 8 January 1917.

129. *Hansard,* 5 April 1916, 2548.

130. DND, *Leadership in the Canadian Forces,* 13.

131. English, "Political Leadership," 84.

132. Lewis, as quoted in Winslow, *Canadian Airborne Regiment,* 52, 65.

133. Winslow, "Misplaced Loyalties," 13–4.

134. Irwin, "Canadian Infantry Platoon Commanders," 23.

135. One could also apply this logic to the reverse scenario: when soldiers are being demobilized they are also in a liminal phase, and command and control is susceptible to collapse. See the Gardner and Coombs chapters in this volume, as well as Desmond Morton's superb "'Kicking and Complaining': Demobilization Riots in the Canadian Expeditionary Force, 1918–1919," *CHR,* Vol. 61, No. 3 (September 1980), 334–60.

136. Conduct values are "norms or standards of desirable behaviour that give direction to and set limits on individual and collective behaviour." In the military, these include civic, legal, ethical, and military values. See DND, *Leadership in the Canadian Forces,* 129.

137. Cited in Desmond Morton, "Aid to the Civil Power: The Canadian Militia in Support of Social Order, 1867–1914," *CHR,* Vol. 51, No. 4 (December 1970), 407.

138. LAC, RG 24, Vol. 1256, File 593-1-87, JAG to Director General Supplies and Transport, 6 September 1916.

139. Chadwick, *Battle for Berlin,* 77.

7 ࣷ

Polished Leathers and Gleaming Steel: Charges of Mutiny in the Canadian Army Service Corps at Bramshott Camp, England, November 1917

CRAIG LESLIE MANTLE

No doubt here all greatly depends on the leaders of those bodies making suitable dispositions; but any one of them may be led into an unavoidable catastrophe by injudicious orders imposed on him by the General-in-Chief.
— Carl von Clausewitz[1]

Few military practitioners would argue with the statement that clear and effective communication between individuals at all levels of a command structure can, and frequently does, influence mission success. Aside from ensuring that orders and information are both transmitted and received in a timely and accurate manner, an efficient communication system also allows for situations in the field to be quickly reported and, if necessary, acted upon. Although the basic means of battlefield communication have evolved over the millennia, its purpose has not, with the collection of intelligence and the control of forces, whether on the large- or small-scale, remaining some of its most important functions. So necessary is the transfer of information that the results can be disastrous, perhaps even catastrophic, when the flow is impeded or the network is compromised. Lucid communication from superior to subordinate and from subordinate to superior, or in other words, "good internal communications,"[2] is an absolute requirement in the day-to-day operations of a military force, whether during times of peace or times of war.

History repeatedly attests to the fact that orders that were poorly transmitted frequently encouraged both confusion and disorganization among the individuals for whom they were intended and, in many cases, caused significant and needless casualties. For instance, historians have described the infamous Charge of the Light Brigade at Balaclava in 1854 as a "legendary disaster,"[3] owing, partly, to poor communications. The imprecise orders sent from Lord Raglan, the British commander in the Crimea, to his cavalry commander, Lord Lucan, encouraged the latter to attack a superior Russian force in error, thus resulting in the loss of significant numbers of both men and horse. Instead of pursuing the fleeing Russian cavalry that had been considerably weakened through the exertions of the Heavy Brigade, the Light Brigade, after some delay, advanced against an emplacement that was well defended by the enemy's infantry, artillery, and cavalry. Owing to the topography of the land, Lucan could not see the Russians to which Raglan was referring, so he ordered an advance directly to his front against those he could see, with disastrous results.[4] Truly, "Someone had blunder'd."[5]

Even at sea, communications between individual ships were sometimes muddled. Early in the First World War, poor signalling at the battles of Dogger Bank and, more famously, Jutland, worked against the British forces, thus allowing their German counterparts to suffer less damage and fewer casualties than they might otherwise have received. The outcome of these engagements might have been different had the orders of Sir David Beatty, who was then in command of a squadron of battlecruisers, been clearer and transmitted with greater accuracy.[6] In ancient times no less, "communication between army (or navy) groups and between field commanders and the central command was very slow and easily interrupted,"[7] a condition that ultimately influenced the outcome of single battles and, more significant, of entire campaigns and even wars. Many additional examples could be cited to provide the same compelling evidence as to the importance of proper signals.

The absence of efficient communication leaves forces misinformed, misdirected, and often encourages a course of action that diverges from the commander's true and original intent. Effective control, then, relies heavily on the effective exchange of information. As one military historian has observed:

Good communications between a commander and a subordinate officer are vital, whether they take the form of a verbal message delivered by a staff officer, a letter, or signals by flag, telegraph or radio. The crucial requirement is that the recipient clearly understand [*sic*] the commander's intentions. There must be no room for misinterpretation.[8]

As will become evident, miscommunication explains many of the dynamics behind a mutiny that involved 18 members of the Canadian Army Service Corps (CASC) who were billeted at Bramshott Camp in Hampshire, England, during the First World War.[9]

Around noon on 5 November 1917, Major Percy Crannell McGillivray, the officer-in-charge of the CASC Depot at Bramshott, inspected the stables occupied by the horse transport (HT)[10] and found that slightly less than three-quarters of the harnesses used by this section were dirty and improperly maintained. He subsequently ordered the officer-in-charge of the HT, Lieutenant Edgar Donald Lougheed, to parade his men at 1800 hours that evening so that the leather straps and steel hardware of *all the* harnesses could be thoroughly cleaned. Although McGillivray "did not intend that the action I told [the lieutenant] to take was to be by way of punishment to the drivers of the horse transport generally,"[11] the neglected state of the equipment certainly made an impression upon him:

> If there had been a set of harness particularly clean I should have noticed it. I did not notice such a set. What I chiefly noticed was that the sweat was caked on the inside of the … collars, and that the shoulder pads were dirty. The parts of the harness which come next to the horses were dirty. Swivels and tugs were dirty. These defects were apparent more or less on each set of harness. I should think that most of the harness which I saw and considered dirty had recently come in from work. Had the harness been in proper condition a morning's work would not have put it into the state in which I saw it.[12]

In McGillivray's estimation, his orders were sufficiently clear and left little room for interpretation:

> If the harness of any particular man had been quite clean by the evening I think that, after [Lieutenant] Lougheed had called a parade and examined the harness, he should have dismissed any man whose harness was quite clean. According to the instructions I gave [Lieutenant] Lougheed he would have gathered that I expected *all the men to be called back to clean harness whether any particular man might or might not have cleaned his harness before evening.*[13]

Later that afternoon, around 1700 hours, Lougheed passed this order onto the Company Sergeant-Major (CSM), Charles William Chubb, who, prior to dismissing the men from their regular stables parade, at which no roll call had been taken, warned all present in a clear and distinct manner to return to the stables in roughly one hour to attend to their equipment yet again. Following the orders of the CSM, Sergeant Thomas Huby, one of three section sergeants belonging to the HT, called at one of the huts where the men lived and, at about 1755, warned the occupants about the upcoming stables parade; he also entered another hut and gave a similar caution. In directing the men to assemble outside, he addressed himself to everyone present, rather than to any one individual in particular. Upon hearing the warning, many of the soldiers stated that they were not disposed to go to the stables. Sergeant Huby and Sergeant William White, another section sergeant, later reported to CSM Chubb that no men were present at the stables at the appointed hour.

After receiving this disturbing news, the CSM immediately went to the stables to investigate the matter for himself. Finding no one there, except for Private John Boskett who had apparently obeyed the order, the CSM directed Sergeant White and Sergeant John Colin McArthur, the final section sergeant who had arrived at the stables a few minutes past 1800, to accompany him to the men's huts.

Upon arriving at the barracks, Chubb and McArthur asked the men in Hut 16, followed by those in Hut 15, if they were going to parade. In both, the men stated that they would not.[14] Sometime between 1800 and 1830, the CSM, now alone, related the situation to Lieutenant Lougheed who was by then supping in the officers' mess. Lougheed eventually informed the adjutant[15] that the men had refused to parade. Accompanied by CSM Chubb and Lieutenant Peters, the assistant officer-in-charge of the HT, Lieutenant Lougheed entered Hut 16 around 1830. The men were called to attention and the horse drivers were separated from the rest of the soldiers who happened to be present. Lougheed then asked them if they would parade and again they refused. He repeated his order but the men stood as they were. Outraged at their disobedience, he immediately ordered the CSM to find a non-commissioned officer (NCO) to place the men under arrest, and shortly thereafter, Sergeant McArthur took 10 men into custody. The two officers, along with the CSM, then entered Hut 15 whereupon all were called to attention and the drivers were separated from the rest. In like manner, Lougheed asked them if they were going to go to the stables and he was again met with a negative response. He repeated his order but, as in the other hut, none of the drivers moved, although Private Bert Young informed the lieutenant that "'we have decided not to go.'"[16] Soon thereafter, Lougheed ordered these men to be placed in the guardroom as well and Sergeant White eventually took all eight into custody. In both huts, *after* the drivers had been placed under arrest, Lieutenant Peters told them that their blatant and insolent refusal constituted an act of mutiny.[17]

Once the men had been confined, Brigadier-General Frank Stephen Meighen, the commander of all Canadian troops at Bramshott, convened a district court-martial to try the soldiers collectively. The proceedings began on the morning of 21 November and lasted for three days.[18] Seeing that all had refused at the same time to proceed to the stables as directed, military authorities charged each with joining in a mutiny for they ...

> on the 5th day of November 1917, when ordered by [Lieutenant] E.D. Lougheed, C.A.S.C. to go to the Stables to clean harness, joined in a Mutiny by combining among themselves to disobey the said Order and did not obey it.[19]

Each man was also charged with "disobeying a lawful command given by his superior officer" for all, when ordered "to go to [the] Stables to clean harness, did not do so."[20]

At the beginning of their court-martial, each of the drivers pleaded not guilty to the charge of mutiny read against him; however, on the suggestion of Lieutenant Charles Sydney Woodrow, the officer appointed to conduct their defence, all the soldiers admitted that they were guilty of disobedience. Later in the trial, after a number of the accused had offered their testimony and the prosecutor, Major Henry Granville Deedes, had finished presenting his evidence, Woodrow begged leave from the court to make abundantly clear

> that the pleas of guilty offered by the accused soldiers, individually, to the alternative charges against each of them [disobedience] were offered on his advice which was based merely on what he knew of the case from reading the summary of evidence.

This summary, it should be known, recorded the testimony of seven different witnesses for the prosecution and, when considered together, made the guilt of all concerned appear evident and indisputable.[21] Had he been "aware of the evidence which had already been given on oath before the court," presumably the more detailed testimony offered by various witnesses during the court-martial proper that alluded to the reasons behind the insolence of the drivers, "he would have advised each of the accused to plead not guilty to the alternative charge against him."[22]

In part, many of the most important aspects of this particular episode of mutiny can be successfully rationalized by examining how the varied expectations held by this group of soldiers (and indeed most within the Canadian Expeditionary Force [CEF] as a whole) conflicted directly with the attitude and conduct of their leaders. Some of the testimony offered by the accused, even that offered by a few of the witnesses for the prosecution, strongly suggests an understood "social contract" operated in the CEF during the First World War that ultimately influenced how some soldiers behaved towards their equals and their immediate superiors. Essentially, in return for their service, sacrifice and, if need be, their lives, soldiers expected their leaders to lead them competently, whether that meant by ensuring their welfare, by ensuring that casualties were not wasted on futile objectives or, more generally, by treating them with a degree of respect and concern. When such leadership was not forthcoming, men sometimes acted inappropriately — anything from malingering to mutiny — to express their dissatisfaction with the prevailing state of affairs.[23]

With this being said, however, the ability to satisfactorily explain the behaviour of *all* the participants through the concept of "reciprocity" is somewhat limited given the especial circumstances of this case. As will become apparent, many of the accused disobeyed the order issued by Lieutenant Lougheed (and transmitted through the CSM and their section sergeants) as a result of miscommunication and not because his directive circumvented one or more of their reasonable expectations. A simple misunderstanding, which was not entirely their fault, led them to erroneously conclude that the order did not apply to them when, in fact, it most certainly did. Given that the 18 individuals involved in this episode possessed a somewhat different perception of the situation with which they were faced, this discrepancy in both motivation and behaviour should come as no surprise.

For the most part, the reluctance of many of the accused to go to the stables at 1800 hours stemmed from their ignorance of the order itself and not from any base desire to disobey. Their confusion partially resulted from the fact that at least 13 (and possibly 14) of the 18 drivers missed the parade at 1700 hours, where the CSM had directed the men to return in roughly one hour's time. Incidentally, since no roll call was taken, Chubb could not later confirm who had been present when he issued his order. The drivers' absence from the stables can be accounted for by the fact that many were either grooming their team of horses or returning their harnesses to their place of storage; others, however, were arriving back from duties elsewhere just as the parade was being dismissed at 1700.[24] The individuals who were on parade consisted of about 30 men who were "not drivers but who were working in the lines on fatigue duty, etc."[25] Consequently, many of the accused had no knowledge of the parade that had been scheduled for later that evening.[26]

In attempting to conclusively prove the charge of mutiny, the prosecutor tried to demonstrate to the court that the men did in fact know about the parade and that their refusal to comply resulted from a broader conspiracy to disobey. In his final summation to the court immediately before sentence was passed, he claimed that the soldiers had spoken with one another about the parade during the intervening hour and therefore knew that they were expected to be at the stables later that evening. Despite these assertions, for which he could offer only scant and unpersuasive evidence, the vast majority of the accused testified that they did not discuss the matter with anyone else, nor did other soldiers speak to them on this point. Some individuals, such as Private Philo Stuart Dunn, claimed that his decision not to go to the stables was entirely his own and that he did not know that the other men were planning to remain behind as well.[27] The handful of men who were present when the initial order was given claimed that they did not discuss the matter with anyone else. Private Boskett, for instance, told the court that "After the order was given at 5 P M for the parade at 6 P M I had no conversation whatsoever with other men about the order."[28]

Only one man, Private Walter Ackling, testified that some individuals did in fact speak about the parade. He claimed that while he was dining between 1700 and 1730, he "heard talk about it at the supper table [but] I could not say for sure whether that talk at the supper table decided me not to go to stables at 6 P.M."[29] Although some may have indeed discussed the situation — Ackling did not indicate who had actually spoken about the order or what specifically was said — no soldier seems to have uttered any mutinous comments and thus the court was left without strong and compelling evidence of a pre-existing conspiracy. This testimony also suggested that no one had tried to persuade his peers to join in an act of disobedience. In all likelihood, since so few of the accused were present at the initial parade, the individuals who were overheard discussing the order were probably not drivers at all, but some of the 30-odd men who were working at the stables on this particular day, and who were not specifically affected by the directive. These individuals may have been discussing the order out of general interest in the course of general conversation.

For those drivers who were present at the parade at 1700 hours, the imprecision in the order to return later that evening led to considerable confusion. Having given his harness the usual cleaning on both Saturday and Sunday — men of the HT habitually cleaned the leather straps on the former and the steel hardware on the latter — Private Thomas Statton believed that his equipment was already in proper form, especially since he did not work his team on either Sunday or Monday. Because he thought that his harness was in an acceptable condition, he assumed that the directive was intended for those who had not cleaned their equipment at all.[30] Other soldiers reached similar conclusions and for similar reasons. Because those who were present on parade apparently decided for themselves whether the directive was intended for them or not, their testimony suggests that either the order itself, as issued by the CSM, was sufficiently vague as to encourage confusion, or that Lougheed, in transmitting his intentions to Chubb, did not properly express himself in a clear and articulate fashion.[31] From the perspective of some of the soldiers, therefore, their decision to remain in their billets did not constitute a blatant act of disobedience for they were unaware of what was actually expected of them.

Although the majority of men missed the initial instructions, provision had in fact been made through alternate means to inform those who were absent. Those in command attempted to ensure that the men's absence from the first parade neither excused nor justified their absence from the second. When questioned as to his actions in regard to this incident, Lieutenant Peters informed the court that "All Horse Transport men were warned on parade, and those who were not warned were supposed to be warned by the [Sergeant-Major] through the Section Sergeants."[32] From testimony given at the court-martial, however, the sergeants seem to have failed in their duty by not informing their men of the upcoming parade. Private Harry Hamilton Spence, for instance, testified that his section leader, Sergeant McArthur, did not warn him at any time during the intervening hour.[33] Possibly, then, the men's ignorance of the order (and their subsequent absence from the stables at 1800 hours) derived from the failure of their immediate superiors to transmit the directive to all concerned.

In all fairness, however, the responsibility of informing the drivers of the upcoming parade may have fallen exclusively to Sergeant Huby. He testified that during the intervening hour, he called on both Hut 15 and Hut 16 to warn those present of the requirement to return to the stables.[34] Although he spoke to the soldiers, his timing and the manner in which he expressed himself and communicated the order did not encourage understanding or, by extension, compliance. Many witnesses testified that he arrived at the huts at 1755, only minutes before the appointed hour of the parade.[35] By so doing, he left little time for the men to prepare themselves, to ask about the directive or to bring their concerns to the attention of their superiors if they so desired.

In addition, he seems to have employed an indirect manner of speech, for some of the men to whom he addressed his comments, especially those that were not of his section, believed that his remarks did not apply to them. To be sure, he addressed himself to all present and did not speak to specific individuals when he cautioned the drivers about the upcoming parade. According to some witnesses, he framed his directive more as a question rather than a precise order. In giving evidence in his own defence, Private Roderick Murchison testified:

> The first I heard of the parade at 6 P M was when [Sergeant] Huby came to the door of the hut and shouted 'is any of you fellows coming to stables' or some such words. He had nothing to do with me and I did not know what he referred to.[36]

Although he was defending his own actions, Private Edward Weller confirmed the questioning tone, the indirect nature and the brevity of Huby's comments, for he asserted that the sergeant simply asked, "… are you fellows going up to stables?"[37]

Whether the responsibility for transmitting the order given at 1700 fell exclusively to Sergeant Huby or to all the section sergeants, a serious failure in communication seems to have occurred. Because most of the drivers had missed the initial order, the lack of a forceful, direct, and clear warning only confused the matter further since many of them did not know to what parade their immediate superiors were referring. Even Lougheed admitted to the court that the spirit and intent of his directive was not communicated effectively to his subordinates:

> I understood that the parade at 6 P M was to be a parade of all the drivers of the horse transport section whether their harness had been clean or not at 12 Noon. At the 6 P M parade I would have inspected the harness and would have released men, probably after half an hour, whose harness was then clean. *This was not explained to the men so far as I know.*[3]

Their ignorance, in effect, contributed to their idleness. Unfortunately, many of the drivers first heard about the upcoming parade when Lieutenant Lougheed entered their billets to find out why they were absent, which was, in this particular case, much too late.

Another individual in a position of responsibility, CSM Chubb, also seems to have neglected his duty and perhaps his ethical obligations as well. His lack of action allowed one of the drivers, whom he apparently knew to be innocent, to be accused of both mutiny and disobedience. Private Boskett testified in his defence that, besides hearing the order for the parade at 1800 hours, he had, as usual, cleaned his harness on both days of the weekend and briefly on Monday. When he had finished his chores late on Monday afternoon, he retired to his hut where, a few moments later, Lieutenant Lougheed, accompanied by Lieutenant Peters and the sergeant-major, directed the drivers to clean their harnesses. According to his testimony, he had in fact obeyed the order since he was at the stables at the appropriate time and was seen by Chubb who, in the course of conversation, asked him if he was going to clean his harness.[39] He also noted for the court, "When [Lieutenant] Lougheed told us to go to clean harness I did not go because I knew that the [Sergeant]-Major had seen me in the harness room and I left it to him to say that I had finished cleaning my harness."[40] For whatever reason, Lougheed was not informed that Boskett had compiled with his directive. In this particular instance, the fact that he had cleaned his harness as ordered made little difference because he appeared disobedient by remaining in his billet with the rest of the drivers. Boskett seems to have been a victim of circumstance in that he returned to his hut immediately before the other men disobeyed the order and was eventually swept in with them all.[41]

As is certain, many of the men heard about the parade at 1800 hours for the first time when Lougheed entered their huts and asked if they were going to go to the stables or not. This fact, repeated by numerous witnesses throughout the entire court-martial, reinforces the assertion that the section sergeants did not warn the men over whom they had control or, if they did, they did so in a haphazard and imprecise manner. When addressing the men in their huts, Lougheed also framed his directive more as a simple and open-ended question rather than a precise instruction. Many of the soldiers did not view his remarks as an order because he supposedly used words and a tone that implied that the men could in fact choose whether or not they would participate in the parade. Although each witness repeated the order somewhat differently during his testimony, all agreed on its vague and ambiguous nature.[42] Private George Desjarlais, for instance, recalled Lougheed asking them, "'will you go down and clean harness?'"[43] Private Weller likewise remembered the order as, "'are you men going over to stables to clean harness?'"[44] The phrasing and tone of Lougheed's statement led the men to believe that they could in fact choose whether or not to go to the stables and many decided that they would not.[45] For many, the decision to remain idle in their hut was obvious seeing that most of them suffered from ill health and had just returned from yet another full day of difficult work.

The imprecise manner in which Lieutenant Lougheed interacted with his subordinates may have resulted from his minimal command experience and his total unfamiliarity with the CASC at Bramshott. Joining the CEF in early 1916 with only six months of previous military service in Canada, he eventually served in France with the 4th Divisional Train for approximately one year, from August 1916 to August 1917. Returning to England from overseas, he spent about three weeks in hospital at Shorncliffe before being transferred in early November 1917 to the CASC encamped at Bramshott. He arrived at his new billet and assumed his new responsibilities only one week before the mutiny occurred. Such a short period would not have allowed him to become accustomed to the manner in which the Depot conducted its daily business, or familiar with the men under his command, especially the NCOs upon whom he would have to rely for the execution of his orders.[46]

Additionally, those individuals who recognized Lougheed's comments as a direct order thought that his remarks did not apply to them.[47] Such a conclusion further suggests a degree of imprecision in his tone. As the vast majority of witnesses testified, when they returned to the stables from their various duties on Monday, most gave their harness the proper care and attention that it required. In fact, many drivers spent a number of hours cleaning their equipment before retiring to their billet. Private Murchison remarked in his defence, "On Monday I made two short trips in the morning and after dinner I made a trip to the Bramshott hospital. I got in from that a little after 2 P M. I then started to clean [my] harness and had it all

Canadian soldiers enjoy the YMCA's canteen at Bramshott Camp in Hampshire, England, sometime during the First World War. (Department of National Defence, Library and Archives Canada PA-5275)

cleaned by 5 P M."[48] Similarly, Private William Alfred Stephens testified that on the same day, "I had my team out from about 8 A M till 10 A M and from about 3 P M to 4 P M. I spent two hours on my harness in the morning and also an hour in the afternoon."[49] Believing that their equipment was properly cared for, these individuals, like many others, assumed that the order to return to the stables to clean their harnesses did not apply to them.[50] Such an impression could only have been arrived at if the order itself was poorly worded and of such a nature as to create confusion. Had the directive been more precise, so as to indicate its true intention, then this assumption would probably not have been made. Their previous efforts, coupled with a less-than effective order, led them to remain stationary when confronted by Lougheed in their billets later that evening.

Although many of the accused failed to obey the lieutenant's directive owing to their lack of understanding, other participants took full advantage of this opportunity to protest the amount of work that they had been required to perform of late and the poor treatment that they had received at the hands of some of their immediate superiors. For a few of the drivers, disobedience represented the surest and quickest method of making their grievances known, especially when those charged with their care appeared disinterested and unconcerned. Throughout the CEF, no other act seems to have focused the attention of those in positions of responsibility on the present state of affairs within their respective commands than the refusal of their subordinates to comply with a lawful order.

For instance, Private John Caldin, who suffered from heart disease and was feeling ill on the night of 5 November, testified, like many of his companions, that he first heard of the stables parade when Lougheed entered his billet. He immediately informed the lieutenant that he ...

> was not feeling well but I got no answer. I heard [Private] Weller make the same remark but he got [no] answer. The officer said that that did not matter. *I put it to myself that as I was not fit to go I could not go.* I thought that the officer would have told me to fall out and have me examined.[51]

Caldin believed that by being ill, he should have been exempted from the upcoming parade; at the very least, he contended, he should have received medical attention. Because his initial attempt to have his grievances redressed in the proper manner failed completely, he thus decided not to parade as ordered. Faced with a non-responsive leader, he disobeyed Lougheed's directive to draw attention to his situation and, to a lesser extent, the impersonal treatment that he had just received. Even the lieutenant testified to the court:

> *I did not take any steps to find out what was the matter with the men or whether there was any grievance.* I merely spoke to them in the manner I have previously stated. I did not tell them that they would be dismissed as soon as their harness was clean.[52]

Only when Lougheed failed to acknowledge his legitimate concerns did illegal conduct appear to Caldin as the only way he could get his grievances noticed and perhaps remedied. If his superior would not care for him, then he would ensure that his own well-being and health did not suffer needlessly. This general pattern, where an individual first attempts to seek adequate resolution through the chain of command and resorts to disobedience only when his complaint does not progress upwards, was repeated many times throughout the CEF.[53] To be certain, additional examples of this phenomenon add considerable weight to the contention that protest seemed to be an acceptable course of action to some who could not, for whatever reason, secure what they believed to be fair treatment and that disobedience was frequently engaged in only as a last resort when the appropriate channels for redress either failed or were closed altogether.

Like many of his comrades, Private Spence also missed the initial order given at 1700 hours and did not hear of the stables parade until the two officers and the sergeant-major came into his billet. He consequently related to the court:

> I did not look on [Lieutenant Lougheed's] remark as a direct order. I had also been doing two men's work which I consider to be a grievance. I had not tried to get the grievance redressed. On this account I decided not to go to stables when [Lieutenant] Lougheed spoke.[54]

In a similar manner, Private Ackling related in his own defence:

> I did not go to clean my harness when ordered by [Lieutenant] Lougheed because I felt I had a grievance, in having to do so seeing that during the previous week I had been coming in late from work daily. I had not come to the conclusion that the best way to have my grievance looked into was to disobey orders. I know the proper course to adopt in the army if I wish a grievance to be inquired into. I cannot say why I did not adopt that course on this occasion.[55]

Why Spence and Ackling failed to seek redress of their legitimate grievances through the proper means is unknown; however, a few possible explanations that account for their silence, and perhaps for that of the other soldiers involved in this affair as well, surface in the testimony offered by some witnesses. When Lougheed entered the men's billets and ordered them to go to the stables, few questioned his directive despite having what they considered to be ample justification to do so. The reluctance of some of the drivers to make their grievances immediately known or to ask about the purpose of the order itself partially resulted from the prevailing military culture that, above all, encouraged "prompt obedience [and] respect for authority."[56] When Lougheed asked if they were going to go to the stables or not, Private Desjarlais, for instance, "said nothing because I know that men are supposed not to speak on parade."[57]

Other soldiers believed strongly that if they had commented on the present situation, they would only have been met with an immediate rebuke from their superiors and that their complaints would have effected little real change. The previous conduct of certain individuals the soldiers frequently dealt with encouraged this belief and ultimately dampened their willingness to bring their concerns to the fore. During his examination by the court, Private Claude Norman Harris testified:

> When [Lieutenant] Lougheed asked if any one was going
> to clean harness I did not answer because I thought there
> was no good in doing so. If I had spoken the [Sergeant]-
> Major would only have told me to 'shut up.' ... I knew
> the [Sergeant]-Major would tell me to shut up because he
> always does so if he is asked anything.[58]

In a similar manner, Private Arthur Peacock observed, "On more than one occasion I had asked the [Sergeant]-Major to let me see the [Commanding Officer] in connection with my grievance. He told me to get on with my work and not to mind."[59] These and other soldiers obviously understood and were willing to use the appropriate channels to have their problems addressed, but when faced with barriers such as these and having few other options available to them, some decided to disobey since their disobedient behaviour would bring attention to their grievances. The unwillingness of both Lieutenant Lougheed and Sergeant-Major Chubb to listen to the legitimate concerns of their charges encouraged the drivers to adopt an aggressive and entirely illegal method of making their problems known; the reluctance of the soldiers' superiors to take note of their difficulties eventually forced the issue to a head.

Despite the conduct of certain leaders, at least one seems to have understood the men's predicament, and openly expressed his sympathy for them. Under oath, Sergeant Huby confirmed that the men under his immediate care had been required to perform a considerable quantity of work in recent days, too much in fact for one man to cope with on his own, especially one who was not entirely fit. He suggested that given their poor health and heavy workload, the order to return to the stables was perhaps both ill-timed and unwise. Although Huby may not have agreed with the conduct of his soldiers, he at least empathized with the difficult circumstances in which they had been placed. While giving evidence to the prosecutor before the beginning of the court-martial, he stated:

> I wish to add that I think if the men had had a fair show, they would have turned out willingly. By this I mean that the work they had done during Sunday night and early Monday morning was a bit stiff. I further wish to add that if these men had had a second driver, it would have made their work much easier. Through the middle of the week, the men have been coming in late at night and they have worked hard as well through the week. They have not had sufficient time to clean their harness.[60]

Appearing to have been based on both prior knowledge and previous experience, Huby's first comment offers insight into some of the expectations generally held by soldiers. In his remarks, he insinuates that if those in command had exercised more fairness, the drivers would have undoubtedly complied with orders that seemed, at the time, unnecessary and overly burdensome. Although his meaning of fair treatment is unknown, one can surmise with confidence that appropriate rest and a work schedule consistent with both their ability and their health may have been sufficient to prevent, or at least to rectify, some of their grievances. Conscientious superiors who attended to the legitimate concerns of their men and who communicated with them effectively might have had a similar result as well. Indeed, as previously demonstrated within the context of the entire CEF, ensuring the well-being of one's subordinates frequently translated into a greater respect for a leader and, by extension, a greater willingness to follow onerous or particularly difficult orders.[61] Huby's testimony also seems to indicate that before this incident, the men had performed their duty well, had worked extremely hard without noticeable complaint and only resorted to illegal conduct when the conditions to which they were exposed became too extreme and surpassed their ability to endure.

In his statement, which was both brief and succinct, Huby also alluded to one of the main reasons why the drivers disobeyed Lougheed's order to return to the stables in the evening. He observed that the absence of additional men to help with the many duties of the day forced the accused, the vast majority in poor health to begin with, to perform this burdensome work entirely on their own. While testifying for the prosecution, Lieutenant Peters indirectly confirmed that the men had been overworked and that, in effect, they had performed the same amount of work that would normally have been assigned to two men:

> If such is available it is usual to have a 2nd driver for a team [of two horses and a waggon] who would share with the [other] driver the work but not the responsibility which rests on the first driver. We have practically no 2nd drivers in England. We are very short of men.[62]

Faced with such a situation, the order to tend to their harnesses yet again, coupled with the belief that many were already clean and in proper form, led many men to decide that they would not parade as directed. Considering their exhausting schedule of late, many thought the work to be needless and unnecessary. Indeed, Private Samuel George Merritt told members of the court, "I had worked all night and was very tired and my harness was perfectly clean."[63] Another of the accused, Private Dunn, similarly noted, "I did not go at 6 P M because I had done about all that I could and was tired out."[64] Their testimony also reinforced the notion that Lougheed's order was imprecise and vague for they seem to have decided unilaterally if they would attend the parade or not.

Although the origin of this mutiny can be attributed primarily to a lack of clear and articulate communication between multiple individuals within the entire command structure, from Lieutenant Lougheed down to the section sergeants, many affronts to the soldiers's reasonable expectations of fair and reasonable treatment also served as a catalyst for action and encouraged certain individuals to overstep the bounds of discipline. Because all the soldiers desired their superiors to behave in a becoming and appropriate manner towards them, the failure of certain leaders to consider their legitimate grievances, that were brought forth in the accepted and encouraged manner, forced many to adopt an aggressive posture to be heard. Indeed, given the absence of other options for redress, an act of protest appeared to be the only method they had to bring their complaints to the notice of their superiors and perhaps gain some degree of rectification. Since they suffered from a want of fitness, their concerns naturally centred on the amount of work that they were required to undertake. Some of the drivers contended that their recent schedule was too intense and that they should not have to perform the duties of two men, especially given their ill health. When their initial attempts to resolve these difficulties failed, however, some of the soldiers tried to rectify these injustices by refusing to perform additional work. Since they desired to be treated with as much respect as military culture would allow, they perceived the dismissal of their concerns as a snub and took immediate action to show their displeasure with the entire situation. Had more attention and concern been paid to them, it is probable that the court-martial would never have occurred at all. In these respects, the notion of a "social contract," where soldiers expect a certain level of treatment in return for their service, seems more than evident.

Immediately before the court retired to decide the case, the prosecutor addressed the members with the express purpose of proving the men's guilt by summarizing much of the evidence that had been offered under oath, especially the particularly damaging testimony. His lengthy statement rested on two cardinal points, namely that the accused did in fact understand Lougheed's words to be an order and that they did conspire among themselves to disobey. Not surprisingly, his address attempted to destroy the claims made by many of the drivers that they knew nothing of the later parade until their superiors approached them; he also attempted to portray Lougheed in a positive and innocent light. Instead of offering irrefutable evidence that the men had spoken to one another about the order and, by extension, that they understood the meaning and spirit of the directive, the prosecutor simply asked the court to rely on its own good logic and common sense:

> Is it feasible or sensible to suppose that this order given at
> 5 pm, was not discussed between that time and 6 pm, or
> was not passed on by those men that knew of it to those
> that did not, particularly when some, if not all were
> smarting under the sense of grievance and overwork [?]
> Are we to think that [Private] Young stepped out and
> answered for the whole without having consulted them
> [?] The suggestion is ridiculous.[65]

Because he doubted that the drivers kept the order to themselves, especially since it required them to perform even more work,[66] he contended that Lougheed's directive "was talked about and freely discussed."[67]

Despite its purpose, however, the prosecutor's statement was exceedingly weak for many of his assertions were untrue and could easily be dismissed. Aside from failing to convincingly prove the charge of conspiracy, as shown above, he asserted that although the "accused men doubtless had grievances ... they made no attempt to have them redressed in the proper manner."[68] On that point he was wrong, for many had attempted to speak with their superiors but were rebuffed. He also believed that their absence "does not count for much" since they were warned minutes before the parade by their sergeants, and that "there had been ample time between 5 pm and 6 pm for the order to circulate among ... Horse Transport drivers," which was again debatable.[69] The prosecutor also claimed that although the harnesses may have been clean and the men may have been overworked, these facts had nothing to do with this particular case! Essentially, he desired to convince the court that all the "accused were ripe for mutiny and only waiting for a chance to give full play to their mutinous and insubordinate characters," yet the evidence he offered in support of this personal accusation was less-than convincing.[70] Being based primarily on assumption and speculation, his statement failed to persuade the members that the accused were guilty of mutiny and, ironically, may even have helped their case in the end. At one point in his address, for example, he confirmed Lougheed's lack of clarity for he related that the lieutenant "took it for granted that the men knew of the order," which to the court, might have indicated a failure to follow-up or to ensure that his directive had been effectively communicated to and understood by all concerned.[71]

On the other hand, Lieutenant Woodrow offered a more compelling argument since his summation reiterated and expanded upon many of the reasons offered by the drivers in defence of their illegal conduct. He laid out reasons why the amount of work required from the men of late was simply too much for them to do alone — caring for two horses and their related equipment and performing a host of other duties in and around the camp was a hefty burden indeed. He further suggested that no conspiracy to participate in a mutiny could have been engaged in as "arrest followed before the men had said a word to each other."[72] Relying somewhat on speculation as well, his most persuasive statements revolved around Lougheed's character and his handling of this incident. After claiming that the detainment of the horse drivers was premature and that the order was too vague to encourage compliance, Woodrow inquired why his brother officer did not ask why the men refused to go to the stables, why he did not warn them as to the nature of the offence that they were committing, namely mutiny, and why he did not issue an order to collectively march the drivers to the stables so that they could perform their assigned duties instead of immediately placing them under arrest and having them escorted to the guardroom.[73] Woodrow's summation proved effective, especially when the court paralleled his statements with some of those made by Lougheed himself. At one point in the trial, the lieutenant recalled, "It did not occur to me to offer a few words of remonstrance to the men before they were arrested."[74]

After weighing the evidence provided by the prosecution and the prisoners, the court rendered its verdict and found all 18 soldiers not guilty of mutiny, the first and most serious offence, but guilty of the second charge, that of disobeying a lawful command. As a consequence of their actions, all were sentenced to 42 days detention, a fairly lenient penalty considering the gravity of the indictment.[75] Later, when confirming the court's findings, Brigadier Meighen remitted 15 days detention for each man since all had already forfeited two weeks' pay while in military custody awaiting trial. Now facing a much-reduced sentence, each driver was incarcerated (most likely at Bramshott Camp) for roughly one month.[76]

The members of the court unfortunately did not record why they reached this particular verdict or why they awarded this particular sentence.

Yet, such a light penalty suggests that both they and the brigadier agreed in some respects with the reasoning and justification that the men offered in defence of their actions. In reaching their verdict, the members may have found fault in the conduct of certain participants, such as Lieutenant Lougheed, the section sergeants or the CSM. Their findings in some degree were undoubtedly influenced by the apparent abrogation of duty by some NCOs and, more important, by the lack of clear and concise orders which, in the end, encouraged the erroneous belief that certain directives did not apply to some drivers. Their leniency may also have stemmed from the fact that owing to their low medical categories, these soldiers were "not well fitted for the hard work of transport drivers at irregular hours." The hard work the court referred to — duties "connected with a pair of horses, two sets of harness, and a waggon" — resulted from the absence of second drivers at Bramshott, a situation that the men were forced to accept and adapt to as best they could.[77] The tribunal evidently believed that the lack of manpower, the poor health of the accused, and the endless work in and around the camp mitigated their actions to a certain extent, but did not exonerate them completely. The court seems to have understood that for these soldiers, additional demands above and beyond their regular daily routine taxed their capacity to endure and ultimately became a source of great frustration. For whatever reason, such a lenient sentence may have been given more for the sake of appearance rather than as a reprimand so as to avoid any suggestion that disobedience, whether justified or not, could go unpunished.

The fact that 10 of the 18 accused (or 55 percent of the total) had committed various offences before the mutiny does not appear to have influenced the sentence awarded to each of the prisoners. Those individuals charged with a prior breach of military law were convicted summarily outside of a formal trial.[78] Throughout the court-martial, no participant, whether for the defence or for the prosecution, alluded to any misconduct committed at an earlier date. Even serious offences such as disobedience and being absent from piquet duty failed to impress the court and carried little weight with the members. In recommending mercy, the officers overseeing the trial noted, "Their conduct sheets show that they may all be regarded as men of good character. In several cases the conduct sheets show no entry."[79] Indeed, the court seemed inclined to deal exclusively with the particulars of this episode, and as such, attached little importance to a soldier's previous conduct.[80]

In this particular case of mutiny, when confronted with numerous difficulties, some men attempted to bring their complaints to the attention of their superiors through the formal chain of command, as was encouraged, while others were much less inclined to do so and disobeyed to demonstrate their displeasure and frustration, an action that obviously ran counter to the expected modes of behaviour.

For the most part, the disobedient attitude adopted by many of the soldiers towards their superiors can be satisfactorily explained through their misunderstanding of the order itself. Their ignorance resulted primarily from the confusing manner in which the directive was initially transmitted at the stables parade and the later failure of other leaders, whoever they were, to ensure that the men had in fact completely understood what was expected of them. For other individuals, however, the unwillingness of some of their superiors to hear their reasonable complaints, regarding their

In July 1916, the Canadian Army Service Corps' 1st Divisional Train lines up for loading. A year later the mutineers in England would have been responsible for similar equipment. (Department of National Defence, Library and Archives Canada PA-224)

rigorous schedule of late and their poor health, encouraged them to engage in illegal conduct to focus attention on their legitimate concerns. Some pursued a disobedient course when their attempts to have their grievances addressed failed altogether and when no other option seemed to remain. To be sure, a combination of factors contributed to an unhealthy situation in which some of the participants felt compelled to disobey. In a sense, this mutiny was the result of a multitude of errors, where one mistake compounded and magnified another. The greatest mistake was a lack of clear and effective communication.

In many respects, this "mutiny" was not a mutiny in the truest and accepted sense of the term. These men did not combine among themselves to disobey a legal order, but remained idle out of ignorance. Being unsure of what was expected led to an erroneous conclusion that the order ultimately given by Major McGillivray and transmitted through others, such as the inexperienced and impatient Lieutenant Lougheed,[81] did not apply to some of them. In part, the sheer amount of movement among the drivers of the HT — each on his own schedule, which saw some going on duty as others were coming off — impeded the efficient communication of an essential order.

Perhaps if those involved in this incident had heeded the spirit of a directive written in mid-1916 concerning the manner in which men should be warned for upcoming parades, the accused might not have been forced into such a compromising and difficult situation, where some felt pressured to commit an illegal act to communicate their dissatisfaction with the present state of affairs:

> Recent cases have come to light where men have been charged with being absent from certain parades. In order to convict a man on such a charge, it must be proved that he was personally warned for such parade or parades. The mere calling out by non-commissioned officers that such and such a platoon will be for such and such a parade within the platoon billets, is not sufficient warning, as a number of the men may not be present at the moment and are therefore not warned within the military meaning. In order to convict a man of being absent, he must be warned

personally for parades and it would be well if two non-commissioned officers could do the warning, instead of one, in order to make sure of convicting offenders.[82]

NOTES

Editor's Note: The present chapter expands upon an earlier paper by the same title. See Craig Leslie Mantle, *Polished Leathers and Gleaming Steel: Charges of Mutiny in the Canadian Army Service Corps at Bramshott Camp, England, November 1917* (Kingston: Canadian Defence Academy [henceforth CDA] — Canadian Forces Leadership Institute [henceforth CFLI], March 2004, Unpublished Paper).

1. Carl von Clausewitz, Colonel J.J. Graham, trans., *On War* (London: Kegan Paul, Trench, Trübner & Co., Ltd., 1908), Volume 2, Book 6, Chapter 30, 397.

2. Canada, Department of National Defence, *Leadership in the Canadian Forces: Conceptual Foundations* (Kingston: CDA — CFLI, 2005), 50.

3. John Keegan and Richard Holmes, *Soldiers: A History of Men in Battle* (London: Hamish Hamilton Ltd., 1985), 93.

4. Geoffrey Regan, *Great Military Disasters: A Historical Survey of Military Incompetence* (New York: M. Evans & Co., Inc., 1987), 67–8.

5. From the poem, *The Charge of the Light Brigade,* by Alfred, Lord Tennyson.

6. Regan, *Great Military Disasters,* 68–70.

7. Barry S. Strauss and Josiah Ober, *The Anatomy of Error: Ancient Military Disasters and Their Lessons for Modern Strategists* (New York: St. Martin's Press, 1990), 6.

8. Regan, *Great Military Disasters,* 67.

9. Library and Archives Canada [henceforth LAC], Record Group [henceforth RG] 150, 8 File 649-C-2595, Microfilm T-8653, District Court-Martial [henceforth DCM] of Private Walter Ackling (718568), Private Arthur Francis Baker (292099), Private John Boskett (681661), Private William Cain (192458), Private John Caldin (65144), Private Cecil Henry Connors (195583), Private George Desjarlais (21461), Private Philo Stuart Dunn (733451), Private Claude Norman Harris (190201), Private Samuel George Merritt (681605), Private Roderick Murchison (437387), Private John Joseph Parks (488759), Private Arthur Peacock (292177), Private Harry Hamilton Spence (252561), Private Thomas Statton (808067), Private William Alfred Stephens

(696637), Private Edward Weller (406211) and Private Bert Young (474351). As a point of interest, all the individuals being tried initially enlisted in the infantry, but were later transferred to the CASC. Since most of the men suffered from ill health (see DCM, Recommendation to Mercy), it seems reasonable to suggest that many were transferred on medical grounds. Unlike other branches of the CEF, the combat arms, namely the infantry, artillery, and engineers, required soldiers to possess an exceedingly high level of fitness owing to the harsh conditions under which they lived and the physical duties that they were expected to perform. Those who were unable to meet these requirements were usually, though not always, transferred to units that allowed a lower standard of health, such as the CASC or various forestry battalions. The personnel files of some of the accused support the claim that medical grounds were the reason for their transfer from the infantry. Private William Cain, for instance, appears to have been transferred to the CASC on account of the wound that he received while serving at the front with the 13th Battalion. See LAC, RG 150, Acc. 1992–93/166, Box 1375, File 29, Personnel file for Private William Cain. With this being said, however, Private Arthur Peacock seems to have been sent to Bramshott on account of being under-age. See *Ibid.*, Box 7676, File 39, Personnel File for Private Arthur Peacock. Private George Desjarlais also seems to have been transferred on account of his health; he had received three wounds on three separate occasions while serving with the 8th Battalion at the front. See DCM, Defence of Private Desjarlais. Moreover, as adjudged by their regimental number, these individuals did not all come from the same infantry battalion, Military District, province, or even region in Canada, but from diverse areas scattered throughout the country. In all likelihood, they made each other's acquaintance during their time in the HT at Bramshott and not before. See Edward H. Wigney, *Serial Numbers of the CEF* (Nepean: Privately Published, 1996).

10. In November 1917, the HT of the CASC at Bramshott consisted of 38 waggons, each with a team of two horses and one driver; the 38 drivers were organized into three sections, each of which was commanded by a sergeant. See DCM, Testimony of Company Sergeant-Major [henceforth CSM] Chubb (First Witness for the Prosecution), and, DCM, Testimony of Sergeant Huby (Second Witness for the Prosecution). The CASC also included a mechanical transport (MT) section that relied upon motorized, rather than equine, vehicles.

11. DCM, Testimony of Major McGillivray (Witness Called by Court).

12. *Ibid.* In his testimony, Lougheed also offered comment on the state of the harnesses and by so doing confirmed their dirty condition. See DCM, Testimony of Lieutenant Lougheed (Fifth Witness for the Prosecution).

13. DCM, Testimony of Major McGillivray. Italics added by present author for effect.

14. The men who lived in Hut 15 included: Ackling, Boskett, Cain, Merritt, Murchison, Peacock, Spence, Statton, and Young; the remainder lived in Hut 16. The living quarters of one man, Baker, could not be determined with the documentation on hand.

15. The adjutant was probably Lieutenant Albert Chilton.

16. DCM, Testimony of Private Young. Also see, DCM, Summary of Evidence, 1, and, DCM, Testimony of CSM Chubb. While testifying in defence of his actions, Private Young explained to the court, "I said 'we have decided not to go' because I saw that no one had moved. I therefore thought that I was justified in saying it. I had not arranged with anyone to say this...." See, DCM, Testimony of Private Young. The inactivity of the drivers prompted Private Cain to remain stationary as well. He testified, "I did not move because I did not see anyone else move. I had not decided to disobey any order." See, DCM, Testimony of Private Cain.

17. For the most part, the more detailed testimony from the court-martial proper was used to compile the above narrative rather than the brief interviews that were conducted for the purposes of assembling the Summary of Evidence prior to the trial. As a point of note, some discrepancy exists as to the precise sequence of events after Lieutenant Lougheed entered Hut 15; the testimony offered at the court-martial does not indicate with absolute certainty in which order the drivers were called to attention, separated from the rest of the men who were present, questioned as to their intentions, et cetera. Even Lieutenant Lougheed himself could not recall his exact actions and words on 5 November. See, DCM, Testimony of Lieutenant Lougheed. Nevertheless, the fact remains that the men in both huts refused to go to the stables for the parade at 1800 hours. For the purposes of the above narrative, the testimony of multiple witnesses was compared in order to determine *the most likely* sequence of events. The official history of the Royal Canadian Army Service Corps, which includes a long section on the First World War, makes no mention of this mutiny, as might be expected. See, Arnold Warren, *Wait For The Waggon: The Story of the Royal Canadian Army Service Corps* (Canada: McClelland and Stewart, 1961).

18. Colonel H.L.B. Acton served as president of the court-martial while the members included Major Charles Burton Hornby, Major James Michael Gillies, Captain Edward Cassils Evans, and Captain William George Ross Gordon. Lieutenant Alexander George Aneurin Clowes acted as the Waiting Member.

19. DCM, Charge Sheet. All the soldiers were charged under Section 7(3) of the Army Act. See Great Britain, War Office, *Manual of Military Law* [henceforth *MML*] (London: His Majesty's Stationery Office, 1914), 384.

20. DCM, Charge Sheet. All the participants were also charged under Section 9(2). See *MML,* 387. The Summary of Evidence found in the proceedings of the DCM lists 25 other ranks who were to be tried for mutiny and disobedience. The names of seven individuals were later crossed off this document and these men were not tried. According to the online database maintained by LAC that indexes all Canadian courts-martial prosecuted during the First World War, which is available at *www.collectionscanada.ca/archivianet/courts-martial/index-e.html,* none of these seven individuals were brought to formal trial on any charge during or immediately after the war.

Four of these soldiers were confined in the guardroom on the night of 5 November 1917; three others joined them early the following morning. Apparently, when drafting the charges and other preliminary documents for the DCM, there was some confusion as to who had participated in the mutiny and who had not. With this being said, however, five of these men — Stark, Wilson, Doan, Baines, and Tanner — were sentenced to a brief term of Field Punishment No. 2 for disobedience because they, on 5 November 1917, did not attend the stables when ordered to do so by their superior officer. See LAC, RG 150, Vol. 234, 16 November 1917. No information could be located that would explain why the remaining two soldiers were not similarly punished. Why these seven men were not charged with mutiny is unknown, although their absence from the huts when Lieutenant Lougheed ordered the drivers to call at the stables probably accounts for this lesser sentence. Might they have been some of the 30-odd men who at the parade at 1700 hours heard the order to return to the stables and to which the order actually applied? Certain details regarding these soldiers are listed below: William Thomas George Baines (276555); Thomas Brennan (781523); Kenneth William Doan (2004331); Frederick Hewitt Hales (811043); James Stark (907081); Roy James Tanner (5136); and Thomas Albert Wilson (681621). Moreover, in the transcript of the court-martial, no mention is made of the other 13 drivers who also belonged to the HT section. Presumably, the order to return to the stables later in the evening applied to all 38 drivers equally. Why these men did not attend the parade at 1800 hours remains a mystery; it is possible, however, that they may have been on duty at this time. As will be recalled, the CSM found no one at the stables when he arrived to investigate the absence of the drivers who had been warned for the parade.

21. DCM, notation situated between the Defence of Private Connors and the Defence of Private Desjarlais. The Summary of Evidence recorded at Bramshott Camp on 5, 6, and 12 November 1917 by Major Henry Granville Deedes of the 25th Reserve Battalion included the testimony of Lieutenant Lougheed, Lieutenant Peters, CSM Chubb, Sergeant White, Sergeant McArthur, Sergeant Huby, and finally, Private John George Fraser, who was in charge of the guardroom that held the accused after their arrest. At these proceedings, the drivers asked numerous questions of the witnesses; understandably, most of their inquiries were of a self-centred nature, that is, they desired to have placed on record whether or not they were at the parade at 1700 hours when the order to return later that evening was given. Aside from asking the witnesses to relate whether or not their harness in particular was dirty, some of the accused also questioned the logic of the order itself. The culture of obedience that permeated the CEF, in which the soldier was expected to follow without question, can be easily observed in these brief exchanges that are recorded in DCM, Summary of Evidence, 5–6. All the responses made by Lieutenant Lougheed to the inquiries that probed the reason behind the order were remarkably similar and illustrated how he viewed the relationship between leader and follower. From his perspective, since an order had been given, the men were expected to obey it, regardless of whether or not it made sense. By reading the entire sequence of questions and answers, as provided in the DCM, one can easily imagine that Lougheed not only became frustrated with the

repetitive questions that were being asked of him, but also adopted a fairly hostile tone towards his inquisitors. A brief excerpt from these exchanges is illustrative:

> Question: "'If a man works on his harness all morning what is the reason that he has to go back at 6:00 p.m. to clean it again?'"
> Answer: "'It was Major McGillivray's orders yesterday....'"
> Q: "'If a man cleans a set of harness in the afternoon is [there] any reason why he should go back at night?'"
> A: "'The order was given to go back by the OC [Officer Commanding].'"
> Q: "'If a harness is cleaned and passed [by] inspection on the Sunday morning and is not used and cleaned again on Monday afternoon, is it necessary to go back at 6:00 p.m. to clean it again?'"
> A: "'The order was given to go back by the O.C.'"

22. DCM, notation situated between the Defence of Private Connors and the Defence of Private Desjarlais. This statement suggests that Woodrow did not spend much time either interviewing the soldiers before their trial or preparing an effective and comprehensive defence; his retraction could not have instilled the accused with much confidence. A lawyer by trade, which is a surprising fact given his conduct during the opening stages of the trial, and a member of the 27th Regiment, Canadian Militia, Woodrow enlisted in the 149th Battalion in early 1917 after serving for 13 years with various regiments of the British Army. He was later promoted to captain.

23. A more detailed examination of the phenomenon of disobedience within the CEF during the First World War, based on an analysis of the needs, wants, expectations and desires of Canadian soldiers, can be found in Craig Leslie Mantle, "The 'Moral Economy' as a Theoretical Model to Explain Acts of Protest in the Canadian Expeditionary Force, 1914–1919" (Kingston: CDA–CFLI, March 2004, Unpublished Paper). Developed by British historian Edward Palmer Thompson, the "Moral Economy" explores the cause-and-effect relationship between financial exploitation in the local marketplace and the behaviour of the British poor during the eighteenth century. Within the confines of the paper cited above, many of the most salient aspects of this theory were extrapolated to the early twentieth century to explain the disobedient behaviour of some Canadian soldiers. In essence, this discussion contends that the frequency (and in some cases the violence) of dissent within the CEF increased when individuals in positions of responsibility, regardless of rank, failed to meet the varied and reasonable expectations of their charges or did not respect the ingrained and cherished values of their subordinates. In sum, a leader could encourage an act of protest by neglecting to provide the necessities of life, by treating his soldiers in an abusive and disrespectful manner, or by failing to lead them competently, either on or off of the battlefield. Historian Bill McAndrew has reached many of the same conclusions regarding the expectations held by Canadian soldiers during the First World War. See Bill McAndrew, "Canadian Officership: An Overview" in Bernd Horn and Stephen J. Harris, eds., *Generalship and the Art of the*

Admiral: Perspectives of Senior Canadian Military Leadership (St. Catharines: Vanwell, 2001), 41.

24. The following four men were present at the parade at 1700 hours: Baker, Boskett, Dunn, and Statton. The remainder of the men involved in this incident were absent from the parade for various reasons. The whereabouts of one driver, Connors, could not be determined with the documentation on hand.

25. Testimony of CSM Chubb. In his testimony, Lieutenant Lougheed also confirmed the composition of the parade. See DCM, Testimony of Lieutenant Lougheed.

26. The testimony of the accused, in which they related if they were present at the parade or not, was relied upon exclusively to determine their whereabouts at 1700 hours on 5 November 1917 since no other documents included in the court-martial proceedings could provide this information. Without corroborating documentation, their word had to be taken as correct. As an aside, many of the witnesses for the prosecution testified that a number of teams had not yet returned from duty at the time that the order was given and therefore they could not place the accused at the parade at 1700 hours.

27. DCM, Defence of Private Dunn.

28. DCM, Defence of Private Boskett. Private Statton offered similar remarks to the court and reinforced the notion that the men did not communicate with one another regarding Lougheed's directive. He stated: "I did not discuss the matter with anyone after I heard at stables the warning for the 6 P M parade. I did not hear any remarks made about the order." See DCM, Defence of Private Statton. Possibly, some of the accused may have testified that they did not discuss the order with anyone else during the intervening hour in an attempt to cast doubt on their guilt. This assertion seems unlikely since the majority of the soldiers testified that they did not speak on this matter; the consensus among the accused on this point could not have, in all probability, been arrived at through coincidence.

29. He also related, "I disobeyed the order of [Lieutenant] Lougheed entirely on my own and without any previous agreement with other men." DCM, Defence of Private Ackling.

30. Even though he heard the warning for the stables parade, he related to the court, "I did not think the order applied to me because my harness was perfectly clean." DCM, Defence of Private Statton.

31. Both Lieutenant Lougheed and Lieutenant Peters were present on parade when the CSM ordered the men to return to the stables at 1800 hours.

32. DCM, Summary of Evidence, 8–9.

33. DCM, Defence of Private Spence.

34. DCM, Testimony of Sergeant Huby.

35. See, for instance, DCM, Defence of Private Parks. Huby also confirmed the time of his arrival. See DCM, Summary of Evidence, 9.

36. DCM, Defence of Private Murchison. Huby admitted to the court, "I was sent by [Sergeant]-Major Chubb to warn all the drivers who were in the three huts [of the parade at 1800 hours], and not only the drivers in my section. I entered each hut. I did not address any man individually. I gave a general order in each hut. I then left at once and had no conversation with any man." DCM, Testimony of Sergeant Huby.

37. DCM, Defence of Private Weller.

38. DCM, Testimony of Lieutenant Lougheed. Italics added by the present author for effect.

39. DCM, Summary of Evidence, 1, and, DCM, Defence of Private Boskett.

40. DCM, Defence of Private Boskett.

41. The prosecutor alluded to a similar fact in his final summation before the court: "[Private] Boskett unfortunately would seem to have returned to his hut and allowed himself to be swayed by stronger wills than his own." DCM, Address by the Prosecutor.

42. While testifying for the prosecution, Lougheed recalled that in hut 15, "I caused the drivers to be fallen in and told them that an order had been given to clean harness and asked them if they were going." Later, while the court examined him, he related, "I considered that I was giving an order to go to the stables to clean harness." See DCM, Testimony of Lieutenant Lougheed.

43. DCM, Defence of Private Desjarlais.

44. DCM, Defence of Private Weller. Private Caldin echoed the testimony offered by his two companions for he recalled the order to be: "'Are you fellows going to the stables?'" DCM, Defence of Private Caldin.

45. See for instance, DCM, Testimony of Private Merritt; DCM, Testimony of Private Harris; DCM, Testimony of Private Cain; DCM, Testimony of Private Dunn; and, DCM, Testimony of Private Parks. In speaking of Lougheed, one soldier recalled, "He gave no distinct order for the men to turn out. He gave no distinct order until he told the men to fall in for the guard room." See DCM, Testimony of Private Connors.

46. LAC, RG 150, Acc. 1992/93–166, Box 5749, File 21, Personnel file for Lieutenant Edgar Donald Lougheed. See also, LAC, RG 9, Vol. 5024, III-D-3, File 811, War Diary, CASC, Bramshott, 29 October 1917. See also, LAC, RG 9, Vol. 5023, III-D-3, File 810, War Diary, CASC, Base Reserve Depot, Shorncliffe, 2 November 1917. As a point of interest, E.D. Lougheed's father, the Honourable (and later Sir) James Alexander Lougheed, was a very prominent Canadian of the late nineteenth and early twentieth centuries. See David J. Hall and Donald B. Smith, "Lougheed, Sir James Alexander" in *Dictionary of Canadian Biography*, Vol. 15 (Toronto: University of Toronto Press), available online at *www.biographi.ca/EN*.

47. See, for instance, DCM, Testimony of Private Murchison; DCM, Testimony of Private Statton; and, DCM, Testimony of Private Desjarlais. One driver related to the court, "I did not go to the stables because my harness was clean and I did not think that the order applied to such men as had cleaned their harness." See DCM, Testimony of Private Stephens.

48. DCM, Defence of Private Murchison.

49. DCM, Defence of Private Stephens.

50. In this regard, one must consider the fact that the order to "clean harness" was given by Major McGillivray around noon and was based upon the condition of some of the equipment at that time; not all the harnesses were examined since many of the drivers were on duty and were therefore absent from the stables. From the available evidence, it does not appear that McGillivray re-inspected the harnesses after he had directed Lougheed to assemble the men in the evening. Moreover, many of the drivers cleaned their equipment in the afternoon of 5 November, as they routinely did each day when they returned from duty. This combination of circumstances, in which the order had in effect been complied with before the appointed hour of the parade, led some of the men to believe, not unreasonably, that because their equipment was in proper form, the order to return to the stables did not apply to them. The failure of Lieutenant Lougheed (and others) to ensure that the drivers had in fact understood his directive only complicated matters further.

51. DCM, Defence of Private Caldin. Italics added by the present author for effect. In his defence, Weller related to the court that after Lougheed had placed the drivers under arrest, he "stepped out one pace so that the officer might see me and said 'Sir I cannot go up to stables tonight as I cannot stand going up to stables.' [Lieutenant] Lougheed said something which I did not catch but I heard him say that 'that does not matter' and then he walked out of the hut." DCM, Defence of Private Weller.

52. DCM, Testimony of Lieutenant Lougheed. As a point of note, Lieutenant Peters acted in a similar manner to Lougheed for he testified, "I did not make any attempt to find out what was keeping the men from going to [the] stables, though the occurrence was unusual." DCM, Testimony of Lieutenant Peters (Sixth Witness for the

Prosecution). Some evidence also exists that Peters used inappropriate language when the drivers refused to follow the order given by Lougheed. See DCM, Summary of Evidence, 7 and 8. When giving evidence in his own defence, Private Dunn recalled that Peters said, "'come God damn it go up to stables.'" DCM, Testimony of Private Dunn. Italics added by present author for effect.

53. For example, see Craig Leslie Mantle, "For Bully and Biscuits: Charges of Mutiny in the 43rd Battalion, Canadian Expeditionary Force, November and December 1917" (Kingston: CDA–CFLI, March 2004, Unpublished Paper).

54. DCM, Defence of Private Spence.

55. He also told the court, "I thought that my harness was in a good enough state and I was not feeling 'at the best.'" DCM, Defence of Private Ackling.

56. Canada, Department of Militia and Defence, *Infantry Training for Use of Canadian Militia* (Ottawa: 1915), 4.

57. DCM, Defence of Private Desjarlais.

58. DCM, Defence of Private Harris.

59. Peacock described his complaint during his testimony. He stated: "I had a grievance viz that I was doing the work of two men, viz 1st and 2nd driver." DCM, Defence of Private Peacock.

60. DCM, Summary of Evidence, 9–10.

61. Mantle, "Moral Economy," 46–51.

62. DCM, Testimony of Lieutenant Peters. See also DCM, Testimony of CSM Chubb, and, DCM, Summary of Evidence, 6.

63. DCM, Defence of Private Merritt.

64. DCM, Defence of Private Dunn. Private Ackling reached a similar conclusion: "I thought that my harness was in a good enough state and I was not feeling 'at the best.'" See DCM, Defence of Private Ackling.

65. DCM, Address by the Prosecutor, 2.

66. He opined, "Would 18 men … keep their thoughts to themselves after receiving this order which meant extra work to them after a hard day, common sense says 'No.'" DCM, Address by the Prosecutor, 2.

67. *Ibid.*, 2.

68. *Ibid.*, 3.

69. *Ibid.*, 1.

70. *Ibid.*, 3.

71. *Ibid.*, 1.

72. DCM, "Note of Points in Address of Lieutenant C.S. Woodrow on behalf of Accused Soldiers," 1. This document lists only the main points of Woodrow's statement and does not reproduce the exact text verbatim. Woodrow stated that the men had recently worked many more hours than the usual six or so that they were required to perform at duty each day, that is, out of stables on the road transporting goods or men from one location to another. Compounded upon these hours was the time spent watering, feeding and caring for their horses, in addition to preparing their harnesses for the next day of work. Regarding the daily duties of HT drivers, see DCM, Testimony of CSM Chubb. For information concerning the average number of hours that drivers routinely spent at work each day, see DCM, Testimony of Major McGillivray.

73. DCM, Note of Points in Address, 2.

74. DCM, Testimony of Lieutenant Lougheed on being recalled by the court.

75. DCM, Findings, and, DCM, Sentences. Without analyzing the particulars of multiple examples of mutiny within the CEF, any statement regarding the severity of a specific penalty is admittedly questionable and somewhat unsupported. Yet, a brief review of the findings of all Canadian courts-martial prosecuted for mutiny both during and immediately after the First World War reveals that one month of detention was, by comparison, a relatively light penalty. The sentences awarded to other soldiers found guilty at their trials either of disobedience or, more rarely, of mutiny, ranged in length from a few days or months of field punishment to many years of incarceration; some were even condemned to death but later had their sentences commuted to penal servitude for life. See Julian Putkowski, *British Army Mutineers, 1914–1922* (London: Francis Boutle, 1998), 90–2. Unfortunately, Putkowski makes no distinction in his index as to what specific charge(s) the participants were actually found guilty of. As historians have observed within the context of the British Army, the punishments awarded for mutinies that occurred in England were consistently and considerably less severe than those awarded for similar episodes in France, a circumstance that undoubtedly resulted from the absence of the enemy. See *Ibid.*, 12. A similar phenomenon with respect to the relationship between the severity of sentences awarded by Canadian courts-martial and the location of the mutiny seems to have existed in the CEF as well. See Mantle, "For Bully and Biscuits," 16–9.

76. DCM, Recommendation to Mercy. A brief review of the personnel files belonging to two of the convicted drivers revealed that they (and probably the other participants) were not removed from Bramshott and incarcerated elsewhere. See LAC, Personnel file of Private William Cain, and, LAC, Personnel file of Private Arthur Peacock.

77. DCM, Recommendation to Mercy.

78. The courts-martial database maintained by the LAC also reveals that none of the 18 accused soldiers were brought to trial on any offence, except for the charge of mutiny with which this analysis is concerned. The name of each soldier who was previously convicted of a breach of military discipline, along with the specific charge and the number of times that they were so charged with the said offence (on separate occasions if more than once), is listed below: Ackling: Disobeying Orders (1); Leaving Post while a Piquet (1); Absent from Parade (2); Baker: Absent without Leave (1); Boskett: Disobeying Standing Orders (1); Cain: Absent without Leave (1); Caldin: Absent without Leave (3); Conduct to the Prejudice of Good Order (1); Committing a Nuisance (1); Desjarlais: Absent without Leave (1); Disobeying Orders (1); Dunn: Absent from Piquet (1); Peacock: Conduct to the Prejudice of Good Order (1); Parks: Absent without Leave (1); Weller: Unknown (1). This summary was compiled using the *Statement as to Character and Particulars of Service of Accused,* a document included in the court-martial proceedings for each individual.

79. DCM, Recommendation to Mercy.

80. Apparently, the members who sat on other CEF courts-martial that were convened for the purpose of trying charges of mutiny also attached little importance to the previous conduct of the accused and do not appear to have allowed the prior conduct of the soldiers who stood before them to greatly influence their decision. For an additional example of such a reality, see Mantle, "For Bully and Biscuits," 16–21.

81. Still remaining with the CASC, Lougheed was later transferred from Bramshott to London in October 1918. See LAC, Personnel file for Lieutenant Edgar Donald Lougheed. As a point of note, Major Hugh Joseph Bacon Freeman immediately replaced McGillivray who was sent to the CASC Base Depot at Shorncliffe. See LAC, RG 150, Vol. 234, Order 279, 22 November 1917, and, *Ibid.,* Order 283, 27 November 1917.

82. LAC, RG 9, III-C-3, Vol. 4121, Folder 2, File 6, 5th Canadian Brigade Staff Captain to 26th Battalion, 29 May 1916.

8

Military Discipline, Punishment, and Leadership in the First World War: The Case of the 2nd Canadian Division

DAVID CAMPBELL

Discipline exists for the safety and protection of the men. All orders are for their own good, and for the good of their comrades. Discipline must be kept at a certain level — like water. Relaxation in any part will lower the whole level, as in water. It may seem hard that a man should be punished for sleeping with his boots on; but guilty of one offense is guilty of all. I have never been late for breakfast, because I am afraid of what one failure would lead to. Discipline is a thing to lean upon, for officers as much as for men.
— Captain Andrew Macphail, Canadian Army Medical Corps.[1]

Issues of military discipline and punishment during the First World War have received considerable popular and scholarly attention within the past decade. In British and Canadian historiography, the focus usually is upon the use of capital punishment as a disciplinary tool. However, cases in which a death sentence was awarded make up a comparatively small percentage of the total number of disciplinary infractions that were committed in the British armies over the course of the war. Those cases actually resulting in executions were an even smaller fraction of that total and thus provide atypical examples of the state of discipline among the troops and of the operation of military justice.[2] Rather than revisit the debate surrounding the justification for employing capital punishment, this chapter charts a wider course by examining the incidence and implications of offences and punishments that were not of a capital nature within the infantry units of a case study formation, the 2nd Canadian Division. The purpose of this study is to gain a clearer understanding of the state of discipline within the division and to show how it was influenced by the quality of leadership exhibited by officers. It will be argued that lapses in military discipline stemmed principally from weaknesses in leadership.

In the Canadian Expeditionary Force (CEF), a division was a formation containing roughly 20,000 officers and other ranks (OR) organized into infantry, artillery, machine gun, engineering, communications, supply, and medical units. Most of the division's personnel were concentrated within 12 infantry battalions that were organized into three brigades of four battalions each. Collectively, the three infantry brigades contained approximately 12,000 officers and ORs. The 2nd Canadian Division was one of four such formations that constituted the bulk of the Canadian Corps, which was the principal fighting arm of the CEF operating within the British Army's order of battle on Europe's Western Front.[3]

Apart from the studies focusing upon capital punishment or mutiny, the broader topic of discipline within the CEF in general and the Canadian Corps in particular has been largely unexplored, except in overview or anecdotal fashion.[4] A major reason for this lies in the scarcity of comprehensive statistical summaries and reports within the Canadian archival record outlining the typology and incidence of offences committed by CEF personnel. This problem is not unique to Canada. Although the British armies on the Western Front collected and assembled detailed reports outlining "the classification and distribution of offenses by corps, division, brigade, regiment and battalion," much of this invaluable documentation "is not readily locatable." Thus far, only scattered fragments have been unearthed for scholarly scrutiny.[5]

To date, historian Jean-Pierre Gagnon has provided the only in-depth statistical analysis of the state of discipline among a group of Canadian soldiers during the First World War. His study focused on a single infantry unit, the 22nd (French Canadian) Battalion, which was part of the 2nd Canadian Division.[6] Although the evidence assembled by Gagnon suggests that the incidence of disciplinary infractions was relatively high in the battalion, this cannot be confirmed without comparative statistics from other units. By utilizing data drawn from a variety of official sources,[7] this chapter, in addition to its primary purpose of assessing the quality of discipline and leadership in the 2nd Canadian Division, also seeks to provide a more substantial comparative context for Gagnon's findings. It does so by charting the frequency of minor offences committed in five other battalions of the division, as well as the incidence of courts-martial in all 12 battalions.

It should be noted that for the purposes of this study, minor offences were those that drew summary punishment from company and battalion commanders. Offences deemed more serious in nature, and thus deserving of harsher punishments than unit commanders were authorized to dispense, were tried by court-martial. Officers could determine the seriousness of an offence by assessing its scale, as well as the accused's previous record. For example, a soldier accused of absence without permission for a short period (such as a few hours) usually received a summary punishment from his company or battalion commander, especially if it was his first offence. However, if a soldier was absent for a much longer period or was a habitual offender, then he could face trial by court-martial.

It must also be recognized that the following findings on the incidence of offences and punishments cannot represent the "entire story" of discipline in the 2nd Canadian Division because a great deal of activity never found its way into official records. An untold number of infractions went unrecorded simply because they did not come to light. Some perpetrators got away with their offences or were witnessed by persons in authority who chose, for whatever reason, to look the other way. At the same time, there also existed a realm of informal punishment, or "rough justice," which might be visited upon disobedient soldiers by the fists of a tough non-commissioned officer (NCO), sometimes with the full knowledge and approval of a senior officer.[8] In addition, because many officers worked under the assumption that "being 'up on a charge' was *prima facie* evidence" of a man's guilt, the number of wrongful convictions and punishments is impossible to determine. The aim of military law, after all, was to maintain discipline for the good of the unit, not to uphold civilian notions of individual justice.[9] Yet, even though the evidence presented here cannot reflect the unknown and informal aspects of disciplinary culture, it is sufficiently extensive to be representative of the overall disciplinary climate within the infantry of the 2nd Canadian Division.

CONTEMPORARY VIEWS ON THE NATURE OF MILITARY
DISCIPLINE AND LEADERSHIP

In its military sense, discipline is a product of internal factors that rely on the cultivation, maintenance, and enhancement of positive states of morale and motivation that impel soldiers, both individually and collectively, towards achieving common goals. Discipline is also the product of external authoritarian factors that seek to impose a system of behaviour that is intended to harness the energies of individual soldiers and weld them into an effective collective force that will successfully execute the orders of its commanders. Desired behaviours ideally are inculcated through training and the positive example of leaders. But, if necessary, they can be imparted through the enforcement of a system of punishment. The threat or operation of punishment thus serves to compel soldiers to conform to the will and the goals of military authorities. However, punishment must only be resorted to when absolutely necessary because its overuse or abuse "can create resistance and outrage that may destroy support and corrode morale,"[10] with disastrous consequences for the maintenance of discipline.

In a lecture delivered at the Canadian Corps Officers' School on 21 July 1916, Brigadier-General P. de B. Radcliffe, the corps' chief of staff, argued that discipline in a volunteer citizen army should be "born of mutual confidence between Officers and men, fostered and increased by public opinion, and the determination of every man to uphold the good name of his regiment and his country and to vie with all others in beating the enemy." According to Radcliffe, "Loyalty, Good comradeship and Esprit de Corps" were other important factors that influenced the quality of discipline. Yet, he was quick to remind his audience that, although it was considered to be a "last resort," punishment still had "to be resorted to [in order] to enforce discipline."[11] Other senior officers shared this view of punishment. In May 1917, the commander of the New Zealand Division, Major-General A.H. Russell, maintained that officers could instill good discipline in their troops, "both by example and by looking after the men's comfort and food, by insisting on the men taking sufficient rest, by devising means of entertainment and amusement and by looking after their men at all times ... Punishment, though necessary," continued Russell, "must not be looked on as a means of prevention. The last resort, it is, after all, a confession of failure on our part to instil the right spirit...."[12]

For contemporary officers, the inspirational and motivational aspects of leadership were vital to the maintenance of good discipline in any unit or formation.[13] These aspects are still enshrined in current Canadian Forces doctrine, which defines effective leadership as, "directing, motivating, and enabling others to accomplish the mission professionally and ethically, while developing or improving capabilities that contribute to mission success."[14] Thus, when considering the relationship of discipline and leadership in the 2nd Canadian Division, we are concerned mainly with the ability of officers to motivate their men to achieve desired standards of discipline. For officers like Radcliffe and Russell, effective unit discipline derived largely from good morale and a sense of trust between officers and ORs. Officers could build up morale by ensuring that soldiers' requirements for decent food, comfortable clothing, serviceable shelter, and physical health were met. Beyond seeing to these basic needs, good officers also did what they could to provide their men with adequate rest, leave, recreation, entertainment, and rewards. The latter could range from simple pleasures like cigarettes or a shot of rum to formal honours and decorations. By exuding confidence and displaying practical skill in tactical and administrative matters, officers inspired trust in their capabilities. At sub-unit levels, such as company and platoon, this trust was an important contributing factor to the sense of cohesion or camaraderie that animated effective group dynamics and helped motivate men to work and fight together on the battlefield.

Ideally, officers in the British military tradition (which included the Canadians) were supposed to act in accordance with a paternalistic code of behaviour that aimed to foster morale and trust largely through personal example and by ensuring that the physical and psychological needs of the ORs were satisfied. As argued by Major-General Russell, it was believed that officers who fulfilled this code could prevent the development of discontent among their men, which, if not checked, might lead to breakdowns in discipline.[15] The relationship between officers and ORs was therefore a reciprocal one. Officers who demonstrated tactical skill, bravery, and conscientiousness in fulfilling the paternal ethic expected, in return, due deference and obedience from those beneath them.

Good discipline was viewed mainly as the product of good leadership by the officers, who were assisted in their work by the NCOs. It followed that if discipline began to break down so that punishments had to be imposed then weakness in leadership was the principal cause. If an officer proved deficient in his ability to enforce regulations and inspire his men to work together for the greater good of their unit, then the tendencies of some men to gratify their own personal interests could lead to an increase in common offences, such as absence or drunkenness. Similarly, if an officer proved unable or unwilling to look after the comfort and well being of his men, then they might protest through acts of insubordination, disobedience, or, if sufficiently aggrieved, outright mutiny. As it turned out, the latter crime was so rare in battalions of the 2nd Canadian Division that it bears no further analysis here. The overall quality of leadership and morale within the division evidently was good enough to preclude the eruption of collective indiscipline on a large scale.[16]

THE MILITIA FACTOR: DISCIPLINE IN CANADA

As soon as they formally entered service in the CEF, officers and ORs were subject to the terms and conditions of the British Army Act, including those concerning offences and punishments. When enforcing discipline, both in Canada and overseas, Canadian officers dealt with the majority of offences in summary fashion, in accordance with the Army Act and *King's Regulations and Orders for the Army.* For various minor offences, company commanders could award private soldiers extra duties on guard or piquet (also spelled *picket*), or up to seven days' confinement to barracks, which also might entail extra fatigues, parades, and pack drills. If an infraction demanded stiffer punishment, the offender could be marched before the battalion commander who was empowered to award up to 28 days of detention or field punishment, confinement to barracks, fines for drunkenness, pay stoppages for lost or damaged equipment, extra guards or piquets, reprimands, and admonitions. Although men had the right to request a court-martial if punishment affected their pay, most simply chose to accept their commanding officer's (CO) decision, fearful that a court-martial would deliver a harsher sentence.[17]

Between October 1914 and May 1915, when the units that would form the 2nd Canadian Division were recruited and underwent basic training in Canada, the most frequent offences were absence and drunkenness. For example, the 19th Battalion, mobilized at Toronto, experienced almost 290 incidents of absence between 1 December 1914 and 31 March 1915. Yet, at the end of February, it was rated by the Inspector-General, Major-General F.L. Lessard, as "the best regiment" he had yet inspected, with an "excellent" state of discipline. On the other hand, the 25th Battalion, mobilized at Halifax, had discharged over 300 men by mid-March 1915. A great many of these "undesirables" had displayed an unhealthy fondness for the bottle, a predilection shared by many who were rejected from battalions across the country.[18]

Forfeiture of pay was a common punishment for cases of short-term absenteeism, with detention being awarded to the minority of offenders guilty of lengthy absences or other more serious offences, such as flagrant disobedience, insubordination or striking a superior officer.[19] At this time, most men deemed incorrigible were simply discharged and sent home. It was ironic that "at the outbreak of war the general ignorance of the horrors of the battlefield made being denied the chance to go overseas a severe reprimand in the eyes of many Canadians."[20] Some of the Ontario battalions reported a 10 percent wastage of manpower because of discharges due to misconduct.[21]

The demands of discipline and the penalties for stepping out of line were not overly harsh during the winter training period in Canada. COs tolerated many offences. They resorted more to admonition, reprimand, and forfeiture of pay than to the full force of military law. This was done likely out of hope that their men, some of whom had never before donned a uniform, would become increasingly obedient to the rigours of army discipline. In addition, some of the ORs who did have previous military experience found themselves occupying positions of leadership (often as NCOs) for the first time. These men, along with novice junior officers, would have required time to become accustomed to their new responsibilities that included the cultivation and maintenance of proper military discipline.[22]

Another possible reason for the initial reluctance of Canadian officers to mete out the full measure of applicable punishments lay in the long-standing disciplinary traditions of the Canadian militia. Owing to the tiny size of Canada's pre-war Permanent Force, the vast majority of the officers and a great many of the ORs in the initial overseas contingents were furnished by, and recruited through, units of the volunteer militia, which contained the bulk of Canada's military personnel.[23] As such, the peacetime disciplinary culture of the reserve force was bound to influence the newly created CEF. According to historian Chris Madsen, "the voluntary nature of enlistment in the Canadian militia ... militated against stern punishments. Aggrieved or disgruntled men simply chose not to re-enlist at the end of their three-year engagements."[24]

A further element that discouraged the use of harsh punishments lay in the social relations among officers and ORs in the pre-war militia. In many units, individuals in both groups knew each other personally in civilian life or were related by blood or marriage. This made it more difficult to uphold the British military tradition of maintaining a social gulf between officers and ORs, which, according to conventional British military wisdom, made it easier for officers to enforce discipline and levy appropriate punishments.[25] Informality, or even intimacy, in relations off of the parade square among Canadian militia officers and ORs could understandably make it more difficult for officers to enforce discipline when on the parade square. Because most unit COs in the 2nd Canadian Division were veterans of the Canadian militia, it is to be expected that many of them would have maintained the disciplinary ethos of the pre-war militia in their new CEF units.

VELVET GLOVES OR IRON HANDS? DISCIPLINE IN ENGLAND AND DURING THE EARLY WEEKS OF OPERATIONAL SERVICE

After the units of the 2nd Canadian Division arrived in England, absence without leave once again was the most prominent offence during the weeks of training that followed. Given the sizable percentage of personnel who were born in the British Isles, this should not have been surprising.[26] The opportunity to visit family, friends, or old haunts not seen for years in some cases proved too tempting a proposition for many. In less than four months (between 6 June and 14 September 1915), 484 cases of absence were recorded in the 19th Battalion alone.[27]

As the incidence of offences increased notably, so did the regularity of summary punishment from company and battalion commanders. Many officers gradually realized that the more easy-going approach to discipline employed in the pre-war Canadian militia was inappropriate for the rigours of wartime service, when volunteers were enlisted for the duration of hostilities. As in Canada, fines, forfeitures of pay, and occasional awards of detention were given regularly to offenders. But in England, Canadian officers began employing field punishment with greater frequency, especially in the form of Field Punishment No. 2 (FP 2). This "meant a note in the pay book, pay forfeit, sleeping under guard, and the performance of such fatigues and pack drills as could be crammed into the day. All the while the offender would be on a diet of water and biscuit. Worse, he would not be allowed to smoke" for the duration of his punishment.[28] He also could be placed in irons, if necessary, to prevent escape. A CO could sentence a man to as many as 28 days of such punishment, although a court-martial could award up to three months.[29] Even though battalion officers were becoming increasingly strict, there were some authorities who felt that unit discipline in England still left something to be desired.

After the 2nd Canadian Division was formally organized in England on 25 May 1915, its military policing establishment was constituted and headed by an officer known as the assistant provost-marshal (APM). It was the APM's job to take "such measures as may be necessary for the proper preservation of good order and discipline" within the division. His duties included overseeing the organization and activities of the military police attached to the division. These activities included the policing and inspection of camps, the enforcement of march discipline among the troops, the collection of stragglers, the regulation of traffic, the policing of water supplies, the protection of civilians and their property, the patrolling of villages, public houses and agricultural property within the divisional area, the handling and investigation of claims lodged against divisional personnel by civilians, cooperation with civil police personnel attached to the division, and liaising with neighbouring civil and military law enforcement officials.[30]

In the 2nd Canadian Division, the position of APM was held throughout the war by Major (later Lieutenant-Colonel) Arthur Murray Jarvis. As a veteran of both the North-West Mounted Police and the South African War, Jarvis's previous experience prepared him well for his new duties.[31] Jarvis was a highly conscientious officer with a passion for upholding the letter of the law regarding the enforcement of order and discipline within his jurisdiction. This frequently led him to decry what was, in his view, the habit of too many battalion commanders failing to award "sufficient punishment" to offenders. For Jarvis, the men could never hope to become efficient until they had been brought into line by a firm system of discipline, with provisions and punishments that were applied fairly, impartially, with consistent force, and according to regulations.[32] Jarvis's complaints reflected his estimation of the quality of leadership among battalion officers, especially the COs. The disciplinary climate within any unit owed a great deal to the temper and diligence of its commander.

One commander with whom Jarvis took particular issue was Lieutenant-Colonel J.A.W. Allan of the 20th Battalion. Before the division departed England in September 1915, Allan was replaced because of his inability to maintain an adequate level of discipline in his unit.[33] Other units, such as the 22nd, 25th, and 26th Battalions, also figured prominently in the APM's reports owing to the comparatively higher incidence of offences committed by their personnel during the division's sojourn in England. Jarvis noted that the 22nd Battalion had accumulated more than 500 crime sheets between 1 June and 23 July 1915. He pointed out that, "On advice from me, Col. Gaudet, O.C. of this Unit is now giving more severe punishments to men who appear before him."[34] Gaudet's increased conscientiousness began to pay off, and his successor, Lieutenant-Colonel Thomas Tremblay, who took over the battalion in January 1916, also worked hard to improve matters.[35] Tremblay was a strict disciplinarian and he jealously guarded the reputation of his battalion throughout the war. He saw his men as the representatives of the French-Canadian people, and as such, they bore the mantle of French-Canadian honour on the battlefields of Europe. Absence and other forms of indiscipline were acts not to be tolerated under his command. Yet, as we shall see, in spite of Tremblay's stern attitude, disciplinary problems continued to flare up periodically in the 22nd Battalion, especially with cases of absence and desertion.[36]

DAVID CAMPBELL

PUNISHMENT AND PATERNALISM: DISCIPLINE IN FRANCE AND FLANDERS

Between September and November 1915, when the battalions of the 2nd Canadian Division experienced their initial tours of trench duty in Belgium, there was a clear retreat from the frequent imposition of such punishments as forfeitures of pay and FP 2. For the remainder of the war, a type of punishment known as Field Punishment No. 1 (FP 1) was administered with much greater frequency and became the dominant penalty levied for offences. Appendix 8.1 illustrates common forms of punishment and the relative incidence at which they were awarded to ORs in the 19th Battalion, while Appendix 8.2 displays the most prevalent types of charges leading to the punishments. Although Canadian regulations did not strictly forbid the use of FP 1 in either Canada or England, British regulations prevented its employment, except in a theatre of active operations. The Canadian authorities followed suit and refrained from authorizing the use of this harsher form of punishment until their men had arrived on the Western Front.[37]

FP 1 was administered in similar fashion to FP 2, in that the prisoner could "be subjected to the like labour, employment, and restraint, and be dealt with in like manner as if he were under a sentence of imprisonment with hard labor." However, according to regulations, a prisoner undergoing FP 1 also could be:

> attached for a period or periods not exceeding two hours in any one day to a fixed object [such as a post or cart wheel] but he must not be so attached during more than three out of any four consecutive days, nor during more than twenty-one days in all. Straps or ropes may be used for the purpose of these rules in lieu of irons.

As was the case with awards of FP 2, COs could award a maximum sentence of 28 days FP 1, while a court-martial could award up to three months.[38] Fines and forfeitures of pay continued to be awarded for very minor infractions, or occasionally, as punishment for a first offence. But these pecuniary penalties more often were awarded in conjunction with other

307

punishments, such as FP 1, which was carried out in full view of the other men, usually in the transport lines, "and served two purposes: public humiliation for the man undergoing sentence and a visible deterrent to the unit."[39]

Not surprisingly, those who were awarded FP 1 gained a special loathing for it. The divisional APM, Major Jarvis, noted: "One obstreperous prisoner, who strenuously objected to being tied up and who used vile and abusive language, had an additional charge put in against him...."[40] Some even went so far as to attempt escape from what they considered to be an unnecessary form of torture. "Our men evidently do not take kindly to Field Punishments," Jarvis remarked in July 1916. " ... [W]ithin the last two weeks several prisoners have shown their dislike of such restrictions of their liberty by taking the earliest opportunity to escape. Fortunately none of them got very far before being recaptured."[41]

The degree to that the administration of field punishment was subject to abuse within the 2nd Canadian Division is not clear. Official instructions for the administration of field punishment clearly stipulated:

> Every portion of a field punishment shall be inflicted in such a manner as is calculated not to cause injury or to leave any permanent mark on the offender; and a portion of a field punishment must be discontinued upon a report by a responsible medical officer that the continuance of that portion would be prejudicial to the offender's health.[42]

But this did not always happen. Some prisoners serving sentences of field punishment in British and Dominion forces were subjected to a variety of abuses by their guards, such as beatings or extended periods restraint in an intolerably uncomfortable or injurious manner. Yet, even when administered "by the book," FP 1 would have been distasteful enough to arouse resentment.

Major Jarvis's comment about prisoners attempting to escape field punishment may indicate some level of physical abuse during its administration in the 2nd Canadian Division. But, if one believes the statements that he made in his war diary during 1916 and 1917, it is evident that Jarvis was diligent in inspecting field punishment arrangements throughout the division. As a result of his supervisory efforts, abuse appears to have been kept to a minimum. "In order to ensure that these punishments are properly administered," he maintained, "I make periodical inspections of the various encampments and examine arrangements in regard to this."[43] When he recorded qualitative assessments of his inspections, he usually pronounced that everything was "all correct" or "according to regulations."[44] Divisional headquarters also ordered medical officers to inspect the condition of the men undergoing field punishment.[45]

The only explicit complaints that Major Jarvis made about the conduct of field punishment were in response to instances when it was being administered in too lax a fashion. On 8 July 1916, he complained that:

> the 21st Battalion, which has several men undergoing No. 1 F.P., was not disciplining these men according to our hard and fast orders. In fact they were not being punished at all and were being put to no worse inconvenience than detention in camp … The results of such lack of firmness is apparent in the conduct of the battalion which has borne a very poor reputation for discipline ever since it left Canada.[46]

This comment was in line with many negative assessments that Jarvis continued to make regarding the appropriateness of punishments awarded by unit commanders. In many instances, he did not name specific units or commanders, preferring instead to comment in general fashion about:

> a great and growing tendency among C.O.'s to deal lightly with men arrested by the Military Police…. If this sort of thing is allowed to continue, it will be impossible for my men to carry out their work, which is difficult at the best of times, and the men will get the impression that the police can be flouted with impunity. As the maintenance of order is entirely in their hands and as they are held directly responsible for any disturbance in the area, this state of things is a matter of the greatest moment.[47]

A worse trend, in Jarvis's view, was the tendency of some COs to interfere with police witnesses during the investigation of offences. According to Jarvis:

> Officers Commanding some Units are getting into the habit of browbeating police witnesses and trying to discredit their evidence and make it difficult for them to press cases, in every possible way. I had a list made of charges for which entirely inadequate punishments were given and the APM Corps is going to go further into the matter. I must have the cooperation of all officers if my work is to have expected results.[48]

This curious conflict between some unit commanders and the military police may have stemmed from the former's own beliefs regarding the maintenance of discipline, beliefs that were much more informal than Jarvis's "by the book" attitude. Concern for the best interests of their men, and a desire to shield them from authority figures who were outside the "regimental family," may have impelled some COs in the 2nd Canadian Division to hamper the efforts of Jarvis and his military police in prosecuting cases and enforcing discipline.

It is axiomatic that each unit was different and that each CO had his own way of dealing with his men. Yet, many COs seem to have believed that displaying leniency had a more desirable effect than the awarding of punishments to the full measure of military law. This may have stemmed from the pre-war militia ethos that discouraged severe punishment of volunteers, except for the most serious breaches of discipline. It has been said that "Most COs, with one eye on their own officers and another on the morale of their NCOs and men, were extremely reluctant to wash regimental dirty linen in public."[49]

A desire to deal with disciplinary matters on an internal basis, in a manner most befitting the personalities involved, and in keeping with the unit's social climate, seems to have spurred some COs in the 2nd Canadian Division to adopt informal methods for dealing with minor offences without recourse to formal disciplinary procedures. The unexplained termination of Major Jarvis's war diary at the end of May 1917 obscures the degree to which such conflicts between informality and regulation continued during the remainder of the war. But a memorandum issued by divisional headquarters in February 1918 that counselled unit commanders on how to deal with repeat offenders, indicates this problem never went away.[50]

Unit commanders could cultivate an image of paternal benevolence, while still maintaining strict discipline, by ensuring that subordinate officers were held responsible for the correct behaviour of their men. Ideally, diligence on the part of junior officers and NCOs ensured that COs often did not need to become personally involved in maintaining discipline. This may have been the case in the 31st Battalion, as evidenced by the post-war remarks of one of its veterans: "… [Our] commanding officer was Col. Arthur Bell … he was very much respected and very much looked up to as a commanding officer, [with a] nice gentlemanly manner and you never heard him get rough with anybody, but I can't say that of all his officers and NCOs…."[51] A 28th Battalion memorandum from March 1918 illustrates the CO's expectations of his junior officers and NCOs and, in addition, displays the strategies he could employ to ensure that his subordinates remained attentive to their duties:

> In view of the requirements for working parties and the hardships which the men have been called upon, of late, to endure, the Commanding Officer does not desire to worry them with parades and inspections, but if the subordinate Officers do not, together with their NCO's, maintain the standard of discipline required in this Unit, he will be compelled to put the men to considerable inconvenience to ensure that this discipline is maintained. This would be a hardship upon the men and the blame would rest entirely on the Officers and NCO's who are not performing their duties as strictly as they should. The Commanding Officer hopes that he will have no further cause to refer to the above.[52]

But expectations among officers worked both ways. If a CO displayed weak judgment with regard to punishment, or failed to support the verdicts of his subordinate officers, he risked losing their support, without which command and control in the unit would degrade. According to W.F. Doolan of the 21st Battalion, "if an officer was not a good disciplinarian, he would lose the respect of his men. That is, he would lose the respect of the men who were worthwhile, sure as daylight."[53] It was imperative, therefore, for a CO to maintain the support of his responsible subordinates, both officers and NCOs, to keep unruly elements under control.

Isabella Losinger has compared the relations between unit commanders and the ORs to a "civilian boss-employee relationship. The commanding officer as 'boss' had the power to reward and punish. In many cases, he maintained friendly, cordial relations with his men but, understandably, avoided intimacy."[54] Since many battalion commanders were business or professional men (as well as militia officers) before the war, this sort of hierarchical relationship would have been familiar to them. To the factory owner who was appointed to lead a battalion, his subordinate officers constituted his management team, while the NCOs essentially functioned as the "shop foremen" who kept the rest of the ORs, or "employees," in line. But where each businessman was free to exercise his own particular style of leadership in civil life, a unit commander was influenced by the exigencies of war and the dictates of military law to temper his personal inclinations to fit army regulations.

Satisfying the men's interests by upholding the traditional British officers' paternalistic code of conduct was the most effective means of maintaining a reasonably favourable state of morale within a unit. This in turn helped to ensure the establishment of acceptable levels of discipline.[55] Ideally, officers were to take an active interest in their men's welfare, ensuring that the ORs' physical well-being and comforts were addressed, even before their own. The highest-ranking Canadian officers, including Lieutenant-General Sir Arthur Currie, who commanded the Canadian Corps from June 1917 to the end of hostilities, readily absorbed this paternal ethic. On one occasion, Currie severely reprimanded Lieutenant Joe O'Neill of the 19th Battalion for his failure to demonstrate adequate personal knowledge of the men in his platoon. According to O'Neill:

> Well he dressed me down from top to bottom, and he
> pointed out that the real job of a junior officer was to
> know his men, to understand them. To work with them

and to understand their problems, and to make them understand that he was their natural leader. Above all things it was up to that officer to know the men personally, and know [that] … one man would react to kindness and another man you had to crowd a bit and so on. But we had to get to understand our men … Well I soon came to understand that [Currie] was right, that one of the most interesting things in life was to know and really like the boys, and really like them and understand them and know their problems, and be their natural leader. I must say I never enjoyed anything more in my life….[56]

The most skilful officers could bring paternalism to bear to nip potential disciplinary problems in the bud. There can be few better examples of such "prophylactic paternalism" than that shown by Major C.E. Sale of the 18th Battalion. In the words of one veteran:

I was very fortunate in having Major C.E. Sale of Goderich as my company commander. Major Sale was a very wonderful man. He was a very human man. The men loved him. I remember back in a rest camp finding one of our men [by the name of Taylor] in the corner of a field crying his eyes out. Apparently he had a row with his wife before leaving home and this woman had sent him a letter enclosing a snapshot of one of his children in its coffin, a dreadful thing to do. This poor fellow was broken-hearted. I came and reported to Major Sale. Major Sale said, "Go and get Shepherd, the cook." I wondered what Shepherd had to do with it and in comes Shepherd and he said, "Shepherd, here's a hundred francs. Take Taylor, here's a hundred francs and a three days pass. Take and get him stupid drunk and bring him back." Now, Taylor was going to go on a binge anyway and the battalion could have been called out at a moment's notice. He'd have been picked up by the police and would have had a very serious charge against him, absent without leave with his battalion in the line. So with [a] three days pass and with trusty Shepherd, he got back in good shape. Now these things percolated down to the men and they loved Major Sale and so did I. The major didn't come back.[57]

Not all officers upheld their paternal obligations. In such instances, passive or even active forms of protest could replace the deference that officers expected from the ORs. One incident, recorded by William Morgan, recounts an episode in which he and his comrades were treated callously by their conducting officer while marching as part of a reinforcement draft to join the 24th Battalion. As Morgan recorded in his diary:

> The "gang" have an independent mood on this morning. Marched off at 7.30 a.m. to join our own Battalion. Officer in charge from 2nd Pioneers carried out his thoughtless tactics of the previous day. Started off up hill under a scorching sun at a great rate. Men started falling out in the first 20 mins. The "gang" fell out at 8.10 a.m. and the officer came back and spoke to us as follows. It is worth putting on record to give one an idea of some of the officers' feelings toward men who have volunteered for service. "What casualties already? " "Is this the God dammed yellow bellied troops they are sending out as soldiers now?" Imagine our feelings. We refused to march off with the company and followed on later, marching into Billets at Camblain L'Abbe in great style.[58]

Morgan did not report any disciplinary action taken against him or the other protesters and it is significant that this treatment was suffered at the hands of an officer who was not of Morgan's own unit. Moreover, his diary shows that the ORs did have recourse to report abusive officers. Almost a week after the incident on the march, Morgan wrote that he had "Put in a written complaint against the Captain of the 2nd Pioneers on request from the Major" of the 24th Battalion.[59]

Although ORs usually could expect more sympathetic treatment from officers of their own unit than from those of other units or from the military police, there were occasions when company or battalion officers did get carried away in their enforcement of discipline. Following Major Jarvis's complaints regarding the lax administration of discipline within certain units, some COs in the 2nd Canadian Division became excessively strict in the estimation of the ORs and, ironically enough, in the opinion of Major Jarvis himself. On 25 June 1916, Jarvis reported:

> Since my complaints to the Corps, about [the] tendency exhibited by Officers Commanding, to award insufficient punishments to men charged by my police, many officers are now going to the other extreme, by giving the stiffest possible sentences for minor offences. This seems to me to be very short-sighted policy and if persisted in, can only succeed in arousing feelings of discontent and disloyalty among the men. I am going to see if the officers concerned cannot be persuaded to use common sense and judgment in dealing with offenders instead of giving sentences dictated by pique and peevishness.[60]

Jarvis even went so far as to advise concerned ORs to visit him personally and register their complaints if they believed that their COs were dealing out unjust punishments.[61] The culture of discipline in the 2nd Canadian Division was a complex one in which the APM could find himself at loggerheads with unit commanders who were being too lenient in some cases and too harsh in others.

What does emerge from the APM's diary is the sense that Jarvis himself held a consistent view about the nature and maintenance of military discipline. This view was based solidly upon the regulations outlined in the Army Act and the *Manual of Military Law*. On the other hand, some commanders of infantry battalions and other units were not as consistent in their approach to the enforcement of discipline. As much as Jarvis and his police were forced to contend with the periodic rise and fall of discipline among the troops of the division, they also had to navigate the shifting behaviours of unit commanders, whose varying views on discipline, particularly during the first half of the war, probably resulted from a combination of ignorance, inexperience, and an unwill-ingness to break from more easy-going pre-war traditions.

During early 1917, the number of complaints regarding unit com-manders' attitudes towards discipline began to dwindle in Jarvis's diary entries and we can only guess at the level of his approval during the peri-od following his diary's mysterious termination at the end of May 1917. Although Jarvis most likely continued to notice some faults, by and large, the increasing professionalism of the Canadian officer corps fol-lowing the Battle of the Somme (July to November 1916) would have seen improved levels of consistency with regard to the administration of discipline in the 2nd Canadian Division and the rest of the Canadian Corps.[62] During the winter of 1916–1917, the critical spirit that ani-mated the re-evaluation of tactics and organization that emerged from the hard experience of fighting at the Somme underscored the need for officers and ORs to discard their amateur ethos and adopt a profession-al, analytical, and more disciplined approach to waging a modern indus-trialized war. As one veteran of the 22nd Battalion put it, "Well, men are always good if officers are good, it all depends on the leaders ... There were plenty of battalions that were good, but when there was something going in a unit they always blame the officers. The boss, if he is not real-ly a boss, he is no good [*sic*]."[63]

PATTERNS OF INDISCIPLINE?

Through examining the incidence of minor offences from records of the 19th Battalion,[64] surviving reports from the 6th Brigade,[65] courts-martial listings, and Jean-Pierre Gagnon's work on the 22nd Battalion, a general pattern with respect to discipline and punishment within the 2nd Canadian Division emerges. In the case of the 19th Battalion, there was an overall decline in the number of charges for minor offences committed by ORs between October 1915 and December 1918 (see Appendix 8.2). This same pattern was observable in the 22nd Battalion (see Appendix 8.3),[66] and in the battalions of the 6th Brigade, particularly during the period from January to October 1918 (see Appendix 8.4).

Canadian troops of the 6th Brigade are interrupted in July 1917 during a service on the 50th anniversary of Dominion Day. Many of these soldiers from the 2nd Division had no doubt committed, or would eventually commit, offences against military law. (Department of National Defence, Library and Archives Canada PA-1447)

There were, to be sure, various peaks and troughs within this overall pattern of declination in each battalion. In general, one might expect that the incidence of offences within a unit would decline during the months when it was heavily engaged in operations and that the number of offences would rise during lulls in the fighting. In many cases, this is precisely what occurred. In the 19th Battalion, April and September 1916, April to May and November 1917, and March to June and September to October 1918, saw some of the lowest monthly number of charges for minor offences in that unit (see Appendix 8.2). Simply put, the troops were too busy fighting in major operations (at St. Eloi, the Somme, Vimy, Fresnoy, Passchendaele, the German 1918 offensives and the final Allied drives) to get into much trouble.[67] On 1 October 1916, as the units of the 2nd Canadian Division experienced the last tragic gasp of their bloody tour at the Somme, Major Jarvis remarked on how well behaved the troops stationed in reserve had been during the recent fighting:

We are having no trouble with our men billeted in the village and the general standard of conduct and discipline was never higher. The men though lively and sober are exceptionally well behaved and are bearing unusual hardships and fatigue with marvelous spirit. To lead such men is a glory — an honour without price.[68]

However, there also were "less active" months in which the 19th Battalion saw an equally low (and sometimes lower) number of charges for minor offences in comparison with periods of active operations. These included November 1915, February to March, and June to July 1916, June and September 1917, and February 1918. Conversely, there were some periods marked by heavy fighting that saw moderate to sharp increases in the number of minor offences committed (such as drunkenness and absence), which were likely in response to stress. This was the case during August 1917, with operations at Hill 70 and Lens, and August 1918, with offensives at Amiens and Arras. Similarly, variable trends were displayed in the 22nd Battalion throughout the war (see Appendix 8.3), and in the 27th, 28th, 29th, and 31st Battalions during 1917 and 1918 (see Appendix 8.4). In addition, offence rates during a particular month could dip sharply for one unit, as for the 19th Battalion in September 1916, while another unit, such as the 22nd Battalion, might see a steep rise in offences during the same month.

In some cases, these differences may be explained by the fact that some battalions were more heavily engaged in certain operations than others; but again, this is not true in all instances. Beyond the very general trend towards a decreasing incidence of minor offences in most battalions as the war progressed, there are few instances when the trends showing a rising or declining number of minor offences at specific points in time can be applied to all battalions for which we have data. Factors such as operational activity levels, casualty rates, influxes of reinforcements, changes in command, or the lengths of time spent in various geographical areas all played varying roles in influencing the offence rates within a given battalion.

Two factors that exerted a prevalent influence over the incidence of offences were command stability and personnel turbulence.[69] In his history of the 22nd Battalion, Jean-Pierre Gagnon noted a serious breakdown in discipline that occurred in that unit during the winter of 1916–1917. He linked the dramatic increases in the incidence of absence and desertion with the heavy casualties that had been sustained by the French Canadians in their attacks at Courcelette and Regina Trench. Hundreds of experienced officers and ORs had been killed and wounded and their places were filled with inexperienced and often ill-disciplined reinforcements. During the four months following the battle at Courcelette in September 1916, the 22nd Battalion absorbed 934 reinforcements, almost its entire strength. Heavy casualties and influxes of new men would have seriously disrupted the established social and disciplinary climate in the unit.[70]

The firm hand of the CO, Lieutenant-Colonel Tremblay, might have proved instrumental in mitigating the negative effects of such personnel turbulence. But Tremblay was invalided back to England in late September 1916 and would not return to the battalion until February 1917. The few veteran officers who had survived the Somme were unable to reassert the good state of discipline that had marked the battalion during the summer of 1916. The interim commander, Major Arthur Dubuc, proved unequal to the task of maintaining control over the increasingly unruly ranks. When Tremblay returned in February 1917, he concluded that unwarranted degrees of leniency had been shown to offenders during his absence and that this had only encouraged further breaches of discipline, especially with respect to absence and desertion.[71] Historian Christopher Pugsley's observation that, "Good battalions would go sour with the loss of a CO or too heavy a casualty list," applies well to the case of the 22nd Battalion in the post-Somme period.[72]

The divisional APM, Major Jarvis, lamented the fate of the 22nd Battalion. It had given him some cause for complaint in 1915 and early 1916, but subsequently had impressed him with its greatly improved discipline during the summer of 1916 and its outstanding performance at the Somme. After the battalion had emerged from the maelstrom of Courcelette, Jarvis enthused about:

> the splendid behaviour of the 22nd Battalion which has been in billets here since the ever memorable fight of September 15th–16th, with the memories of a terrible experience fresh in their minds and temptation pressing

on all sides, they having just been paid, they have shown splendid discipline and restraint and my men have not had to make a single arrest.[73]

This record changed dramatically over the winter of 1916–1917, such that by March of the latter year, Jarvis complained:

More men of the 22nd Battalion have been reported as under arrest at Bethune and St. Pol respectively. The excellent discipline shown by this Battalion while in Belgium [before their tours at the Somme] has been considerably marred by the advent of new reinforcements, almost all having proved very unsatisfactory and unreliable.[74]

The 22nd Battalion was not alone in experiencing rising rates of indiscipline during periods in which large numbers of reinforcements were absorbed. The 19th Battalion also saw an increasing incidence of offences following significant influxes of new personnel. Between September and December 1916, the battalion absorbed 712 ORs to make good the losses incurred at the Somme (see Appendix 8.5). At the same time, the monthly number of minor offences within the 19th Battalion steadily increased from a low point of 10 in September 1916 to a peak of 24 in January 1917 (see Appendix 8.2). Thereafter, offences trailed off somewhat from February to March and then fell abruptly in April 1917 with the advent of heavy fighting at Vimy. This same pattern occurred again following the arrival of 379 ORs as reinforcements in June 1917 (see Appendix 8.5). Offences within the unit rose from a low of six in June to a peak of 26 in August, which also saw attacks at Hill 70 and the environs of Lens.[75]

As early as January 1916, Major Jarvis had noted the pernicious influence that reinforcements could have upon the good discipline of a unit. In complaining of a case of theft and assault committed by a 22nd Battalion man at an estaminet (small café), he remarked that "Crimes of this nature are becoming altogether too frequent…. In nearly all recent cases I find that the culprits are men who have come over with new drafts. They seem to be an undisciplined mob with a large percentage of really vicious characters amongst them."[76] In June 1916, Jarvis continued to comment on the disruptive influence of reinforcements: "The new drafts which are coming to the country are not nearly up to the standard of the original Canadian battalions either physically or in discipline and they are now the cause of nearly all our troubles."[77]

Yet, acts of indiscipline were not limited to reinforcement personnel. During 1916, the 19th Battalion saw more minor offences committed by original personnel than by reinforcements. But beginning in August of that year, reinforcement personnel began to outnumber original men in the lists of punishment cases appearing in unit records. By the end of the year, out of a total of 185 instances where individuals from the 19th Battalion were awarded punishment for minor offences, 96 involved original personnel, while 89 involved reinforcements. As the ranks of the originals dwindled during 1917, the vast majority of punishments for minor offences were awarded to men who had joined the battalion after its departure from Canada. Of a total of 202 cases involving minor offences in 1917, only 36 involved original men, while in 1918, a mere 10 cases of a total of 121 involved surviving original men.[78] These ratios simply reflected the relative proportions of original and reinforcement personnel in the 19th Battalion over the course of the war. Since most of the original personnel in the 2nd Canadian Division had departed the division during and immediately after its tours at the Somme, these ratios are to be expected.

For all of his complaints about ill-disciplined reinforcements, Major Jarvis was not blind to instances in which offences by original men appeared to be on the rise. As late as 18 May 1917, Jarvis remarked that absenteeism "seems to be on the increase but the reason is hard to state from this week's return as the majority are 'Original' men."[79] This phenomenon may have been indicative of growing rates of battle exhaustion among those who had served in the division since 1915.

Other important factors impacting upon shifting levels of indiscipline were the availability of alcohol and the opportunity for interaction with civilians behind the lines. During the relatively "quiet" weeks from January to March 1916, after the 2nd Canadian Division had been stationed in the Kemmel sector of Flanders for some time, Major Jarvis remarked that the troops had "been able to get on terms of intimacy" with the inhabitants of various villages behind Canadian lines, "and those with expensive thirsts have found the Estaminet keepers willing to give them credit. Lack of hard work, freedom from worry and a comparatively easy life in general has certainly, in my opinion, not been conducive to either the physical or moral well being of the men."[80] Alcohol was of particular concern to Jarvis, especially the trafficking of English beer and stout by local civilians. When an order came through prohibiting the sale of English beer in areas occupied by the Allied armies in France, Jarvis felt it was:

> a very good move and should come into force in Belgium also, as nine-tenths of our troubles with the men are caused by this stuff, which is originally very strong and is in most cases doctored with other heady mixtures by the Estaminet keepers. It is almost as bad in its effects as liquor and must be very injurious to the health. The native brews, French and Belgian, are over two-thirds water and are entirely innocuous. If we can manage to have English beer prohibited in this area, it will prove a great factor in preventing offences against civilians and their property, which is my chief source of worry.[81]

Historian Craig Gibson, in his examination of civil-military relations in the 2nd Canadian Division between September 1915 and May 1917, concluded that both soldiers and civilians were to blame for the frequently tense relations that existed behind Canadian lines. Regarding the Canadian experience in Belgium, according to Gibson, "the local Flemish, who from [Major Jarvis's] point of view were greedy, sullen and a threat to security, resented the intrusion of a military presence which controlled their mobility, regulated their businesses, damaged their fields and farms and stole from their *estaminets*."[82]

The war brought about an unfortunate coexistence of frustrated civilians, who were being told by foreign military officials how to conduct their affairs in their own country, and bewildered Canadian soldiers, who could not understand why their efforts to liberate Belgium failed to meet with more enthusiasm from the locals. This confusion on the Canadians' part combined with frequent ignorance and intolerance of local customs and was capped with a ferocious resentment of any attempts by civilians to "cheat" or "gouge" them during commercial transactions. In doing their utmost to profit by whatever means they could from the unfortunate circumstances in which they found themselves, many civilians in the occupied zones ended up fuelling indiscipline among the troops. Making alcohol available to troops outside of sanctioned drinking hours, or selling it in prohibited areas, only encouraged the troops to flout regulations. This occasionally contributed to both petty and major criminal offences against civilians by uncontrolled troops. Caught in the middle was Major Jarvis who met with varying amounts of success in enforcing regulations regarding the timing and location of alcohol sales and in keeping offences by Canadian troops to a minimum.

Of additional significance were the superior rates of pay received by Canadian troops in relation to their British or French counterparts, which made them especially susceptible to the commercial ambitions of countless civilian hawkers of virtually any commodity on both sides of the English Channel. When units were rotated for periods of rest behind the lines, payday, not surprisingly, became equated with rowdiness and general lapses in good discipline. "Most of the units in the area have been paid today," Jarvis remarked on 13 April 1916, "and I am anticipating a busy time in the village [Reninghelst] tonight as the conduct of the men has been entirely too good to continue...."[83]

The heady mixture of liquor and soldiers demonstrated that even good leadership from the officer corps sometimes had its limits as a positive influence on discipline. Behind the front lines it was difficult to eliminate illegal activities involving civilians, even with the assistance of local law enforcement officials. One solution may have been the total segregation of military personnel from the civilian population, but this would not have been practical in many cases, especially from a billeting perspective, for civilian homes often were required to house troops stationed in reserve. The best that officers could do was to try to police local communities, ferret out individuals dealing liquor in an unauthorized fashion and keep a lid on troops eager to imbibe to let off steam or calm frayed nerves. Policing liquor consumption in the trenches generally was far easier, for it was the officers who controlled the issue of regular rum rations. Drunkenness in the lines was not as big a concern among the ORs, except on rare occasions when individuals managed to pool their rum rations illicitly for a binge.[84]

COMPARING UNITS

Based upon the total numbers of minor offences committed in each unit, it is possible to make some general comparisons of relative discipline levels among the infantry battalions of the 2nd Canadian Division. We shall first compare incidence of minor offences in the 22nd and 19th Battalions from October 1915 to October 1918, inclusive (Appendix 8.6, Table 1), and then do the same with the 19th, 27th, 28th, 29th, and 31st Battalions from January 1917 to December 1918, inclusive (Appendix 8.6, Table 2).[85]

Over the course of the war, it is obvious that the incidence of minor offences was higher in the 22nd Battalion than in the other units. Although the difference in timescales in the source material prevents direct comparison between the units of the 6th Brigade and the 22nd Battalion, it is unlikely that the totals for any of the 6th Brigade's units would have come remotely close to matching those of the 22nd Battalion. If we consider that the number of minor offences in the 19th Battalion during the period from January 1917 to December 1918 is almost half of the total number given for the same unit during the entire period from October 1915 to November 1918, we can estimate that by doubling the numbers presented here for the battalions of the 6th Brigade, an approximation of the total number of minor offences could be obtained for those units from October 1915 to November 1918. Such calculations would furnish the following results: 27th Battalion, 484 minor offences; 28th Battalion, 638 minor offences; 29th Battalion, 810 minor offences; and 31st Battalion, 312 minor offences. In any case, it is clear that among these units, the 22nd Battalion displayed the greatest number of offences while the 31st Battalion exhibited the lowest.

This pattern remains consistent when we compare numbers of courts-martial and the incidence of offences tried within all 12 infantry battalions of the 2nd Canadian Division between 1915 and 1919 (Appendix 8.6, Table 3 and Table 4). Although these figures may not represent the total number of courts-martial for each battalion, they are drawn from a sample that is large enough to be statistically representative of those totals. Once again, the 22nd Battalion emerges with the highest incidence of courts-martial and offences brought to trial while the 31st Battalion presents the fewest on both counts.

Part of the reason for the 31st Battalion's impressive record can stem from the remarkable stability of its leadership. Lieutenant-Colonel Arthur Bell, a professional soldier with considerable pre-war experience, held command of the unit from its formation until April 1918 when he was promoted brigadier-general in command of the 6th Brigade.[86] Until the end of hostilities, command of the 31st Battalion would change only once more, in October 1918. Similar levels of command stability also marked the experiences of the 27th and 28th Battalions, which saw a lower incidence of courts-martial and minor offences than many other battalions in the division (see Appendix 8.6, Table 5).

This relative stability or continuity in senior command could have compensated for the greater levels of personnel turbulence among the junior officers and NCOs. Senior officers, from company commanders on up, tended to remain in their positions longer and were afforded the time to gain experience and to develop their power of command. For the most part, when a change in battalion command occurred, the new commander already had seen extensive service in that same unit as a major or a captain. This was especially true during 1917 and 1918. In some cases, such as that of Lieutenant-Colonel John Wise of the 25th Battalion, they had even risen from the ranks.[87]

Experienced senior officers, who knew their own jobs, as well as the jobs of their subordinates, would not have been as likely to tolerate indiscipline as less experienced or less confident men. Seasoned commanders also were intimately familiar with the traditions and social customs of their units, as well as with the personalities and habits of many of their personnel. Such knowledge was crucial if they were to satisfy their men's needs and preserve what was best in their unit's culture. It also helped them recognize the most effective ways of dealing with men when they fell afoul of military law. An officer had to know and understand the men he commanded to extract the best performance from them. As Lieutenant Joe O'Neill quickly learned from Lieutenant-General Currie, "Officers and N.C.O.s who could not handle the discipline in their own units were considered misfits and very inefficient...."[88]

CONCLUSION: DISCIPLINE AND LEADERSHIP

Generally speaking, the infantry battalions examined from the 2nd Canadian Division experienced an overall decline in the incidence of indiscipline. Numbers of offences diminished from peak periods in the summer and early fall of 1915 and then increased periodically from late 1916 through to the end of 1917. This was followed by a general improvement in discipline throughout 1918.

Each successive personnel cohort in a unit required varying amounts of time before they became effectively disciplined. Offences by the original personnel of the division, frequent during training periods in Canada and England, gradually diminished after the division's arrival in France. Subsequent sporadic influxes of reinforcements brought significant numbers of new men, many of whom had belonged to other units that were broken up to supply drafts for battalions fighting at the front. Such dislocations sometimes bred resentment or despondency among reinforcements. These attitudes could spill over into acts of indiscipline until the men became socialized to their new units and gained some respect for, and trust in, their new officers.

The quality of leadership was the most important factor in determining discipline within the division. Each unit in the division had its own experience and each unit commander played a key role in setting the disciplinary agenda for his command. Units with strong leadership from their senior officers stood a better chance of maintaining discipline during the stressful preparatory periods before major operations, as well as during the reorganization process that usually followed if a unit suffered heavy losses. The instability engendered by higher turnover rates for experienced junior officers,[89] who, with the NCOs, were the primary instruments for keeping the ORs in line, could be offset by greater stability in the more senior officer cadre. These senior officers, along with surviving veterans of all ranks, could work to maintain or re-establish the cohesion and discipline of the unit. This process did not function optimally in all units at all times. But it does appear to have worked often enough, such that the operational effectiveness of the division as a whole was never seriously impaired, even if a small number of individual units suffered greater degrees of difficulty with discipline and efficiency.

The exercise of the paternalistic officer ethic, especially among company officers, placed a premium upon the maintenance of discipline through ensuring that the basic comforts and needs of the majority of men were satisfied as often as possible. Not all company officers were equally diligent in this respect, just as not all COs were consistent in their attitudes towards administering discipline within their units. But consistency in the quality of leadership at the most senior levels appears to have improved from the end of 1916 onward, with formation commanders keeping a close eye on the quality of their subordinates' work. Lieutenant O'Neill's encounter with Lieutenant-General Currie illustrates how well the values of paternalism were understood at even the highest levels within the Canadian Corps. It also illustrates the degree to which the most senior commanders took an interest in the work of their most junior subordinates. Although rates of indiscipline periodically rose during 1917, this may have resulted from bursts of personnel turbulence among junior officers and ORs during periods of heavy operational activity. There would have been a certain amount of lag time when less-experienced reinforcement officers and NCOs would become increasingly conscientious and competent in the execution of their responsibilities and duties, thereby leading to improvements in discipline. The supervisory efforts of senior commanders likely speeded this process along.

General officers regularly took subordinates to task, either individually or collectively, for observable signs of disciplinary lapses. These could include laxness in saluting, dress, and deportment, or incorrect observation of regulations, like those pertaining to the proper use of gas masks or precautions against trench foot.[90] General officers and unit commanders alike could institute sanctions against subordinates as punishment for failing to comply with policy or to maintain discipline. One example was the warning on 2 March 1918 from 28th Battalion Headquarters that the men would be put to "considerable trouble" with extra parades and inspections should there be no improvement in the discipline and deportment of the unit. This directive was designed to spur junior officers to greater individual effort to spare their men from unnecessary ceremony and themselves from the consequent blame that would fall on them from the ORs, who, it was said, would resent the officers for not cracking down on the minority of troublemakers that were subjecting all personnel to greater inconvenience. In training instructions issued by 2nd

Canadian Division Headquarters in 1918, it was argued that "Discipline is strengthened by insisting at all times on the thorough performance of all duties, by demanding smartness in appearance, tidiness in camp, punctuality, care in saluting, and attention to all the minutiae associated with the soldier's daily life."[91]

Living and working under the intense scrutiny of both superiors and subordinates took its toll on the physical and mental health of many officers. The pressures on, and expectations of, platoon and company commanders in particular were enormous, and some of those who did break under the strain did so through committing disciplinary infractions of their own. Among the courts-martial entries examined in a database at the Library and Archives Canada were 36 cases in which infantry officers of the 2nd Canadian Division were tried for breaches of discipline. Most involved drunkenness.[92]

If the courage of a few officers was liquid in nature, disciplinary states within units, both individually and collectively, were fluid, as were perceptions of them at the time. Even as he recorded his myriad complaints about the quality of discipline in certain units, the divisional APM, Major Jarvis, remarked with pride on the overall high level of discipline within the 2nd Canadian Division. On 15 June 1916, Jarvis pointed out that although the percentage of crime was "unusually low" in the division during that month, the division's crime rates had "always been much lower than those of any other in the entire Expeditionary Force. In fact, heretofore there has been ground for no comparison between our Crime Record and those of other Divisions. We never had more than a fraction of one per cent undergoing No. 1 F.P."[93] There was some self-congratulation in such statements, since low crime rates reflected not only upon the efforts of officers and ORs in each unit of the division, but also upon the vigilance of the military police and the APM himself.

It is important to remember that only a minority of troops were involved in acts of indiscipline.[94] But even a relatively small percentage of delinquents could exert an impact upon both the disciplinary climate and command culture of the division that was out of proportion to their numbers. Senior officers regarded any diminution in the quality of discipline as a threat to the efficiency of their commands, which in turn, reflected upon their own capabilities. Despite the reputed low quality of reinforcements received during the post-Somme period, the disciplinary crisis that afflict-ed the 22nd Battalion during the winter and spring of 1917 was attributed mainly to the inexperience and indulgence of its officers, and in particular, to that of its interim commander.

Based upon the surviving evidence examined to date, the disciplinary record of the 22nd Battalion appears demonstrably worse than those of other individual infantry battalions in the 2nd Canadian Division, and is even worse than the combined record of several battalions. Even when allowing for the differing degrees of operational stress and personnel tur-bulence experienced by each unit over the course of the war, every battal-ion in the division experienced the same pressures to maintain efficiency in the face of accelerating operational tempo and personnel turnover rates. That some units handled these pressures either more or less effectively than others resulted from the success or failure of leadership within those units. By August 1918, the experience and skill levels of commanding and general officers were at their height. This factor, when combined with the galvanizing effect of almost constant operational activity through the course of the final Hundred Days campaign, contributed to rates of indis-cipline in the 2nd Canadian Division that were far lower than those seen during any earlier period of comparable length.

NOTES

1. Library and Archives Canada [henceforth LAC], Manuscript Group [henceforth MG] 30 — D150, Vol. 4, Sir Andrew Macphail Papers, Personal diary, Vol. 3, 3 January 1917.

2. Of the more than 8.5 million troops of the British Empire that served during and immediately after the war, 304,262 officers and other ranks (ORs) were tried by court-martial between 4 August 1914 and 31 March 1920. Of those tried, 3,080 received sentences of death, most of which were commuted to lesser sentences. The total number of men executed in the British armies was 346. Included in these totals are the approximately 17,000 Canadians who were tried by court-martial, of whom 222 were sentenced to death, with 25 executions actually taking place. See War Office [henceforth WO], *Statistics of the Military Effort of the British Empire During the Great War* (London: His Majesty's Stationery Office [henceforth HMSO], 1922), 643, 649, and 756; Gerard Oram, *Death Sentences Passed by Military Courts of the British Army, 1914–1924* (London: Francis Boutle, 1998), 14. Oram, a British historian, disputes

the number of death sentences quoted above by the WO and instead proposes a figure of 3,118. See Oram, *Death Sentences*. For the source of the number of Canadian courts-martial, see endnote 7 below. It is important to point out that not all offences were tried by court-martial. Indeed, the majority of offences were addressed and punished by unit officers, and only serious cases were brought before a court-martial. Therefore, the total number of offences committed by troops of the British Empire (including Canadians) would be far higher than the total number of courts-martial quoted above. The total number of minor offences committed during the course of the war is not known thus far.

3. A division was commanded by a major-general and administered by a headquarters staff. An infantry brigade containing four battalions was commanded by a brigadier-general, who was assisted by a headquarters staff. Each infantry battalion, in turn, was commanded by a lieutenant-colonel and contained roughly 1,000 all ranks. The battalion was subdivided into four companies, each under the command of a major or captain, and consisted of four platoons. A platoon was commanded by a lieutenant (who was assisted by two sergeants) and it contained four sections, each of 10 to 14 men under the leadership of a corporal or lance-corporal. The 12 infantry battalions of the 2nd Canadian Division, and the brigades in which they were organized, were as follows: 18th, 19th, 20th, and 21st Battalions (4th Infantry Brigade); 22nd, 24th, 25th, and 26th Battalions (5th Infantry Brigade); and 27th, 28th, 29th, and 31st Battalions (6th Infantry Brigade).

4. For a general discussion of discipline in the Canadian Expeditionary Force, see Desmond Morton, *When Your Number's Up: The Canadian Soldier in the First World War* (Toronto: Random House, 1993), 82–4 and 247–52. Morton also produced earlier essays examining specific disciplinary issues. See Desmond Morton, "The Supreme Penalty: Canadian Deaths by Firing Squad in the First World War," *Queen's Quarterly*, Vol. 79, No. 3 (1972), 345–352; Desmond Morton, "'Kicking and Complaining': Demobilization Riots in the Canadian Expeditionary Force, 1918–19," *Canadian Historical Review*, Vol. 61, No. 3 (1980), 334–360. Morton has stood relatively alone in the field until the past decade, which has seen other scholars and students devote increasing attention to disciplinary culture in the CEF. The focus, however, remains overwhelmingly upon issues of mutiny, protest, and capital punishment. For example, see, Andrew B. Godefroy, *For Freedom and Honour? The Story of the 25 Canadian Volunteers Executed in the Great War* (Nepean: CEF Books, 1998); Howard G. Coombs, *Dimensions of Military Leadership: The Kinmel Park Mutiny of 4–5 March 1919* (Kingston: Canadian Defence Academy [henceforth CDA], Canadian Forces Leadership Institute [henceforth CFLI], unpublished paper*; Craig Leslie Mantle, *For Bully and Biscuits: Charges of Mutiny in the 43rd Battalion, Canadian Expeditionary Force, November and December 1917* (Kingston: CDA-CFLI, unpublished paper)*; Craig Leslie Mantle, *Polished Leathers and Gleaming Steel: Charges of Mutiny in the Canadian Army Service Corps at Bramshott Camp, England, November 1917* (Kingston: CDA-CFLI, unpublished paper)*; Craig Leslie Mantle, *The "Moral Economy" as a Theoretical Model to Explain Acts of Protest in the*

Canadian Expeditionary Force, 1914–1919 (Kingston: CDA-CFLI, unpublished paper); Teresa Iacobelli, *Arbitrary Justice?: A Comparative Analysis of Death Sentences Passed and Commuted During the First World War* (Unpublished M.A. Thesis, Wilfrid Laurier, 2004). [**Editor's Note**: Those papers marked above with an asterisk (*) have, with some minor editing and alterations, been published in this volume.]

5. David Englander, "Discipline and Morale in the British Army, 1917–1918," in John Horne, ed., *State, Society and Mobilization in Europe During the First World War* (Cambridge: Cambridge University Press, 1997), 133.

6. Jean-Pierre Gagnon, *Le 22e Bataillon (Canadien-français), Étude socio-militaire* (Ottawa et Québec: Les Presses de l'Université Laval en collaboration avec le ministère de la Défense Nationale et le Centre d'édition du gouvernement du Canada, 1986), Chapter 8, 279–311.

7. The data on discipline and punishment in this chapter has been derived from several sources. First, the war diary of the assistant provost-marshal (APM) of the 2nd Canadian Division, Major (later Lieutenant-Colonel) Arthur Murray Jarvis, proved extremely useful for its candid revelation of Jarvis's attitudes towards discipline within the division. Although the APM's war diary does contain some statistical information regarding offences and punishments, these details are not recorded on a consistent basis. What is more, the diary ends abruptly in May 1917 and the reason for this is not yet clear. For these reasons, the APM's diary cannot be used as a comprehensive source of statistical information on rates of indiscipline within the division. Yet, for the two full years that the diary does cover, it stands as a key source of information on official attitudes to discipline and punishment within the 2nd Canadian Division. See LAC, Record Group [henceforth RG] 9, III-D-3, Vol. 5050, War Diary, 2nd Canadian Division A.P.M., 1 June 1915 to 31 May 1917. A second source of information was the Part II Daily Orders from a sample infantry battalion — the 19th from Ontario. See LAC, RG 150, Series 1, Vol. 71, Files "19th Battalion (Parts 1–4)," Part 2 Daily Orders, 1915–1918. Part 2 Orders contain all information regarding matters affecting an individual's status, rank, and pay within a unit. They were prepared by the administrative personnel of each unit and consist of lists of officers and ORs taken-on and struck-off-strength, promotions, demotions, appointments, awards, and honours, personnel who were sick, killed, wounded, taken prisoner, or missing, and any personnel who were punished or tried by court-martial. Despite their name, these orders were not always issued daily. Sometimes they were issued weekly. With regard to discipline, Part II Orders contain specific details on the numbers of individuals undergoing punishment at any given time, the offences that they committed, the nature of the punishments that were awarded by company and battalion commanders or by courts-martial, and the dates when the offences and/or the punishments occurred. Part II Orders of the 19th Battalion were examined in the course of research for a commemorative history of that particular unit. Aside from furnishing useful insights into patterns of discipline within the 2nd Canadian Division as a whole, they also provide a detailed comparison with Gagnon's work on

discipline within the 22nd Battalion. A third source is an on-line database available from the LAC that serves as a finding aid to a series of microfilm reels with reproductions of the courts-martial proceedings of tried CEF members. There are 11,887 entries in this database, many of which may refer to multiple proceedings, as the known number of CEF courts-martial is approximately 17,000. The latter figure was quoted by the Judge Advocate-General, Colonel R.J. Orde, in a memorandum to the Canadian Army's Official Historian, Colonel A.F. Duguid. See LAC, RG 24, C-1, Vol. 1502, File HQ 683–1-30–2, Orde to Duguid, 9 April 1936. Even if it is assumed that each entry in the courts-martial database refers to only a single court-martial, the number of entries would still represent almost three-quarters of the of the known number of courts-martial proceedings, which would make it highly representative of the actual total. As it is designed primarily as a finding aid to the collection of filmed proceedings, the information on this database is limited in scope. It includes the name of the accused, his regimental number (or rank in the case of officers), his unit, the date of either the offence or the court-martial, and the section of the Army Act violated. No information is given on the verdict reached by the court, or on any sentences passed if the verdict was one of guilt. However, this database is useful for establishing the relative incidence of courts-martial among units and for tracking the types of charges laid against the accused men. However, the dating system employed is inconsistent, with many entries supplying only a year instead of a complete date. Some cross-referencing of courts-martial known through other sources also has revealed that the dates given in the database entries do not always refer to the same thing. Although most dates appear to refer to the date of the actual court-martial, other dates seem to refer to the date of the offence. This lack of consistency, and the fact that many entries do not supply the month or day, but only the year of the offence or the trial, make it difficult to use this database as a tool to track incidence of courts-martial during each month of the war. Nevertheless, it can be used to track incidence within a given year. See *www.collectionscanada.ca/archivianet/courts-martial/index-e.html*. A statistical ledger that outlines minor offences in the 6th Canadian Infantry Brigade on a monthly basis during 1917 and 1918 constitutes a fourth significant source of information. It provides some basis for comparison with data drawn from the 19th Battalion Part II Orders and from Gagnon's history of the 22nd Battalion. See LAC, RG 9, III-C-3, Vol. 4123, Folder 1, File 11, 6th Canadian Infantry Brigade Headquarters, Discipline, January 1917 to November 1918.

8.   For anecdotal evidence of "rough justice" in the British Army, see Richard Holmes, *Tommy: The British Soldier on the Western Front, 1914–1918* (London: HarperCollins, 2004), 555–56. According to Holmes, although it was "an offence under military law for a superior to strike an inferior, many units tolerated unofficial violence." After all, it was an age when a certain amount of corporal punishment was tolerated, even in civil society. School children were subjected to it regularly and foremen working in factories, mines, or shipyards sometimes "ruled by their fists." See, Holmes, *Tommy,* 555; Cathryn Corns and John Hughes-Wilson, *Blindfold and Alone: British Military Executions in the Great War* (London: Cassell, 2001), 85.

9. Morton, *When Your Number's Up*, 83. As historian Chris Madsen has pointed out, "military law serves strictly utilitarian and practical purposes in the maintenance of discipline within armed forces. Its endearing qualities are few. The application of military law is sometimes arbitrary and is heavily influenced by situation; it places the interests of service and group before the individual, and tends towards severe punishments." See Chris Madsen, *Another Kind of Justice: Canadian Military Law from Confederation to Somalia* (Vancouver: University of British Columbia [henceforth UBC] Press, 1999), 3.

10. John A. Lynn, *The Bayonets of the Republic: Motivation and Tactics in the Army of Revolutionary France, 1791–94* (Boulder: Westview, 1996; originally published in 1984), 36.

11. LAC, RG 9, III-C-3, Vol. 4129, Folder 3, File 1, "The Duties and Responsibility of an Officer," Brigadier-General, General Staff, Canadian Corps, 21 July 1916.

12. Confidential letter from Major-General Russell to brigadiers and battalion commanders of the New Zealand Division, 24 May 1917, as quoted by Christopher Pugsley, *On the Fringe of Hell: New Zealanders and Military Discipline in the First World War* (Auckland: Hodder and Stoughton, 1991), 188.

13. For historical perspectives on the concept of military leadership, see G.D. Sheffield, ed., *Leadership and Command: The Anglo-American Military Experience Since 1861* (London: Brassey's, 1997).

14. Canada, Department of National Defence, *Leadership in the Canadian Forces: Doctrine* (Kingston: Canadian Defence Academy — Canadian Forces Leadership Institute, 2005), 5.

15. For an in-depth study of the function and role of paternalism among British officers and ORs during the First World War, see G.D. Sheffield, *Leadership in the Trenches: Officer-Man Relations, Morale and Discipline in the British Army in the Era of the First World War* (London: Macmillan, 2000).

16. A search of the LAC's court-martial database reveals what appear to be six cases of mutiny committed by infantrymen of the 2nd Canadian Division. Only three of these LAC entries, however, match with the case listings found in Julian Putkowski's published study of mutineers in the British Army during the First World War. The three individuals in question, Privates L. Coons, H. Osborn, and V. Souliere, all belonged to the 21st Battalion. The first was tried for mutiny in March 1919 and the remaining two were tried in May of the same year. Coons and Souliere were convicted, while Osborn was acquitted. Two other cases listed in the LAC database do not match with entries in Putkowski's book. The first, Private John Chambers, is identified by the LAC as a member of the 22nd Battalion, but is listed by Putkowski as a member of the 23rd Reserve Battalion. The second, Private J.R. Kidder, is identified

by the LAC as a member of the 20th Battalion, but does not appear in Putkowski's listings at all. The sixth case found in the LAC database is Private J. Schmidt, who is listed as a member of both the 28th Battalion and the 2nd Battalion, Canadian Machine Gun Corps. In Putkowski's book, he is listed as a member of the Canadian Machine Gun Depot, so he most likely was not serving in the 28th Battalion at the time of his offence. Putkowski also presents around a dozen other listings that apparently refer to men from infantry battalions of the 2nd Canadian Division. But some of these individuals show up in the LAC database as belonging to reserve battalions in England. The others either do not show up as mutiny cases in the LAC database, or they do not appear there at all. To determine which source is more accurate, the original file for each case would have to be consulted. Accessed at *www.collection-scanada.ca/archivianet/courts-martial/index-e.html,* and Julian Putkowski, *British Army Mutineers, 1914–1922* (London: Francis Boutle, 1998), 91.

17. Colonel A.F. Duguid, *Official History of the Canadian Forces in the Great War, 1914–1919, General Series.* Vol. 1: *Chronicle, August 1914–September, 1915* (Ottawa: King's Printer, 1938), 25; *The King's Regulations and Orders for the Army, 1912* (London: HMSO, reprinted 1914), Paragraphs 493–501, 112–15; Holmes, *Tommy,* 557; Gordon Corrigan, *Mud, Blood and Poppycock: Britain and the First World War* (London: Cassell, 2003), 221–22. The *King's Regulations* detailed a number of additional regulations governing the awarding of punishments to non-commissioned officers (NCOs), the respective jurisdictions of company or battalion commanders in disciplining NCOs, and the types of punishments that could be awarded to different ranks of NCOs. See *King's Regulations, 1912,* Paragraphs 493 and 499, 112–14. A more succinct discussion of a commanding officer's powers of punishment over NCOs may be found in the *Manual of Military Law,* which states: "Under the terms of the Army Act (s. 46 (2)) a non-commissioned officer cannot be awarded field punishment or forfeiture of pay by his commanding officer, and under the King's Regulations a non-commissioned officer is not to be subjected to summary or minor punishments by his commanding officer. He may be admonished, reprimanded or ordered to revert from an acting or lance rank to his permanent grade, or may be removed from an appointment to his permanent grade, but this power of removal, if the non-commissioned officer's permanent rank is higher than that of corporal, is not to be exercised without reference to superior authority." See WO, *Manual of Military Law* [henceforth *MML*] (London: HMSO, 1914, reprinted 1917), Chapter IV, paragraph 31, 32.

18. LAC, RG 150, Series 1, Vol. 71, File "19th Battalion (Part 1)," Part II Daily Orders, December 1914 to March 1915; LAC, RG 9, II-B-5, Vol. 5, Inspectors-General Reports on CEF Battalions; Robert Craig Brown and Donald Loveridge, "Unrequited Faith: Recruiting the C.E.F., 1914–1918," *Revue Internationale d'Histoire Militaire,* No. 51 (1982), 58.

19. LAC, RG 150, Series 1, Vol. 71, File "19th Battalion (Part 1)," Part II Daily Orders, December 1914 to March 1915.

20. Godefroy, *For Freedom and Honour,* 6.

21. Brown and Loveridge, "Unrequited Faith," 58.

22. There are no comprehensive statistics on the levels of military experience among per-
    sonnel of the Second Canadian Contingent. However, a survey of attestation papers
    from 51 officers and 308 other ranks in the Contingent's infantry battalions revealed
    that all but one of the officers and just over two-thirds of the ORs (210 men) claimed
    some measure of current or previous military service. By the end of the war, the pro-
    portion of men in the CEF as a whole who claimed previous military experience was
    closer to one-third of the total number. Yet, although this survey of Second
    Contingent personnel revealed an impressive number of experienced men, the levels
    of their experience varied widely. Only 24 officers and 105 ORs of those surveyed
    provided some information on their attestation papers regarding the duration of their
    current or previous service. Of those who did, 16 officers admitted between one and
    10 years of experience, while 76 ORs claimed service of four years or less. Some ORs
    had only several weeks of service, while a few claimed just a few days. Only 15 ORs
    boasted any longer-term service, of between 11 and 15 years each. Eight of the offi-
    cers had served for 11 years or more, three of which had over 20 years of experience.
    However, in the majority of cases, these experienced officers had served on a part-time
    basis in units of the Canadian militia. See David Campbell, "The Divisional
    Experience in the C.E.F.: A Social and Operational History of the 2nd Canadian
    Division, 1915–1918" (Unpublished Ph.D. Thesis, University of Calgary, 2003),
    28–30; Morton, *When Your Number's Up,* 279. Without more extensive statistical and
    anecdotal evidence, it is difficult to determine the degree to which inexperience or
    ignorance of military law may have affected the quality of sentencing displayed by the
    Second Contingent's officer corps when dealing with cases of indiscipline.

23. In the summer of 1914, the established strength of Canada's land forces was 3,110 in
    the Permanent Force and 74,213 in the militia. Actual strengths were, in fact, lower.
    Between 1914 and 1920, total enlistments in the CEF numbered 619,636 all ranks.
    See Colonel G.W.L. Nicholson, *Canadian Expeditionary Force, 1914–1919: The
    Official History of the Canadian Army in the First World War* (Ottawa: Queen's Printer,
    1962), 12 and 546.

24. Madsen, *Another Kind of Justice,* 13. During the nineteenth century, a memorandum
    issued for the guidance of officers stated, "maximum punishments were to be the
    exception rather than the rule and were only to be imposed 'when the offence com-
    mitted [was] the worst of its class, and [was] committed by an habitual offender, or
    [was] committed under circumstances which require[d] an example to be made by
    reason of the unusual prevalence of that offence in the force to which the offender
    belong[ed].'" See Parliamentary Counsel's Office, *Military Law 1878–9,*
    "Memorandum Explanatory of the Army Discipline and Regulation Act, 1879," 16
    July 1879, quoted in *Ibid.*

25. *Ibid.*

26. In the First Canadian Contingent, which departed Canada in 1914, approximately 60 percent of personnel were born in the British Isles. Statistics are lacking for the Second Contingent that left Canada during the spring of 1915 and furnished personnel for the 2nd Canadian Division. Although the proportion of Canadian-born in the Second Contingent may have been slightly higher, it appears that the majority were born elsewhere, with the British Isles again being the dominant place of origin. See Colonel A.F. Duguid, *Official History of the Canadian Forces in the Great War, 1914–1919, General Series.* Vol. 1: *Chronology, Appendices and Maps* (Ottawa: King's Printer, 1938), Appendix 86, 58; Campbell, "The Divisional Experience," 17–23 and Appendix A.

27. In addition to the large number of absences, there were 29 cases of drunkenness, eight cases of striking, threatening, or using insubordinate language to superiors, 13 cases of disobedience or neglect to obey orders, and 30 other various types of infractions. See LAC, RG 150, Series 1, Vol. 71, File "19th Battalion (Part 1)," Part II Daily Orders, June to September 1915.

28. Denis Winter, *Death's Men: Soldiers of the Great War* (London: Penguin, 1979), 43.

29. "Rules for Field Punishment," in *MML,* 721.

30. LAC, RG 9, III-D-3, Vol. 4848, War Diary, Assistant-Adjutant and Quartermaster-General [henceforth AA & QMG], 2nd Canadian Division, August 1915, Appendix 2, "Instructions to the Assistant Provost Marshal, 2nd Canadian Division."

31. For a synopsis of Jarvis's pre-war career, see Craig Gibson, "'My Chief Source of Worry': An Assistant Provost Marshall's View of Relations between 2nd Canadian Division and Local Inhabitants on the Western Front, 1915–1917," *War in History,* Vol. 7, No. 4 (2000), 416, fn. 6.

32. LAC, RG 9, III-D-3, Vol. 5050, War Diary, 2nd Canadian Division A.P.M., 1 June 1915 to 31 May 1917.

33. Jarvis was not alone in his estimation of Allan's inadequacies as a disciplinarian. Brigadier-General Lord Brooke (then commanding the 4th Infantry Brigade), the divisional staff officers in charge of training and the divisional commander (at that time Major-General Sam Steele), had noticed that all was not correct in this particular unit. Steele pronounced that Allan would not "ever be fitted to command a Battalion" and Lord Brooke remarked that Allan lacked "the necessary hold on his battalion to ensure proper discipline." Brooke pointed out, however, that Allan "has been badly supported by his officers and although I have spoken severely to the officers of the 20th Battalion I see no improvement." See LAC, RG 9, III-A-1, Vol. 43, File 8–5-8, Steele to Carson, 14 August 1915; *Ibid.,* Lord Brooke to General Officer Commanding [henceforth GOC], 2nd Canadian Division, 16 August 1915.

34. LAC, RG 9, III-D-3, Vol. 5050, War Diary, 2nd Canadian Division A.P.M., diary text, 23 July 1915.

35. LAC, RG 150, Acc. 1992-93/166, Box 3442, File 21, Personnel file of Colonel F.M. Gaudet.

36. Gagnon, *Le 22e Bataillon,* 302.

37. The rules for Field Punishment (FP), as outlined in the *MML,* forbade its use except under conditions of active service. Since British troops were not considered to be on active service until their arrival in France, these punishments were not legally applicable in England. Although Canadian troops were considered to be on active service during their time in England, the aspect of public humiliation inherent in FP 1, to say nothing of its attendant physical discomforts, likely rendered it so unpalatable to civil populations (to say nothing of the sensibilities of the soldiers who had recently volunteered) that the legal proscription against its use on British troops in England became a customary proscription in Canadian practice. As with the British, this would change once the men of the 2nd Canadian Division landed in France.

38. "Rules for Field Punishment," in *MML,* 721.

39. Pugsley, *On the Fringe of Hell,* 91–2. Pugsley also reports, "In France, the award of detention was forbidden and any sentences of detention were to be commuted to field punishment." *Ibid.,* 92.

40. LAC, RG 9, III-D-3, Vol. 5050, War Diary, 2nd Canadian Division A.P.M., diary text, 11 July 1916.

41. *Ibid.,* 1 July 1916.

42. "Rules for Field Punishment," in MML, 721.

43. LAC, RG 9, III-D-3, Vol. 5050, War Diary, 2nd Canadian Division A.P.M., diary text, 16 March 1916.

44. *Ibid.,* for example, see, 10 July 1916, 24 November 1916 and 23 January 1917.

45. LAC, RG 9, III-D-3, Vol. 4084, Folder 7, File 1, Administrative directive regarding 2nd Canadian Field Punishment Station, 13 May 1918.

46. LAC, RG 9, III-D-3, Vol. 5050, War Diary, 2nd Canadian Division A.P.M., diary text, 8 July 1916.

47. *Ibid.,* 4 March 1916. For examples of further complaints about unit commanders, see Jarvis's war diary entries on the following dates: 16 and 30 November 1915; 11 and

17 January, 11 February, 3 and 4 March, 18 April, 20 June, 8 and 9 July, and 3 November 1916.

48. *Ibid.*, 20 June 1916.

49. Corns and Hughes-Wilson, *Blindfold and Alone,* 89.

50. The memorandum was generated by Canadian Corps Headquarters and forwarded to all units through divisions. See LAC, RG 9, III-C-3, Vol. 4129, Folder 4, File 5, 2nd Canadian Division A(a) 22 to all units, 17 February 1918. It read as follows:

> It has recently been observed in cases where men have been tried for serious offences by FGCM, that frequently the man's conduct sheet discloses a considerable number of entries for which only a light punishment has been awarded by his Commanding Officer.
>
> Two cases have recently occurred, amongst others where men have been charged with desertion, found guilty, and sentenced to death. In both cases the men's conduct sheets were full of entries, in one case six previous absences were recorded, and as a rule only very light punishments were awarded.
>
> As a general rule, in fairness to a man and in order to maintain discipline in a unit, it will be found more beneficial in every way, to inflict a substantial punishment in cases where a man has been given every chance to reform, but persists in rebelling against discipline.
>
> While it is in no way intended to interfere with Commanding Officers in dealing with men under their command, yet if the above points are borne in mind serious offences would be considerably lessened....

51. LAC, RG 41, Records of the CBC, B-III-1, Vol. 12, *In Flanders Fields,* 31st Battalion, Transcript of interview with R. Ferrie, Tape 1, 1.

52. LAC, RG 9, III-C-3, Vol. 4138, Folder 4, File 4, Memorandum, 28th Battalion, 2 March 1918.

53. LAC, RG 41, B-III-1, Vol. 10, *In Flanders Fields,* 21st Battalion, Transcript of interview with W.F. Doolan, Tape 1, 12. According to Major-General Russell, GOC New Zealand Division, it was a small minority (about 10 percent) of personnel who were consistently getting into trouble, and it was these men that gave platoon commanders and NCOs "all the headaches." See Pugsley, *On the Fringe of Hell,* 206.

54. Isabella Losinger, "Officer-Man Relations in the Canadian Expeditionary Force, 1914–1919" (Unpublished M.A. Thesis, Carleton University, 1990), 53–4.

55. Sheffield, *Leadership in the Trenches,* Chapters 1 and 10.

56. LAC, RG 41, B-III-1, Vol. 10, *In Flanders Fields,* 19th Battalion, Transcript of interview with Joe O'Neill, Tape 1, 8–9.

57. *Ibid.,* 18th Battalion, Transcript of interview with Shuttleworth, Tape 1, 11.

58. LAC, MG 30–E 488, William Clement Morgan Papers, Diary, 5 June 1917.

59. *Ibid.,* 11 June 1917.

60. LAC, RG 9, III-D-3, Vol. 5050, War Diary, 2nd Canadian Division A.P.M., diary text, 25 June 1916.

61. *Ibid.,* 7 July 1916.

62. For an analysis of the development of this professional spirit, see Stephen J. Harris, *Canadian Brass: The Making of a Professional Army, 1860–1939* (Toronto: University of Toronto Press, 1988), Chapters 6 and 7.

63. LAC, RG 41, B-III-1, Vol. 11, *In Flanders Fields,* 22nd Battalion, Transcript of interview with W.R. Lindsay, Tape 1, 9–10.

64. LAC, RG 150, Series 1, Vol. 71, Files "19th Battalion (Parts 1–4)," Part II Daily Orders, 1915 to 1918.

65. LAC, RG 9, III-C-3, Vol. 4123, Folder 1, File 11, 6th Canadian Infantry Brigade Headquarters, Discipline, January 1917 to November 1918.

66. Gagnon, *Le 22e Bataillon,* Graphique 8, 284.

67. In his study of the New Zealand Division, Christopher Pugsley noted, "Disciplinary problems all but vanished during the Somme: everybody was too concerned with the fighting.... It was more in the lull before and after battle that disciplinary matters became of concern...." See Pugsley, *On the Fringe of Hell,* 123. Historian Niall Ferguson has written of the "anaesthetic quality of combat," with regard to troop morale — a principle that also may be applicable to discipline. Ferguson argued, "soldiers in the most exposed positions were rarely those whose morale cracked. For morale to crack, men needed time to weigh their chances of survival. In combat there was no opportunity to do so. Instead of a rational assessment of survival chances, men acted on impulse: usually they fought, trusting that they as individuals would be lucky." See Niall Ferguson, *The Pity of War* (New York: Basic Books, 1999), 366.

68. LAC, RG 9, III-D-3, Vol. 5050, War Diary, 2nd Canadian Division A.P.M., diary text, 1 October 1916.

69. According to T.O. Jacobs, "personnel turbulence is endemic in military units. In war,

it results from casualties. In peace it results from personnel movements." See T.O. Jacobs, "Introduction to Section 4," in Reuven Gal and A. David Mangelsdorff, eds., *Handbook of Military Psychology* (New York: John Wiley, 1991), 391. It should be noted that a great deal of personnel movement occurs in any given unit during wartime as well (i.e., promotions, transfers, temporary attachments to other units or staffs).

70. Gagnon, *Le 22e Bataillon,* 285 and 301.

71. *Ibid.,* 301–03.

72. Pugsley, *On the Fringe of Hell,* 171.

73. LAC, RG 9, III-D-3, Vol. 5050, War Diary, 2nd Canadian Division A.P.M., diary text, 22 September 1916.

74. *Ibid.,* 7 March 1917. Jarvis later declared, "The latest drafts sent to this Battalion have been of a very low morale and the excellent reputation gained by the originals has been very sadly tarnished." See *Ibid.,* 14 March 1917.

75. Numbers of other ranks taken on strength as found in LAC, RG 24, C-6-i, Vol. 1874, File 22, 1, "Monthly Strength, Infantry, 2nd Division."

76. LAC, RG 9, III-D-3, Vol. 5050, War Diary, 2nd Canadian Division A.P.M., diary text, 3 January 1916.

77. *Ibid.,* 19 June 1916.

78. These numbers include men who were attached temporarily to other units, but who still belonged to the 19th Battalion. They also include repeat offenders. Many individual "cases," or "instances," as they have been termed here, involved multiple offences committed by accused individuals, who frequently were awarded multiple punishments, such as FP, along with fines or forfeitures of pay. See LAC, RG 150, Series 1, Vol. 71, Files "19th Battalion (Parts 2–4)," Part 2 Daily Orders, 1916 to 1918. When examining cases of punishments for minor offences or courts-martial cases in unit Part II Orders, one can distinguish between original personnel and personnel who joined the unit after its departure from Canada by looking at an individual's regimental number. This number is provided in the listings along with the individual's name and rank. Original other ranks from the 19th Battalion were issued regimental numbers within the following range: 55001 — 57000. Men with regimental numbers falling outside of that range joined the battalion after its departure from Canada. For serial number blocks assigned to each unit of the CEF, see Edward H. Wigney, *Serial Numbers of the C.E.F.* (Nepean: Privately Published, 1996).

79. LAC, RG 9, III-D-3, Vol. 5050, War Diary, 2nd Canadian Division A.P.M., diary text, 18 May 1917.

80. *Ibid.*, 16 March 1916.

81. *Ibid.*, 30 January 1916.

82. Gibson, "'My Chief Source of Worry,'" 413.

83. LAC, RG 9, III-D-3, Vol. 5050, War Diary, 2nd Canadian Division A.P.M., diary text, 13 April 1916.

84. Tim Cook, "'More a Medicine than a Beverage': 'Demon Rum' and the Canadian Trench Soldier of the First World War," *Canadian Military History,* Vol. 9, No. 1 (2000), 16–7.

85. For the purpose of this study, the 19th Battalion is the only unit for which monthly figures on minor offences were collected from Part II Daily Orders. For comparative purposes, the figures for this unit have been calculated twice, in accordance with the different time scales presented in Gagnon's history of the 22nd Battalion and in the archival source that relates the numbers for the battalions of the 6th Infantry Brigade.

86. Bell took over the brigade following Brigadier-General Ketchen's departure for Canada to assume command of Military District 10.

87. LAC, RG 41, B-III-1, Vol. 11, *In Flanders Fields,* 25th Battalion, Transcript of interview with Colonel John Wise, Tape 2, 3–4.

88. LAC, RG 41, B-III-1, Vol. 10, *In Flanders Fields,* 19th Battalion, Transcript of interview with Joe O'Neill, Tape 1, 6.

89. During the First World War, Canadian officers suffered a casualty rate of 54 percent, as opposed to a casualty rate of 37 percent among the ORs. See Nicholson, *Canadian Expeditionary Force,* Appendix C, 546, 548.

90. For an analysis of the development and maintenance of effective anti-gas policy and discipline within the Canadian Corps, see Tim Cook, *No Place to Run: The Canadian Corps and Gas Warfare in the First World War* (Vancouver: UBC Press, 1999).

91. LAC, RG 9, III, Vol. 5307, 2nd Division training instructions, 1918, as cited by Desmond Morton, *When Your Number's Up,* 247.

92. According to historian Isabella Losinger, "One is tempted to attribute what seems to have been an inordinately high level of drinking activity amongst officers to the burden of their responsibilities." Yet, it is "nonetheless difficult to justify the consumption of 'three whiskys [*sic*] daily before breakfast.'" See Losinger, "Officer-Man Relations," 266.

93. LAC, RG 9, III-D-3, Vol. 5050, War Diary, 2nd Canadian Division A.P.M., diary text, 15 June 1916. Based on Jarvis's comments at the end of December 1916, it appears that the "normal" number of arrests made by his police during a seven-day period ranged between 10 and 20. See *Ibid.*, 29 December 1916.

94. Determining the exact number of men who committed offences, and particularly the number of repeat offenders, would involve an exhaustive study of Part II Orders from each unit. However, from a survey of 308 ORs' personnel files from infantry battalions of the 2nd Canadian Division, it was found that 136 men were charged with one or more offences between May 1915 and November 1918. These men accrued a total of 282 charges, which works out to an average of just over two charges per man. Most of those charged were found guilty and received some form of punishment. Only three men were found not guilty of the charges brought against them and there were five cases in which the personnel records were unclear as to the finding of guilt or innocence. Of the 136 men charged with offences, 67 were charged once during their entire period of service; 31 were charged two times; 20 were charged three times; nine were charged four times; five were charged five times; and four were charged more than five times (one man of the 22nd Battalion was charged eight times; one man from the 25th Battalion was charged six times; one man from the 29th Battalion was charged 11 times; and one man from the 31st Battalion was charged seven times). Of the 282 charges brought against the ORs surveyed, the single most prevalent charge was absence without leave (155 instances), followed by various other forms of absence, such as from parades, work parties, fatigues, billets, et cetera (39 instances). Drunkenness was the next most common charge (22 instances). Other charges included desertion (nine instances); deficiency in or injury to equipment (eight instances); disobedience (eight instances); striking, threatening or using insubordinate language (seven instances); insubordination and resisting arrest (four instances); and being drunk and leaving guard without permission (two instances). There were 13 instances of "conduct to the prejudice of good order and military discipline" and 15 charges for other miscellaneous offences. See Campbell, "The Divisional Experience," 425–27.

9

For Bully and Biscuits: Charges of Mutiny in the 43rd Battalion, Canadian Expeditionary Force, November and December 1917

CRAIG LESLIE MANTLE

Guard what has been entrusted to your care.
— 1 Timothy 6:20, New International Version

While billeted at Shoreham-by-Sea, a training camp located in the south of England, Arthur Lapointe recorded in his diary in early January 1917 that he and his fellow soldiers from the 22nd Battalion, Canadian Expeditionary Force (CEF), had just endured an "endless night of shivering cold!" He lamented:

> I dozed for an hour, but that was all the cold would allow. This morning, after the distribution of a miserable ration, which none of us could eat, the men in our hut refused to parade. A sergeant ordered us out, but we told him: "Better treatment, or we won't budge." An officer then came to see what it was all about. We showed him the [broken] window, the broken stove, and the sickly meal, which was a mess not fit to offer a dog. The officer saw, and promised us better treatment, but could not get a second ration issued, and we had to parade with stomachs cryingly empty.[1]

Their experience of suffering was not uncommon, and apparently, neither was their resulting attitude towards such treatment. Other soldiers likewise believed that housing men miles behind the lines under conditions that closely resembled those at the front was "very poor policy" indeed and "only helps to … sow seeds of discord in the ranks."[2] So important were the smallest of comforts to the soldier, especially to those who served in the trenches, that the inability to enjoy the simplest of pleasures tended to impact negatively upon morale and, in a few cases, discipline.[3] To be sure, men derived great satisfaction from such amenities as a warm meal, a dry place to sleep or an extra tot of rum simply because military life was generally without "luxury" and was both physically and mentally exhausting.

Although the reasons that account for the behaviour of Lapointe and his *amis* seem fairly clear and straightforward, they serve to illuminate a complex an important phenomenon that mediated the relationship between leader and follower during the First World War. These men, like others throughout the CEF and those that followed them in subsequent generations, undoubtedly believed that they had entered into a reciprocal and unwritten "contract" with the military in which both sides were responsible to the other. In return for their individuality, their service, and if required, their lives, soldiers believed that they should be accorded a degree of fair and proper treatment. Just what exactly constituted "fair and proper treatment" varied somewhat among individuals, but the vast majority seems to have implicitly agreed on a useable definition. Most believed, for instance, that they should be competently led by men who recognized the sanctity of life and who tried to prevent needless casualties; they also contended that they should be provided with the necessities of life, that they should be accorded just treatment in all that affected their welfare and that personal interactions should, on the whole, be cordial.[4] Soldiers of the First World War, like those who came before and after, did not possess unreasonable expectations. They had a few desires that would, if satisfactorily met, make their lives somewhat more comfortable while they prosecuted whatever task was at hand. In many respects, then, they expected sound and competent leadership.[5]

When adequate treatment was not forthcoming, however, the likelihood that soldiers would unilaterally seek a solution to their difficulty increased substantially; morale, and eventually discipline, suffered greatly when soldiers were inadequately cared for or incompetently led. As noted military historian Richard Holmes once observed, "A sense of broken contract usually lies close to the heart of a mutiny."[6]

Because soldiers naturally expected to be treated with respect and dignity, rather than with disdain and contempt, that is, in a manner consistent with their sacrifices, many engaged in disobedient acts as a means of communicating to those in positions of responsibility that their basic needs had not been met satisfactorily. The refusal of Lapointe and his chums to comply with an entirely legal order seems to be attributable to their conception of contract and, by extension, their impressions of fair and proper treatment.

The small mutiny in which he and his companions participated was not an isolated incident, for the historical record is filled with similar episodes. Throughout the First World War, Canadian soldiers constantly resorted to various forms of protest that ranged in severity from malingering and insubordination to mutiny and possibly even attempted murder to demonstrate their displeasure with a specific situation or particular individual.[7] Veteran soldiers such as Will Bird,[8] Donald Fraser,[9] Frank Ferguson[10], and E.L.M. Burns[11] all offer relevant examples of such behaviour in their wartime or post-war writings; many more instances surely went unrecorded and thus are now unfortunately lost. Soldiers did not protest every unfair circumstance, but reserved their complaints for those situations that could be altered, that exceeded their already-remarkable ability to cope, or were of such importance that they could not be left without immediate comment or action. In most cases, the problem was quickly resolved without further difficulty or opposition, but in others, the result was much less satisfactory, as many individuals who opted to transgress the bounds of discipline and to challenge authority in an attempt to improve their present circumstances eventually found themselves confronted with a summary punishment, or more seriously, a court-martial. Such was the case with a small group of soldiers who joined the 43rd Battalion (Cameron Highlanders of Canada), CEF, shortly after it had weathered the muddy storm that was Passchendaele.

On 26 October 1917, as part of a larger attack launched by elements of the 3rd and 4th Canadian Infantry Divisions, the 43rd Battalion[12] advanced up the western slope of the ridge after a four-day artillery barrage intended to soften German positions. Although moving swiftly through the mud and meeting with early success, the assault soon floundered on a piece of sharply rising terrain known as the Bellevue Spur; later in the day, Lieutenant Robert Shankland won the Victoria Cross for stoically defending this outcrop and saving the battalion's gains.[13] After many tenuous hours, the Highlanders finally consolidated their position and awaited relief. With its strength now significantly reduced, the 43rd retired from the line and, in a few days hence, marched to the French village of Westrehem where reinforcements joined them in due course.[14] So depleted were the 43rd's ranks that one new arrival, Albert Cook West, remarked with astonishment that although he had received "a very warm reception" from a few of the surviving soldiers, the battalion itself was now "so small."[15]

Nearly one month after the battle, however, a number of soldiers found themselves incarcerated in a makeshift guardroom located somewhere in the village.[16] At an earlier date, various military authorities at different locations throughout France had summarily awarded varying terms of Field Punishment No. 1 (FP 1) to Privates Albert William Bonang, Charles Clergy, Sidney Herbert Cuff, Henry James Primmett, Wilfred John Graham and Charles Moar for being absent without leave. The first

In July 1917, Canadian soldiers from the 43rd Battalion march into the line. (Department of National Defence, Library and Archives Canada PA-1415)

346

four men had absented themselves on the same day and for approximately the same length of time, thus suggesting that they had acted in unison, while the other two soldiers had committed their offences individually.[17] The four soldiers were probably charged somewhere on the lines of communication while they were making their way to join the battalion in the field; they arrived under arrest and were no doubt immediately placed in the guardroom to serve the remainder of their sentence. The other two soldiers, Graham and Moar, were already serving with the battalion and had been for some time when they were charged. The nature of the punishment imposed upon all included confinement in a specially segregated area, a restricted diet that did not include the daily nose of rum, and an exhausting schedule of manual labour and drills in full marching order. The most humiliating and painful aspect of their daily routine, dubbed "crucifixion" by the soldiers, occurred when the prisoners were tied to posts or cartwheels for several hours.[18]

At 1545 hours on 25 November, the provost-corporal of the 43rd Battalion, Charles McPerry,[19] entered the guardroom and directed the six prisoners who were present, most of whom had just returned from a full day of work, to prepare themselves for yet another hour of pack drill. Incensed by this order and speaking on behalf of the larger group, Private Bonang immediately exclaimed that neither he nor his fellow prisoners would parade until they had received a full and proper meal. Their harsh daily routine had apparently prevented them from receiving nourishment for some time. Four other soldiers concurred with these insubordinate sentiments; only Private Moar acted as instructed, a decision that ultimately saved him from further punishment.[20] After the battalion adjutant and certain senior officers received word of this episode, two Field General Courts-Martial were convened on 9 December, the first to judge the alleged ringleader and the second to try the remaining four participants collectively, an arrangement to which they did not object.[21] Three charges were levelled against Bonang for his role in this incident, the most serious was "causing a mutiny" since he voiced his opinion first. His actions also warranted charges of "endeavouring to persuade persons ... to join in a mutiny" and "wilful defiance [of] a lawful command."[22] The other four soldiers were similarly indicted with joining in a mutiny and disobedience.[23] Considering themselves to be correct and justified in refusing McPerry's order, each man pleaded not guilty to all the charges brought against him.

In the early phases of each court-martial, both of which took place in the field,[24] the prosecution tried to build a strong and convincing case against the mutineers by calling forth and examining a number of individuals who witnessed their disobedience. Not surprisingly, much of this testimony centred on the soldiers' insubordination and illustrated how they had refused a legal order. Rather than offer evidence regarding the root cause of the mutiny (the apparent lack of food and some other reasons that will become apparent), the prosecution attempted to establish the singular and indisputable fact that every man had rebelled.

Appearing first at both trials, Corporal McPerry, who knew "nothing about the feeding of the prisoners," related that he had entered the guardroom at precisely 1545 and told those present, in a voice loud enough so all could hear, to "'get ready ... and fall in for pack drill.'" According to McPerry, Private Bonang, in response to his order, asked his companions generally and aloud, "'What about that boys? Are you going to do that?'" Then, facing each in turn, he questioned them individually, asking if they would participate. Only Moar, who was standing away from the others, opted to obey and he soon proceeded outside after assembling his equipment; unfortunately, no testimony was offered at either court-martial to explain why he pursued this particular course.[25] With an air of confident satisfaction, Bonang supposedly related to the corporal that the men answer "buggers your pack drill." To ensure that the soldiers had both understood and refused his command, the latter asked all of them if they intended to parade and each of the five replied in the negative. Aside from noting that none of the prisoners (except Moar) made any effort to prepare themselves for the drill, McPerry told the court that if the men "had changed their minds and decided to obey my order they could have called me or spoken to the sentry" who was standing just outside the guardroom door. Once he had issued his order, McPerry apparently left the guardroom and remained outside until after 1600, when the parade was scheduled to begin. His testimony also confirmed that the men had had a sufficient amount of time, about 10 minutes or so, "to get ready, fall in and be proved before the parade started."[26]

To strengthen its already solid case, in which the guilt of the accused seemed more than evident, the prosecution proceeded to call Corporal

Harold Reuben Smith[27] who was in charge of the regimental guard at Westrehem on 25 November. Being present in the guardroom at the time of the incident, his testimony corroborated most the facts related by McPerry, such as the prisoners' inactivity once the order had been issued, and confirmed the clear nature of the directive given by the provost-corporal.[28] In his estimation, there could have been no misunderstanding as to what was required of the prisoners. More important, however, Smith alluded to some of the reasons that accounted for the soldiers' disobedience. He recalled that when McPerry ordered the prisoners to quickly prepare themselves for one hour of pack drill, the accused replied that "they would not go ... until they had had their supper." From his perspective, they "seemed quite positive they were not going on parade." He also related that the drill would overlap the prisoners' regular supper hour that commenced daily at 1630. Despite having been in charge of the prisoners for only 15 minutes, from approximately 1530 to 1545, Smith testified that no one had complained to him about the amount of food that they had received up to that point.[29]

Echoing earlier testimony regarding the sequence of events and the nature of the verbal exchanges, the third and final witness for the prosecution, Private Moar, the only soldier who complied with McPerry's order,[30] offered additional insight into the origin of the mutiny by describing the actual quantity of food that the prisoners had received. He recalled that on 25 November:

> we had biscuits and bully for breakfast and a couple of tins of bully for dinner. We only had two tins for both meals. I had [one-half of] a biscuit myself.... I cannot say where the food came from on this occasion. I did not see any of the accused get any. If they had wanted it I can suggest no reason why they shouldn't have it. There was a grab for the food.[31]

In tacitly supporting the actions of his companions, Moar's statements indicated that other individuals had appropriated the majority of the provisions that were intended for the prisoners, many of whom were now on trial. The records of the 43rd Battalion reveal that at least four other soldiers were confined in the regimental guardroom at Westrehem in late November. Each of these men had been sentenced to a term of FP 1 for being absent without leave, and judging by both the dates and times that they left and returned to the battalion, they do not appear to have been absent together.[32] From all available accounts, they do not seem to have been present at the time of the mutiny in the afternoon of 25 November, although it is more than probable that they were in close proximity to the accused in the morning as all prisoners undergoing punishment would have been held more or less together. While the seizure of the food cannot be attributed to these individuals with absolute certainty — the testimony offered by Moar, and by all others, is too imprecise to properly identify the perpetrators — it seems likely, owing to their presence, that they were somehow involved. Indeed, being subjected to the same regimen as the mutineers, they too would have been hungry. By taking control of most of the provisions that were delivered to the guardroom, these men satisfied their personal needs, but in so doing, allowed some of their fellow soldiers to go without.[33]

Later, while commenting upon the findings of the two courts-martial, the Acting Officer Commanding, 43rd Battalion, Major William Kellman Chandler, recorded that:

> The prisoner's [sic] statements that they were without food had been previously investigated and evidence was on hand at the trial to show that they had been supplied with 24 hours [Field Punishment] rations the night before. This evidence however was objected to by the Court as immaterial.[34]

Unfortunately, the evidence he referred to is unknown as no documentation to this effect was included in either court-martial proceeding. Apart from clearly illustrating the court's desire to explore the singular issue of disobedience, these comments lend considerable weight to Moar's testimony regarding the presence of food in the guardroom, although its distribution still remains somewhat of a mystery.

In turn, each man eventually offered a few words in defence of his actions. As might be expected, Bonang contradicted much of the testimony offered against him when given the opportunity to defend himself once the prosecution had concluded its evidence. According to his recollection of events, he simply stated in response to McPerry's order that "'It cannot be done.'" In due course, he also denied asking the other prisoners if they too would refuse to participate and asserted that the other men had acted entirely on their own accord without any direction from him. To further demonstrate his innocence, he refuted all claims that he had used insolent expressions towards his jailer.[35] Finally, in an attempt to reassure the court of his character and perhaps to gain a degree of sympathy, Bonang recounted his record of military service that, much to his credit, dated from August 1914.[36]

Hoping to gain compassion and leniency, all the prisoners attributed their disobedience to the lack of food. At his trial, Bonang also said he "had been working hard at the transport lines and had had no meals for 24 hours," and as such, "I was feeling too weak for want of food to go on parade."[37] Private Graham, like other soldiers, claimed, "If I had got some food I would have gone on pack drill."[38] The assertions made by the accused with respect to their diet are consistent with the general experiences of other soldiers who were subjected to the same form of punishment during the war. Consequently, their claims must not be hastily dismissed. As historian Julian Putkowski observes in his study of mutiny within the British Army during the First World War, "most who underwent field punishment recall *hunger*, degradation and the brutality of the guards."[39]

Although each prisoner insisted that his actions resulted from the prolonged absence of provisions, a claim that Moar corroborated, a few suggested in the hope of demonstrating further justification for their imprudence that McPerry had employed an inappropriate tone when ordering them to parade. Private Primmett asserted that his jailer "said he would give us two minutes to *get the hell* out on pack drill."[40] Likewise, Private Clergy, who at the moment the order was issued "was rather weak from want of food," echoed his companion's remarks, for he too did not believe that "the way the order was given was proper."[41] By army standards, this language, if it was used at all, was probably not overly offensive, and so it seems at this point that the prisoners were searching for additional flaws in McPerry's character and conduct that they could turn to their advantage.

Throughout their testimony, many of the soldiers also suggested that the inability to bring their complaints before a higher authority encouraged their protest since no one could "get any satisfaction."[42] The lack of provisions seems to have prompted the men to attempt to speak with the orderly officer who, in their estimation, could have rectified this apparent oversight; none of the soldiers, however, claimed explicitly at their trial that they wished to speak with him on the matter of food.[43] While this officer had called at the guardroom early in the morning of 25 November, when all the men except Moar were out on fatigue as part of their punishment, it does not appear that any prisoner met with him throughout the remainder of the day.[44] Thus, when confronted with McPerry's order and the prospect of missing yet another meal, the soldiers demanded an audience since the opportunity to have their concerns heard had been lost through no fault of their own. As elsewhere in the trials, different witnesses offered conflicting testimony regarding the true response of the provost-corporal to this request. Although McPerry told the court that he intended to allow the men to see the orderly officer later in the day, thereby implying that the drill would come first at the expense of their meal, Smith noted that this request was in fact refused altogether. On the other hand, Primmett was apparently told that he could bring forth his complaint in the morning.[45] Regardless of McPerry's actual response, none of the above solutions would have proven satisfactory to the prisoners since their grievances could not have been immediately rectified.

While the absence of food undoubtedly prompted the prisoners' desire to speak with the orderly officer, Bonang testified that he wanted to see him because McPerry was in fact drunk at the time that he ordered the men to prepare themselves for the upcoming parade.[46] This inflammatory assertion, however, seems designed to gain currency with the court by discrediting the corporal upon whom the prosecution depended heavily as a key witness. In reviewing both courts-martial, Major Chandler noted, "The accusations of the prisoners to the effect that … McPerry was drunk are groundless. This N.C.O. [non-commissioned officer] reported to the Adjutant a short time after the incident in the Guard Room, and was sober then."[47] In addition, Smith testified that he did not notice anything unusual about McPerry[48] who, in his own defence, stated that even though some soldiers claimed to have seen him enter an estaminet (small café) that was conveniently located across from the guardroom, he had "had nothing to drink that afternoon."[49]

In sum, the testimony offered by all the accused and other key witnesses clearly reveals the reasons that account for the outbreak of this particular example of mutiny and explain the behaviour of the participants; the concept of a contractual relationship is further reinforced as well. On the whole, the prisoners desired proper treatment or, more precisely, an appropriate amount of food, from those individuals responsible for their care. They surely wished that those in positions of responsibility would waken "to the fact that fighting men require food to be in battling trim."[50] Indeed, soldiers frequently insisted that their immediate superiors behave in a fair manner when dealing with them, and when such was not forthcoming, the likelihood of disobedience increased significantly.[51] Rather than precipitating the mutiny, the absence of food on 25 November seems to have brought previous maltreatment to the fore, which, incidentally, had also revolved around the lack of provisions. At their courts-martial, many prisoners testified that they had not received nourishment for *some time* and were consequently very weak. Their hunger and exhaustion combined to add further importance to supper on this particular day. Faced with the bleak prospect of missing yet another meal, these soldiers believed that they could suffer these conditions no longer and ultimately mutinied to voice their displeasure at the less than adequate treatment that they had received. From their perspective, engaging in an illegal act served as a means of communicating their dissatisfaction and their reasonable grievances to those in positions of responsibility. Although they willingly endured many of the privations associated with Field Punishment, these individuals disobeyed a legal order only after the conditions under which they lived could be tolerated no longer.

In addition, the prisoners did not desire anything more beyond what was absolutely necessary for their general well-being and comfort; they tried to rectify only the specific circumstance that did not meet their expectations of fair and reasonable treatment.[52] Significantly, they did not protest against the harshness of Field Punishment itself, but only acted against those conditions that unnecessarily exposed them to harm. Judging from the lack of recorded complaints on other matters relating to their punishment — like other soldiers, they undoubtedly "groused" among themselves about their circumstances, but did not press the issue with their superiors — the men seemed willing, on the whole, to carry out their term of isolation, deprivation, and physical exertion. That they desired little else than the rectification of their single grievance is clearly reflected in the testimony of Private Graham who stated in his defence that if his hunger had been satiated, he would have followed the initial order to parade.[53] Although statements such as these may have been given to the court in an attempt to win sympathy and to curry favour, they must also be considered as a sincere expression of their intent, especially given the soldiers' singular desire to supplement the amount of food that they were currently receiving.

The testimony offered at both courts-martial also reveals that these soldiers desired responsive superiors who would attempt to rectify their legitimate concerns whenever possible.[54] A few of the accused, such as Private Primmett, took great pains to relate to the court that before the mutiny occurred, they had attempted to remedy the situation by following the proper method of bringing complaints to the attention of their superiors, that is, through the formal chain of command. Indeed, all the prisoners told Corporal McPerry that they wished to speak with the orderly officer who, in their estimation, could have dealt with their problems himself or could have, in turn, informed his superiors of the situation. When their initial attempts at resolution failed, however, they resorted to a more aggressive form of protest by refusing to parade until they were heard on this matter. The fact that the prisoners first sought amends through the appropriate channels strongly suggests that mutiny was not seriously entertained in the beginning; only when satisfaction could not be achieved did they decide to transgress the bounds of discipline because, in their opinion, they had run out of ways to seek redress. For them, disobeying a direct order represented the surest way of making their grievances known to those in command, especially since earlier attempts to rectify the situation had all but failed. As is certain, the inability to speak with the orderly officer encouraged their disobedient course for this additional grievance compounded their problems and, to them, further justified their conduct.

Finally, the prisoners also appear to have valued some aspects of their daily schedule, despite its rigour and intensity, and had undoubtedly become accustomed to enjoying a brief respite from the severity imposed by Field Punishment during their regularly scheduled mealtime. As previously observed, Corporal Smith suggested in his testimony that the men followed a fairly standard routine each day and that they sat down to supper at a relatively consistent hour.[55] That they would have formed through past experience a reasonable expectation that their food would arrive at a particular time seems plausible since four of the six soldiers began serving their sentence on 19 November, nearly one week before the mutiny; the other two had spent a lesser amount of time under punishment. Although the amount of liberty and freedom that the prisoners could reasonably hope for while in confinement was not substantial, they were after all being punished for infractions of military law, it seems reasonable to propose that they had come to expect that their meal on 25 November would arrive at the same hour as it had on previous days. To be sure, soldiers took great enjoyment from pleasurable practices and often protested when a particular routine that they had come to rely on for relief was, in their minds, needlessly altered by those set over them.[56] The cause of their disobedience, then, lies partially in the fact that a pleasurable and routine reprieve, their highly anticipated meal, would either be postponed or eliminated altogether owing to the requirement for an additional parade. McPerry's order conflicted directly with the prisoners' expectations of proper treatment and, to a lesser extent, a consistent schedule. This divergence ultimately encouraged the men to act in a disobedient manner.[57]

After the witnesses had concluded their testimony, the members of the court paused to consider the previous conduct of each prisoner before rendering their verdict. Lieutenant Albert Edward Grimes[58] of the 43rd Battalion, who prosecuted both trials, presented the lengthy conduct sheets of all the accused as evidence of their past infractions of military discipline. Each soldier had previously committed a number of offences while billeted at Dibgate Camp, England, that included being absent without leave, overstaying a leave pass, drunkenness, malingering, making false statements, and breaking out of either barracks or camp; few, however, were charged while on active service in the field.[59] Although these men were not model soldiers — the above charges seem to indicate impatience with army life and a strong desire to enjoy the local surroundings — only a handful of indictments were levelled against these individuals for disobedience and insubordination. Regardless of the nature of their previous convictions, however, these records did little to improve the court's impression of the soldiers who now stood before them.

A Canadian finds that a Boche shell has disarranged his home during the Battle of Passchendaele in November 1917. (Department of National Defence, Library and Archives Canada PA-2217)

Private Bonang, the individual who in the eyes of his superiors had instigated the episode, was found not guilty of the two most serious charges of causing a mutiny and persuading others to join in an act of resistance; he was convicted of wilful defiance and sentenced to two years imprisonment with hard labour owing to his role in speaking on behalf of the larger group. In like manner, the court found the remaining four participants not guilty of participating in a mutiny but convicted each of disobedience. Receiving a somewhat lighter penalty, all were sentenced to 18 months imprisonment with hard labour.[60] The court unfortunately offered no reasoning to account for its decisions, although the fact that the accused were sober at the time of the incident and that their protest was brief, non-violent, and had occurred well away from the enemy surely influenced its judgments.[61]

All men received a relatively harsh punishment considering that they were convicted of the lesser charge of disobedience only. In similar instances where individual soldiers from the 43rd Battalion refused to obey a lawful command, the court awarded a fairly lenient penalty.

Sergeant John Campbell Walker, for example, was sentenced "to be reduced to Corporal" after being convicted of "using insubordinate language to his superior officer in that he … when ordered to go to his billet … replied 'I wont' or words to that effect."[62] In a case remarkably similar to the present mutiny, a court found Private John Veitch guilty of "disobeying a lawful command," in that he, "when ordered … to parade with a Lewis Gun refused saying 'I wont have nothing to do with it' or words to that effect and did not subsequently parade as ordered." He forfeited 28 days pay as punishment.[63] Although these incidents occurred in mid-1918, they do indicate that the military responded to individual acts of resistance with a relatively light punishment, while collective acts of insubordination warranted a charge of mutiny and a much harsher sentence.[64]

In reviewing the findings of both courts-martial, the General Officer Commanding 3rd Division, Major-General Louis James Lipsett, commented:

> This is a serious case and the first case of this description that we have had in the Division…. I would ask that an example be made. Such offences must be checked at the first appearance…. Judging from their action the men have very lax ideas of discipline.[65]

Lieutenant-Colonel Dennis Colburn Draper, Acting Officer Commanding, 9th Brigade, offered a concurring opinion that the sentences should stand as awarded and recommended neither compassion nor mercy:

> Having in view the gravity of the offence of which each of these soldiers was found guilty I consider, in the interests of discipline, [that] the sentences as awarded should be carried out. In my opinion the effect of leniency in these cases would be injurious to the discipline of the Unit concerned. These men were already undergoing punishment and their defiance, constituting an attempt to make a mockery of such penalty, in these circumstances must be considered to possess an additionally serious aspect.[66]

The severity of their punishments, to be sure, stemmed not from the fact that the men had been found guilty of disobedience, but that they had acted collectively in refusing a lawful order. The seriousness and novelty of this incident, an apparent first within the division, worried senior military commanders at all levels who naturally desired the maintenance of a stringent regimen of discipline. In the hope of stemming further acts of mass action through deterrence, the court seems to have made examples of all five soldiers to demonstrate that such behaviour would not be tolerated and those who defied properly constituted authority in unison with others could expect severe punishment. By reducing or commuting the sentences in such a grave matter as this, so the reviewing officers believed, other soldiers might be tempted to act in a similar manner to these men since the possible benefits to be gained from disobeying an order could be perceived in some instances to far outweigh the expected penalty. At a battalion parade on 13 December in the village of Westrehem, the sentences of the five men were promulgated and read to all present for effect.[67] So swift was military justice in this case that barely four days had elapsed between the convening of the courts-martial and the publishing of the sentences.

Two weeks after the trials, the new battalion commander, Major Hugh Macintyre Urquhart, who was appointed on 23 December 1917,[68] issued a detailed set of orders listing the individuals ultimately responsible for the delivery of rations to those soldiers in confinement. Such a task fell to the duty company when the battalion was out of the line and to the quartermaster when in. The directive also stated that "rations for Field Punishment men consist of Bully beef, biscuits and tea. Prisoners awaiting trial or awaiting sentence will receive full rations." These orders clarified the procedures and responsibilities that seem to have been misunderstood or neglected at the time of the mutiny. Their presence in Routine Orders strongly suggests that food and its distribution was indeed the root cause of the incident. The fact that the battalion issued these directives immediately after the event, and once a sufficient amount of time had elapsed for Urquhart to accustom himself both to his new command and to this particular situation, lends considerable weight to the claims of the convicted men regarding the inappropriate amount of provisions that they had received while in confinement.[69] Without drawing an undue amount of attention to itself, the battalion admitted the existence of a problem in its daily routine through the publication of this order. Because the 43rd issued detailed instructions that explained the procedures relating to the allocation of food to men undergoing Field Punishment, this episode seems to be much more than a group of soldiers being insolent without just cause. With this being said, however, the true significance of or the motivation behind a published order cannot be known with absolute certainty simply by its existence alone, yet its presence strongly suggests that "something" was truly amiss that ultimately led these soldiers to rebel by taking unilateral action.

Although the court awarded long prison terms to each participant, none of the five served their entire sentence. Committed in early January 1918 to Number 10 Military Prison at Dunkirk, France, most individuals remained incarcerated for only a few months. After their trials, a recommendation was made to the director of military prisons in the field by the general officer commanding the British First Army, that if the men "behave themselves in prison, their sentences [should] be put before the Commander-in-Chief at the conclusion of three months."[70] Receiving the harshest punishment, Bonang served the longest term of all and eventually regained his freedom in mid-February 1919 after being incarcerated for slightly more than one year. Released in the spring and summer of 1918, Clergy, Primmett, Cuff, and Graham returned to the 43rd Battalion; the latter two were wounded in the hard-fought battles that concluded the war. Incidentally, in June 1919, Clergy was committed to Wandsworth Detention Barracks at Witley Camp, England, to serve the remainder of his sentence. His additional period of incarceration, which lasted for one month only, probably resulted from the fact that he escaped from a working party but was quickly recaptured by prison guards while interned at Dunkirk.[71]

During the First World War, acts of protest represented an effective, if somewhat risky, method for men to express their dissatisfaction with the present state of affairs. Far from being passive and completely obedient, as the military culture of the time would have them be, men of the CEF constantly held the military to account in certain situations they deemed manifestly unfair, or needlessly threatening to their well-being. To the Army's surprise, soldiers frequently "demonstrated a will of their own."[72] As is certain, insubordinate activities naturally attracted the attention of the military and, in some cases, forced senior commanders to confront a problem and to implement a solution. Because behaviour of this sort aroused concern, soldiers became all the more willing to resort to disobedience if the conditions they laboured under could be suffered no longer or their chain of command proved completely unresponsive to their legitimate needs and concerns.

This particular episode of mutiny is almost unique within the historical record of the CEF, as it is one of the very few times when soldiers took collective action against their leaders while billeted in the field. The vast majority of insubordination did not occur at the front, but in support areas or in training camps such as Kinmel, Bramshott and Ripon. Between 1914 and 1919, the CEF officially charged 167 of its members with mutiny and prosecuted 51 of these cases before November 1918. Of the 167 men who were brought to trial, the majority were either non-combatant troops or soldiers on the strength of reserve infantry formations, 127 were found guilty either of mutiny or of a lesser charge.[73]

All the soldiers involved in this particular case resorted to a form of protest when they felt that their personal welfare suffered without reason. Although a combination of factors contributed in varying degrees to their disobedience, the want of proper treatment, as manifested through the lack of food, strongly induced the prisoners to refuse the demands of their superior that, in the end, would further exacerbate their hunger and discomfort. Despite accepting responsibility for their previous actions, these men refused to tolerate undue maltreatment and believed that expressing their concerns was both justified and necessary. Moreover, the inability to bring their complaints before their superiors encouraged their protest of a situation that in their opinion could easily be rectified; the promise of being allowed to address the appropriate authorities after the parade had been completed held no weight with men who desired an immediate and satisfactory remedy. The possible use of intemperate language by one of their jailers may also have played a role in encouraging the men to disobey, although this seems unlikely. The above assessment also reinforces the notion that acts of disobedience were oftentimes triggered by an additional affront to the participants' expectations and values and that such instances usually occurred when the conditions to which soldiers were exposed could be endured no longer; rarely was one difficulty the sole, exclusive, and primary cause of a mutiny.

All in all, these soldiers expected fair treatment from their superiors or, more precisely, an adequate amount of food to sustain them. Faced with what they considered to be an intolerable situation, they tried to make their grievance known through the proper chain of command. When their initial attempts at resolution failed, they escalated their response and ultimately adopted a more aggressive (and entirely illegal) form of protest. Despite engaging in mutiny, they attempted to alter only those conditions that posed a serious and unacceptable threat to their overall well-being. As other students of disobedience have noted, "unit or group expectations that go unfulfilled, such as expected leave, timely relief, or *adequate rations* may promote a sense of a broken contract with higher levels of command," and, when combined with poor leadership, can encourage non-compliance.[74] The testimony offered by many of the prisoners suggests that when an individual in a position of authority simultaneously transgressed multiple expectations or values, acts of protest, in whatever form, became all the more likely. The lack of food initially encouraged the soldiers to adopt a hostile attitude, but the failure of their leaders to be responsive to their reasonable demands added additional weight to their claims of unfair treatment and, in the end, further justified their conduct from their perspective.

In contrast, however, the military establishment looked with trepidation upon their behaviour. For them, the sheer fact that these soldiers had collectively disobeyed a direct order while under punishment for earlier offences proved infinitely more important and serious than the quantity of food received by a handful of unruly and recalcitrant prisoners. Fearing that such displays of hostility towards properly constituted authority would spread, the officers overseeing both courts-martial sought to make examples of these individuals for the instruction of others who might be tempted to pursue a similar course of action. Whether such punishments actually served as a deterrent or not is a point still to be reconciled for it seems that soldiers frequently resorted to acts of protest despite the risks to rectify the needlessly difficult circumstances that they faced or the inadequate leadership with which they were sometimes burdened.[75] Notwithstanding the lack of attention paid by the court to the causes of this disturbance, the new battalion commander, who seems to have recognized that discipline could in fact be maintained and upheld by treating soldiers appropriately and with fairness, tried to prevent the occurrence of similar episodes in the future.

NOTES

Editor's Note: The present chapter expands upon an earlier paper by the same title. See Craig Leslie Mantle, "For Bully and Biscuits: Charges of Mutiny in the 43rd Battalion, Canadian Expeditionary Force, November and December 1917" (Kingston: Canadian Defence Academy [henceforth CDA]–Canadian Forces Leadership Institute [henceforth CFLI], March 2004, Unpublished Paper).

1. Arthur Lapointe, R.C. Fetherstonhaugh, trans., *Soldier of Quebec* (Montreal: Editions Edouard Garand, 1931), 8 January 1917, 15.

2. Donald Fraser, Reginald H. Roy, ed., *The Journal of Private Fraser, 1914–1918* (Victoria: Sono Nis Press, 1985), 93.

3. Historian Tim Cook, for instance, has observed the importance of the daily rum ration. He notes: "During the bitter winter months, rum acted as an important stimulant for keeping up morale...." He observes further: "Soldiers expected the rum ration and many considered it as owed to them for their hard life in the ditches of the Western Front.... When rum was issued, men were content. If it were withheld, it could lead to a plunge in morale." See Tim Cook, "'More a medicine than a beverage': 'Demon Rum' and the Canadian Trench Soldier of the First World War," *Canadian Military History,* Vol. 9, No. 1 (Winter 2000), 10 and 15, respectively.

4. A more detailed examination of the phenomenon of disobedience within the CEF during the First World War can be found in Craig Leslie Mantle, "The 'Moral Economy' as a Theoretical Model to Explain Acts of Protest in the Canadian Expeditionary Force, 1914–1919" (Kingston: CDA–CFLI, March 2004, Unpublished Paper). Developed by British historian Edward Palmer Thompson, the "Moral Economy" explores the cause-and-effect relationship between financial exploitation in the local marketplace and the behaviour of the British poor during the eighteenth century. Within the confines of the paper cited above, many of the most salient aspects of this theory were extrapolated to the early twentieth century to explain the disobedient behaviour of some Canadian soldiers. In essence, this discussion contends that the frequency (and in some cases the violence) of dissent within the CEF increased when individuals in positions of responsibility, regardless of rank, failed to meet the varied and reasonable expectations of their charges or did not respect the ingrained and cherished values of their subordinates. To be sure, a leader could encourage an act of protest by neglecting to provide the necessities of life, by treating his soldiers in an abusive and disrespectful manner or by failing to lead them competently, either on or off of the battlefield. Historian Bill McAndrew has reached many of the same conclusions regarding the expectations held by Canadian soldiers during the First World War. See Bill McAndrew, "Canadian Officership: An Overview" in Bernd Horn and Stephen J. Harris, eds., *Generalship and the Art of the*

Admiral: Perspectives of Senior Canadian Military Leadership (St. Catharines: Vanwell, 2001), 41.

5. The idea that soldiers possessed a set of expectations that could encourage disobedient conduct if they were not adequately met is the subject of Craig Leslie Mantle, "Loyal Mutineers: An Examination of the Connection between Leadership and Disobedience in the Canadian Army since 1885," Craig Leslie Mantle, ed., *The Unwilling and The Reluctant: Theoretical Perspectives on Disobedience in the Military* (Kingston: CDA Press, 2006).

6. Richard Holmes, *Acts of War: The Behavior of Men in Battle* (New York: The Free Press, 1985), 321.

7. The possibility of assassination, however remote and unlikely, must be considered since some evidence exists on point. See Stephen Pike, Gene Dow, ed., *World War One Reminiscences of a New Brunswick Veteran* (New Brunswick: Privately Published, 1990), 46–7. Within the British Expeditionary Force (BEF), subordinates sometimes deliberately murdered their leaders. See Holmes, *Acts of War,* 331.

8. William Richard Bird, *Ghosts Have Warm Hands: A Memoir of the Great War, 1916–1919* (Nepean: CEF Books, 2002), 53–4 and 128–29.

9. Fraser, *Journal,* 214–15.

10. Frank Byron Ferguson, Peter G. Rogers, ed., *Gunner Ferguson's Diary: The Diary of Gunner Frank Byron Ferguson: 1st Canadian Siege Battery, Canadian Expeditionary Force, 1915–1918* (Hantsport, Nova Scotia: Lancelot Press, 1985), 60 and 85.

11. Eedson Louis Millard Burns, *General Mud: Memoirs of Two World Wars* (Toronto: Clarke, Irwin & Co., 1970), 14–5.

12. In the 9th Brigade of the 3rd Division, as of October 1917, the 43rd Battalion from Winnipeg, Manitoba, fought alongside the 52nd, 58th, and 116th Battalions, all of which were initially headquartered in Ontario at Port Arthur, Niagara-on-the-Lake, and Uxbridge, respectively.

13. A brief summary of the deeds that earned Lieutenant Robert Shankland his Victoria Cross are provided in Arthur Bishop, *Our Bravest and Our Best: The Stories of Canada's Victoria Cross Winners* (Toronto: McGraw-Hill Ryerson, 1995), 70–1. See also, *London Gazette,* Issue 30433.

14. For a brief summary of the casualties suffered by the 43rd Battalion at Passchendaele, see Library and Archives Canada [henceforth LAC] , Record Group [henceforth RG] 9, III-D-3, Vol. 4938, File 434, Part 2, 43rd Battalion War Diary entry for 27 October 1917.

15. LAC, Manuscript Group 30 — E32, Albert Cook West fonds 3. West (693265) originally enlisted in the 174th Battalion, Cameron Highlanders of Canada, from Winnipeg, Manitoba. After being promoted to corporal, he was awarded the Military Medal for his bravery during the closing battles of 1918. See *London Gazette,* Issue 31227.

16. According to West, the billets occupied by the 43rd Battalion were scattered throughout the town. His diary entry for 23 November 1917 to 20 December 1917 records: "We live fairly well except our cook-kitchen is a kilometer or more from our billet and food gets cold before billet 61 [presumably the one in which he lived] gets there." See LAC, West fonds, 5.

17. Private Henry James Primmett (1000981) was sentenced on 19/11/1917 to 14 days, FP 1, for being: (a) Absent Without Leave from 8:00 a.m. until 9:30 p.m., 16/11/1917; (b) Absent from 8:00 a.m. parade until apprehended at 1:20 p.m., 17/11/1917; and (c) Absent from Company Orderly Room at 1:00 p.m., 17/11/1917. See LAC, RG 150, Vol. 82, 43rd Battalion Part II Orders, File 4, Sheet 2, 6 December 1917. Private Charles Clergy (489185) was sentenced on 19/11/1917 to 14 days, FP 1, for being: (a) Absent Without Leave from 8:00 a.m. until 9:30 p.m., 16/11/1917; and (b) Absent from 8:00 a.m. parade until 1:00 p.m., 17/11/1917. See *Ibid.* Private Sidney Herbert Cuff (859385) was sentenced on 19/11/1917 to 14 days, FP 1, for being: (a) Absent Without Leave from 8:00 a.m. until 9:30 p.m., 16/11/1917; and (b) Absent from 8:00 a.m. parade until 1:00 p.m., 17/11/1917. See *Ibid.*, Sheet 3, 6 December 1917. Private Albert William Bonang (488709) was sentenced on 19/11/1917 to 14 days, FP 1, for being: (a) Absent Without Leave from 8:00 a.m. until 9:30 p.m., 16/11/1917; (b) Absent from 8:00 a.m. parade until apprehended at 1:20 p.m., 17/11/1917; and (c) Absent from Company Orderly Room at 1:00 p.m., 17/11/1917. See *Ibid.* Private Charles Moar (1000201) was sentenced on 24/11/1917 to 7 days, FP 1, for being Absent Without Leave from 9:00 p.m., 22/11/1917 until 6:30 a.m., 24/11/1917. See *Ibid.*, Sheet 1, 8 December 1917. Private Wilfred John Graham (922369) was sentenced on 23/11/1917 to 7 days, FP 1, for being Absent Without Leave from 7:00 a.m., 21/11/1917 until 8:45 a.m., 22/11/1917. See *Ibid.*, Sheet 1, 8 December 1917.

18. The particulars of FP 1 are described in Julian Putkowski, *British Army Mutineers, 1914–1922* (London: Francis Boutle, 1998), 11 and 14; Desmond Morton, *When Your Number's Up: The Canadian Soldier in the First World War* (Toronto: Random House of Canada, Ltd., 1993), 84; and, Cook, "Rum," 15. An artistic depiction of a soldier being subjected to "crucifixion" has been used on the front cover of this volume.

19. McPerry (420761) was an original member of the 43rd Battalion.

20. Private Charles Moar was neither charged nor brought to trial in connection with this incident. He eventually resumed his duties with the 43rd Battalion, presumably after

he completed his initial sentence of FP 1. He died on 6 March 1918 from the effects of being gassed and was buried in Barlin Communal Cemetery Extension located in the Pas de Calais in northern France. See Edward H. Wigney, ed., *The C.E.F. Roll of Honour — Members and Former Members of the Canadian Expeditionary Force who Died as a Result of Service in the Great War, 1914–1919* (Ottawa: Eugene Ursual, 1996), 535.

21. Often composed of a president and three members, all of whom were commissioned officers, a field general court-martial (FGCM) could try both officers and other ranks for serious offences committed while on active service and could, if necessary, award the death penalty. See Putkowski, *Mutineers,* 10. In this specific instance, the same officers presided over both trials. Major Duncan James Hunter Ferguson, an accountant by trade and an officer in the 43rd Battalion, served as president, while the members included Captain Warner Elmo Cusler, a banker from the 58th Battalion, Lieutenant Burpee Clair Churchill from the 52nd Battalion, and Captain J.H. Thorpe of the British Army's 7th Manchester Regiment. Thorpe lectured to various units of the CEF on the topic of courts-martial. See LAC, RG 9, III-D-3, Vol. 4934, File 421, Part 1, 26th Battalion War Diary entry for 30 September 1917. Lieutenant E. Ward of the 43rd Battalion acted as the "prisoner's friend" at both courts-martial, and as such, assisted the accused in both the preparation and presentation of their defence. According to the database maintained by the LAC that indexes courts-martial prosecuted during the First World War-era, available online at *www.collection-scanada.ca/archivianet/courts-martial/index-e.html,* none of the five men who participated in this mutiny were brought to trial for earlier or later offences; this was their first and only court-martial, a fact for which they were no doubt grateful.

22. LAC, RG 150, 8, 649-B-4231, Schedule, Court-Martial proceedings for Albert William Bonang (488709), Microfilm T-8652. [This court-martial hereinafter referred to as CM1.] Bonang was charged under Sections 7(1), 7(2), and 9(1) of the Army Act. See Great Britain, War Office, *Manual of Military Law* [henceforth *MML*] (London: His Majesty's Stationery Office, 1914), 384 and 387.

23. LAC, RG 150, 8, 649-C-29813, Schedule, Court-Martial proceedings for Charles Clergy (489185), Sidney Herbert Cuff (859385), Wilfred John Graham (922369), and Henry James Primmett (1000981), Microfilm T-8659. [This court-martial hereinafter referred to as CM2.] These four soldiers were charged under Sections 7(3) and 9(1) of the Army Act. See *MML,* 384 and 387.

24. Bonang was tried on 10 December 1917, while the remaining four participants were tried on 11 December 1917. See CM1 and CM2, Certificate of President as to Proceedings, respectively.

25. Moar may have decided not to participate in the mutiny since he may have viewed himself as an "outsider" with respect to the larger group. As will be recalled, four of the six men seem to have committed their offence together. Such a common

experience would have undoubtedly created, or at least reinforced a strong bond of attachment between all the participants and might have, in the end, encouraged them to participate in yet another act of disobedience together. Since Moar does not appear to have been involved in this earlier episode, his will to follow a similar course as the others may therefore have been less strong and compelling. His emotional distance from the group may also have resulted from the fact that he, on the morning of the incident, remained in the guardroom unlike the rest of the accused who were out on fatigue. Finally, his fear of additional punishment may also have encouraged his compliance. Explaining Graham's participation is more problematic as he too was not involved in the earlier incident and was sentenced to Field Punishment after the other four soldiers had received their sentence; duress or his reasonable desire to gain group acceptance, especially since one seems to have existed, may have encouraged him to follow Bonang and the others.

26. For the entire paragraph, see CM2, McPerry Testimony, I & II, and, CM1, McPerry Testimony, I & II. The testimony offered by McPerry at both trials was remarkably similar. Some witnesses told the court that McPerry entered and left the guardroom on two separate occasions between 1545 and 1600 on 25 November 1917. Since the transcripts of both courts-martial offer so little evidence on this point, no definite conclusions as to his actual whereabouts during these 15 minutes can be offered here. Despite this limitation, however, the fact remains that the men disobeyed his order.

27. H. R. Smith (859542) was an original member of the 179th Battalion.

28. The order must have been clear and understandable for Private Cuff testified, "I took the order to be one which meant we were to get out on pack drill as soon as possible." CM2, Cuff Testimony, VIII.

29. CM2, Smith Testimony, III-V, and, CM1, Smith Testimony, III-IV. At the latter trial, Smith said he had been in charge of the guardroom since 1500 that afternoon. The actual amount of time over which he had control of the prisoners is somewhat immaterial for while he was present "there were no complaints laid to me about food."

30. When the orderly-sergeant arrived to drill the men at 1600, he promptly cancelled the parade since only one prisoner had obeyed the corporal's command. McPerry eventually ordered Moar to remove his cumbersome equipment, which was to be worn during the drill, and to dig a latrine. CM2, McPerry Testimony, II.

31. CM2, Moar Testimony, V & VI.

32. Private Peter LaPierre (198401) was sentenced on 1/11/1917 to 28 days, FP 1, for being Absent Without Leave from 5:00 p.m., 23/10/1917 until 11:30 a.m., 25/10/1917. See LAC, RG 150, Vol. 82, File 4, 43rd Battalion Part II Orders, Sheet 1, 20 November 1917. Private Francis Xavier Lepine (700399) was sentenced on 23/11/1917 to 7 days, FP 1, for being Absent Without Leave from 6:30 a.m.,

21/11/1917 until 6:30 a.m., 22/11/1917. See *Ibid.*, Sheet 1, 8 December 1917. Private John Hill (871072) was sentenced on 23/11/1917 to 7 days, FP 1, for being Absent Without Leave from 9:00 p.m., 20/11/1917 until 11:00 p.m., 22/11/1917. See *Ibid.*, Sheet 1, 8 December 1917. Private Robert Hatcher (693251) was sentenced on 23/11/1917 to 7 days, FP 1, for being Absent Without Leave from 6:30 a.m., 21/11/1917 until 3:00 p.m., 21/11/1917. See *Ibid.*, Sheet 1, 8 December 1917.

33. This selfish act, which would seem to contradict the notion that soldiers generally ensured each other's well-being and looked out for one another's interests, may possibly be explained by the fact that the majority of the prisoners who were brought to trial were new arrivals to the battalion; they arrived under punishment and probably did not interact with other soldiers as they were, no doubt, immediately incarcerated. As such, the "old sweats" who had served for a longer period in the 43rd and who now found themselves imprisoned as well, may have looked down upon them and decided to have "nothing to do with the newcomers." See, for instance, Bird, *Ghosts*, 36. These veterans may have felt that their previous service somehow entitled them to a greater proportion of the food. Without confirming the actual amount of time that the other four prisoners had been with the battalion, the above statements remain somewhat speculative. Within an infantry battalion, casualties, and the resulting influx of replacements, was a constant of life. Over time, those replacements who survived eventually became the veterans and, in due course, began to impose their will on new soldiers, just as had happened to them upon their arrival. Bird, once a replacement himself, recorded in his memoir that on one occasion, two men "were assigned to our cellar, and calmly tried to take possession of the best corner until gently shown the error of their ways." See *Ibid.*, 75. With this being said, however, some replacements stood firm and, whether through bluff or resolve, indicated that they would not be manipulated for the benefit of those who claimed a longer record of service and experience. See *Ibid.*, 10. Indeed, many of the 43rd Battalion men subjected to FP 1 in November had spent minimal time together under punishment, judging by the dates of their incarceration, and so, when combined with the fact that many were new to the battalion altogether, it should not be surprising that they were fairly unfamiliar with one another. One would think that the men who had had their food stolen would be able to identify those who were responsible for the theft, but these facts may explain this inability. It is also possible, of course, that the men who stole the food intended for the prisoners were not themselves prisoners, but from the 43rd Battalion itself. This statement, using the transcripts of the courts-martial alone, cannot be proven, and little evidence exists elsewhere to verify or deny such an assertion.

34. CM1, Major W.K. Chandler, Acting Officer Commanding, 43rd Battalion, to 9th Brigade, 13 December 1917.

35. CM1, Bonang Testimony, VI &VII.

36. He stated to the court, "I enlisted [in] August 1914. I came to France [in] June 1916 and went into the line at Ypres. I was wounded in June. I went to England sick in [November] 1916 and rejoined [the 43rd Battalion] in [November] 1917." CM1, IX.

37. CM1, Bonang Testimony, VI & VII. Private Cuff offered similar testimony for he stated to the court, "Supper, the previous night, was our last meal." CM1, Cuff Testimony, VIII.

38. CM2, Graham Testimony, VII.

39. Putkowski, *Mutineers,* 11. Italics added for emphasis by the present author.

40. CM2, Primmett Testimony, VI. Italics added for emphasis by the present author. Primmett also echoed much of his peers' testimony regarding the lack of food for he stated to the court, "I did not go on the pack drill as I had had nothing to eat." CM2, Primmett Testimony, VI.

41. CM2, Clergy Testimony, VII. He also asserted, "I would have gone on parade if my request [for food] had been attended to." CM2, Clergy Testimony, VII. Private Bonang expressed similar sentiments when he asserted, "If the [corporal] had asked us a second time to go on parade in a proper manner I would have done so." CM1, Bonang Testimony, VII.

42. CM2, Cuff Testimony, VIII.

43. During the trial of the four remaining prisoners, Corporal Smith, who was present in the guardroom at the time of the mutiny, offered no clarification on this point either; he simply testified, "I don't remember their reason for wanting to see the Orderly Officer." CM2, Smith Testimony, IV.

44. CM1, Moar Testimony, V, and, CM1, Smith Testimony, IV.

45. CM1, Smith Testimony, IV, CM2, Primmett Testimony, VI, and, CM1, McPerry Testimony, II.

46. CM1, Bonang Testimony, VI & VII. When examined by the court, Bonang stated that Corporal McPerry "was not staggering but he had been drinking." At his court-martial, Clergy stated: "When the [corporal] came in to us he was intoxicated." CM2, Clergy Testimony, VII. Neither Bonang nor Clergy offered convincing proof that McPerry was drunk at the time that he entered the guardroom.

47. CM1, Chandler to 9th Brigade, 13 December 1917.

48. CM2, Smith Testimony, IV.

49. CM2, McPerry Testimony, II.

50. Fraser, *Journal,* 297.

51. Mantle, "Moral Economy," 49–51 especially, but throughout as well.

52. This phenomenon has been observed elsewhere. E.L.M. Burns, a signals officer during the First World War, relates in his memoirs that "good officers paid attention to what the men were grousing about, and if there were reasonable grounds for it the officer tried to put it right. The men did not usually expect more than this." See Burns, *General Mud,* 63.

53. CM2, Graham Testimony, VII. He told the court, "If I had got some food I would have gone on pack drill." Cuff, who "had just come off fatigue when we were ordered to go on pack drill," expressed a similar willingness to comply. He stated at his trial, "If I had received a meal or a promise of one I should have gone on parade." CM2, Cuff Testimony, VIII.

54. For an example of how a responsive chain of command could benefit morale, see Mantle, "Moral Economy," 49–51 especially, but throughout as well.

55. CM2, Smith Testimony, IV. He testified to the court, "The prisoners have their supper at 4:30 p.m."

56. See again, Burns, *General Mud,* 14–5.

57. In all fairness, however, McPerry seems to have been carrying out the orders of a superior when he directed the prisoners to prepare themselves for pack drill. As noted in both trials, one of his duties late in the afternoon of 25 November was to assemble the men on parade for the orderly-sergeant to drill at 1600. CM2, McPerry Testimony, II, and, CM1, McPerry Testimony, II-III.

58. Lieutenant A.E. Grimes, a Roman Catholic gentleman who was born in Paris, France, originally enlisted in the 113th Battalion (Lethbridge Highlanders); he previously belonged to the 15th Light Horse of the Canadian Militia.

59. The number of separate occasions on which each soldier received punishment for a breach of military discipline follows their name: Bonang, 9; Clergy, 8; Cuff, 6; Graham, 3; Primmett, 10. In many instances, a soldier committed more than one indictable offence on each occasion. See CM1, Conduct Sheets, and, CM2, Conduct Sheets.

60. CM1, Schedule, and, CM2, Schedule.

61. These factors seem to have played a role in minimizing the sentences handed down by British courts-martial and probably did so at Canadian trials as well. Putkowski, *Mutineers,* 12.

62. LAC, RG 150, Vol. 83, File 5, 43rd Battalion Part II Orders, Sheet 1, 8 June 1918. J.C. Walker (153514) was an original member of the 79th Regiment Draft. The

transcript of his court-martial is available at LAC, RG 150, 8, 649-W-26664, Microfilm T-8690. This document was not reviewed for the purposes of this study.

63. LAC, RG 150, Vol. 82, File 5, 43rd Battalion Part II Orders, Sheet 1, 27 July 1918. J. Veitch (693223) originally enlisted in the 174th Battalion. The transcript of his court-martial is available at LAC, RG 150, 8, 649-V-1952, Microfilm T-8686. This document was not reviewed for the purposes of this study.

64. This statement also holds true for the period before the mutiny. On 28 February 1917, for instance, a FGCM sentenced Private Robert James McGowan (859722), an original member of the 179th Battalion, to 60 days FP 1 for "disobeying a lawful command given by his superior officer." See LAC, RG 150, Vol. 82, File 4, 43rd Battalion Part II Orders, Sheet 2, 9 April 1917. The transcript of his court-martial is available at LAC, RG 150, 8, 649-M-14400, Microfilm T-8675. This document was not reviewed for the purposes of this study.

65. CM1, Major-General L.J. Lipsett, General Officer Commanding [henceforth GOC], 3rd Division, to Canadian Corps, 19 December 1917. As an aside, Lieutenant Clifford Almon Wells, an officer of the 11th Reserve Battalion who eventually served with the 8th Battalion in France, thought highly of Lipsett, as did many others. In a letter home, he related: "He is, I think, the best known, best liked, and one of the most efficient officers of the C.E.F. The officers and men of the 8th believe he is in a class by himself. He was a very strict disciplinarian, which is by no means incompatible with popularity. He mingled with the men on all possible occasions." See O.C.S. Wallace, ed., *From Montreal to Vimy Ridge and Beyond: The Correspondence of Lieut. Clifford Almon Wells, B.A., of the 8th Battalion Canadians, B.E.F. November 1915 — April 1917* (Toronto: McClelland, Goodchild & Stewart, 1917), 5 July 1916, 168.

66. CM1, Lieutenant-Colonel D.C. Draper, Acting Officer Commanding, 9th Brigade, to 3rd Division, 11 December 1917.

67. LAC, RG 9, III-D-3, Vol. 4938, Part 2, File 434, 43rd Battalion War Diary entry for 13 December 1917.

68. Major (later Lieutenant-Colonel) H.M. Urquhart served as Brigade Major of the 1st Brigade immediately before being appointed to command of the 43rd Battalion. See LAC, RG 9, III-C-3, Vol. 4196, 43rd Battalion Routine Orders, Folder 7, File 1, 24 December 1917, Number 489. For his services and bravery throughout the war, he was awarded the Distinguished Service Order (and bar) and the Military Cross. The citations for these decorations can be found in David K. Riddle and Donald G. Mitchell, *The Distinguished Service Order — Awarded to Members of the Canadian Expeditionary Force and Canadians in the Royal Naval Air Service, Royal Flying Corps and Royal Air Force, 1915–1920* (Winnipeg: The Kirkby-Marlton Press, 1991), 106; David K. Riddle and Donald G. Mitchell, *The Military Cross — Awarded to Members of the Canadian Expeditionary Force, 1915–1921* (Winnipeg: The Kirkby-Marlton Press, 1991), 339.

69. LAC, RG 9, III-C-3, Vol. 4196, 43rd Battalion Routine Orders, Folder 7, File 1, 31 December 1917, Number 504.

70. CM1, Deputy Assistant Adjutant-General [henceforth DAAG] for GOC, First Army, to Director, Military Prisons in the Field [henceforth DMPF], 27 December 1917. This recommendation applied to all the soldiers except Private Bonang; the First Army desired that he serve his entire sentence. CM1, DAAG for GOC, First Army, to DMPF, 13 January 1918. In reviewing the findings of the courts-martial prior to forwarding them to higher levels of command, Lipsett offered a similar recommendation for he desired "that the men be committed to prison. If, for lack of space, it is deemed impossible to commit them all, I deem it essential that [Private] BONANG, who was evidently the ringleader, should be sent to prison and the other sentences commuted to 90 days F.P. No. 1." CM1, Lipsett to Canadian Corps, 19 December 1917. Sir Henry Sinclair Horne commanded the First Army of the BEF at the time of this particular mutiny.

71. LAC, RG 150, Acc. 1992–93/166, Box 865, File 24 (A.W. Bonang); *Ibid.*, Box 1793, File 50 (C. Clergy); *Ibid.*, Box 7986, File 2 (H.J. Primmett); *Ibid.*, Box 2196, File 50 (S.H. Cuff); *Ibid.*, Box 3713, File 35 (W.J. Graham).

72. Morton, *When Your Number's Up*, 19.

73. The present author compiled the statistics presented in the text. See Putkowski, *Mutineers*, 90–2. As earlier historians of the First World War have noted, mutinies caused by inadequate rations and unsuitable accommodations were far from rare in the larger British Army. See *Ibid.*, 12.

74. Joel E. Hamby, "The Mutiny Wagon Wheel: A Leadership Model for Mutiny in Combat," *Armed Forces & Society*, Vol. 28, No. 4 (Summer 2002), 581. Italics added for emphasis by the present author.

75. Mantle, "Moral Economy," 55–6.

10 ❧

Crisis in Leadership: The Seventh Brigade and the Nivelles "Mutiny," 1918

IAN MCCULLOCH

It was the fate of 7th Brigade, in its last great action of the war, to encounter enemy formations well rested, strong and full of fight.[1]
— G.R. Stevens, *A City Goes to War*

It was also the fate of 7th Canadian Infantry Brigade (CIB) to have a new brigade commander for Cambrai, the last great action of the war, and to lose two experienced battalion commanders in the early hours of the campaign. It meant that command and control were seriously affected and needless casualties were incurred.

The General Officer Commanding (GOC) 7th CIB, Brigadier-General John Arthur Clark, former CO of the 72nd Battalion (Seaforth Highlanders) from 4th Canadian Infantry Division (CID), looking back 45 years later would say:

> Never have I felt so depressed as I felt after that battle. It seemed impossible to break the morale and fighting spirit of the German troops. We felt that this *Boche* could not be beaten, certainly not in 1918. He fought magnificently and in a most determined fashion. He discouraged a great many soldiers in the Corps.[2]

General Currie, who visited the 42nd Battalion (Royal Highlanders of Canada) officers in a rest area after the battle in late October, also felt the discouragement. He asked them to tell him what had gone wrong:

> I want you to forget that I am the Corps Commander and to tell me quite frankly just what you think went wrong with the last show. I want to know exactly what you are thinking, whether you believe mistakes have been made by higher commanders or not. I want you to feel quite free to speak to me man to man and nothing you will say will be held against you.[3]

Currie was lucky that the Highlanders' CO, Royal Ewing, was on leave during his visit, for the embittered Ewing, no doubt, would have given the corps commander an earful. Charles Stewart of the Princess Patricia's Canadian Light Infantry (PPCLI) had been killed, Dick Willets of the Royal Canadian Regiment (RCR) had been severely wounded, and Robert Palmer of the 49th Battalion had been on leave. This made Ewing the only surviving battalion commander of the brigade involved in the battle under discussion. What the Highlanders said in their CO's absence is not recorded.

The corps would persevere and on 9 October, Cambrai fell to the Canadians. The brigade would take part in the pursuit of the retreating German army, at one point leading the corps through the Forest of Raismes. It would have the ultimate honour of being the first Canadian brigade to enter Mons (where the first major battle of the Western Front was fought) on 10 November, the day before the Armistice was declared. It would also be the first and only brigade to mutiny in the Canadian Corps. It would, however, continue to exist in name until the day its battalions got on the ships to return home to Canada. Before doing so, it would not be forgotten by its first two commanders. Brigadier-General Hugh Dyer came for a last goodbye to a brigade parade held in his honour at Bramshott. The charismatic "Batty Mac" (Archibald Macdonnell) remembering the "Fighting Seventh" would pen one last heartfelt message: "It is a proud boast for me to be able to say that at one time I commanded such a Brigade. I have no fear but that they will succeed in civil life and will ever exhibit the same qualities of courage, initiative, thoroughness and tenacity of purpose that they showed to such a large degree on the battlefield."[4]

PROMOTIONS AND PROBLEMS

The problems in 7th CIB began when its much loved GOC, Brigadier-General "Daddy" Dyer, was replaced by newly promoted Brigadier-General Clark on 12 September in the short lull between the battles of Arras and the battles for Cambrai. Dyer's leaving is noted by the various regimental histories and war diaries, which all extol his virtues and profess love and admiration for the man, but no reasons for his sudden departure are given. The Official History only states that Major-General Lipsett's departure and General Loomis's promotion "led to a number of changes in the command of infantry brigades within the corps." Dyer had served for 12 months under Loomis as a battalion commander and had been promoted during that period to command a brigade, no doubt on Loomis's recommendation, so it was definitely not a case of the new GOC not wanting Dyer.

Dyer's handling of 7th CIB at Passchendaele, Amiens and Monchy-le-Preux had been effective but not brilliant, so incompetence is ruled out. Health was more likely the cause, Dyer having sustained a serious wound at the 2nd battle for Ypres. Burns notes in *General Mud*[5] that the average tenure of command for a First World War brigade commander was 17 months. Dyer, with an unbroken 15 months of brigade command, preceded by demanding battalion work from the outset of the war, was due for a long needed rest. He had done his time honourably and was now accordingly sent back to England to the less stressful command of the Canadian Training HQ at Seaford.[6] Whether it was the best decision for 7th CIB "to change horses in midstream" is another matter. As will be seen, the battles of the last 100 days became more chaotic and unpredictable, making demands upon those in command and control to have well-tested and smooth operating procedures in place, and the knowledge to execute them effectively.

Dyer's replacement, the younger 32-year-old Clark, was a lawyer and militia officer from Vancouver, who had commanded the Seaforths from the outset of the war. As a battalion commander he had won the DSO three times but would appear from the outset to have been uncomfortable as a brigade commander.[7] An RCR officer in his memoirs revealed that Clark spoke to him after the war and "mentioned how uncomfortable it was for a new brigadier to ask so much from well-known regiments, to be under such pressure himself and scarcely more than a name to the brigade."[8] Clark himself would reveal in an interview in the 1960s, that to take over command of a brigade just before a complex operation such as the breaking of the D-Q (Drocourt-Quéant) line and the crossing of the Canal du Nord, was a daunting prospect.

"I was quite a young Brigade commander," he recalled for the Canadian Broadcasting Corporation (CBC). "I was 32 at the time and most of these COs were older than I was and I felt more or less a stranger in the brigade."[9] Clark thus came to lean heavily on the CO of the PPCLI, Lieutenant-Colonel Charles Stewart, the most experienced and flamboyant of the four battalion commanders. When Stewart was killed at the Canal du Nord action on 28 September 1918, Clark admitted that he "felt his loss particularly." Stewart had given him "a most generous welcome and the most loyal possible support. I'd grown to rely on him and I always felt his cheery nature buoyed me up and gave me a lot of encouragement."[10] That Lieutenant-Colonel Stewart could have had this effect on his senior commander in the space of a little over two weeks is a testament to his charisma and natural leadership abilities.

In the vicious fighting that followed Stewart's death, Clark would flounder and incur the disrespect of at least two of his four battalions — the PPCLI and the 42nd Battalion. Later, after the Armistice, his brigade would mutiny at Nivelles in Belgium in December 1918, ostensibly for orders requiring the men to march with full kit, but there were deeper and blacker reasons — resentment and hatred for Clark's ineptness in handling the brigade at Tilloy. Clark himself claims to have been demoralized by his first and only stint as a brigade commander in prolonged offensive operations. "When the 7th Brigade was relieved, I felt tired and depressed," he recalled. "Our losses were heavy. I felt somehow, that I had failed in the leadership that the troops were entitled to."[11]

At least one CO, Lieutenant-Colonel Royal Ewing, had exactly the same thoughts and took the first opportunity after the battles for Cambrai to make his thoughts known in a back-handed way — the end-month submission of his battalion war diary. The entry on Brigadier-General Hugh

Dyer's departure, which takes up almost the entire page, is placed over a small entry acknowledging the arrival of Clark on 12 September. The wording and style is unmistakably Ewing's and is a blatant message to Clark that he does not fit the bill. It is worthwhile quoting both entries in full:

> The departure of Gen Dyer from the 7th Cdn Inf. Brigade occasioned the most widespread and sincere regret. Not only had his leadership won the admiration of the men and officers under his command, but his personality had endeared him to all who knew him. His sound and balanced judgement — his sure appreciation of a military situation — together with his keen sense of the supreme value of human life made him a leader in whom we were able to impose implicit trust, while his genial and kindly spirit — his deep interest in the life of his men and his personal gallantry in action won for him the affectionate admiration of all.[12]

Almost as a footnote under this eulogy is the original entry that Ewing knew the new commander would be sure to read. It simply states: "Lt Col J.A. Clark, DSO, OC 72nd Battalion Seaforth Highlanders took over the Brigade. Col Clark comes with a fine record of service and we feel confident that the brigade will achieve further successes under his leadership."[13]

Ewing was not alone in his dislike of Clark. Another CO, Captain G.W. Little of the PPCLI, who temporarily replaced Stewart, was so embittered by his experiences with Clark, that in a 1960s interview with CBC, he exclaimed, "My brigadier, the son of a bitch, is still alive — I'll kill him if I see him."[14]

PLANS AND PROCEDURES

Sir Arthur Currie, perhaps the greatest general Canada has ever produced, considered his 26 August to 3 September offensive in 1918, crowned with the victory of breaking the D-Q Line, his corps' greatest achievement for several reasons.

[At Amiens] we went up against an enemy who was prepared for the offensive; here he was prepared for the defensive. There his trenches were not particularly good ones; he
had no concrete emplacements; he had little wire; his guns
were all well forward in order to help him in the advance he
proposed to make…. Here we went up against his old system, that which he has never had anything stronger any-
where. His guns were echeloned in great depth, and so we
were continually under artillery fire…. It is practically his
last, and certainly his strongest system west of Cambrai.[15]

"Few would disagree with Sir Arthur," states the Official History.
"The Corps' success in destroying the hinge of the German defence system
had not only made it possible for the Third Army to advance; the repercussions were to be felt along the whole front."[16]

The same day the Canadians were receiving congratulations for breaking the D-Q Line, Field-Marshal Foch ordered an offensive on a front of
125 miles, with heavy attacks to be delivered by British, French, U.S., and
Belgian forces. By 10 September 1918, six armies, three French, and three
British, had closed up on the last line of German defences as the Germans
withdrew. After the breaking of the D-Q line, Currie was told by the chief
of the general staff (CGS) that "the Commander-in-Chief was well pleased
with the conduct of the Canadians, and that he hoped it would not be
necessary to employ us in any further big operations during the year."[17]
But, unfortunately, this was a false hope, as Haig wanted to win the war
in 1918 and needed the Canadian Corps to help keep pressure on a crum-
bling German front.

On 15 September, General Currie was informed that the corps would
be the spearhead of First Army in forcing a crossing of the Canal du Nord
and striking at Cambrai, a vital centre of communications. Currie's daring
plan to accomplish the mission will not be given in detail here; suffice it
to say, it worked. The 1st CID and 4th CID led off for the Canadian
Corps. On the left, 1st CID overran its immediate objectives and pushed
on. In the south, 4th CID had less luck, meeting strong resistance at
Bourlon village and Bourlon Wood. The latter was taken only after it was
heavily saturated with poison gas by Canadian artillery. As a result, 3rd

CID was called forward before its time: On the morning of September 27th it was ordered forward to relieve elements of 4th CID and to sustain the momentum of the assault by helping to take Fontaine-Notre-Dame.[18]

Crossing the Canal du Nord in the wake of the other two divisions, 7th CIB found itself in Bourlon village and the eastern wood line of Bourlon Wood by 1800 hours. Brigadier-General John Clark was commanding the brigade in his first action. The new commander had been given a very detailed and ambitious task by an equally new divisional commander, Major-General F.O.W. Loomis, who had replaced Major-General L.J. Lipsett. Passing through the 11th CIB, Clark's 7th CIB was to force the Marcoing Line from the village of Sailly in the north to the angle of the Arras-Cambrai and Bapaume-Cambrai roads in the south. Once this was accomplished, he was to move his brigade to the north-east and pass the northern outskirts of Cambrai. Then the brigade was to cross the Douai road and railway embankment, take Tilloy and Tilloy Hill, and finally descend into the valley at Ramillies, capture the canal crossings, "and if possible secure the village of Ramillies and establish bridge-heads over the Scheldt Canal." The PPCLI historian notes drily that "it is easy to see after the fact that such a programme underrated both the opposition that the Germans would put up to save the bridge-heads, and the immense strength of their prepared positions on railway and hill."[19] In other words, 7th CIB was being launched into unreconnoitred territory for which there was no detailed intelligence.

Clark decided to use only one battalion to break through the Marcoing Line in his sector with the PPCLI detailed to provide support if necessary. The verbal orders he gave to the CO of the RCR later that evening for the first phase of the plan, however, did not leave much time for battle procedure. The RCR History relates the night's events:

> Soon after midnight, LCol C.R.E. Willets, D.S.O. returned to the unit from Brigade Headquarters and, summoning his company commanders to a conference in a shell hole behind a broken wall, explained the outline of the next day's operations. There was no time or opportunity to enter into detail. By the light of an electric torch, LCol Willets marked on a number of maps the

frontage and general direction of each company's attack, the boundaries that had been decided upon, and the objectives which it was hoped the attack would attain. The first objective was the Marcoing Line, beyond which the attack would swing north-east towards Tilloy if possible. Probably in the whole experience of The Royal Canadian Regiment no orders for a major operation had ever been more concise, as the Commanding Officer, knowing how little time there was to spare, wasted as few words as possible.[20]

Time was all important and company commanders tried to conduct reconnoitres forward but were hampered by the pitch darkness and the Germans' shelling of the area with mustard gas. At 0530 hours on 28 September, the three designated RCR assault companies attacked with one in reserve. The RCR were supported by four tanks and "a very effective barrage" and went straight from the edge of Bourlon Wood to the Marcoing Line, which lay behind a railway embankment and was sited on a reverse slope to their view. As they crested the rise "the men realized the grim nature of the task before them," recounts the regimental history. "Defended by great belts of wire and by many strong points, each with a garrison of trained machine-gunners and two or more guns, the German position constituted a barrier which obviously could be stormed only by an effort of supreme valour and determination."[21]

Mid-morning found the regiment pinned down under heavy fire from the front and the village of Sailly on the left flank. The CO was seriously wounded by a shell, and his adjutant was killed. The battalion appeared to be floundering. The RCR were inspired by the leadership and gallantry of one junior officer, Lieutenant Milton "Groggy" Gregg, who, when the advance had been held up by uncut wire, went forward alone, found a gap, and brought his men forward into the German positions. Then he led bombing attacks along the German trench system and when the bombs ran out, personally went back for more. His bold attack allowed the other companies to move up and get through. Gregg would later be awarded the RCR's only VC of the war for his gallantry.[22]

The PPCLI, sent forward by Brigadier-General Clark to assist the stalled RCR, lost its devil-may-care CO, Lieutenant-Colonel Stewart, to a stray shell as it moved up past Raillencourt. Nevertheless, companies, already briefed, carried on with the tasks at hand and by early afternoon both battalions were through the Line and mopping up support positions between the Arras and Bapaume roads.[23] But further progress was impossible for the time being as the 9th CIB's attack on their right flank had bogged down. The 49th Battalion came through the Marcoing line and took up positions on the right of the PPCLI to continue the advance towards Tilloy at 1900 hours. The supporting barrage favoured the 9th CIB on the right that got the village of St. Olle as its objective. The 49th and PPCLI went forward without the tanks they had been promised and encountered no serious resistance until they were in view of the Cambrai-Douai railway embankment. Then the PPCLI ran into an unmarked overgrown belt of wire and the advance was halted. The 49th Battalion lead companies were pinned down by heavy machine gun (MG) fire, not only from the front, but also from German MGs on their right flank in St Olle, which 9th CIB had failed to clear. That evening Clark ordered the 42nd Battalion and the 49th to resume the attack in the morning at 0800 hours.[24]

"When the supporting barrage opened at 0800 hours it was thin and ineffective," reports the 49th Battalion History of the ill-fated 29 September attack. "A and B companies advanced against machine guns firing at point blank range. Both company commanders were killed, but their men drove steadily on." After heavy losses the 49th Battalion closed up to the Cambrai-Douai road just the other side of the belts of wire. The 42nd Battalion, attacking on its left flank, fared no better, decimated by machine guns firing from the embankment while they were entangled in the wire. Major C.B. Topp, the 42nd Battalion's ground commander for the attack, recalled that the leading companies began the advance "on the stroke of eight" and that the barrage was "comparatively weak in volume."[25] Nonetheless they advanced:

> long thin lines of sections in extended order ... the supporting companies following in the same order some distance behind. The advance continued in this order almost as a parade ground movement for more than 1000 yards.

Not a shot was fired and it was thought for a time that the enemy had evacuated the position during the night; then the Highlanders reached the wire in front of the dump, two long broad belts loosely strung and almost concealed in the grass. The first ranks crossed the wire stepping labouriously over it strand by strand. The men in the second line were making their way through and the remainder of the Battalion was fast closing up. Then, as though by signal, dozens of machine guns opened fire at point blank range from along the Douai road from the railway embankment and from the high ground on the flank. So sudden was the burst of fire it was impossible for the men even to throw themselves on the ground in time to escape it. The leading ranks went down like ninepins, many, their clothing caught in the wire, hung there helpless under the stream of bullets. From that moment organized control of the attack was impossible, and it is to the lasting credit of the noncommissioned officers and the men themselves that even in the face of this devastating machine gun fire there was no attempt to turn back.[26]

The 42nd suffered 50 percent casualties in the short space of about 15 minutes, but like the 49th Battalion, its men struggled on through singly, in pairs and by sections, firing as they went. Survivors took up fire positions and captured dugouts along the Cambrai-Douai road facing the Cambrai-Douai railway embankment some 300 to 400 yards away. That "dozens" of MGs had caused the Highlanders attack to fail was proven the following morning when the 42nd advanced after the PPCLI and the RCR had passed through to capture Tilloy village. One of the two composite companies of survivors found 36 MGs abandoned among the German dead in a 100-yard stretch of railway cutting to its immediate front.[27] These were then put to good use and turned on the enemy.

After the failure of the 29 September attacks, Brigadier-General Clark's 7th CIB was ordered to take Tilloy the following morning. Historian Dan Dancocks has observed: "The choice of this brigade was questionable: it was tired and depleted, seeing action for a third consecutive day."[28]

Corporal Will Bird recorded the reaction of the bitter men on the ground at the time: "Sellars and his men said it was impossible that we had been ordered to attack again, that it was suicide."[29] The PPCLI attacked with just a little over single-company strength. The 42nd were reduced to six weak rifle platoons cobbled together into two weak companies. The RCR was not much better.

The PPCLI history records that the final battle for Tilloy was "beyond every other action of the later years of the war, a fight to the finish." The 49th history concurred when it stated the battle became an "intimate encounter — man against man and seldom more than section against section or platoon against platoon. The machine gun, either in attack or defence, was the key weapon." The "Left-Out-of-Battle" men of all the battalions were brought up the night of 29 September and the PPCLI and RCR were in their attack assembly areas by 0330 hours on 30 September. They jumped off at 0600 hours, supported by a tremendous barrage, as well as MG and trench mortar batteries in support, and stormed the railway embankment with relative ease.[30]

Brigadier-General Clark, 7th Infantry Brigade, with battalion commanders and their seconds-in-command at Mons in November 1918. Armistice Day is near, and the strain of war is evident on many of their faces. (Department of National Defence, Library and Archives Canada PA-3593)

Crossing the embankment, and again exposed to German MG posts and nests configured in depth, the two battalions soon shuddered to a halt. The PPCLI according to its acting CO caught the Germans in Tilloy "with their pants down" and had consolidated the village by 0730 hours, capturing a battery of 77-millimetre guns and 50 German MGs. Reinforced with the remnants of the 49th Battalion, the PPCLI hung grimly on to its meagre gains under heavy shellfire until relieved that night by 9th CIB, which fared no better than the 7th CIB in getting forward the following day. The RCR on the left of the PPCLI, while debouching from the railway line, was hit by a storm of MG fire, much of it coming from the direction of Blecourt, where the 4th CID was bogged down. In effect, by mid-morning, 7th CIB had been fought to a stand-still by the Germans and had ceased to be an effective fighting formation. Brigadier-General Clark knew it, his officers knew it and his men knew it.[31]

PERSONALITIES AND PRESSURE

Until Cambrai and the unfortunate aftermath of the Armistice, the "Fighting Seventh" had been one of the most dependable and hardest-fighting brigades in the corps. After Passchendaele, Brigadier-General "Daddy" Dyer had rebuilt its strength with new drafts of officers and men, honing its aggressive skills while in the line by fierce raiding and patrolling and training for open warfare when out of the line.

Three infantry battalions had new COs for 1918, the RCR receiving theirs immediately before Passchendaele, the PPCLI a few months later, and the 42nd mid-summer, when Lieutenant-Colonel Bartlett McLennan was killed by a stray shell.

In the RCR, Lieutenant-Colonel Claude Hill, DSO, "the martinet" who arrived just before Sanctuary Wood, was replaced by his second-in-command (2 I/C), Major C.R.E. "Dick" Willets, DSO, a competent and experienced "Original" company commander of the overseas battalion and a Permanent Force officer of some 10 years. Assigned a supporting role of providing ammo carrying and stretcher bearing parties at "Pash," his battalion performed well. His first test of command, however, would not come until after the battle of Amiens, which he had missed by being on leave (16

July-18 August) — no doubt a victim of the carefully controlled deception plan and secrecy that had shrouded the operation. The RCR would be led by a captain in this important battle. Willets was back for the tough fighting in and around Arras, though his battalion appears to have been caught napping before the battles for Orange Hill and Monchy-le-Preux. "Owing to the fact that orders for the move up to the line had arrived unexpectedly," notes the regimental history, "all officers entered the attack wearing the uniforms usually worn only when out of the line. In the close fighting that followed, this was not without its effect, for the officers, with belts and buttons shining and lightcoloured breeches, afforded a conspicuous and easily identifiable target to enemy snipers." It seems that Willets was carrying on his predecessor's legacy for maintaining Permanent Force standards at the front. When Willets was wounded by a direct hit on his battalion HQ at the battle for the Marcoing Line in September, his place would be temporarily taken by Major C.B. Topp, DSO, 2 I/C of the 42nd, who just happened to be on a liaison visit at the time. Subsequently a RCR captain became CO. Once the regiment was out of the action, Major G.W. MacLeod, DSO, a 49th Battalion officer serving with 3rd Canadian Machine Gun Battalion would be promoted to take command of the regiment, probably much to the consternation of several Permanent Force officers.[32]

In the PPCLI, Lieutenant-Colonel Agar Adamson, the eccentric 52-year-old CO known affectionately to his men as "Ack-Ack," was burnt out. "The previous summer, he'd spent a week in hospital with trench fever," notes his biographer. "Later, he'd been hospitalized by a dose of mustard gas. So poor was his vision, even in his good eye, that he was helpless without the monocle that was now enshrined in regimental folklore, and, even with it screwed in, continually fell into holes and bumped into obstacles when inspecting the trenches at night." He was also suffering from nervous exhaustion and the brigade commander stepped in. "The brigadier was very nice about it," he wrote to his wife. "Whoever is in command should be full of health and youth. My blind eye and age were against me." Adamson resigned his command on the pretext of his wife's ill health in the U.K., but in fact, it was his own.[33]

Dyer's view on his COs being fit and dynamic ensured that the regiment's founder, Lieutenant-Colonel Hamilton Gault, sporting a wooden leg from wounds received at Sanctuary Wood, was kept out of the running to replace Adamson. As Gault's biographer notes "the question of Adamson's successor had received little attention in the midst of the German offensives,"[34] but when it did, it illustrates the process and careful deliberation that went into selecting a battalion commander in 1918.

Brigadier-General Dyer believed Gault to be unfit and recommended the acting CO, Major C.J.T. "Charlie" Stewart for command. Major-General Lipsett, GOC 3rd CID agreed, but Currie, the corps commander, thought Stewart lacked the necessary balance of character and told Lipsett to consult Gault. Biographer Jeffery Williams takes up the story:

> There was no doubt in Gault's mind that Stewart would fight the battalion boldly and well in any kind of action. But out of the line, when the flow of adrenalin eased he had shown little interest in its day-to-day management. He was a soldier of Falstaffian tastes who too frequently shed mundane administration for a roaring party in the Mess. More than once the Regiment had had to extract him from trouble when he was on leave in London. More than once, after drinking too much, he had been hidden from a visiting general. He was impulsive and prone to speak on serious subjects without much thought. He was unlikely to represent the Regiment well within the Corps and would probably be regarded as a lightweight, if not a buffoon. He seemed incapable of maintaining a judicious distance from his subordinates — to draw the line between friendliness and familiarity, between authority and indiscipline — an essential quality of a commander. But in Gault's view, one of the worse results of the careless running of the regiment would be that the men would suffer.[35]

Stewart's tactical competence and ability to do what was right in action was beyond reproach, but it was administration, an equally important aspect of command, that was considered his major failing. Without a firm grip on administration, Stewart was not considered completely "professional," nor was he a true "gentleman" with his "unbalanced" and flawed character. Gault recommended that he, as senior major, should take command and the corps commander agreed. The 18 June 1918 Canadian Corps orders announced: "Major (Acting Lieutenant-Colonel) A.H. Gault to be temporary lieutenant-colonel and to command PPCLI with effect from 28 March 1918." When Gault arrived at the regiment however, he found Stewart on leave and was met by the acting 2 I/C, Major George Macdonald (former staff captain "I" of 7th CIB who had recovered from wounds), who asked to speak to him privately. By a twist of fate, the final "informal" political aspect of the battalion commander selection process kicked in. Bluntly, Macdonald told Gault that the regiment as a whole no longer knew him and the officers thought him physically unfit to command. "They wanted Stewart, a first-rate fighting soldier, who had commanded them for the past three months, was known to them and enjoyed their confidence," notes the biographer. The final revelation was that Dyer, the brigade commander, who had not yet spoken to Gault, thought that Gault was unfit to command and had asked for Stewart.[36]

Gault was stunned and went to an interview with the GOC 7th CIB where he learned the full truth. "Much as 'Daddy' Dyer admired Gault and regarded him as a friend, he was indeed of the opinion, that, with only one leg, he was unfit to command," records Williams.

> As gently as he could, [Dyer] told him so and confirmed that he had asked for Stewart.... When [Gault] left brigade headquarters, he was near to despair. Since his marriage had been destroyed, he had focused all his love and aspirations on the regiment which now had rejected him.... If his officers and brigadier regarded him as being unfit to lead, to him there was no alternative but to refuse the command that had become his life's ambition.[37]

Gault would command the regiment after the Armistice, but not before the ill-disciplined rot of Stewart's tenure of command had set in with unfortunate results.

In all fairness, Stewart was well-liked by both his brigade commanders and the other battalion commanders. The PPCLI History states that he possessed "a very unusual personality" and that he "was one of the best known battalion officers in the Canadian Corps" because of his "endless tales of his life as a rolling stone, as a Royal North-West Mounted Policeman, as a campaigner in Belgium and France, [and] of whimsical dare-devilry in the four corners of the earth." One of his platoon commanders remembered: "The tales of Charlie Stewart were legend. He had been a soldier of fortune, a Nova Scotian by birth, and had fought, it seemed, in half the armies in the world. He was quite an original character as was Adamson [who] had all the qualities of leadership which he chose to hide under a whimsical and offhand manner."[38] Adamson, the former CO, as selfless in his devotion to the regiment as Gault, was incensed with his former battalion officers. He was convinced that too many officers were becoming greedy for promotion and he wrote to his wife that "the best of them is inclined to forget what he came out here for." He added:

> I consider that Charlie Stewart is selfish in the matter and … I am ashamed of C.S. and the other officers whom he should never have allowed to be on equal terms with him in matters of policy. He will never be anything but an irresponsible boy without any of the reserve and dignity that should go with the Command of a Regiment and will never be able to do more than command a fighting company, and that he would always do well and gallantly.[39]

The 42nd Battalion would lose its beloved CO, Lieutenant-Colonel McLennan, to a freak shell while on his reconnaissance four days before the battle of Amiens. His young 2 I/C, Major Royal Ewing, was a militia officer and insurance broker before the war, an "Original" officer who had served continuously in France as platoon commander, adjutant, and company commander. The 42nd padre summed up everyone's feelings regarding McLennan's death in his diary:

> Our loss cannot be reckoned in words. All that he has been to us and done for us we shall never know fully, and only with the passing of days shall we begin to realize how his spirit was the dynamic of all our life and the foundation-stone of all that is true and worthy in our battalion…. His life here bore its own witness. In honour without stain, in

chivalry beyond reproach, in duty without fear, in leadership supreme, in friendship surpassingly loyal, he lived among us the perfect type of soldier and gentleman.[40]

The problems in 7th CIB started with the death of Lieutenant-Colonel Stewart on 28 September, whom most officers in the brigade had thought was indestructible. Morale in Stewart's battalion visibly sagged and Clark became concerned when the PPCLI were held up by a wide belt of barbed wire blocking the way to the Douai-Cambrai road. The barrier in question was a formidable obstacle, so overgrown with vegetation that it could not be detected on aerial photographs. Despite the descending darkness, the PPCLI had made a determined effort to overcome this concealed barrier and had discovered a small gap. It was, however, an intentional gap with several German machine guns accurately trained on it. Soldiers tried to rush it in the failing light, but were mown down. More than 40 PPCLI dead were found later at this gap, heaped in a 20-yard radius. Under the cover of darkness, the PPCLI withdrew 200 yards to lick their wounds. Captain Little, the senior company commander and acting CO as of 1600 hours that afternoon, now takes up the tale:

> In our first attacks at Tilloy we were held up in a sunken road by wire and … we couldn't move, so we came back about 200 yards. In the first interview I had with the Brigadier, he said, "Little, do you know the first principles of war?" I said, "I'm not sure. What are they?" "Well," he says, "One of them is to keep whatever you've got." I said, "We never had it, so don't worry." Then he said, "The 42nd is going to do it." So he told Royal Ewing [CO 42nd] that they were going to do it and Royal Ewing said, "We don't want to do it, the PPCLI couldn't do it, we can't do it." "Why?" asked Clark. "Because there's too much wire there." "How do you know there's too much wire there?" "The PPCLI told us." [Clark] said, "I have aerial photographs. There's no wire there." Royal said, "If the PPCLI tell us there's wire, we believe them sir. If we told them there was wire, they'd believe us too!"[41]

That this shared intelligence on the wire obstacle had been brought to Clark's attention, but not acted upon, is borne out by Little's comments in his after-action report when he states: "It is not sufficient to rely alone on aerial photographs for the locating of wire. Personal recce seems to be absolutely necessary." Another reference to the above conversation was the telling statement: "The closest possible liaison between battalions is of greatest value. Battalion HQs were close together, and necessary information from participating units was readily at hand."[42] In other words there was no excuse to ignore the reality of a significant obstacle, which required artillery bombardment. On the other hand, the brigade had a mission and Clark in effect was telling his subordinates to get on with it.

At the end of Little and Ewing's heated exchange with Clark, Ewing reportedly agreed to make the attack, but under protest. Ewing was so worried that he travelled to the RCR BHQ to retrieve his 2 I/C, Major Charles ("Toppo") Topp, who was the acting CO of the RCR after a shell had seriously wounded Lieutenant-Colonel C.R.E. "Dick" Willets the preceding day. Topp recalled later in a letter to Duguid, the official war historian and a close personal friend, that Ewing came to see him at 0200 hours, 29 September, the night "black as the ace of spades," and:

> [Ewing] told me that the 42nd had been ordered to attack at 8 am to the left of the RCR position: that he was extremely worried, having not seen the ground and having had no opportunity whatsoever of locating routes to the assembly position. No one, he said, seemed able to guide the battalion and he concluded with the request — "For God's sakes, Toppo. Come along with us. We're in a hell of a jam!" ... I knew the ground already because I'd been there with the RCR, so I left my command without permission, simply notified the brigade that I was returning to the 42nd....[43]

One might ask where were the brigade observers, who were supposed to act as guides for such operations. These important brigade assets may have been casualties in earlier battles, with no trained personnel remaining to fill their important role. On the other hand, normal command and control measures by the brigade may have simply been discarded for the sake of maintaining momentum. The 42nd jumped off from the forward positions of the PPCLI with minimal artillery support, as did the 49th on the right, and advanced to where the PPCLI had been stopped. "The 42nd had 340 casualties in 10 minutes," states Little (the actual official records show 288 all ranks). "Toppo," the designated commander on the ground for the attack, the four company commanders and the four company 2 I/Cs were all casualties. The 49th were also badly battered as they forced a way through the wire obstacle and forced German machine-gunners to fall back to the railway embankment and village of Tilloy.[44]

Ewing's rage is scarcely concealed in his after-action report as to where the exact problem areas in the attack occurred. Most can be laid directly at Clark's door, and significantly, not a single one appears as a brigade comment in its after-action report to division. Ewing noted among other things "the desireability [sic] of an opportunity to make a reconnaissance before an attack if at all possible"; "faulty info as in the attack of the 29th Sept when a belt of wire was run into which was not known to exist"; "the necessity for more accurate information as to the existing line, and as to position from which the jump off is to be made, before making an attack, and the consequent impossibility of laying down a proper line for the artillery"; and, "the necessity of more time being given to battalion commanders prior to an intended attack to go into the matter thoroughly with their company commanders, and the latter in turn with their companies, and that ample time be given to the latter to get into position."[45]

In this latter point Ewing was not alone. Major Chattell, acting CO of the 49th Battalion, who had attacked on the 42nd's right the same morning, caustically noted his chief concern was:

> The importance of receiving definite and final orders for the successive attacks in sufficient time to admit of those most interested and involved being fully acquainted with the situation. The difficulties of communicating with frontline Company Commanders does not appear to be fully appreciated.[46]

Launching into the unknown without prior recce, thorough preparation, and good artillery support was a revisitation of the Somme experience. It was not surprising that some experienced veterans, who knew what resources were available and how artillery-infantry cooperation was supposed to work, would become bitterly convinced that their lives were being thrown away on the whims of higher command.

Clark had not fully grasped the battle procedure required for a brigade in mobile operations and was falling back on the command experience he understood best. He was treating his battalion commanders as if they were company commanders. Captain Little noted that:

> [Clark] was a great battalion commander but he didn't realize that when he became brigadier he had four battalion commanders working for him…. We weren't given the opportunity [of commanding]. The higher command had a strategic plan that they were going to win the war before they knew it, before anybody else knew it, and we were told to do impossible things.[47]

The inexperienced Clark hinted in an earlier quote that he was under pressure from above to push on as fast as he could. His battalion commanders did not feel this should be accomplished by eliminating battle procedure or without some "sure appreciation of the military situation" as his predecessor had been wont to do. Ewing openly criticized Clark in his after-action report when he stated:

> had it been possible to delay the attack on the morning of the 29th in order to get full information as to conditions, I am of the opinion that with a bombardment by the heavies on the dumps and the railway line, followed by a barrage, it would have been possible to have got forward without anything like as heavy casualties.[48]

Clark, in his mind, was responsible for the butcher's bill for not having the courage to tell Loomis that he needed more time and resources.

In some fairness to Clark, however, the 2000 hours attack of the

42nd was not an isolated affair. All 3rd CID's brigades were attacking, the reasoning being that maintaining pressure and attacking on a broad front was the best defence against German counter-attack. However the brigade attacks were not coordinated. As Dancocks has commented in *Spearhead to Victory,* his study of the corps' operations in 1918 down to the brigade level:

> it might have been expected ... that the Third Division would have problems. The three senior officers directing its operations on [28–30] September were all rookies. The divisional commander, Major-General Frederick Loomis, had been promoted barely two weeks earlier and both brigades [7th CIB and 9th CIB] were led by men unfamiliar with their commands.[49]
>
> The lack of time for units to prepare or to allow their supporting artillery to close up with the frontline and prepare the way resulted in the 29th [of] September being a day of extremely bitter fighting with very little ground gained for any CEF units.[50]

Little recalls that after the 42nd got the hell knocked out of them he had his second interview with Brigadier-General Clark on the evening of 29 September:

> He said "Okay, Little, you're going to do it again. You didn't do it the first time, so you're going to do it now." I said, "I don't think we have enough men to do it."
>
> "If you haven't, Little, then you have a lot of stragglers."
>
> Well, I hope you can see that saying that to a fellow who was in the PPCLI as I, was exactly like calling a fellow the worst name you can in front of his mother. That infuriated me beyond any sensibility.

Little was now verging on open insolence, but his remarks show that Clark was not in the least way capable of mounting a coordinated brigade attack or prepared to try. Little thought to himself:

"To hell with him. We'll show the bugger that we can still do it even though he killed half of the 42nd …" He then asked Clark: "If we're still going to do it, is there a brigade plan or do I do it."

"You do it," said Clark.

"Well, we're not going to do it the way its been done so far."[51]

A close examination of the one-page brigade operations order for the PPCLI-RCR attack on Tilloy and Tilloy Hill (issued only six hours before the attack) is revealing. It has absolutely no coordinating instructions in it. Significantly, the artillery, trench mortars, and MGs are all ordered to co-operate with the assaulting battalions. If one wishes to be charitable to Clark, one could say he was following Currie's lead in allowing his battalion commanders, the men on the ground, to formulate the plan.[52] Thus, Little took what was left of his battered battalion and swung them left over the railway embankment on the 30th September and caught German defenders in the right flank. With heavy machine guns (HMGs) providing supporting fire from Chapel Hill, Stokes mortars firing in close support, and the RCR covering his left flank after he swung right, Little reported that "we caught them more or less with their pants down and they suffered pretty severely." But the depleted battalion, which according to their regimental history had "a rifle strength of very little more than a full-sized company" was under observation from German MGs sited on the high ground in depth behind Tilloy, which now joined in.[53]

"We had a hell of a time getting up that hill, but we say we got there. I don't think we ever [physically] got there. They went out more than we went in, but they punished us like the devil." The PPCLI and RCR never did take Tilloy Hill and when 9th CIB passed through the next day at 0500 hours the PPCLI history records, "the tremendous ordeal was over."[54]

The 7th CIB had been bled dry by three continual days of non-stop fighting. Despite left out of battle (LOB) procedures in the battalions, for the battles in and around Cambrai, the strongest and most effective junior leaders were killed off quickly in the battalions. By 30 September, the 49th Battalion had no junior officers left and had to recall its liaison officers to maintain some semblance of command.[55] Lieutenant-Colonel

Ewing wrote on 2 October 1918: "The troops are being used too continuously without an opportunity to properly re-organize, which is particularly a necessity with regard to NCOs [non-commissioned officers] amongst whom the casualties had been heavy."[56] Junior officers, as noted, had also been hard hit and this lack of junior leadership in 7th CIB would have serious ramifications, especially among the men of the PPCLI, after the Armistice.

PACKS AND PROVOCATION

One PPCLI historian notes that after Mons had fallen and the guns had fallen silent:

> all was not well. Since the disaster at Tilloy, the Battalion had not regained its full strength. New officers with no previous association with the PPCLI had been drafted in from a pool of reinforcements and there had not been time to mould its new men into the ways of the Regiment. With the Armistice of 11 November, the fundamental incentive essential to discipline in a citizen army was removed. Men accepted that they must soldier on, but began to wonder "for how long?" Increasingly they found military routines and duties irksome. The key to morale, as ever, was leadership.[57]

In short, with the necessity for operational discipline gone, inexperienced battalion officers and NCOs fell back on peacetime "chickenshit" to keep the soldiers occupied. Key officers disappeared on leave. The PPCLI experience was shared by the other 7th CIB battalions. When the brigade marched from Mons to Nivelles, arriving at their destination on 13 December 1918, several hundred men of various brigade units met in the park the following day to discuss their grievances. "The immediate cause of the dissatisfaction lay in marching with full packs, a procedure that had been discarded during the operational periods of the war," recalled a PPCLI platoon commander. "Moreover, the other ranks had not been told of their destination; many believed that they were on the way to Germany and hence destined for protracted service abroad. Finally, a few radical ring leaders had been infected by the Russian example and wished to institute Soldier's Councils empowered to negotiate with commanding officers."[58]

During the evening, the crowd in the park increased and about 200 gathered at the brigade HQ. A small group, including an American PPCLI private, Eric McKnight (later the author of the classic *Lassie*) were allowed in and spoke with the brigadier. "I went and talked to the Brigadier," recalled McKnight in a letter to Gault many years after the war. "He seemed heart-broken, and I was tremendously sorry for him." But Clark would not accept any of the protesting soldiers' demands. Early the next morning, a crowd from other units visited the PPCLI billets inciting the men to attend a mass meeting at 0830 hours in the town square. When the battalion paraded at 0900 hours, an entire company was missing and presumed to be at the meeting. With a few exceptions, the men of the other three companies remained in their billets, ready to turn out on parade.[59]

The 42nd Battalion rests in the Grand Place at Mons on the morning of 11 November 1918. The photograph was taken on Armistice Day. Some battalion soldiers mutinied a mere month later. (Department of National Defence, Library and Archives Canada PA-3571)

At the town square, after being addressed by several agitators, the crowd made a second visitation to all the units' lines, attempting to enlist widespread support for their cause, as well as breaking into guardrooms and setting prisoners free. The fact that the PPCLI and RCR regimental histories do not mention the mutiny at all, while the 49th and 42nd cover it in some detail, lends credence to historian Jeffery Williams's claim that in "the official reports of the brigade and the battalions concerned ... one can detect a cover-up — commanding officers defending both their men and their own actions in the sorry affair."[60] The 42nd regimental history claims not to have had any men who participated in the mutiny. The history goes as far to point out that when "rioters" smashed in the doors of the battalion guardroom, "their object being to release prisoners," the prisoners helped out the quarter guard commander by claiming they were actual members of the guard. Afterwards the released prisoners, "of their own accord, returned to the guardroom." However, there is some evidence that some 42nd soldiers attended the meetings and rallies. Private Frank Flory, 96, remembers:

> [I] was approached by some members of the 49th and asked to make propaganda in the 42nd. I don't know where the lead was coming from, only one evening the call went out for everyone to participate by meeting at the headquarters for a general request for the elimination of packs to carry on route marches. The ground was full to capacity and I don't know how the complaint was presented in the turmoil.... I don't know if there was any punishment for the ringleaders or not, but I do know as one from the Black Watch, I had to appear in front of our commanding Colonel. After all the questions and answers, I only got 7 days Guard Duty.... After that, whenever the [Brigade] went from place to place, we were always accompanied by MPs & mounted police. All went well from there on ... and a good thing this was over or it may have come to terrible consequences.[61]

The proof that most the 42nd remained steady is evidenced by Brigadier-General Clark's orders to Lieutenant-Colonel Ewing to police the brigade after it mutinied "which we were not in the least anxious to do," admitted Ewing to Currie's biographer, Hugh Urquhart, after the war. In effect, Clark faced not only mutinous other ranks, but a mutinous battalion commander as well. Undoubtedly, Clark was the individual that Topp, the 42nd regimental historian, was referring to when he stated "some authorities had advocated the use of force to quell the disturbance, but cooler heads prevailed." Ewing, an obvious "cooler head," wrote to Urquhart:

> We were absolutely fair to Clark in this matter but, Clark, to my mind, made an unfair report to the Corps Commander, who brought me to the mat. Currie was absolutely fair and while undoubtedly he must have liked Clark, I am sure that he saw through his weakness on the occasion…. If Clark had only handled the decision in December in [a] deliberate way he would have had no trouble, but he bounced in and tried to make a big man of himself and couldn't bring it off. General Currie, in the interview I had with him, led me to believe — not by what he said, but more or less by how he acted — that he understood this part of the situation quite well.[62]

Loomis, GOC 3rd CID, storming back from leave on the night of the 16th December was under no illusions. He first vented his spleen on the assembled battalion commanders of 7th CIB, then visited every unit and spoke to the men. His formal report to his immediate superior, the GOC 4th British Corps was to the point:

> The alleged complaints which were voiced by the men were trivial. There were no real grounds for complaint. The whole matter was one of discipline, training and efficient Officers and Non-Commissioned Officers. It was not a condition of recent growth. The measures which I am taking are not exactly those which I would recommend if the Division were not preparing to move back home and if the fighting were not finished. The benefit of the doubt is now, in large measure, being given to cer-

tain officers who, if the Division was not shortly to be demobilized, I would strongly recommend that they be removed from their commands for inefficiency.[63]

It can only be speculated upon whether Loomis would have removed Clark, as well as most of the battalion commanders (including one from his own regiment), from command. We know that at least one PPCLI company commander was sacked and sent home immediately after the mutiny by his returning CO — Gault — who had hastened back from leave with Loomis. The irascible Captain Little was struck off strength on 17 December as it had been his company which refused to parade on 15 December. What Little's personal involvement in the Nivelles "mutiny" actually was will never be known, but it is certain that Gault held him personally responsible for his company's actions, and acted swiftly to set an example.[64]

Thus the Great War for "The Fighting Seventh" ended on a sour note. Its experienced veterans, including the few remaining "Originals," and the newer recruits, with many Military Service Act (MSA) men, ended their record of service by being ignominiously accompanied from place to place on their demobilization journey home by armed police escorts. Immediately following the Armistice, when discipline was at its most vulnerable, 7th CIB officers were called upon to lead by example. The battalion officers, who had always seen to the welfare of their men while in the trenches, out of the line, or on operations, however, chose to turn their backs on their men. They took prolonged leaves and insisted on meaningless military ritual. Ultimately, they suffered the consequences of that betrayal. The Nivelles "mutiny" is a perfect example of how authoritarian control can never be an adequate substitute for the human dynamic of command known as leadership.

NOTES

1. G.R. Stevens, *A City Goes to War* [henceforth *49th History*] (Brampton: Charters Publishing Company, 1964), 132.

2. Library and Archives Canada [henceforth LAC], Record Group [henceforth RG] 41, Canadian Broadcasting Corporation Radio Transcripts of *In Flanders Fields* [henceforth CBC], "Generals," J.A. Clark.

3. Currie cited in Charles Beresford Topp, *The 42nd Battalion, O.E.F. Royal Highlanders of Canada in the Great War* [henceforth *42nd History*] (Montreal: Montreal Gazette Printing Co., 1931), 282.

4. *42nd History,* 307–308.

5. E.L.M. Burns, *General Mud: Memoirs of Two World Wars* (Toronto: Clarke, Irwin & Company, 1970).

6. G.W.L. Nicholson, *Official History of the Canadian Army in the First World War: Canadian Expeditionary Force, 1914–19,* [henceforth *CEF*] (Ottawa: Queen's Printer, 1962), 441; Burns, *General Mud,* 64; *Canada in the Great World War: An Authentic Account of the Military History of Canada from the Earliest Days to the Close of the War of the Nations* (Toronto: Makers of Canada Publishers, 1917–1921), Vol. 6, 317.

7. B.M. Greene, ed., *Who's Who in Canada* (Toronto, 1920), 946.

8. Robert England, *Recollections of a Nonagenarian in the Service of the Royal Canadian Regiment* (Victoria: privately published, 1983), 11.

9. CBC, "Generals," J.A. Clark.

10. *Ibid.*

11. *Ibid.*

12. 42nd War Diary, 12 September 1918.

13. *Ibid.*

14. CBC, "PPCLI," G.W. Little.

15. LAC, Manuscript Group [MG] 30-E100, Currie Papers, Letter to D. Oliver dated 11 August 1918.

16. *CEF,* 440.

17. Chief of General Staff cited in Daniel G. Dancocks, *Spearhead to Victory: Canada and the Great War* [henceforth *Spearhead*] (Edmonton: Hurtig, 1987), 123.

18. *CEF,* 443–48.

19. Ralph Hodder-Williams, *Princess Patricia's Canadian Light Infantry* [henceforth *PPCLI History*] (London: Hodder and Stoughton, 1923), Vol. 1, 361.

20. Robert Collier Fetherstonhaugh, *The Royal Canadian Regiment, 1883–1933* [henceforth *Royal Canadian Regiment History*] (Centennial Print & Litho, 1936), 353.

21. *Ibid.*, 354.

22. *Royal Canadian Regiment History,* 355–56.

23. *CEF,* 448–49; *Royal Canadian Regiment History,* 354–58.

24. *PPCLI History,* 366–69.

25. *49th History,* 133; *42nd History,* 268–71.

26. *42nd History,* 269.

27. *Ibid.*, 273.

28. Dancocks, *Spearhead,* 159.

29. William Richard Bird, *And We Go On* (Toronto: Hunter-Rose Co., 1930, or later), 195.

30. *PPCLI History,* 380; *49th History,* 135.

31. CBC, "PPCLI," G.W. Little; *PPCLI History,* 373–77.

32. *Royal Canadian Regiment History,* 342, 359–60, 420, in passim.

33. Adamson cited in Sandra Gwyn, *Tapestry of War: A Private View of Canadians in the Great War* (Toronto: Harper Collins, 1992), 424, 428–29. *PPCLI History,* 283, adds that Adamson "was pronounced by a medical board for further front-line service."

34. Jeffery Williams, *First in the Field: Gault of the Patricias* (London: L.Cooper, 1995), 134–35.

35. *Ibid.*, 134–35.

36. *Ibid.*, 135.

37. *Ibid.*, 135–36.

38. *PPCLI History,* 364; CBC, "PPCLI," G.R. Stevens.

39. Letter dated 21 June 1918, Agar Adamson, Norm Christie, ed. *The Letters of Agar Adamson* (Nepean: CEF Books, 1997).

40. George Gordon Dinwiddie Kilpatrick, *Odds and Ends from a Regimental Diary* (1923), 18.

41. *Ibid.*

42. Princess Patricia's Canadian Light Infantry War Diary, "Ops from September 27th until October 1st, 1918 inclusive."

43. Black Watch of Canada Regimental Archives, MS 004, Undated Letter attached to 42nd War Diary excerpt, September 1918.

44. *42nd History,* 270, 275.

45. Black Watch of Canada Regimental Archives, MS 004, Ops Orders Folder, "Lessons Learned from Recent Operations" dated 2 October 1918.

46. *Ibid.*

47. CBC, "PPCLI," G.W. Little.

48. Black Watch of Canada Regimental Archives, MS 004, Ops Orders Folder, "Lessons Learned ...," 2 October 1918.

49. Dancocks, *Spearhead,* 148.

50. *CEF,* 450.

51. CBC, "PPCLI," G.W. Little.

52. Black Watch of Canada Regimental Archives, MS 004, Ops Orders Folder, 7th CIB Instructions No. BM 100/3.

53. CBC, op.cit.; *PPCLI History,* 371–78.

54. CBC, "PPCLI," G.W. Little; *PPCLI History,* 378.

55. *49th History,* 134; 49th War Diary, 30 September 1918.

56. Black Watch of Canada Regimental Archives, MS 004, Ops Orders Folder, "Lessons Learned ...," 2 October 1918.

57. Williams, *First in the Field,* 141–42.

58. Stevens, *49th History,* 146.

59. Knight quoted in Williams, op.cit., 144.

60. *42nd History,* 304–306.

61. Frank Flory, Letter to author dated 26 March 1996.

62. McGill University Archives [henceforth MUA], *UP,* Ewing Interview.

63. Loomis quoted in Williams, op.cit., 145.

64. MUA, MG 3054, 1918 Diary of Lt A.J. Kelly, Intelligence Officer, PPCLI, December 1918; *PPCLI History,* Vol. 2, 82.

11 ↝

Dimensions of Military Leadership: The Kinmel Park Mutiny of 4–5 March 1919

HOWARD G. COOMBS

The mutineers were our own men, stuck in the mud of North Wales, waiting impatiently to get back to Canada — four months after the end of the war. The 15,000 Canadian troops that concentrated at Kinmel didn't know about the strikes that had held up the fuelling of ships and that had caused food shortages. The men were on half rations, there was no coal for the stove in the cold grey huts, and they hadn't been paid for over a month. Forty-two had to sleep in a hut meant for thirty, so they each took turns sleeping on the floor, with one blanket each.[1]

Mutiny is a subject that evokes strong emotions. For some, it has connotations of disobedience and disloyalty, while for others, it is a justifiable reaction to the draconian discipline associated with military life. Unfortunately, few attempts have been made to analyse military revolt within a Canadian context. Official records reflect the viewpoint and processes of the service involved — army, navy, or air force — and at the same time, few of the participants leave written accounts. One mutiny deserving of further study occurred at the Canadian camp located at Kinmel Park in Rhyl, Wales, on 4–5 March 1919. This event, ostensibly precipitated by frustration with delays in demobilization and redeployment to Canada, involved hundreds of soldiers and resulted in five Canadian deaths, as well as a considerable number of courts-martial.

The violence at Kinmel Park aptly illustrates that military leadership has formal and informal dimensions. Formal leaders have *de jure* authority vested in them by legislation and informal leaders have *de facto* influence that can arise from many sources. The formal leadership of any organization must always ensure that it minimizes any possible divergence between the actions of informal leadership and institutional aims. Maintaining and facilitating communication is an effective method for preventing the disastrous consequences associated with a separation of formal and informal leadership. The Kinmel Park mutiny clearly demonstrates the necessity of the establishment and continuance of an interactive information flow within a military organization, particularly under conditions that produce uncertainty. Previous studies of this disturbance have not examined the role that leadership should have played at Kinmel Park in mitigating the negative influences experienced by the soldiers through the effective communication of critical information.

Colonel G.W.L. Nicholson, in the *Official History of the Canadian Army in the First World War*, briefly describes the Kinmel mutiny as part of a larger series of events that occurred during the post-war redeployment of Canadian troops:

> In all, between November 1918 and June 1919, there were thirteen instances of riots or disturbances involving Canadian troops in England. The most serious of these occurred at Kinmel Park on 4 and 5 March 1919, when dissatisfaction over delays in sailing resulted in five men being killed and 23 wounded. Seventy eight men were arrested, of whom 25 were convicted of mutiny and given sentences varying from 90 days' detention to ten years' penal servitude.[2]

The synopsis provided by Nicholson is extremely brief and he rapidly transitions to other topics. Although his reasons are not explicit, one can surmise that in the aftermath of the First World War, official military history would have preferred to avoid a critical examination of any fail-ures, including potential organizational issues, to praise success.[3] An analysis provided by the Canadian Army Historical Section suggested that in the case of Canadian Demobilization Camps, they "had been well organized and some of the disturbances could hardly have been guarded against."[4] This rather off-hand statement illustrates the proposition that mutiny among military forces is a subject either deliberately ignored or superficially researched.[5]

Nicholson's seeming reluctance to interpret the events at Kinmel Park within the official history of Canadian Army participation in the First World War is completely understandable. For any nation, the thought of its military forces revolting against legally constituted authority is unpalat-able, and this arises from the unique position that the military occupies within society.[6] Militaries act on behalf of the state and the state expects that violence will only be applied as directed. Mutiny, however, does not fall into that category and is normally summarily addressed by the author-ities with little introspection concerning the genesis of the event. Members of the military have established a covenant with the nation and are expect-ed to adhere to the rules and regulations of that institution, no matter how unreasonable they may seem.[7]

In the context of the First World War, this idea can be discerned in the definition of mutiny contained within the 1914 British *Manual of Military Law*. This body of military law was adopted and used by the Canadian Army throughout the war. A mutiny was considered to be "a combination of two or more persons to resist or induce others to resist lawful military authority." Charges of mutiny could also be laid even if efforts to incite mutiny did not succeed and nothing concrete transpired. In cases where an individual was present during a mutiny and did not take part, such charges could still be preferred. The *Manual* lists the conditions under which a soldier could be charged as follows:

> every person subject to military law who ...

> 1. causes or conspires with any other persons to cause, any mutiny or sedition in any forces belonging to His Majesty's regular, reserve, or auxiliary forces, or Navy; or

2. endeavours to seduce any person in His Majesty's regular, reserve, or auxiliary forces, or Navy, from allegiance to His Majesty, or to persuade any person in His Majesty's regular, reserve, or auxiliary forces, or Navy, to join in any Mutiny or sedition; or joins in, or, being present, does not use his utmost endeavours to suppress, any mutiny or sedition in any forces belonging to His Majesty's regular, reserve, or auxiliary forces, or Navy; or coming to the knowledge of any actual or intended mutiny or sedition in any forces belonging to His Majesty's regular, reserve, or auxiliary forces, or Navy, does not without delay inform his commanding officer of the same.[8]

Although, the *Manual* clearly defined mutiny as a treasonable act, the term has a different meaning when examined from the perspective of the participants. British historian Lawrence James proposes that mutiny is a collective action undertaken by members of the military when they feel that they have no other recourse. In his work on mutiny, James examines a number of such instances in British and Commonwealth forces between 1796 and 1956. He indicates that mutineers viewed their participation in this act as completely justified given the nature of their complaints. The most prevalent sources of discontent were rooted in aspects of military routine and quality of life. Grievances could arise from onerous quantities of work, unacceptable quality or quantity of rations, curbing of previously accepted privileges, inadequate quarters, perceptions of poor leadership, inappropriate methods and types of punishment, and difficulties with pay. Although the genesis of a mutiny could be attributed to trivial matters, the form and level of the resultant collective action could be completely disproportionate to the original cause. Once an individual or group voiced their complaints and encouraged others to participate, additional causes of unhappiness were aired and the mutiny would quickly gain momentum. Successful challenges to authority begat other confrontations and suggests an escalating scale of violence.[9]

James also proposes that the development and conduct of the collective action tended to be dependent on the initial reaction of military authorities. Leadership that demonstrated a heavy-handed response to a minor

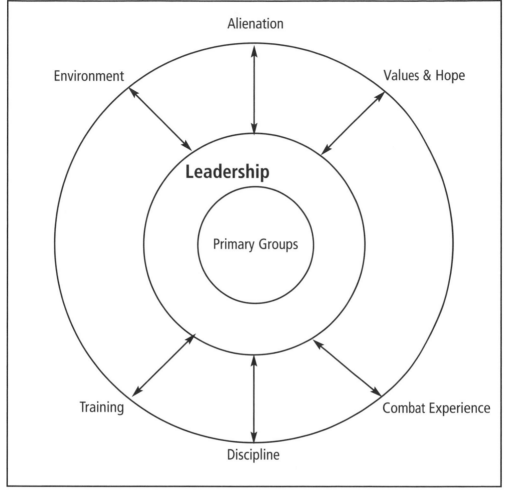

Figure 11.1: The Mutiny Wagon Wheel[17]

instance of protest could produce an uncontrollable escalation upwards of the mutiny, in both size and violence. Additionally, he attributes outside influences as sometimes giving form to mutiny. Socialism was viewed as being a potential catalyst for military disturbances and was perceived with concern in the first decades of the twentieth century. This belief was apparent in the aftermath of the disturbances at Kinmel Park.[10]

In focusing on the response of military officials to the disturbance, James's interpretation, as does others, minimizes the role of military leadership in the genesis of a mutiny. Throughout his work, he examines the conditions of service and the reaction of authorities to the event, rather than the prior action or inaction of leaders that may have reinforced the negative factors that prompted the mutiny in the first place. Still, his explanation of mutiny as a group response of last resort to perceived intolerable circumstances is probably the most useful interpretation. In certain ways, it can be visualized as a form of communication through collective action.[11]

To examine the role of duly constituted leaders in the origins of a mutiny, one can turn to Joel Hamby's "The Mutiny Wagon Wheel: A Leadership Model for Mutiny in Combat." Hamby hypothesizes that leadership, training, and military discipline are tools necessary to prevent "military rebellion" or mutiny. His theory is useful in examining the underlying elements of a mutiny and suggests what commanders can do to mitigate the conditions that are precursors to such action. In the case of Kinmel Park, this model is of great value in identifying the critical failures that led to revolt.[12]

Hamby proposes that there are eight influences in the genesis of a mutiny. These factors are depicted in Figure 11.1, "The Mutiny Wagon Wheel," on the previous page and are listed as follows:

(1) Alienation;
(2) Environment;
(3) Values and Hope;
(4) Combat Experience;
(5) Training;
(6) Discipline;
(7) Primary Groups; and
(8) Leadership.[13]

These factors can act to provide or destroy group cohesion, as mutiny is more likely when leadership is not used to mitigate negative influences. Moreover, Hamby notes that leaders who exert a positive influence will moderate the impact of those negative factors that undermine the morale of a military unit and lead to mutiny.[14]

Alienation is described as that which inhibits the effectiveness of individuals and groups and has five common manifestations. First, there is a feeling of powerlessness with regard to effecting possible outcomes; second, there is an impression of meaninglessness in that the individual or group is confused as to what to believe; third, normlessness results when individual behaviour is no longer shaped by previously accepted social norms and earlier customary standards of conduct have become irrelevant; fourth, a sense of isolation is produced when members of a group no longer value societal beliefs that attach importance to certain philosophies; and fifth, self-estrangement results when individuals are unable to find satisfaction in the tasks and duties that must be completed. Together, these factors can create a separation between the purpose of the soldier and that of the unit and promote "inertia in individuals and units."[15]

This alienation can only be increased by the impact of other forces. The hardships and privations produced by the physical environment can elicit emotions of despair that will affect both individual and group morale. Simultaneously, values and hope determine a soldier's level of commitment. These personal convictions as to the worth of the larger society assist in determining an individual's effort and dedication. A loss of faith in the nation will diminish commitment. In combat, veterans, knowing what awaits them, are more apt to mutiny when an "exceptional stress" occurs that reduces their belief in the chain of command and causes individual doubts to spread throughout the group.[16]

Even though sound leadership is the primary method of maintaining cohesion, training that is deemed effective by the primary group is a positive influence in mitigating disintegrating factors. A further dynamic that minimizes disruptive influences is fair and balanced discipline. Nevertheless, despite the fact that effective discipline can instill pride and spirit, discipline that is deemed despotic will be disregarded and in the process produce feelings of dissatisfaction.[18]

To moderate negative stimuli, efforts to maintain cohesion must be aimed at primary groups for the reason that these clusters of individuals are the primary reason soldiers fight. The underlying bonds of loyalty to each other, the will and determination to live, and the expectations of comrades, keep individuals motivated in combat. The primary group forms and regulates accepted standards of behaviour. It is necessary to maintain alignment between the objectives of these primary groups and the larger organization because a divergence in goals will result in a lessening of efficiency and may contribute to a mutiny.[19]

The most important dynamic in ensuring congruence is leadership, which provides motivation and sustains soldiers throughout all situations.

Hamby presents the four "authority factors" of Lieutenant-Colonel David Grossman, as detailed in the latter's work, *On Killing,* as being paramount when determining the effectiveness of leadership.[20] They are: first, proximity of the leader; second, intensity of demands; third, legitimacy of the authority; and fourth, respect. Of these four factors, respect is the most important and leaders must provide and care for their soldiers to earn their respect. If the formal leadership is unable to do this, the group will seek informal leaders to provide them with effective direction. Based on an analysis of the Kinmel Park mutiny, informal and formal mechanisms of candid communication are critical within this leadership model and this aspect is not addressed by Hamby's model.[21]

An amended version of "The Mutiny Wagon Wheel," which emphasizes the role of leadership and the communication of information, is outlined in Figure 11.2. This model, which explains the Kinmel Park mutiny of March 1919, emphasizes that leadership exists in two spheres, the formal leadership of duly constituted authority and the informal leadership of primary groups. With a lack of effectual formal leadership, disintegrating factors cause the catastrophic failure of formal authority, thus enabling informal leaders to determine the actions of the primary groups. This divergence of aims and expected behaviours can manifest itself precipitously, as in mutiny. The exchange of information is of vital importance in maintaining an alignment of formal and informal leadership. The establishment of methods of communication in a military organization is a key variable in preventing mutiny.

Regrettably, the officers charged with the responsibility of managing Kinmel Park did not ensure that the soldiers knew that their concerns were understood and, if not addressed, acknowledged. This was truly unfortunate because demobilization was not a haphazard event since planning had commenced as early as 1916. The Department of Militia and Defence, as well as the Ministry of Overseas Military Forces of Canada (OMFC), had attempted to provide for an efficient redeployment to Canada.[22] Considered in this process were the requirements to make the return occur without delay, to ensure that it was as comfortable as possible and to create an equitable system to determine the priority of return.[23]

It was originally envisioned that the soldiers of the Canadian Expeditionary Force (CEF) would embark in France and sail directly to

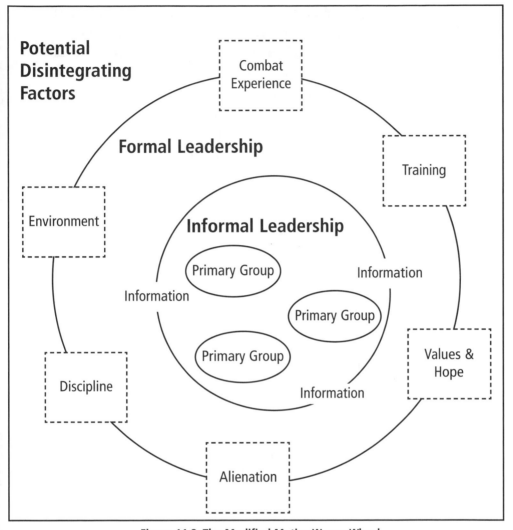

Figure 11.2: The Modified Mutiny Wagon Wheel

Canada, but a great many Canadians had relatives in the United Kingdom whom they wished to visit before leaving Europe. Since transportation to and from the British Isles was problematic, it was impractical to grant them leave in the United Kingdom before embarking in France. For that reason, on 23 January 1919, the commander of the Canadian Corps, Lieutenant-General Sir Arthur Currie, made strong representation to the British adjutant-general and the secretary of state for war that Canadian troops should transit to the United Kingdom before their repatriation. Consequently, camps were established in England to facilitate the movement of the CEF and a large staging area was created at Kinmel Park near Rhyl, Wales.[24]

Kinmel Park was not a single encampment, but a concentration of 20 cantonments organized into 11 autonomous wings that mirrored the geographic Military Districts (MD) of Canada.[25] The wings had staffs that were responsible for administration, rations, quartering, recreation, and training while the transients passed through Kinmel Park.[26] A diagram of the sub-camps and associated geographic region, or MD, is presented below as Figure 11.3.

OMFC had forecasted the potential for trouble. Sir Edward Kemp was concerned about the mixture of troops staging through England. Within the formed units and formations of the CEF, the formal leadership could maintain discipline. In the combustible combination of *ad hoc* units and organizations in England, however, there were innumerable soldiers who would not hesitate to voice their grievances based on pre-war collective bargaining experience. Kemp opined, "Where you mix up all kinds of combatant and non-combatant troops into drafts that fit into the demobilization necessities in Canada and these men are held pending shipping arrangements they become most difficult to control."[27] Others, such as Lieutenant-General Sir Richard Turner, chief of the general staff of the Overseas Ministry, echoed this sentiment but with no effect.[28]

Historian Desmond Morton suggests that for staging camps, such as that at Kinmel, the best solution would have been to keep transients moving through. Regrettably for the authorities, modifications to the shipping schedules reduced the number of departing soldiers to a fraction of that which should have been redeployed to Canada. In February, cold weather, continuous rain and fuel shortages made for an uncomfortable environment at Kinmel Park, and this was exacerbated by a monotonous, although adequate, diet. Kinmel's "Tin Town," the area outside the main gates created by local entrepreneurs, could have been used by the transient troops to obtain diversion or to supplement their meals, but the majority had no remaining pay after an extended stay in the camp. Regulations provided only one last payment before repatriation, so extra food, alcohol, or recreation became beyond the means of soldiers who were delayed in transit and had spent all their money.[29]

On 26 or 27 February, it became common knowledge that a number of large liners had been reallocated from the CEF to the Americans who had not served overseas for nearly the same amount of time. Then news arrived at Kinmel of the third postponement of the *SS Haverford*. Some 300 members of Sailing Party 21, who were in Camps 3 and 4 (MD 10), wished to protest to the camp commandant, Colonel Malcolm A. Colquhoun. After these representations were forwarded to camp headquarters, the adjutant, Lieutenant-Colonel R.G. Thackeray, agreed to meet with three representatives who would voice the concerns of this group of soldiers. After the meeting, Thackeray felt that he had explained the delays satisfactorily, though was soon alarmed when other ships were allocated to the 3rd Canadian Infantry Division. Thackeray realized that soldiers at Kinmel Park would see this development as an abrogation of the "first over, first back compact."[31]

On 1 March, Lieutenant-Colonel J.P. French, the commander of Camp 2 (MD 12), reported hearing rumours that all canteens would be looted; however disenchanted soldiers took no action. On the same day, soldiers from Camp 1 (MD 7) refused to go on a route march, but later paraded on 2 March after that day's march had been cancelled. Also on 2 March, Sailing Party 21 again sent a delegation to headquarters because the *Haverford* had been delayed for a fourth time. This caused Colonel Colquhoun to send his adjutant to London with instructions to communicate the seriousness of the

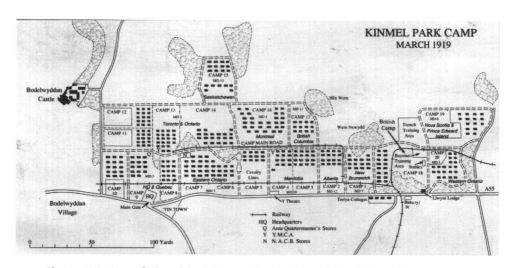

Figure 11.3: Map of Kinmel Park Camp showing the various military district wings and subordinate camps.[30]

situation at Kinmel Park. Major H.W. Cooper, the commander of Camps 3 and 4 (MD 10), later met with soldiers from Sailing Party 21. He duly reported that their unhappiness lay with the slow administration in regards to demobilization.

Colquhoun advised all subordinate wing commanders that if they requested, he would personally explain the cancellations to the soldiers. He received no requests from the wing commanders to speak to the men in the various sub-camps.[32] Later, during the evening of 3 March, groups of soldiers gathered in Tin Town. Their unhappiness with the situation was palpable. Private A.L. Wallace of MD 2 was later quoted as saying:

> many men were broke and couldn't buy cigarettes or soap, but were all looking forward to get away home … then came the cancellation of sailings — then came the news that the 3rd Division were going home first — that they were the fighting division of the Canadians — this was the climax. On the day before the riot it was on everybody's lips — it was the general feeling — every man I met was talking the same thing.[33]

On the morning of 4 March, the men of Sailing Party 21 boycotted the regular morning route march. Major Cooper spoke to them and one of their numbers was chosen to speak by telephone to Major G.L. MacGillivray, the assistant adjutant. This representative was informed that Colonel Colquhoun would speak to them as a group if necessary. They dispersed soon after, seemingly satisfied that their grievances were being addressed.[34]

Morton emphasizes the impact that the cancellation of the *Haveford* had on the troops awaiting repatriation at Kinmel Park. This act was no mere whim of capricious fate however, since an inspection board had deemed the ship substandard and unfit for troop movement. This policy of verifying the suitability of shipping for military transport had been instituted as a result of an incident that had caused the Canadian government great public embarrassment. A previous transport ship, the *SS Northland*, had received such negative reports in the press about its onboard state that the authorities were determined that there would be no reoccurrence.

In the case of the *Haveford*, the berthing areas were unventilated, the heads were unsuitable in quality and quantity, and there were inadequate feeding arrangements. Regrettably, the reasons for the cancellation were not disseminated to the troops scheduled to sail on this transport. Compounding this situation was the failure of the camp staff to circulate news of Lieutenant-Colonel Thackeray's accomplishments in London at the Overseas Ministry. He had persuaded Brigadier-General Donald Hogarth, the quartermaster-general, that the situation at Kinmel was serious, and shipping was eventually reassigned from the 1st Division to the sailing parties awaiting transit at the camp. Thackeray telegraphed the news to Colquhoun and then proceeded to spend the evening sampling the entertainment of the metropolis. This telegram arrived at Kinmel after Colquhoun had departed for an evening in the local town of Rhyl and there is no indication that it was ever shared with the troops. Despite rumours of impending trouble, the junior officers who overheard such gossip were reluctant to disturb a senior officer with mere murmurings of discontent after normal duty hours.[35]

The mutiny at Kinmel Park commenced on the evening of 4 March in a series of meetings that resulted in Sapper William Tsarevitch being chosen as the leader of the nascent collective action.[36] David Lamb alludes to a report in *The Times* that the mutiny had commenced with the shout of "Come on the Bolsheviks!" and quickly gained ground throughout the area.[37] These reports, which were considered exaggerated by Canadian authorities, are contained in Appendix 11.1 for the sake of interest. Although some civilians had joined the mutineers in vandalizing and looting the collection of stores at Tin Town, Camps 19 and 20, which contained administrative facilities and officers' quarters, successfully resisted attempts to take control. The nearby populace of Rhyl viewed the resultant fires and disturbances with concern.[38]

Desmond Morton offers a similar account, but does not lay the emphasis on Sapper Tsarevitch. According to Morton, at 1930 hours, a group of soldiers vandalized the canteen at MD 3, the camp for soldiers from eastern Ontario. Corporal Bert Morrison, who had been recently demoted from his position as provost-marshal at the camp, led them. They attacked another canteen and then proceeded to Tin Town and destroyed those stores as well. Once finished in Tin Town, the soldiers flowed back

Some of the soldiers involved in the rioting at Kinmel Park in 1919. (Canadian War Museum AN19890086-591 #1)

into the camp, continued with their destruction and looted the officers' and sergeants' messes and canteens, as well as the canteens managed by the Navy and Army Canteen Board (NACB). By 2200, the mutiny had moved to the eastern edge of the camp and returned to empty the NACB main store and tobacco depot. Staff officers attempted to intervene and one major was struck in the face, but this type of physical contact was unusual. At midnight, a few hundred soldiers attacked the camp's quartermaster stores. Officers using sticks attempted to drive the soldiers off, but looting continued until 0430 on 5 March.[39]

At a conference with his senior officers on the morning of 5 March, Colquhoun took stock of the situation. The NACB stores, 11 canteens and messes, 11 stores in Tin Town and two Young Men's Christian Association (YMCA) buildings had been vandalized and looted. No injuries had been reported and about two-dozen soldiers were in custody. Colquhoun then directed his 11 wing commanders to avoid bloodshed and ordered all ammunition to be collected and guarded at camp headquarters.[40] Moreover, he ordered that all stocks of spirituous beverages were to be drained immediately and directed an immediate pay advance of two pounds per soldier.[41] A reserve of 25 troopers was formed from the Canadian Reserve Cavalry Regiment. After concluding his conference, Colonel Colquhoun was able to roam the camp unmolested throughout the morning and, even though his efforts to convince the mutineers to desist met with varying reactions, he was not offered physical violence.[42]

By the morning of 5 March, the mutineers were relatively dormant while camp authorities were commencing vigorous actions to quell the disturbances. Lieutenant J.A. Gauthier took off his rank insignia and moved among the mutineers in an effort to identify the leaders of the group.[43] A defensive perimeter that included trenches had been established in the area of Camp 20 to deter any further attack. In the early afternoon, rifles and ammunition were issued to 40 officers and trusted men. Lieutenant Gauthier warned mutineers about making another attempt on Camp 20, but was ignored.

Organized into three groups, the mutineers approached the entrance to the camp.[44] The first group moved towards the camp and was followed by a second of similar size. Both groups carried what appeared to be red flags, but may in fact have been "a strip of red YMCA curtain hung on pool cues."[45] Behind the second group was another, larger mass of mutineers. This third group was reported to be bearing rifles and carrying stones. An earlier report had mentioned homemade weapons of straight razors attached to sticks. The camp's defenders made a pre-emptive foray into the first group and 20 mutineers were seized and quickly removed to Camp 20. Unfortunately, this provoked a rescue attempt on the guardroom and records office. One witness described the mutineers as being led by two men with a red flag between the poles. The guardroom was entered and an attempt made to liberate the prisoners. This effort was unsuccessful and the crowd subsequently moved to the area of the canteen in Camp 18. A group armed with sticks, stones, and some rifles then collected near the road and attempted an attack on Camp 20, rushing through to the Camp 18 huts. Members of Camp 20 repelled the assault, and as the initial rush subsided, they withdrew to their perimeter. At that point, an exchange of rifle fire occurred. As a result of this engagement, four were killed and 21 were wounded.[46]

A court of inquiry, under Brigadier-General James MacBrien, heard evidence that there had been rumours that some soldiers had used bribery to obtain an earlier departure. MacBrien also heard that the troops had not been kept informed about the reasons behind the delays in repatriation and that officers, rather than taking care of their troops, had absented themselves to enjoy leave in London. Allegations were made that the mutiny would have been contained if either a standing piquet of sufficient size had been maintained or the camp leadership had taken an active role in suppressing the collective violence.[47]

Statements contained in the proceedings of the court of inquiry provide further insight into the origins of the Kinmel Park mutiny. Colonel Colquhoun testified that he had been the camp commandant since September 1918 and acknowledged that there had been problems with a boy's battalion and some canteen robberies. He said there had been difficulties with sailings and many challenges because of the varied composition of the camp's population. Of a total of 17,400 persons, all had been in France except about 2,000 draftees and some soldiers who belonged to the Forestry Corps or the Railway Troops. Colquhoun had been aware of the feelings in the camp regarding the latest sailing cancellations and he, in response, had dispatched Thackeray to London. When Major MacGillivray had informed him that the men were restless in the camps belonging to MD 10, he offered on 3 March, as previously indicated, to address the wings and to explain the cancellation of the sailings, but none of the wing commanders thought it necessary. Colquhoun received no indication that there was likely to be further trouble. The lack of communication between officers and men was evident in Colquhoun's testimony and this theme was to be reiterated time and time again during the Inquiry. Private A.L. Wallace of the 15th Battalion remarked:

> I registered in this Camp on 21st February 1919. I live in hut 15 in sailing Lines, M.D.2. I am a re-patriated prisoner of war. The situation in this camp as I understand it was this: — There were the usual mumerings of soldiers, there were discomforts of various sorts, many men were broke and couldn't buy cigarettes or soap, but we were all looking forward to get away home and all these things were suffered with the hope in view of something better to come in the shape of sailing for home. Then came the

cancellation of sailings — then came the news that the 3rd Division was going home first — that they were the fighting division of the Canadians — this was the climax. On the day before the riot it was on everyone's lips — it was a general feeling — every man I met was talking the same thing. I do not think it was organised, but once the thing was started others joined in and it turned into a demonstration about the sailings being cancelled and it became a protest designed to reach the attention of the highest authorities. The sailings were the real cause — the want of pay was secondary. In my hut I don't think there was five shillings among the 30 men. One man had not received pay since 5th Feb. I had not received pay myself since 8th February, but personally I have no complaint about pay. I have drawn $300 since coming back from Germany. I have still some $600 coming to me. I knew I could have drawn pay at any time.

I think if the men had been told about the sailings, why they were postponed or cancelled there would have been no trouble. The first explanation given us was by Gen. Turner.[48] Now it is posted on boards. — things are improved. *Had the men known the true situation they would have thought different....*[49]

Private Wallace's compatriots made similarly cogent observations regarding the flow of information. Corporal G.J. Clout of the 10th Canadian Railway Troops testified:

I have been addressed by Officers about the regulations as to pay since the riot — not before. Orders were read out. *Previous to the riot we had no explanations about cancellations of sailings* — nor about the washing system — nor about requiring a pass to go to Rhyl — nor about dress.[50]

Some of the subordinate wing commanders also indicated a degree of dissatisfaction that was apparent before the mutiny, but in their testimony did not provide the same emphasis to the issues described by Wallace and Clout. Lieutenant-Colonel French stated:

> From talking to the rioters I found them complaining about the cancellation of the boats and the 3rd Division going home first — also some complaints about lack of food and about coming here without proper documents, and consequent delays here.[51]

Major Cooper acknowledged that he had been aware of the dissatisfaction and had attempted to find some diversion to distract the soldiers from their concerns.[52] Cooper and other senior officers also discussed the difficulty in obtaining staff for their camps and the unreliability of those that they did have. There seems to be consensus that capable leadership, at both the commissioned and non-commissioned levels, was difficult to obtain and keep. Additionally, tensions were created within the camp by differences in pay between the lower ranking permanent cadre and conscripts who were receiving specialty pay:

> There is a shortage of suitable N.C.Os [non-commissioned officers]. There is no inducement to keep them here. I have not applied to H.Qrs. [headquarters] for N.C.Os, but the reason is that my experience in applying for Officers was that the Officers sent were no good.
> I am 12 Sergts [sergeants] below Establishment, 21 Cpls [corporals] and 35 L/Cpls [lance-corporals]. Seven of my Officers received their commissions in Nov. 1918.
> I am receiving constant applications from my permanent cadre to go home. There is no inducement for them to stay. There is dissatisfaction among the L/Cpls that they cannot get the pay that M.S.A [Military Service Act] clerks get. I have 100 M.S.A men employed in my Wing.[53]

Examining the testimony of the different camp commanders, it is interesting to note that while the fluidity of the various staffs was cited as an issue, none acknowledged that this problem could also have extended itself upwards throughout the entire chain of command. Almost all camp commanders who testified could claim three or less months in their positions. *Ad hoc* organizations, lacking experienced leaders in key positions and processing large numbers of individual soldiers, were bound to experience difficulties. This observation, interestingly, was not listed in the findings of the court of inquiry.[54]

A question that arises is one regarding the role of the non-commissioned officers (NCOs) during the period prior to the mutiny. Acting Company Sergeant-Major E.J. Williams of Number 1 Company, MD 10, stated to the court, "The men of 21 Sailing had frequent parades on their own. Every time the Sailing was postponed, and when it was cancelled, the 21 Sailing men paraded by themselves."[55] He was not asked what he did with the information about these gatherings or if he or others had taken any steps to allay the concerns that had led to these impromptu meetings. In fact, from the Sergeant-Major's testimony, one gets the sense of "non-involvement."

Other historical resources reinforce the lack of information and the presence of inexperienced or new staff in the camps. Newspaper interviews in the *Toronto Daily Star* after the mutiny provide similar perspectives: "The fault lay with the staff at Rhyl, he [an unnamed returned sergeant] declared. He dubbed it the worst camp in England. 'Most of the staff are drawing good pay,' he declared, 'and they don't care how long they do it. They have no interest in the men.'"[56] Later, a different soldier was questioned as to the probability of disturbances when he was processed at Kinmel Park three weeks previously: "Oh yes, I was sure a riot would break out any time. There was a lot of grousing. In fact, the soldiers said there'd be a riot if they did not get away."[57] Another article alleged: "Things were both good and bad. I will have a lot to tell you later on. There is a total lack of organization at Ryhl Camp and the men are up in the air about it."[58]

Apart from the testimony offered by the witnesses, the members of the court obtained documentary evidence that emphasized the necessity of informing the troops at Kinmel Park of the reason behind shipping delays and the potential issues resulting from any violation of the principle of "first over, first back" during repatriation. Camp headquarters had sent a letter to the secretary of the OMFC complaining of the tardiness of official information pertaining to amendments in the shipping schedules.

They had also articulated concerns that this information was in the local papers several days before being issued by the Ministry. Consequently, the soldiers were aware of probable sailing dates before they were issued by headquarters at Kinmel Park, a situation that put the camp staff in a "very wrong light." But despite the request that this information be communicated to the camp in a timely manner, no concrete action was taken by the ministry to rectify this problem.[59]

The court of inquiry conducted its initial investigation at Kinmel Park immediately after the mutiny and later reconvened at OMFC Headquarters in London on 31 March. The findings of the inquiry attributed the causes of the mutiny to a number of issues:

- Delays and postponements of sailings, coupled with rumours of cancellations until the 3rd Division returned to Canada. To this was added the fact that the last sailing previous to the mutiny was 25 February and no information regarding future sailings arrived prior to 4 March, too late to assuage the discontent;
- Soldiers having an impression that their stay at Kinmel Park would be brief, which was not always the case. Coupled with these extended stays was the administrative problem arising from the fact that individuals did not receive pay after their initial repatriation issue until embarkation for Canada;
- Delays in repatriation due to the loss of personal documents;
- Delays in pay owing to lost papers;
- An inability to procure tobacco on credit;
- Poor food due to a lack of qualified cooks.[60]

The recommendations of the court of inquiry focused on actions that occurred during the disturbance:

- Colquhoun was criticized for not having a standing piquet for contingencies and neither taking more "vigorous" action upon the commencement of the mutiny nor placing guards on vulnerable buildings before the uprising.
- Although the systemic problems regarding communication of

information and camp staffing were not addressed *per se,* the court acknowledged some issues in that area.

- It was believed that Colquhoun was probably not aware of the breach of discipline that had occurred in MD 10 on the morning of 4 March and that Major Cooper did not know about it either, since he had only taken over the previous day.
- Thackeray was criticized for telegraphing the information that he had obtained in London regarding the two 15 March sailings for Kinmel troops. It should have been telephoned to the camp and, while not explicitly stated by the court, given emphasis by Thackeray to ensure that it was quickly disseminated.
- Finally, the lack of timeliness in the arrival of information regarding amendments to sailings was cited as contributing to the mutiny.

Despite these findings, disciplinary action against some of the mutineers was the order of the day in the end.[61]

In the subsequent courts-martial, 51 participants in the mutiny were charged and tried under the British Army Act.[62] Canadian historian Chris Madsen raises the possibility that the British press, through lurid reporting of the violence, may have caused military authorities to be pressured into a desire to be perceived as acting decisively in the aftermath of the mutiny. Various sentences were meted out, with those convicted receiving differing lengths of detention or imprisonment. Madsen mentions a defending officer for British Columbia soldiers, Captain George Black, who sent a letter to Prime Minister Sir Robert Borden that detailed a number of problems with the trials. These irregularities included concerns regarding bias against the accused by members of the court, the briefness of the trial proceedings themselves, as well as violations of legal procedure and evidence. As a result, Captain Black requested that the Canadian government ask for the release of jailed soldiers.[63]

Even if Kemp had guaranteed cooperation with the Flintshire coroner, F.L. Jones, the civilian investigation was hampered by a lack of witnesses. Many of them had left England by the time the inquest commenced near the end of March, and the court of inquiry would not provide copies of the statements from these witnesses:

Three days before the inquest, on March 17, 1919 the Coroner had received a note from the Canadian President of the Canadian Army's Court of Inquiry saying: "I regret very much that I cannot furnish you with any statements from officers, which you ask for, as our proceedings are confidential and cannot be made public at present."[64]

Because of the paucity of evidence and pressure to allow the Canadians to resolve this matter themselves, the coroner recommended that no criminal charges be laid.[65] In the intervening years, this fact has resulted in the suggestion that there was a conspiracy to conceal the details of the deaths.

In the final analysis, whatever the findings of the court of inquiry and coroner's inquest, the mutiny did achieve some positive results for the soldiers. Repatriation was accelerated, and by 25 March, approximately 15,000 soldiers had departed Kinmel Park.[66] Contemporary sources confirm that Canadian authorities expedited sailings for the soldiers of Kinmel, and immediately after the riot, the *SS Adriatic* and the *SS Celtic* were reallocated to the troops of the camp, thus providing berths for approximately 5,000 soldiers.[67]

Desmond Morton believes that there was no conspiracy to mutiny. There was "no plan and many leaders." Individuals garnered support by appealing to the anger of other disenchanted individuals. Once the soldiers found that they could act at will, they fortified themselves with alcohol and continued to vandalize and loot institutions within the camp.[68] Although the proceedings of the court of inquiry allude to alcohol as a factor in the destruction that occurred, it does not list intoxication as a significant factor in the genesis of this event. In fact, the soldiers who testified at the inquiry support Morton's thesis regarding the spontaneity of the mutiny.[69] Although there are various interpretations as to the origins of the dissatisfaction at Kinmel Park, the mutiny during 4 and 5 March should not have come as a surprise. There had been indications of great dissatisfaction since the beginning of the year and these incidents had increased in intensity.[70] The culmination of this escalating scale of protest was the violence of the mutiny and it was entirely preventable.

Some historians, such as Colonel G.W.L. Nicholson, proposed that amendments to the "first over, first back" redeployment policy, coupled with delays in shipping, were the primary causes of the riots that occurred at several Canadian camps, including Kinmel Park.[71] This point of view is reinforced by Desmond Morton and Jack Granatstein in *Marching to Armageddon*. They suggest that in addition to shipping delays and cancellations, the mutiny at Kinmel Park resulted from the news that Military Service Act conscripts of 3rd Division units, with minimal time overseas, were being returned early. In combination with this was an environment of "cold weather, shortages, strikes and influenza" to produce what Sir Edward Kemp said amounted to poor living conditions: "You cannot blame the soldiers for kicking and complaining…. You are living in paradise in Canada as compared with this place."[72] Lawrence James adds that Canadian troops were incensed that ships seemed to be available for American forces, most of whom were comparative newcomers to the war, unlike the Canadians.[73] Moreover, rumours persisted of discrimination in the employment market in favour of officers and there was news of lay-offs and wage-cuts in response to a recession caused by the war debt. Soldiers realized that the longer they were delayed in England, the more difficult a time they would have securing employment in a dwindling job market. Unfortunately, by late February, unemployment in Canada rose sharply. All these factors combined to create an environment conducive to mutiny.[74]

Another point of view is advocated by British researcher Julian Putkowski who rejects arguments that it was the living conditions at Kinmel Park that sparked the mutiny. He sees such interpretations to be simply another version of the conclusions of the court of inquiry. Putkowski believes that the key cause of unhappiness was that the Canadian troops viewed themselves as being stuck in England. He indicates that precursors had earlier signalled the soldiers' unhappiness with shipping delays and that attempts to communicate this dissatisfaction had been made to the camp authorities. Representations had been offered to Colonel Colquhoun on 27 February and there had been a refusal to parade by some soldiers on the morning of 4 March. The mutiny did not spontaneously occur, but resulted from repudiation by camp authorities of soldiers' attempts to communicate their grievances.[75]

Putkowski also argues that the social and political environment in England in early 1919 was conducive to forms of collective action by disaffected soldiers. Continuing turbulence within the civilian populace affected the military. There was not a major camp that had not been influenced by strikes, demonstrations, and protest marches. Most of this unrest was linked to conditions of life and terms of service.[76] Putkowski believes that three particular crises impacted negatively on the situation at Kinmel Park: (1) strikes in the civilian sector; (2) a renewed Irish Republican Army campaign to cause the British to leave Northern Ireland; and (3) many soldier-strikes across the British Army. The empire was straining to keep itself together and attempting to ensure that Germany did not resume the conflict. Approximately 100 soldier-strikes, involving almost 100,000 British servicemen, took place in France and England. The core of contention revolved around the complicated British demobilization process that released servicemen based on an array of categories as opposed to length of service. This collective action resulted in the system being amended to demobilize men based on the time that they had in the Army. Putkowski goes on to say that these soldier-strikes were widely reported in the press and undoubtedly were viewed by British and Canadian soldiers as the primary reason that the demobilization policy changed. Their success reinforced the idea of mutiny as a form of "collective bargaining."[77]

Incidents at Kinmel Park increased in frequency and magnitude before the eruption of violence in March 1919. Morton, for instance, records a series of disturbances in January and February. On 7 January, an inter-racial disturbance occurred when a black sergeant-major of the 2nd (Coloured) Canadian Construction Company attempted to put an insubordinate white soldier in custody. The black soldiers of the construction company were attacked as they prepared for their ablutions. In the fracas, razors were used to slash five white soldiers and rocks injured some black soldiers. Several days later, on 10 January, some soldiers from Nova Scotia attempted to liberate a friend from a guardroom. In the melee, a "drunken" corporal struck an officer with the butt of an appropriated rifle. In February, there was a disturbance in the form of rock throwing and fights between Canadians of the Young Soldiers' Battalion and British officer cadets when the Canadians were turned away from a local dance. The subsequent court of inquiry laid blame on the British officers. It is noteworthy that this battalion was returned to Canada as soon as practicable.[78] Another incident occurred on 28 February, when Canadian soldiers, at the Rhyl railway station, unsuccessfully attempted to rescue a friend who had been arrested.[79]

Together, Nicholson, Lamb, Morton, Granatstein, Putkowski and others, in combination with contemporary sources of the period, ably illustrate the eight issues that, in accordance with The Mutiny Wagon Wheel model, act as disintegrators and provide impetus to the origins of mutiny. Alienation was produced by separation from parent units and primary groups for the return to Canada; the constant delays in shipping schedules; feelings of unequal treatment; monotony; and boredom. Even though it paled in comparison to life in the trenches, the physical environment of the camp — rudimentary accommodations and diversions, and poor weather — contributed, as well. A loss of faith was created when the social turbulence of the period shattered previously accepted values and hopes of the returning veterans. This disillusionment prompted men who had survived the rigours of combat to voice their unhappiness when the situation became unacceptable to them. Normlessness was prompted by an absence of effective discipline, in that the common standards of acceptable military comportment did not seem to be enforced at Kinmel Park. This lack of discipline and the refusal by the camp leadership to take effective action in response to various incidents also reinforced the escalating scale of protest. Even training activities that could have assisted in diverting attention from the existing conditions were unimaginative and repetitious. Most important, the command structure of the camp was fluid and changes in leadership were frequent. Individual soldiers transiting through the camp did not have the benefit of being members of a formed unit with its own officers and NCOs, and at the same time, did not have a permanent camp staff to assist them.

Yet, these factors do not address the primary cause of the mutiny. In the case of Kinmel Park, the critical issue was a failure of the leadership in the camp to inform the soldiers moving through of the origins of the amendments to the shipping schedules that affected their transit back to Canada. This lack of communication, in combination with other disintegrating factors, led directly to the violence of 4 and 5 March. The importance of this omission has been neglected by previous investigations.

It is apparent from the court of inquiry that the soldiers at Kinmel Park did not understand the seemingly constant shift in shipping. The third and fourth delays of the *SS Haverford,* and the subsequent protests and representations of Sailing Party 21, were indicative of this lack of comprehension. Such actions, although not within military norms, were likely viewed as the only method that was capable of achieving results. Over time, the explanations and promises of the camp commander and his staff became empty platitudes, as no resolution seemed to be forthcoming. Soldiers then ceased believing their commanders and used mutiny to express their discontent.

There have been differing reports regarding the atmosphere of the camp, but in the end, it was probably no worse than others. Still, the combination of inclement weather, boredom, lack of money, monotonous meals, and a deficiency of meaningful work created a great deal of discontent. This, discontent, blended with an extremely slow demobilization process and heightened by perceived changes to the "first over, first back" policy, likely produced feelings of disenfranchisement or alienation. Consider, as well, the fast diminishing hope for prosperity in the post-war era. Growing unemployment in Canada and a perception of a shrinking pool of employment were not the rewards these veterans sought. This, on top of a perceived inequality of post-war benefits between soldiers and officers caused the troops to be less concerned about the maintenance of their compact with the nation, particularly in a staging camp with leadership that appeared unknowing and uncaring.

The volatile mix of individuals at Kinmel Park included veteran combat troops who were afflicted with restlessness and discontent. They had won the war, they were alive, and they believed themselves deserving of better treatment than they had received. But regardless of who was most prone to mutiny, in the context of Kinmel Park, the mix of experienced and other soldiers was explosive and, as some had feared, only needed a spark to ignite.

Individuals unconstrained by unit loyalties, doubting the camp chain of command and suffering from restlessness, would have been more likely to take action to voice their disapproval of perceived wrongs in March 1919.

Even though training could be used to promote unit cohesion, this was not true at Kinmel Park. In the aftermath of the First World War, training at the staging camp consisted of the morning route march and little else. There was no impetus to devise something more imaginative and interesting to occupy the soldiers. Besides contributing to the boredom of camp life, such repetitious and unimaginative activity must have bred resentment.[80] The refusals to participate in the route marches on 1 and 4 March provide further evidence that the discipline imposed on the soldiery at Kinmel Park was not

Tin Town after the riot at Kinmel Park. (Canadian War Museum AN19890086-591 #4)

effective. In a number of instances since February, soldiers had protected their own from the authorities at the camp. Not only were troops resisting the arrest and incarceration of their peers, but the leadership at the camp took no effective action, such as a piquet within the camp, to enforce discipline.

Enabling all these disintegrating factors and providing the impetus to the mutiny was the lack of communication between camp staff and transiting soldiers. The scarcity of relevant information regarding the shipping delays caused the uncertain leadership of the camp to fail catastrophically. The formal leadership was unable to gain the trust of the soldiers or to respond to the individual and collective protests and representations, leaving the stage clear for informal leaders. These informal leaders galvanized the Kinmel Park troops to mutiny and gained the attention of both Canadian and British authorities.[81]

The events at Kinmel Park on 4 and 5 March 1919 should be considered for their primary lessons. For those involved, it was the option of last resort to make their concerns known. Many indications of escalating dissatisfaction had been, for most part, misinterpreted or ignored. The leadership did not try to be aware of the soldiers' concerns, or address their apprehensions in any meaningful manner. An accurate and opportune two-way flow of information would have impeded these disintegrating factors and prevented the divergence of the objectives of the *de jure* and *de facto* leadership of the camp. In the final analysis, the Kinmel Park mutiny of 4 and 5 March 1919 emphasizes that in the presence of centrifugal forces that can lead to a breakdown of organizational effectiveness, the communication of information is a powerful cohesive element that military leaders neglect at their own risk.

NOTES

Editor's Note: The research and writing of this paper would not have been possible without the sponsorship of the Canadian Forces Leadership Institute. Its support is gratefully acknowledged.

1. Noel Barbour, "Gallant Protestors," *The Legion,* Vol. 48, No. 10 (March 1973), 45.

2. Colonel G.W.L. Nicholson, *Official History of the Canadian Army in the First World War: Canadian Expeditionary Force 1914–1919* (Ottawa: Queen's Printer, 1962), 532.

3. Eliot A. Cohen and John Gooch, *Military Misfortunes: The Anatomy of Failure in War* (New York: Free Press, 1990), 28.

4. Library and Archives Canada [henceforth LAC], Record Group [henceforth RG] 24, Series III, C-1, File 8779, Document 2770, Colonel A. Fortescue Duguid, "Disturbances in Canadian Camps and Areas 1918–19," Canadian Army Historical Section, March 1941, Reel 1, C-8375.

5. Joel Hamby suggests that "Militaries in general seem not to like dealing with deep systemic problems, and prefer to mete out justice once, and them move on with the prosecution of whatever operation is at hand." See Joel E. Hamby, "The Mutiny Wagon Wheel: A Leadership Model for Mutiny in Combat," *Armed Forces & Society,* Vol. 28, No. 4 (Summer 2002), 592.

6. The military is a unique institution; it is part of the larger society, yet by the nature of its function, distinct. Death and serious injury can easily occur to those involved in the military profession while in the service of the state and General Sir John Hackett's concept of a "contract of unlimited liability" aptly summarizes this idea. See Sir John Winthrop Hackett, "Today and Tomorrow," in Melham W. Wakin, ed., *War, Morality and The Military Profession,* 2nd ed. (Boulder, Colorado: Westview Press, 1989), 99.

7. "The rights of representation, free speech and collective action which had extended during the nineteenth and twentieth centuries meant little to soldiers and sailors, for whom they were severely curtailed. The profession of arms looked to the different values of duty, courage and honour." See Lawrence James, *Mutiny: In the British and Commonwealth Forces, 1797–1956* (London: Buchan & Enright, 1987), 32.

8. References to British military law cited in Julian Putkowski, *British Army Mutineers 1914–1922* (London: Francis Boutle, 1998), 9.

9. E.P. Thompson, *The Making of the English Working Class* (London: Victor Gollancz, 1965), 13–5.

10. *Ibid.*, 14–8.

11. Noted British scholar E.P. Thompson believed in much the same way that mobilization occurs when class interests are established. He wrote: "… class happens when some men, as a result of common experiences (inherited and shared), feel and articulate the identity of the interests as between themselves, and as against other men whose interests are different from (and usually opposed to) theirs." *Ibid.*, 9.

12. Hamby, "The Mutiny Wagon Wheel," 575–78 and 591.

13. *Ibid.*, 577.

14. *Ibid.*, 575–78.

15. *Ibid.*, 578–79.

16. *Ibid.*, 579–84.

17. Figure 11.1 was taken directly from *Ibid.*, 577.

18. *Ibid.*, 584–86.

19. *Ibid.*, 587–88.

20. David Grossman, *On Killing: The Psychological Cost of Learning to Kill in War and Society* (Boston: Little Brown, 1995), 143–46.

21. Hamby, "The Mutiny Wagon Wheel," 588–91.

22. By April 1917, the new Ministry of the Overseas Military Forces of Canada (OMFC), under the Overseas Minister, Sir Edward Kemp, had commenced demobilization planning. See Desmond Morton, "'Kicking and Complaining': Demobilization Riots

in the Canadian Expeditionary Force, 1918–19," *Canadian Historical Review,* Vol. 61, No. 3 (September 1980), 335.

23. "With the exception of the Canadian Corps, which, as we have seen, was returned by units, [on the recommendation of Lieutenant-General Sir Arthur Currie, the Corps Commander] the principle of 'first in, first out' was adopted. The full duration of the war was divided into seventeen three-month periods, with two service groups assigned to each. The first seventeen consisted of married men, the last seventeen of single, the married groups having priority over the single. Thus while the guiding principle for release was the order of enlistment, men who had families dependent on them took precedence over the single men." See Nicholson, *Official History,* 531.

24. In these staging camps, soldiers completed their medical and dental clearances, and any other final documentation. Demobilization leave of eight days to two weeks could then be approved. Upon return to the staging camp, they were assigned to an embarkation company to await transportation to Canada. According to Nicholson, the average soldier spent about a month in England, although it is noted that the policy was sometimes amended in individual cases for compassionate reasons. Nicholson states that these few early returnees were a reason for "dissatisfaction" among soldiers who were not aware of the reasons behind these early repatriations. Adding to their resentment, in order to obtain maximum use of the available shipping, recently arrived drafts of soldiers were sometimes returned to Canada soon after their arrival in the United Kingdom. See *Ibid.*, 530–32.

25. James, *Mutiny,* 115.

26. Morton, "'Kicking and Complaining,'" 342.

27. Cited in *Ibid.*, 340.

28. Contained within a letter to Kemp, 11 February 1919. Cited in *Ibid.*, 340–41.

29. "Regulations were clear: soldiers awaiting discharge were entitled to a pound or two each fortnight." See *Ibid.*, 344.

30. Figure 11.3 was provided by Mr. William Constable.

31. Putkowski, "The Kinmel Park Camp Riots 1919," 15.

32. "On Monday a deputation went to the headquarters of MD No. 2 in a perfectly regular manner with a spokesman who addressed the Major. They were referred to Capt. Patterson who blustered and bulldozed them, and said that he would have none of this nonsense. They said that if Argyll House [Headquarters of the OMFC in London] was not appealed to before 10.30 p.m. on Tuesday [4 March] they would

riot. Col. Colquhoun said that he had appealed to Argyll House several times and been able to accomplish nothing." Cited in *Ibid.*, 16.

33. Cited in *Ibid.*, 16–7.

34. *Ibid.*, 17.

35. Morton, "'Kicking and Complaining,'" 344–45.

36. David Lamb spells "Tsarevitch" as "Tarasevitch" and says that the press used "Tarashaitch" or "Tarouke" as other variations. See David Lamb, "Mutinies." London: Solidarity United Kingdom, 2002, 28 [internet document], *www.geocities.com/cordobakaf/mutinies.html*, accessed 18 October 2002.

37. *Ibid.*, 28–31.

38. James, *Mutiny,* 115.

39. To reduce unpopular duties, Colquhoun had eliminated the piquet that would have been used to react to emergencies such as fires or, as in this case, a disturbance. Camp military police were in Rhyl and other nearby communities to prevent trouble between Canadian soldiers and locals. There were no formed units in the camp, except the Canadian Reserve Cavalry Regiment, to react on behalf of the camp authorities. In the case of the Reserve Cavalry Regiment, they reported they had no soldiers in barracks to use as a reaction force. See Morton, "'Kicking and Complaining,'" 345–46.

40. All officers did not obey this order. Major J.C. Stevenson of MD 4 kept a box of ammunition, which he shared with bordering camps. See *Ibid.*, 347.

41. According to Morton, this was not completed efficiently and soldiers found two unguarded carloads of liquor and beer that was duly distributed and consumed. See *Ibid.*, 346.

42. Morton notes that although some instances of assault occurred, they were rare. He also writes that the soldiers of the Canadian Expeditionary Force remembered their debt to the Salvation Army and did not target its facilities. On the other hand, the YMCA and NACB were disdained for their perceived exorbitant costs and haughtiness. See *Ibid.*, 346–47.

43. Lieutenant J.A. Gauthier organized the defence of Camp 20. After viewing the initial disturbances of 4 March, he returned to Camp 20 and organized his movement draft of 50 to protect it. On the morning of 5 March, he removed his insignia of rank and circulated among the mutinous troops. Upon seeing that they were going to attack Camp 20, he tried to convince them not to do so. Morton writes that although Major

Charles Maclean was the commander of MD 1, it was Gauthier who inspired the defence. Gauthier convinced the soldiers that it was necessary to protect records to prevent further disruptions to repatriation and this caused several hundred soldiers to assist the camp authorities. See *Ibid.*, 349.

44. James writes that rifles were issued at 1330 hours, Gauthier's warning occurred at approximately 1400, and the mutineers moved to Camp 20 about 1430. See James, *Mutiny*, 115–16.

45. Morton, "'Kicking and Complaining,'" 349.

46. Lawrence James provides a succinct list together with the circumstances of the casualties: "A Private Hickman was shot dead in Camp 18 and several men in one of its huts was wounded. Private Gillan, one of the guards, was hit in the crossfire as he was moving towards a group of mutineers who were in the ASC [Army Service Corps] stables. Gunner Haney was shot in the head, Corporal Young killed by a bayonet wound in the head and Tsarevitch, allegedly the leader, died from a bayonet wound in the lower stomach. The last two men must have been wounded during the sharp hand-to-hand fighting between the guards and the mutineers. The fierceness of the resistance led to the mutineers hoisting a white flag. Four had been killed, twenty-one wounded, and seventy-five were arrested. Fifty men were charged with mutiny, of which twenty-seven were convicted and sentenced to between 90 days and ten years." See James, *Mutiny*, 116–17.

47. Morton, "'Kicking and Complaining,'" 352–53.

48. Turner toured the camp immediately after the mutiny.

49. LAC, RG 9, Series III, Vol. 2770, File D-199–33, Kinmel Park Camp Court of Inquiry. Italics added by present author for emphasis.

50. *Ibid.* Italics added by present author for emphasis.

51. *Ibid.*

52. Not all officers were forewarned of potential unrest. Captain R.J. Davidson of the 21st Battalion and second-in-command of MD 2 said, "I was surprised at the outbreak. I knew there was unrest about the sailings, but I did not expect any outbreak. I do not think the outbreak was organised to any great extent...." See *Ibid.*

53. *Ibid.*

54. Although Colonel Colquhoun had been at Kinmel Park since September 1918, he was the exception. Lieutenant-Colonel French had commanded since December 1918 and Major Cooper had occupied his position only since 3 March 1919, but had been employed at Kinmel Park prior to this date. *Ibid.*

55. *Ibid.*

56. "Toronto Men Explain Riots at Kinmel Camp," 1, 8 March 1919, *Toronto Daily Star* [henceforth *TDS*].

57. *Ibid.*, 24.

58. *Ibid.*, 1.

59. LAC, RG 9, Series III, Vol. 2770, File D-199–33, Kinmel Park Camp Court of Inquiry.

60. *Ibid.*

61. As of 10 March, there had been 61 arrested and sent out of the area. See *Ibid.*

62. Courts-martial were legal proceedings in that there was no jury. The president and members of the court had to be commissioned officers. There was no formal system of appeals regarding the sentences that were handed down. There were four types of court-martial: (1) regimental; (2) district; (3) general; and (4) field general, with the main difference being the severity of the offence and the powers of sentencing that were provided to each kind. The most severe, general and field general courts-martial, could try all ranks and could award sentences up to and including death. A general court-martial had a board of between five and nine officers and a field general court-martial required three officers and these two types of court-martial normally tried charges of mutiny. Given the seriousness of these types of charges, there was normally a court-martial officer appointed whose duty was to advise the court on procedures and issues of military law. However, the prosecution and members could come from the accused's unit or from elsewhere. Most of the officers involved had minimal legal training. See Putkowski, *British Army Mutineers,* 10. Morton provides the figure of 59 soldiers being jailed at Liverpool to await court-martial, with the others being tried summarily by their commanding officers. See Morton, "'Kicking and Complaining,'" 350.

63. Chris Madsen, *Another Kind of Justice: Canadian Military Law from Confederation to Somalia* (Vancouver: University of British Columbia Press, 1999), 51.

64. Cited in Lamb, "Mutinies," 39.

65. Morton, "'Kicking and Complaining,'" 353.

66. James Lamb suggests, " … the men underestimated the ruthlessness and determination of the officers. When a mutiny is under way there can be no unarmed approaches to armed officers. Unless a mutiny is 100% solid the authorities will use all means at their disposal to crush it. When 'necessary' they will not flinch from bloodshed." See Lamb, "Mutinies," 38–39.

67. LAC, RG 9, Series III, Vol. 2770, File D-199–33, Kinmel Park Camp Court of Inquiry.

68. Morton, "'Kicking and Complaining,'" 351–52.

69. LAC, RG 9, Series III, Vol. 2770, File D-199–33, Kinmel Park Camp Court of Inquiry.

70. Friends of Colquhoun were cited as saying that they had received letters from him describing the unrest in the camp and that "riots of small scale" occurred almost daily. See "Small-Scale Riots Common Occurrence," 1, 8 March 1919, *TDS*.

71. The Canadian Army Historical Section concurred and stated the reasons for the outbreak were sailing delays and postponements, tobacco shortages, poor food, and concerns regarding post-war employment. See LAC, RG 24, C-1, Series III, File 8779, Document 2770, Duguid, Appendix, Reel C-8375.

72. Kemp, as cited in Desmond Morton and J.L. Granatstein, *Marching to Armageddon: Canadians and the Great War 1914–1919* (Toronto: Metropole Litho, 1989), 252–53.

73. James, *Mutiny,* 115.

74. *Ibid.*, 26–8.

75. Internet document. E-mail from Julian Putkowski to *wwi-1@raven.cc.ukans.edu,* 4 December 1999, accessed at *www.ukans.edu/-kansite/WWI-L/1999/12/msg00150.html,* 12 October 2002. See also, Putkowski, "The Kinmel Park Camp Riots 1919," 14–5.

76. Putkowski, *British Army Mutineers,* 13–4.

77. Putkowski, "The Kinmel Park Camp Riots 1919," 8–9.

78. Morton, "'Kicking and Complaining,'" 339–43.

79. Putkowski, "The Kinmel Park Camp Riots 1919," 14–15.

80. *Ibid.*

81. Drastic actions of last resort to change soldiers' conditions continue in the Canadian Army to this day. The allegations surrounding actions of soldiers in the Warrant Officer Matt Stopford incident with the 1st Princess Patricia's Canadian Light Infantry Battle Group in Croatia during Operation HARMONY Roto 2 can be taken as evidence of this.

12 ✣

Disaffection and Disobedience in the Aftermath of the First World War: The Canadian Assault on the Epsom Police Station, 17 June 1919

NIKOLAS GARDNER

Canadian soldiers did not go home quietly at the end of the First World War. During the spring of 1919, Canadians at holding camps across Great Britain rioted and clashed with local civilians and police, sometimes with fatal consequences. Historians have interpreted these eruptions of violence primarily as a manifestation of the soldiers' frustration that stemmed from repeated delays in their return to Canada.

Although frustration undoubtedly sparked many of these incidents, particularly the Kinmel Park riot of March 1919, it does not explain them all. This is especially true of the Canadian attack on the police station in the town of Epsom, Surrey, on the night of 17 June 1919. Following the arrest of two Canadians in Epsom that evening, up to 800 soldiers from the nearby Woodcote Park Convalescent Hospital launched a prolonged assault against the station, killing one police officer and injuring 14 others, in an effort to free their comrades.

Desmond Morton has discussed this episode briefly in an article on the "demobilization riots" of 1919 and treats it largely as a consequence of continued Canadian anger at their extended sojourn in Britain.[1] A closer examination of the Epsom incident, however, reveals a more complex picture. This chapter will therefore begin by assessing relations between Canadian soldiers and the Surrey population in 1919. It will then discuss the nature of the Woodcote Park Convalescent Hospital, the patients who resided there and their interactions with local residents. This chapter will also examine the attack on the Epsom police station itself, demonstrating that it resulted from mounting tension between Canadian soldiers and the residents of Epsom in the context of indifferent and largely inadequate military discipline at Woodcote Park. In conclusion, it will consider what the Epsom incident reveals about relations between Canadian soldiers and the command structure above them in 1919.

ANGLO-CANADIAN RELATIONS IN SURREY, 1919

At the conclusion of the First World War, thousands of Canadian soldiers passed through the county of Surrey as they awaited repatriation. The county, which is immediately southwest of London, hosted a large staging camp at Witley, and the smaller Woodcote Park Convalescent Hospital at Epsom. Soldiers from Bramshott camp in adjacent Hampshire also visited the towns of Surrey regularly. As 1919 progressed, however, the relationship between Canadian soldiers and the local inhabitants deteriorated. As Desmond Morton has explained, a shortage of adequate shipping, strikes by British workers, and the limited capacity of the Canadian rail system to transport personnel out of Atlantic Canada delayed the return of thousands of soldiers. The *ad hoc* administration of the demobilization process in England gave these soldiers scope to vent their growing frustration. Thousands of Canadians from different units mixed in large staging camps under the supervision of unfamiliar officers, non-commissioned officers (NCOs), and staff, all of whom proved unable to maintain discipline as discontent mounted. In June, disciplinary problems increased at Witley because of the arrival of hundreds of men recently released from military prisons, and others barred from sailing home earlier for disciplinary offences. Thus, in mid-June 1919, thousands of angry Canadian soldiers rioted at Witley, and in the process, destroyed "Tin Town," an agglomeration of shops set up by local merchants in the camp.[2]

Such unrest, however, did not occur in a vacuum, particularly in Surrey, where soldiers had frequent contact with the local population. Hundreds of Canadians left their camps daily, seeking entertainment in such towns as Epsom, Guildford and Woking. While local businesses benefited significantly from the visitors, a variety of factors increased tensions between the Canadians and their hosts during the spring of 1919. The informal demeanour of Canadian soldiers at leisure annoyed some local residents. As one resident complained in a letter to a local newspaper, "I see that the Canadians are walking about Guildford with greasy trousers, coats all open, and white cricketing shoes. I wonder what our military authorities would say to a British 'tommy' walking about like this!"[3] Another lamented the poor discipline of Canadian soldiers, commenting, "In the course of a good few years of soldiering, I have never seen such utter contempt shown to officers by NCOs and men under their control."[4] Besides their apparent indifference to military authority and protocol, soldiers in Surrey fell afoul of the law with relative frequency. Throughout the spring of 1919, local newspapers regularly detailed the convictions of Canadians for offences such as theft, assault, and public disorder. One poorly advised Canadian sapper was charged after trying to purchase 30 grams of cocaine from a local pharmacist.[5]

These infractions did little to endear the soldiers to the local population. Animosity toward the Canadians ran particularly high among young males in the area. As British soldiers from Surrey returned home in 1919, often to gloomy economic prospects, the presence of the Canadians, who were better paid than their Imperial counterparts, caused considerable resentment. The fact that the foreigners proved to be "great favourites" with local women undoubtedly fuelled the hostility of British veterans, many of whom returned home to broken relationships. The popularity of the Canadians also irritated local men who had not served in uniform.[6] Moreover, according to one local newspaper, members of the locally-recruited Royal West Surrey Regiment begrudged what they perceived to be the disproportionate praise heaped on the Canadian Corps for its capture of Vimy Ridge in 1917.[7]

Given the extent of anti-Canadian sentiment in Surrey, it is hardly surprising that neither the mid-June riot at Witley, nor the subsequent attack on the Epsom Police Station, were isolated incidents. Indeed, Canadian soldiers clashed repeatedly with local civilians and police officers during the spring and summer of 1919. April and May saw violent incidents in Guildford involving soldiers from the Witley camp and local civilians, all of which culminated in a series of brawls on the nights of 9 to 12 May. Although the Canadians clearly contributed to the violence, *The*

Surrey Weekly Press attributed it to "scores of Guildford's young 'hot heads' more than Canadians. They have been 'spoiling' for a real, downright row...."[8] On 25 June, the nearby town of Woking saw a series of fights between Canadians and local civilians, as well as soldiers from New Zealand. The following night, Guildford police arrested two drunken civilians who had declared their intention to "fight any Canadian at once."[9] Thus, rather than simply a manifestation of the soldiers' frustration with the delays in the repatriation process, the Canadian attack on the Epsom Police Station forms part of a broader pattern of Anglo-Canadian hostility in Surrey in 1919.

THE WOODCOTE PARK CONVALESCENT HOSPITAL

Anglo-Canadian tension prevailed in Epsom, home of the Woodcote Park Convalescent Hospital. Significantly, however, the nature of the hospital's patients and the lax disciplinary regime imposed on them complicated the relationship between the residents of Epsom and the Canadians. In the months following the end of the First World War, the population of the hospital fluctuated between 2,000 and 4,000 patients and staff, with hundreds transferring in and out each week. In mid-June 1919, the hospital housed approximately 1,500 patients and 700 staff.[10] The exact purpose of this facility has been subject to speculation among both contemporary observers and historians. Writing to the British home secretary immediately after the Canadian attack on the Epsom Police Station, the commissioner of the Metropolitan Police suggested that the hospital existed "mainly for Venereal Cases...."[11] Similarly, in correspondence with Desmond Morton, historian Julian Putkowski referred to Woodcote Park as "the VD [venereal disease] unit...." In his own brief account of the attack on the police station, Morton makes no reference to this issue. In a letter to Putkowski, he explained, "I know of no evidence that the convalescents at Epsom were VD cases and I suspect that this was invented to blacken them."[12]

The truth lies somewhere between these two views. The Woodcote Park Convalescent Hospital did not exist solely, or even primarily, to accommodate those soldiers who were suffering from VD. The hospital's war diary indicates that dental work occupied at least as many of its staff as did the treatment of sexually transmitted diseases. Confusion regarding the purpose of the Woodcote Park facility may have stemmed from the proximity of the nearby Canadian Special Hospital at Witley, which apparently dealt exclusively with VD cases.[13] Nonetheless, a significant proportion of the patients at Woodcote Park received treatment for such ailments. It is unlikely that these patients suffered from the derision of their peers. Indeed, the extent to which soldiers took advantage of the hospital's prophylactic program (i.e., receiving preventive treatments for VD before and after leave in Epsom or London) suggests that such maladies were an accepted hazard as soldiers awaited their return to Canada.[14]

Those soldiers afflicted with VD were subject to prolonged and uncomfortable treatments that did nothing to alleviate their frustration with the repeated delays in their repatriation. More significant, they were compelled to wear blue uniforms and were confined to the hospital's grounds, while other patients, who wore khaki uniforms, were able to leave Woodcote Park, often for days at a time.[15] The hospital attempted to intern and clearly identify VD patients, at least partly to assuage public concerns about their ability to mix with the general population outside Woodcote Park. Rather than alleviating these worries, however, such policies likely had the effect of tainting the entire hospital in the eyes of the local community since it housed a largely hidden population of patients of questionable character who could conceivably corrupt their peers inside the facility.

Also, this policy of segregation undoubtedly caused annoyance among the VD patients themselves. The frustration of one such patient is evident in the following newspaper account of his trial for assault in February 1919. According to the *Surrey Advertiser and County Times,* Private Winter entered the Star Beer House in Epsom, but "as he was in hospital blues, the landlord refused to serve him." Winter responded by striking the landlord, and was ejected from the premises. He then "put his foot through the window" of the Beer House. When confronted by the police, Winter "closed with PC [Police Constable] Loudwell and they fell to the ground. The ambulance was fetched, and as the prisoner was being put on it he struck PC Major, who had come to the assistance of his colleague." After being dragged to the police station, he "deliberately put his shoulder through a window."[16] Winter may have been uncharacteristically belligerent. Nevertheless, the makeup of the patient community at Woodcote Park had a significant impact on Anglo-Canadian relations in Epsom. Those patients receiving treatment for VD had reason to feel stigmatized and excluded from the local community. At the same time, their presence at the hospital likely contributed to public suspicion regarding its patients as a group.

As the case of Private Winter suggests, maintaining discipline among the patients at Woodcote Park, regardless of their condition, proved to be a constant challenge. The hospital's staff offered a wide range of activities to alleviate the boredom and frustration felt by the soldiers. Patients could participate in many sports, including boxing and badminton. Staff and patients alike fielded a soccer team that competed against teams from other hospitals in the London area. Even more popular was a baseball team that participated in the "Anglo-American Baseball League" in the spring of 1919; on one memorable occasion, it defeated a team from the U.S. Navy. The hospital also featured nightly cinema shows and a band, as well as canteens and tearooms that local charitable societies provided. In addition, patients could take advantage of guided trips to local landmarks such as Windsor Castle and hear lectures offered by the Khaki University, an educational program for soldiers.[17]

While Woodcote Park clearly offered a number of diversions for its patients, it had few other means of controlling their behaviour. As a senior police officer commented in a report following the attack on the Epsom Police Station, "The whole camp appeared to be run on very lackadaisical lines...."[18] In theory, patients resided in huts with dozens of others under the supervision of a corporal or a sergeant. This NCO was responsible for calling roll at 2130 hours every night, shutting the lights out at 2215 and calling roll again between 0630 and 0700 the next morning.[19] In practice, this system did little to constrain the movements of either patients or staff. Given the rapid turnover of patients, it was virtually impossible for officers to form meaningful relationships with NCOs and staff, some of whom were often patients themselves. Moreover, the few officers at Woodcote Park were largely medical or administrative personnel whose responsibilities did not require them to exercise authority over the patients and staff on a daily basis. In the absence of strong leadership by the officers, the NCOs showed little enthusiasm for their responsibilities, which they held only temporarily as they awaited their return to Canada. Thus, in some cases, soldiers absent at roll call were apparently ignored. As Corporal Walter Hall

Lees related during the investigation of the attack on the Epsom Police Station, he called roll on the night of 17 June and found that one patient was not present. According to Lees, "I thought he was somewhere about the camp and I did not report him absent."[20]

Beyond roll call, there existed few measures to ensure that soldiers remained on the hospital's grounds. In the spring of 1919, only four military policemen (MPs) were on duty at Woodcote Park at any given time. Given that there were five entrances to the grounds, at least one of which remained open at all times, their numbers were clearly insufficient to control the soldiers' movements. In addition, as some of the MPs were patients themselves, there is reason to doubt the zeal with which they enforced the rules at Woodcote Park. Indeed, at least one MP actually participated in the attack on the Epsom Police Station.[21]

Even if the NCOs and MPs were entirely conscientious in the execution of their duties, the relatively permissive leave regulations at Woodcote Park made it impossible to monitor the activities of many soldiers. All patients in khaki uniforms were allowed to leave the hospital grounds and venture into the town of Epsom between 1600 and 2130 hours every day.[22] In addition, the hundreds of patients who served on the hospital's staff while undergoing treatment themselves received a permanent pass that allowed them to remain outside the hospital's grounds until 2300 hours. Given that the NCOs in charge of the huts usually went to sleep after lights-out, staff could effectively return at any time before roll call the next morning. Patients also received furloughs that allowed them to leave the hospital for days at a time. At least one patient paid to stay at a guesthouse in Epsom on multiple occasions in 1919, despite its close proximity to the hospital.[23]

Outside the camp, patients were effectively unsupervised. The MPs who patrolled the hospital's grounds did not venture into the town of Epsom, despite the presence of hundreds of soldiers there every evening. Thus, the tiny Epsom branch of the London Metropolitan Police shouldered the responsibility for keeping the peace between the soldiers and an increasingly hostile local population. With less than 20 officers and constables on duty at any given time, this detachment struggled to defuse large-scale altercations. Canadians at Woodcote Park were not prisoners and it is entirely reasonable that they were allowed to leave the hospital's grounds as they awaited their return to Canada. Nonetheless, given the permissive atmosphere that prevailed at the hospital, and the limited police presence in Epsom, tensions between unruly soldiers and members of the local community could easily spiral out of control. Such tensions were evident from early 1919. In late January, two patients from Woodcote Park, Sapper Franklin Brown and Private Conrad Carl Deacon, stood trial in Epsom after committing a serious and apparently unprovoked assault on Private Arthur Jones, a British soldier. According to a local newspaper:

> Jones said on Wednesday evening [that] he was going down the High-street when the prisoners were arguing and using bad language. He asked Deacon to go home and to keep a civil tongue. Deacon enquired if he was a Canadian, and he replied that he was not, he was a Tommy. Deacon then used a filthy expression towards him, and struck him, knocking him down. When on the ground the other prisoner kicked him. Deacon said, 'leave him to me, and I will finish him off,' at the same time giving him another blow to the face. After other evidence, [the] prisoners said they were both drunk and did not know what happened.[24]

Clashes between Canadian soldiers and local civilians in nearby Witley overshadowed events in Epsom over the next four months. Nonetheless, altercations involving Canadians in Epsom were sufficiently common that the local police and the authorities at Woodcote Park developed a system to expedite the processing of delinquent soldiers. Rather than pressing charges against those who were intoxicated or violent, the police simply telephoned the authorities at Woodcote Park and requested an escort to retrieve the offenders from the police station. The inadequacy of this system as a means of maintaining order in the town was evident to Major P.J.S. Bird, the adjutant at Woodcote Park. During the spring of 1919, he asked for additional MPs to patrol the streets of Epsom, and he asked that Canadians be barred from public houses in the town.[25] Neither Canadian nor British military authorities granted these requests.

A parade at the Convalescent Hospital in Epsom. (Department of National Defence, Library and Archives Canada PA-22679)

In early June, violent confrontations became nightly occurrences on the streets of Epsom. The soldiers were not always the instigators. Testifying at the trial of a civilian who was charged after picking a fight with a Canadian on the night of 16 June, Police Sergeant Blayden expounded on the causes of the trouble. He explained, "The young men demobilised come into contact with the Canadians. That is the origin of it. They get drinking about, and quarrels start." Pressed further by the court, Blayden continued, "There is a little bit of feeling between the two — Imperials and Canadians."[26] Thus, on the 16th, the night before the attack on the police station, "a gang of stable lads," presumably with veterans among them, "came down to give the Canadians a hiding if they could." The situation escalated until nearly 100 soldiers and civilians were involved in a confrontation in the street. Although the police were able to defuse the situation with only one arrest, this was hardly an isolated incident. In the week leading up to the attack on the station, repeated disturbances forced the Epsom Police to deploy extra constables every night.[27]

Even more ominous than the increasing tension in the streets of Epsom in June was a growing Canadian disregard for the authority of the local police. On the night of the 12th, Private Clifton Duby was arrested after using obscene language, for attempting to instigate a fight with local civilians and for refusing to leave the area when instructed to do so by a police constable. When PC Stanford attempted to detain him, Duby threw him to the ground, while another Canadian soldier jumped on the back of PC Barltrop and struck him in the head with a stick. At Duby's trial, Inspector Pawley, the officer in charge of the Epsom Police Station, lamented that such behaviour was part of a broader trend, complaining that whenever his officers "took a Canadian into custody, no matter how justifiable their action, comrades of the arrested man attacked them."[28] The 17 June assault on the Epsom Police Station, therefore, was not simply a spontaneous display of Canadian frustration because of delays in repatriation. Boredom and irritation at their prolonged stay in England undoubtedly contributed to the belligerence of Canadian soldiers in 1919. Well before 17 June, however, the management of the Woodcote Park Convalescent Hospital and the mounting tension between its patients and the local civilian population created the conditions for an eruption of violence to occur in Epsom.

THE ATTACK ON THE EPSOM POLICE STATION, 17 JUNE 1919

After the incidents of the preceding week, the resumption of hostilities in Epsom on the night of 17 June did not come as a complete surprise. As the *Surrey County Herald* related: "What occurred on Tuesday night was the culmination of a nightly series of disturbances in the streets, in which not only Canadian soldiers, but some of the young men of Epsom were concerned. There had been several clashes between them, and on Tuesday night further trouble was anticipated."[29]

The day of the Epsom Derby, 17 June, saw large numbers of soldiers and civilians rubbing shoulders in the town's drinking establishments. The flashpoint of the violence that evening remains shrouded in rumour. According to one account, a Canadian private was seated in a pub with his wife when a civilian assaulted him. When the police arrived, they arrested the private, thereby provoking an angry response by his comrades.[30] In another version, a sergeant joined the private and his wife. A fight followed between the two Canadians that was broken-up by the police. While the sergeant subsequently left, the private verbally abused the police until he was arrested.[31] In the investigation that followed the attack on the Epsom station, the police involved made no reference to a dispute between Canadian soldiers. With this being said, some Canadians evidently became involved in an altercation with civilians inside the Rifleman Beer House on the evening of the 17th. When police constables attempted to disperse the offenders at approximately 2145 hours, a Canadian, Private McDonald, refused, used obscenities and attempted to instigate a fight with a civilian. Unable to pacify the aggressive soldier, the police escorted him to the Epsom Police Station. Following the trend of previous nights, McDonald's comrades followed, threatening to release him by force. Two other constables then intervened, arresting a second soldier, named A. Veinotte, for disorderly conduct and obstructing police in the execution of their duty.[32]

Intended to reduce the tension in the streets, the two arrests had the unfortunate consequence of heightening it. Canadian soldiers clearly felt that McDonald and Veinotte had been detained unjustly and were quick to protest. After the two soldiers entered the Epsom Police Station, a small group of about 20 Canadians gathered outside. The police shooed them away, but at approximately 2230 hours, a larger and more hostile crowd of around 70 soldiers assembled on the street in front of the station. According to Police Sergeant Herbert Shuttleworth, the soldiers intended to secure the release of the two prisoners, particularly McDonald, shouting, "Come on, we will have Mac out of this!" Attempting to placate the angry Canadians, police officers informed them that the arrested soldiers would be handed over to a military escort from Woodcote Park. The crowd, however, became increasingly agitated and started throwing missiles at the station. This compelled the officer-in-charge, Inspector Pawley, to order his subordinates to aggressively disperse the Canadians.[33] This effort succeeded, and with the threat to the station evidently alleviated, Pawley dismissed the extra constables that he had retained that evening in anticipation of trouble.[34]

Pawley's decision proved to be premature. After being chased from the police station, the Canadians returned to Woodcote Park, determined to mobilize their comrades. When Police Sergeant George Greenfield telephoned the hospital at 2245 hours to arrange for the transfer of the two incarcerated soldiers, a Canadian officer hurriedly told him, "We have some trouble here right now, let it go a bit and I will ring you."[35] Authorities at Woodcote Park, however, were unable to respond effectively to the return of dozens of soldiers who were highly agitated by the arrests of McDonald and Veinotte. Unimpeded by the MPs, the soldiers roused sleeping patients and staff by running sticks along the sides of their corrugated iron huts, while a bugler sounded repeated calls to "fall in."[36] Attempts by officers and NCOs to stop the angry mob of soldiers from assembling were largely half-hearted and entirely ineffectual. Few of the NCOs tried to stop the soldiers in their huts from joining the expedition to the station. Those who did were not particularly forceful. The only NCO subsequently interviewed by the Metropolitan Police who even claimed to have attempted to stop the departure of his charges was Corporal Walter Hall Lees who simply "pointed out to the boys that there would be little hope of getting him out of the police station … and that it would be wrong to get him out by force."[37]

While Lees limited his intervention to the passive proffering of advice, the senior officer on duty at Woodcote Park, Major James Ross, made more strenuous efforts to avert the attack on the police station. After hearing the commotion in the camp, Ross confronted the soldiers as they assembled inside the hospital's grounds. As he related:

> I, with some difficulty, addressed them and appealed to them on the reputation that the Canadians had made at the front to desist from doing anything that would in any way bring discredit upon the Canadians. I promised that their grievances, if any, could be looked into by the proper military authorities.

Despite his endeavours, Ross, the hospital accountant, apparently had little influence over staff or patients. Thus, he admitted, "My council did not prevail."[38]

Unable to talk down the angry soldiers, Ross hurried off to Epsom in an attempt to warn the police of their impending arrival. After directing Regimental Sergeant-Major John Parson, the senior NCO at Woodcote Park, to lead the crowd by a circuitous route through the streets of Epsom, Ross took a shortcut through a park. Parson, however, could exert no more authority over the soldiers than Ross, and the crowd simply followed the major to the police station. After failing to dissuade or divert the soldiers, Ross and Parson tried to keep them quiet as they entered Epsom, but even this failed. The mob became increasingly rowdy as it neared the station, with the bugler ignoring repeated admonitions to remain silent. Soldiers armed themselves by tearing apart the wooden fences that fronted a private home and a chapel. They also threw rocks and chunks of wood through the windows of a local hotel, as well as at an ambulance that was hurriedly despatched from Woodcote Park, thereby preventing it from collecting the prisoners from the police station.[39]

The crowd of between 400 and 800 soldiers, "about half in khaki and half in blue," was clearly audible as it approached Epsom Police Station at approximately 2330 hours. Preparing for the worst, Inspector Pawley summoned off-duty officers and constables from their homes, as well as available personnel from other stations in the vicinity. He also assembled his entire force at the gate outside the front garden of the station to meet the riotous soldiers.[40] As they arrived, Major Ross came forward to confer with Pawley in a final effort to avert a violent clash between soldiers and police. Vastly outnumbered, Pawley agreed that he would transfer the prisoners into Ross's custody. The two men then entered the station to release McDonald and Veinotte. Explaining this development to the crowd, however, proved prohibitively difficult. As Sergeant-Major Parson related in a statement to the police, "The men immediately around the gate understood that Major Ross was acting in the interests of all concerned, but some men at the rear of the crowd began throwing sticks and other missiles." Standing at the door of the station, Parson attempted to placate the mob outside the gates while Ross secured the release of the men. According to Parson, "As Major Ross did not appear for some moments the crowd began to throw missiles. I again appealed to the men to be quiet. The men near me stopped and asked the others to stop and for a moment they complied."[41]

This uncharacteristic discretion on the part of the crowd was short lived. When Ross did not reappear almost immediately, the soldiers apparently concluded that he too had been arrested. Parson soon found himself in the line of fire, as soldiers began launching missiles at the station from the back of the crowd. After a piece of brick struck him in the back of the head, Parson beat a hasty retreat to the gate.[42] Though neither Parson nor Ross had been able to exercise much control over the crowd, the soldiers had at least shown some restraint in their presence. With Ross now inside the station, however, and Parson only visible to a few individuals who were around the front gate, the aggressive instincts of the mob took over. Soldiers began to throw wood and rocks through the windows of the station, endangering those inside. Ironically, given the intent of the crowd, this prevented Major Ross and Inspector Pawley from freeing the two Canadian prisoners, as the door to the passageway to the station's cell stood directly in front of one of the windows targeted by the soldiers.[43]

Ross decided to return to the front gate in an effort to calm the crowd. The hail of missiles striking the front of the station, however, forced him to exit through a back door and climb over several walls and fences. By the time he reappeared at the gate, he could do little to intervene as the bombardment of the station had evolved into a full-scale assault. According to one eyewitness, most of the crowd did not participate in the attack, but simply watched the proceedings from a nearby park.[44] The number of soldiers with violent intentions, however, exceeded the strength of the police by a considerable margin. Thus, as the soldiers broke through the gates into the garden in front of the station, police constables had little choice but to retreat inside the building. Hurriedly reinforced by timber, the front door of the station withstood the efforts of the angry mob to break it down. At the side of the station, however, the Canadians managed to gain entry into the passageway leading to the prisoners' cells after ripping the iron bars out of a window. Once inside, they forced the lock on Private McDonald's cell and freed him.[45]

Oblivious to the success of their comrades at the side of the building, the soldiers in front of the station grew increasingly frustrated as the front door held fast while the police inside repelled their efforts to gain entry through adjacent windows. Apparently disregarding the welfare of the Canadian prisoners that they had come to liberate, soldiers began threatening to set fire to the station. According to Police Sergeant Greenfield, "I heard several Canadian soldiers shout, 'Let's fire the fucking building and we'll burn you and your buggers.... ' The soldiers started throwing wood into the charge room through the window, and there was every appearance of their threat being carried out."[46]

In this context, Police Sergeant Thomas Green, an off-duty officer who had entered the station through the back after the attack had commenced, suggested mounting a charge to clear the front garden. Given the size and temperament of the mob, Pawley was initially reluctant to leave the station. With the Canadians threatening to break down the front door or set fire to the station, however, he saw no other choice. Leaving several policemen to defend the front of the building, Pawley led about a dozen others in a charge against the Canadians outside. The most violent episode of the evening occurred as the police exited the back of the station and attacked the crowd on the side and front of the building using truncheons and improvised clubs. Many of the Canadians fought back with their own makeshift weapons.[47] In the ensuing melée, many soldiers and policemen sustained injuries. Sergeant Green incurred multiple wounds, but continued to fight, even after being knocked down once. Subsequently, however, Canadian Private Allan McMaster struck him in the head, apparently with an iron bar. His skull fractured, Green never regained consciousness.[48]

Despite the loss of Sergeant Green and several others who sustained injuries during the charge, the phalanx of policemen managed to drive the soldiers out of the garden in front of the station. Finding themselves "hopelessly outnumbered" upon reaching the street, they quickly returned to the building. The charge had broken the momentum of the Canadian attack, because several of its leaders had suffered head wounds themselves. Thus, the Canadians showed little enthusiasm for a renewed assault on the station. This respite allowed the police to free the remaining prisoner, Veinotte.[49] To their credit, several Canadian soldiers recognized that Sergeant Green was in critical condition and carried him to a nearby house. According to its owner, Charles Polhill:

> When the six soldiers carried Sergt. Green to me at the gate one of them said, "We want some place to put him." I said, "take him round the back" as I thought he was an injured Canadian soldier. They said, "Open that front door. He has to go in there and if you don't open it we will smash it open!"

Upon gaining entrance to Polhill's house, the Canadians remained with Green for half an hour, bathing his forehead with cold water and rubbing his hands with salt before departing at about 0030 hours on 18 June.[50]

Aside from this small group, few Canadian soldiers lingered at the scene of the crime. After the attack on the station lost its impetus, most made their way back to Woodcote Park in small groups between midnight and 0100. Captain John Hutchinson, a medical officer at the hospital, stopped several of these groups and inquired as to their whereabouts earlier in the evening. Questioned by an officer, the soldiers showed little concern or compunction. As Hutchinson related, "I stopped 2 or 3 small groups and asked where they had been. They said at Epsom … and we have had a first rate time. We got what we went after and we are now going back to bed."[51]

THE AFTERMATH OF THE ATTACK

Punishment was neither harsh nor particularly just for the Canadians who were involved in the attack. Colonel Frederick Guest, the commandant at Woodcote Park, assembled the patients and staff at the hospital on the morning of 18 June and informed them of Sergeant Green's demise. He chastised the soldiers, but refrained from putting Epsom out of bounds, instead requesting that patients and staff stay out of the town. It was only later on the 18th that Canadian Military Headquarters declared the town off-limits to Canadian troops.[52] The commandant's reluctance to punish the soldiers under his supervision probably stemmed in part from the fact that not all of them had participated in the attack. Significantly, however, it also reflected Guest's fear of antagonizing the patients and staff at Woodcote Park, over whom he had little, if any, control. Although Metropolitan Police Inspector John Ferrier was eager to start his investigation into the attack as early as possible, Guest asked him not to question any Canadians at Woodcote Park "until such times as an armed force of 400 men could be obtained from Ripon, as it was feared any interrogation might provoke another outburst."[53]

A substantial armed guard deployed at the hospital within 24 hours of the attack on the police station. While this effectively precluded any further aggression by patients and staff, Canadian officers and NCOs still offered only limited assistance to the police investigation. Even those officers and NCOs who had spoken to soldiers involved in the attack claimed that they could identify none of them afterwards. Despite talking with several small groups of soldiers as they returned to Woodcote Park, Captain Hutchinson maintained, "I can't identify any of the men. The patients I don't know at all and I was not near enough any of the staff men to recognize them."[54] Similarly, Sergeant-Major Parson, who was present throughout the attack, could identify only two soldiers who sustained injuries in Epsom. Even Major Ross, who had accompanied the soldiers to the police station and addressed them repeatedly in an effort to avert the attack, claimed to be unable to recognize any of the perpetrators. As Ross averred:

> Owing to absolute darkness in the camp at the time I addressed the men, and the fact that I was speaking to the crowd in general, and not to any individual person, I am unable to identify any man who was a member of the crowd with the exception of a bugler, whom I had seen in the camp before.[55]

Other than the bugler and the soldiers who had sought treatment for wounds after the attack, officers and NCOs at Woodcote Park were unable to identify any of those who had participated in the assault on the station. In light of the lack of contact between medical and administrative officers and patients at the hospital, as well as the high turnover of patients, it is not surprising that Ross and others could not identify the culprits by name. Given the extent of their interaction with the crowd on the night of 17 June, however, these claims warrant some scepticism. Ferrier certainly had his suspicions, as he complained in a report published in July:

> In view of the extreme reluctance shewn [sic] by nearly every member of Woodcote Park Camp it was a very difficult matter to obtain information, of a tangible nature, which would assist in establishing the identity of the men, who had broke Camp that night and attacked the Police Station.[56]

Faced with few eyewitnesses able to identify soldiers involved in the attack, the police used medical evidence instead. On 19 June, Ferrier visited the Canadian Military Hospital at Orpington and questioned patients and staff from Woodcote Park who had sustained head injuries on the night of the 17th. Those who could explain their whereabouts that evening, as well as the causes of their wounds, faced no charges. On 20 June, however, the police laid charges of riot and manslaughter against six injured Canadians, as well as the bugler identified by Major Ross. These men were not the only soldiers involved in the attack. As one of the accused protested upon learning of the charges, "It's only the fellows that got hit that's taken; there were others; it's not fair."[57]

Protests aside, this proved to be a reasonably accurate method of identifying at least some of the soldiers who were involved in the attack. While none of the accused admitted participating, they could not explain the origin of their head injuries, which were more than likely inflicted by police truncheons in the garden of the Epsom station. Moreover, among the accused was Private Allan McMaster, the soldier responsible for Green's death. In late July, five of the seven charged, including McMaster, were acquitted of manslaughter, but convicted of riot. On reaching this verdict, a rather sympathetic jury suggested that the judge "should take into consideration these men's military services and that it is possible that they were ignorant of the laws of this country and did not appreciate the gravity of the offences they had committed." The judge apparently agreed. Before passing sentence, he informed the soldiers:

> that he was pleased the Jury had not returned a verdict of Manslaughter against them, and that he was exceedingly sorry to see men who had served the country as soldiers and who were not in the ordinary sense of the word criminals — in such a serious position....

He then sentenced them each to 12 months in prison from the time of their initial incarceration.[58] Ultimately, the Canadians served only five months before receiving a pardon from the Prince of Wales in December 1919. The relatively light punishment apparently did not sit well with Private McMaster. On 31 July 1929, he presented himself to the Winnipeg police and confessed to the murder of Sergeant Green, stating, "This matter had worried me for a long time and I have made up my mind to confess as to clear my conscience."[59] The Metropolitan Police, however, showed no interest in reopening the case, wiring their Winnipeg counterparts that in light of his 1919 conviction for riot and subsequent imprisonment, "McMaster is not wanted here."[60]

CONCLUSION

The frustration of Canadian soldiers in Great Britain during the spring of 1919 is wholly understandable. After months and often years overseas, where they made a significant contribution to the defeat of the Central Powers, soldiers faced repeated delays in being repatriated. Growing impatience undoubtedly contributed to the outbursts of violence at Canadian holding camps such as Kinmel Park and Witley, as well as in towns such as Guildford and Epsom. Frustration alone, however, is not sufficient to explain the Canadian attack on the Epsom Police Station. Throughout Surrey in 1919, tension prevailed between Canadian soldiers and local residents, particularly demobilized British soldiers. Altercations between the two groups during the spring intensified this mutual animosity. In Epsom, the nature of the Woodcote Park Convalescent Hospital compounded Anglo-Canadian pressures. In particular, the presence of quarantined soldiers undergoing treatment for sexually transmitted diseases fuelled local suspicions about the Canadians, while the blue-clad patients chafed at their imprisonment inside the hospital's grounds.

The relative weakness of military and civilian authorities in Epsom allowed ample scope for the expression of frustrations and animosities. Neither personnel nor procedures at Woodcote Park were adequate to control the thousands of patients and staff who occupied the hospital at any given time in 1919. Even if the authorities at the hospital had possessed the means to control the patients and staff, it seems unlikely that they would have attempted to do so, for fear of provoking an angry backlash from soldiers anxious to return to Canada. In the absence of sufficient control by the military authorities, the local police shouldered the burden of containing Canadian excesses in Epsom. The Epsom detachment, however, was far too small to cope with the hundreds of soldiers who visited the town on a daily basis. Moreover, it is likely that respect for the Canadians's wartime service, along with the recognition of the economic boon that they represented, encouraged the police and local judiciary to indulge their rowdy behaviour when possible. In the resulting vacuum of authority, mounting tensions between Canadian soldiers and local civilians exploded on 17 June, causing extensive damage to property, many injuries, and the untimely death of a police officer in the line of duty.

Besides demonstrating the consequences of Anglo-Canadian tensions and insufficient disciplinary measures, the attack on the police station also sheds light on the relationship between Canadian soldiers and the command structure above them in 1919. Recent studies of discipline and disobedience in armies during the First World War have conceived of this relationship in contractual terms. According to this model, soldiers performed specific tasks and adhered to a clearly defined code of conduct. In return, they expected a certain standard of care and leadership from their superiors. When soldiers perceived the command structure to be in breach of this implicit contract, either through the imposition of additional demands on the rank and file, or through neglect of its responsibilities toward them, they responded with collective acts of disobedience.[61]

While this model helps to explain the behaviour of frustrated soldiers at various Canadian holding camps, the attack on the Epsom Police Station was clearly not an act of disobedience aimed at the Canadian command structure. Rather, the Epsom incident demonstrates the problems that can arise when the contract binding soldiers and the command structure becomes obsolete. In 1919, officers at Woodcote Park had little interest in imposing wartime standards of discipline on soldiers who had contributed to the defeat of the enemy and, like the officers themselves, wished to return home as quickly as possible. Moreover, the rapid turnover of patients at the hospital made the imposition of strict disciplinary standards extremely difficult in any case. This situation proved problematic for convalescents and staff at the hospital. With the defeat of Germany in November 1918, these men had accomplished their principal task as soldiers. In 1919, they found themselves at Woodcote Park for a prolonged period with little purpose or guidance. In this context, they behaved much like newly enlisted soldiers did in Canada in 1916 (see Chapter 6 in this book). In these instances, under the tentative oversight of inexperienced officers, new recruits with few responsibilities targeted individuals and businesses in their local communities that were suspected of "enemy" loyalties.[62] Similarly, soldiers at Woodcote Park existed in an environment in which neither their roles and responsibilities, nor those of their superiors, were clearly defined or enforced. In the absence of this implicit contract, they found "enemies" in the local community and acted against them with relative impunity. Disciplinary problems were difficult to avoid given the ambiguous situation in which thousands of Canadian soldiers found themselves at the end of the First World War in England. Nonetheless, such a situation had fatal consequences in Epsom in June 1919.

NOTES

1. Desmond Morton, "'Kicking and Complaining': The Demobilization Riots in the Canadian Expeditionary Force in England, 1918–1919," *Canadian Historical Review*, Vol. 61, No. 3 (September 1980), 334–60.

2. Morton, "Demobilization Riots." See also, Julian Putkowski, *The Kinmel Park Camp Riots* (Hawarden, Wales: Flintshire Historical Society, 1989).

3. W.R. Horne to the Editor, *The Surrey Weekly Press* [henceforth *SWP*], 27 June 1919, 8.

4. "J.W." to the Editor, *Surrey County Herald* [henceforth *SCH*], 20 June 1919, 3.

5. "The Doping Evil," *SWP*, 2 May 1919, 2.

6. "Soldiers & Civilians," *SWP*, 16 May 1919, 5; Imperial War Museum [henceforth IWM], Department of Documents, Miscellaneous File 130 (2007), Julian Putkowski to Desmond Morton, 14 May 1980.

7. "Soldiers & Civilians," *SWP*, 16 May 1919, 5.

8. "Men and Matters," *SWP*, 16 May 1919, 4; IWM, Department of Documents, Miscellaneous File 130 (2007), Putkowski to Morton, 14 May 1980.

9. "Civilians & Canadians," *SWP*, 27 June 1919, 7; "Canadian at Woking," 2, 27 June 1919, *The Surrey Herald and Egham and Staines News.*

10. Library and Archives Canada [henceforth LAC], Record Group [henceforth RG] 9, III-D-3, Vol. 5039, Canadian Convalescent Hospital, Woodcote Park, Epsom, War Diaries, January to May 1919, microfilm T-10930; "The Raid on the Epsom Police Station," *SCH*, 17 June 1919, 3.

11. The National Archives of the United Kingdom [henceforth TNA], MEPO 2/1962, Commissioner, Metropolitan Police to Secretary of State, Home Office, 18 June 1919.

12. IWM, Department of Documents, Miscellaneous File 130 (2007), Morton to Putkowski, 23 May 1980; *Ibid.*, Putkowski to Morton, 14 May 1980.

13. LAC, RG 9, III-D-3, Vol. 5041, Canadian Special Hospital, Witley, War Diaries, January to March 1919, microfilm T-10932.

14. LAC, RG 9, III-D-3, Vol. 5039, Canadian Convalescent Hospital, Woodcote Park, Epsom, War Diary, May 1919, microfilm T-10930. On soldiers' attitudes towards sexually transmitted diseases, see Philippa Levine, *Prostitution, Race and Politics: Policing Venereal Disease in the British Empire* (New York and London: Routledge, 2003), 150.

15. "Epsom. Urban Council Matters," *Surrey Advertiser and County Times* [henceforth *SACT*], 28 June 1919, 7; "The Raid on the Epsom Police Station," *SCH*, 27 June 1919, 3. On treatments for venereal disease, see Levine, *Prostitution, Race and Politics,* 149 and 370n.

16. "Ewell. A Violent Canadian," *SACT*, 22 February 1919, 6.

17. LAC, RG 9, III-D-3, Vol. 5039, Canadian Convalescent Hospital, Woodcote Park, Epsom, War Diaries, January to May 1919, microfilm T-10930.

18. TNA, MEPO 2/1962, Divisional Detective Inspector John Ferrier, "Special Report," Wandsworth Station, 25 July 1919.

19. TNA, MEPO 3/331, Statement of Corporal Francis George Clowery, 26 June 1919; *Ibid.*, Statement of William Henry Dower, 26 June 1919; *Ibid.*, Statement of Horace Nunn, 27 June 1919.

20. *Ibid.*, Statement of Corporal Walter Hall Lees, undated.

21. *Ibid.*, Statement of P.J.S. Bird, Adjutant, 5 July 1919.

22. "The Raid on the Epsom Police Station," *SCH*, 27 June 1919, 3.

23. TNA, MEPO 3/331, Statement of Maud Elizabeth Maidment, undated; *Ibid.*, Statement of William Lloyd, 19 June 1919; *Ibid.*, Statement of William Henry Dower, 19 June 1919.

24. "Assault by Canadian Soldiers," *SACT*, 1 February 1919, 7.

25. "The Raid on the Epsom Police Station," *SCH*, 27 June 1919, 3.

26. "Canadians and Civilians," *SCH*, 20 June 1919, 3.

27. *Ibid.*; TNA, MEPO 3/331, Ferrier, "Special Report," Wandsworth Station, 21 June 1919.

28. "Canadians and Epsom Police," *SCH*, 20 June 1919, 3.

29. "Epsom Police Station Raided," *Ibid.*, 6.

30. "Fatal Rioting at Epsom," *SACT*, 21 June 1919, 5.

31. IWM, Department of Documents, Miscellaneous File 130 (2007), Putkowski to Morton, 14 May 1980.

32. TNA, MEPO 3/331, Statement of Police Sergeant Herbert Shuttleworth, 18 June 1919; TNA, MEPO 2/1962, Report by Inspector Charles Pawley, 20 June 1919.

33. TNA, MEPO 3/331, Statement of Police Sergeant Herbert Shuttleworth, 18 June 1919; *Ibid.*, Statement of Police Constable George Barton, 18 June 1919.

34. *Ibid.*, Statement of Inspector Charles Pawley, 21 June 1919.

35. *Ibid.*, Statement of Police Sergeant George Greenfield, 19 June 1919.

36. *Ibid.*, Statement of Major James Ross, 20 June 1919; *Ibid.*, Statement of Corporal Francis George Clowery, 26 June 1919.

37. *Ibid.*, Statement of Corporal Walter Hall Lees, 24 June 1919.

38. *Ibid.*, Statement of Major James Ross, 20 June 1919. See also "Epsom Police Station Raided," *SCH*, 20 June 1919, 6.

39. TNA, MEPO 3/331, Ferrier, "Special Report," Wandsworth Station, 21 June 1919; *Ibid.*, Further Statement of Regimental Sergeant-Major John Norton Parson, 3 July 1919; *Ibid.*, Statement of Stephen Stables, Driver, 28 June 1919.

40. *Ibid.*, Statement of Inspector Charles Pawley, 21 June 1919.

41. *Ibid.*, Further Statement of Major James Ross, 3 July 1919.

42. *Ibid.*, Further Statement of Major James Ross, 3 July 1919; *Ibid.*, Statement of Robert Todd, 21 June 1919.

43. *Ibid.*, Ferrier, "Special Report," Wandsworth Station, 21 June 1919; "The Raid on the Epsom Police Station," *SCH*, 27 June 1919, 2.

44. TNA, MEPO 3/331, Ferrier, "Special Report," Wandsworth Station, 21 June 1919; *Ibid.*, Statement of Private Edward Le Pointe, 23 June 1919.

45. *Ibid.*, Ferrier, "Special Report," Wandsworth Station, 21 June 1919.

46. *Ibid.*, Statement of Police Sergeant George Greenfield, 17 July 1919. See also, *Ibid.*, Statement of Police Sergeant William Kersey, 17 July 1919.

47. TNA, MEPO 2/1962, Ferrier, "Special Report," Wandsworth Station, 25 July 1919; TNA, MEPO 3/331, Statement of Police Sergeant George Greenfield, 17 July 1919.

48. TNA, MEPO 3/331, Ferrier, "Special Report," Wandsworth Station, 21 June 1919; *Ibid.*, Statement of Acting Police Sergeant Shirley, 6 June 1919; TNA, MEPO 2/1962, Chris Newton, Chief Constable, Winnipeg Police to the Commissioner of Police of the Metropolis, 1 August 1929.

49. TNA, MEPO 3/331, Statement of Police Sergeant George Greenfield, 17 July 1919.

50. *Ibid.*, Statement of Charles Polhill, 11 July 2005.

51. *Ibid.*, Statement of Captain John Hutchinson, 27 June 1919.

52. "Epsom Police Station Raided," *SCH*, 20 June 1919, 6.

53. TNA, MEPO 2/1962, Ferrier, "Special Report," Wandsworth Station, 25 July 1919.

54. TNA, MEPO 3/331, Statement of Captain John Hutchinson, 27 June 1919.

55. *Ibid.*, Statement of Major James Ross, 20 June 1919; *Ibid.*, Statement of Regimental Sergeant-Major John Norton Parson, undated.

56. TNA, MEPO 2/1962, Ferrier, "Special Report," Wandsworth Station, 25 July 1919.

57. TNA, MEPO 3/331, Ferrier, "Special Report," Wandsworth Station, 21 June 1919.

58. *Ibid.*, Ferrier, "Special Report," Wandsworth Station, 24 July 1919.

59. TNA, MEPO 2/1962, Newton to the Commissioner of Police, 1 August 1929.

60. *Ibid.*, Assistant Commissioner, Metropolitan Police to Newton, 3 August 1929.

61. See for example, L.V. Smith, *Between Mutiny and Obedience: The Case of the French Fifth Infantry Division During World War I* (Princeton: Princeton University Press, 1994); G.D. Sheffield, *Leadership in the Trenches: Officer-Man Relations, Morale and Discipline in the British Army in the Era of the First World War* (London: Macmillan,

2000); and Nikolas Gardner, "Sepoys and the Siege of Kut-al-Amara, December 1915-April 1916," *War in History,* Vol. 11, No. 3 (July 2004), 307–26.

62. P.W. Lackenbauer and N. Gardner, "Citizen-Soldiers as 'Liminaries': the CEF Soldier Riots of 1916 Reconsidered," in Yves Tremblay, ed., *Canadian Military History Since the 17th Century* (Ottawa: Department of National Defence, 2001), 155–66.

Common Punishments for Minor Offences: 19th Battalion, 1915-1918

Legend: ■ FP 1 ▨ FP 2 ▥ Fine/Forfeiture of Pay ▨ Reduction in Rank □ Reprimand

Note: These numbers do not include punishments awarded to 19th Battalion personnel temporarily attached to other commands.

Source: Library and Archives Canada, Record Group 150, Series 1, Vol. 71, "19th Battalion (Parts 1–4)," Part 2 Daily Orders, 1915–1918.

APPENDIX 8.2

Minor Offences: Numbers and Types of Charges, 19th Battalion, 1915–1918

Legend: ■ Drunkenness ▨ Absence ■ Insubordination/Striking ▨ Disobedience/Neglect □ Other

X-axis: Number of Charges

Note: These numbers do not include charges against 19th Battalion personnel temporarily attached to other commands.

Source: Library and Archives Canada, Record Group 150, Series 1, Vol. 71, "19th Battalion (Parts 1–4)," Part 2 Daily Orders, 1915–1918.

APPENDIX 8.3

Minor Infractions and Absences Without Permission in the 22nd Battalion During the Unit's Stay at the Front

Legend: —— = Minor Infraction   --- = Absences Without Permission

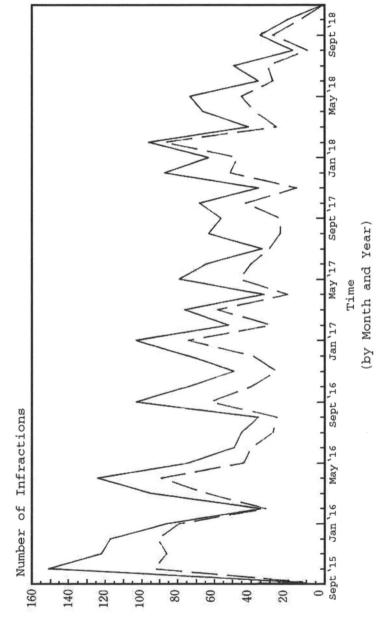

Source: Jean-Pierre Gagnon, *Le 22e Bataillon (Canadien-français), Étude socio-militaire* (Ottawa et Quebec, 1986), Graphique 8, 284.

APPENDIX 8.4

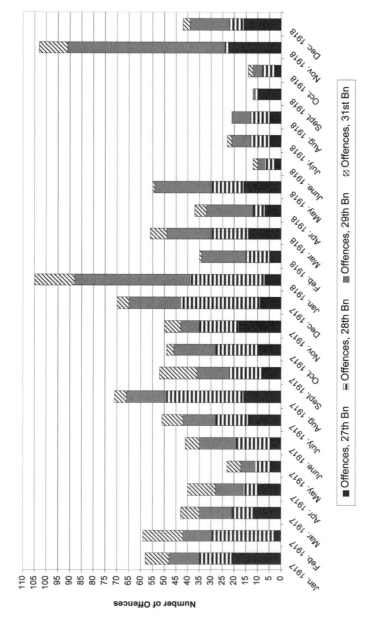

Minor Offences: 6th Brigade, 1917-1918

■ Offences, 27th Bn   ▤ Offences, 28th Bn   ▦ Offences, 29th Bn   ▨ Offences, 31st Bn

Source: Library and Archives Canada, Record Group 9, III-C-3, Vol. 4123, Folder 1, File 11, 6th Canadian Infantry Brigade Headquarters, Discipline, January 1917 to November 1918.

Personnel Turbulence: 19th Battalion, 1915-1918

Legend: —○— Taken on Strength – ■ – Casualties

Source: Library and Archives Canada [henceforth LAC], Record Group [henceforth RG] 24, C-6-I, Vol. 1874, File 22, Vol. 1, Monthly Strengths; and LAC, RG 150, Vol. 492–495, Files "Casualties by Days — France and Belgium."

APPENDIX 8.6

Table 1: Minor Offences, October 1915 to October 1918

Battalion[1]	Absence Without Permission	Drunkenness	Other Infractions	Total
22nd	1660	262	553	2475
19th	278	54	215	547

Table 2: Minor Offences, January 1917 to December 1918

Battalion[2]	Absence Without Permission	Drunkenness	Other Infractions	Total
19th	140	20	111	271
27th	71	26	145	242
28th	125	36	158	319
29th	149	69	187	405
31st	58	22	76	156

Table 3: Number of Courts-Martial by Year[3]

Battalion	1915	1916	1917	1918	1919	Total
18th	5	16	32	24	8	85
19th	1	6	26	20	2	55
20th	3	7	35	38	8	91
21st	2	26	26	22	9	85
22nd	9	27	80	54	15	185
24th	2	19	29	37	22	109
25th	4	29	25	29	6	93
26th	1	10	26	33	6	76
27th	2	11	14	17	2	46
28th	7	13	19	16	10	65
29th	3	18	23	29	8	81
31st	8	5	8	7	6	34
Total	47	187	343	326	102	1005

Table 4: Offences Tried by Courts-Martial, 1915–1919[4]

Battalion	Absence	Desertion	Drunkenness	Insubordination and Disobedience[5]	Other Offences[6]	Total Offences Tried
18th	29	13	19	25	38	124
19th	12	10	10	8	30	70
20th	27	22	12	23	51	135
21st	20	23	11	17	43	114
22nd	28	63	20	27	93	241
24th	13	20	11	41	57	142
25th	12	11	2	22	47	120
26th	11	14	10	13	57	105
27th	5	15	6	9	24	59
28th	9	16	19	27	29	100
29th	16	8	24	26	32	106
31st	3	2	15	8	18	46
Total	195	217	185	246	519	1362

Table 5: Discipline and Command

Battalion	Number of Courts-Martial, 1915 to 1919	Number of Minor Offences[7], 1917 to 1918	Number of Changes in Command[8] prior to 11 Nov 1918
18th	85	?	3
19th	55	375	4
20th	91	?	3
21st	85	?	4
22nd	185	1438	5
24th	109	?	6
25th	93	?	6
26th	76	?	6
27th	46	242	2
28th	65	319	2
29th	81	405	6
31st	34	156	2

NOTES TO APPENDIX 8.6

1. Gagnon, *Le 22e Bataillon,* Tableau 24, 287; Library and Archives Canada [henceforth LAC], Record Group [henceforth RG] 150, Series 1, Vol. 71, "19th Battalion (Parts 1–4)," Part 2 Daily Orders, 1915–1918. The numbers given here do not include those offences committed by 19th Battalion personnel when they were attached temporarily to other units or commands.

2. Figures for the 19th Battalion, as taken from *Ibid.* Figures for the 27th, 28th, 29th and 31st Battalions, as taken from LAC, RG 9, III-C-3, Vol. 4123, File 11, 6th Canadian Infantry Brigade Headquarters, Discipline, January 1917 to November 1918.

3. Numbers derived from LAC database entitled *Courts-Martial of the First World War.* Accessed at *www.collectionscanada.ca/archivianet/courts-martial/index-e.html.*

4. *Ibid.* An individual could be charged with, and tried for, multiple offences.

5. For the sake of convenience, offences against Sections 6, 8, 9, and 10 of the Army Act were grouped together under this heading.

6. Includes the very prevalent charge, "Conduct to the prejudice of good order and military discipline." See Section 40 of the Army Act.

7. These figures for the 19th, 27th, 28th, 29th and 31st Battalions are taken from Table 3 above. The figure given here for the 22nd Battalion is derived from Gagnon's history and covers the period October 1916 to October 1918. See Gagnon, *Le 22e Bataillon,* Tableau 24, 287. Numbers of minor offences in the other battalions have yet to be calculated.

8. These numbers were derived from lists of units and commanding officers found in LAC, RG 24, C-6-d, Vol. 1886, File 85.

APPENDIX 11

Excerpt from "Riot in Canadian Camp: Twelve Killed and Many Injured. V.C. Trampled to Death," 7 March 1919, *The Times.*

On Tuesday night, the men held a mass meeting, which was followed by a mad riot. The outbreak began in Montreal Camp at 9.30 p.m. with a cry "Come on the Bolsheviks," which is said to have been given by a Canadian soldier who is Russian. The men rushed to the officers' quarters, helped themselves to all the liquor they could find, then went for the stores, disarmed the guards, and with their rifles smashed doors and windows, helping themselves to the content of the stores. Boxes of cigarettes and cigars were thrown all about the ground. Then they went out to wreck the whole camp. One portion, where tradesmen's shops supplied soldiers, was stripped and in a few moments not a shop was left standing. The Church Army and Salvation Army buildings, however, were not touched. The rioters then proceeded to the quarters occupied by the girls, who were in bed, and carried away their clothes. The girls were not injured, but had to remain in bed the next day because they could not dress themselves. Next day, the rioters were masquerading about the camp in girls' clothing.

By mid-day on Wednesday the camp appeared as if it had been passed over by legions of tanks. Unfortunately a brewer's dray containing 48 barrels of beer arrived at the camp. The men took fire buckets, broke the barrels and drank the beer. Then they started shooting all round. In one of the distant parts of the camp a young soldier stood on guard and attempted to do his duty. In reply to his challenge one of the rioters shot him dead.

A little later a major from New Brunswick, who had gained the VC, attempted to interfere, but in his endeavour to hold the rioters back from such portion of the officers' quarters that was not demolished, he was thrown down and trampled to death. Another officer, going amongst the rioters, was so badly mauled that he died a few hours later. [Editor's Note: These two fatalities did not occur.]

During this time some of the men had been arrested. The rioters demanded the release of the men. The colonel refused, and the rioters released the men themselves. The whole disturbance was quelled by night and the ringleaders, numbering about twenty, and stated to be mostly of foreign extraction, were taken away. The Canadian soldiers in the camp, while explaining the cause of the affair, are now regretting it. They say that they did not anticipate that it would go to such lengths, and the mob went further than it meant to.

The disturbance caused great alarm in Rhyl, when it was reported that 5,000 to 6,000 men of the camp were going to raze the town.

Yesterday an officer from the War Office arrived at the camp by aeroplane and found everything calm. He addressed the men, telling them it was murder for Canadians to kill Canadians. He gave them an assurance that within a few days about half of the Canadians in the camp should be on their way home. The others would follow quickly. This statement was cheered by the men who said it was all they wanted.

Excerpts from "The Camp Riot: Further Details," 8 March 1919, *The Times*.

All was quiet yesterday at Kinmel Park, North Wales. It was officially stated that the casualties were five killed and twenty one wounded. The inquest on the victims was opened yesterday, and adjourned until next week. Brigadier General M. A. Colquhoun, in a statement yesterday morning, said that no attack was made on the officers who were treated with the greatest courtesy. "I myself," he went on to say, "went in and out amongst the men freely. Some of them actually put down their loot in order to salute me, and then picked up their loot again." Reports of the damage are greatly exaggerated. Some fifty or sixty men got out of hand, and attacked some canteens. The men in one camp, anticipating danger, armed themselves and, contrary to express orders, fired. That was on

Wednesday, when the fatalities occurred. The girls' camp was not attacked. As a matter of fact the girls were treated with the utmost chivalry. No man entered the girls' bedrooms while they were occupied. One man raised the red flag in an attempt to introduce Bolshevism, but was shot.

In view of the splendid discipline and record uniformly maintained by Canadian troops since the beginning of the war in England and France, the "incident" at Kinmel Park is regretted. It is considered that by comparison with others discipline amongst the Canadian troops is of a high order. It is also regretted that reports of the incident have been exaggerated. Immediately after the Armistice, Kinmel Park was secured as a concentration area through which Canadian troops stationed near Liverpool could pass through to Canada. All documentation is completed there, and the troops are sorted into drafts, according to their destination in Canada. Considering the shortage of shipping, the Canadian authorities congratulate themselves upon the splendid record they have for sending troops to Canada.

In the month of February [1919], however, the Ministry of Shipping were unable to furnish sufficient ships to carry out the programme as promised to the Canadians. Owing to this the programme in February and early March had fallen short by one third. This had caused the "backing up" of troops from Kinmel Park through to areas in England, through to France. This had caused disappointment to the Canadians, some of whom had been overseas, without seeing home, for four years …

Immediately upon the matter being reported to the Chief of the General Staff, Lieutenant-General Sir Richard Turner VC, KCB, he went to Kinmel Park and addressed the men in fifteen different places. They seemed to appreciate his explanations and there is not likely to be any further disturbances …

If the number of men originally planned for February had been allowed to embark, it is thought that there would have been no trouble. But the shipping situation, owing to strikes and other reasons, is admittedly a difficult matter to control. It is however hoped that there will not be a recurrence of the delays which have hitherto taken place.

It is not attempted, in the slightest degree, to excuse the misconduct of the men who took part in the disturbance. Many of the offenders have already been placed under arrest and these, with others involved, will be rigorously dealt with.

During the disturbance a certain amount of damage was done, and it was discovered that civilians were concerned. Up to the present twelve of these civilians have been arrested and handed over to the local authorities.

During the disturbance three rioters were killed and two men on picket duty. Twenty one soldiers were wounded, of whom two were officers. There is no foundation to the report that a Major, who was a VC, was killed or injured. The troops at Kinmel Park are concentrated in units representing the military districts of Canada to which they will proceed. They are not in their original units, these wings being composite formations consisting of personnel belonging to many different units. This sorting out is done in deference to the wishes of the authorities in Canada, in order to avoid delay when they reach the Dominion.

A court of inquiry, of which Brigadier J.O. MacBrian CB, CMG, DSO, is President, has been convened to make a thorough investigation into all circumstances in connection with the disturbance.

GLOSSARY

AA & QMG	Assistant Adjutant and Quartermaster-General
AD	Archives Deschâtelets
ADSO	Assistant Deputy Sub-Divisional Officer
APM	Assistant Provost-Marshal
BEF	British Expeditionary Force
BHQ	Battalion Headquarters
Capt	Captain
CASC	Canadian Army Service Corps
CBC	Canadian Broadcasting Corporation
CDA	Canadian Defence Academy
CEF	Canadian Expeditionary Force
CFLI	Canadian Forces Leadership Institute
CGS	Chief of the General Staff
CHR	*Canadian Historical Review*
CIB	Canadian Infantry Brigade
CID	Canadian Infantry Division
CMR	Canadian Mounted Rifles
CO	Colonial Office; Commanding Officer
CSM	Company Sergeant-Major
CSP	*Canada Sessional Papers*
DAAG	Deputy Assistant Adjutant-General
DCM	Distinguished Conduct Medal; District Court-Martial
DH	*Documentary History*
DHH	Directorate of History and Heritage
DM	Deputy Minister
DMPF	Director Military Prisons in the Field
DND	Department of National Defence
DOC	District Officer Commanding

D-Q	Drocourt-Quéant
DSO	Distinguished Service Order
FGCM	Field General Court-Martial
FP	Field Punishment
GMP	Garrison Military Police
GOC	General Officer Commanding
HBC	Hudson's Bay Company
HMG	Heavy Machine Gun
HMS	His Majesty's Ship
HMSO	His Majesty's Stationery Office
HQ	Headquarters
HT	Horse Transport
IWM	Imperial War Museum
JAG	Judge Advocate-General
LAC	Library and Archives Canada
LCol	Lieutenant-Colonel
LOB	Left Out of Battle
Lt	Lieutenant
MD	Military District
MG	Machine Gun; Manuscript Group
MML	*Manual of Military Law*
MP	Military Police
MQUP	McGill-Queen's University Press
MSA	Military Service Act
MT	Mechanical Transport
MUA	McGill University Archives
NACB	Navy and Army Canteen Board
NCO	Non-Commissioned Officer

NDA	National Defence Act
NMM	National Maritime Museum
OA	Officer Administering
OC	Officer Commanding
OMFC	Overseas Military Forces of Canada
OR	Other Ranks
OUP	Oxford University Press
PC	Police Constable
PM	Provost-Marshal
PPCLI	Princess Patricia's Canadian Light Infantry
QUA	Queen's University Archives
RCD	Royal Canadian Dragoons
RCFA	Royal Canadian Field Artillery
RCR	Royal Canadian Regiment
RCRI	Royal Canadian Regiment of Infantry
RG	Record Group
RN	*Records of Niagara*
RN	Royal Navy
RNWMP	Royal North-West Mounted Police
SAC	South African Constabulary
SACT	*Surrey Advertiser and County Times*
SCH	*Surrey County Herald*
SD	Standard Deviation
SWP	*Surrey Weekly Press*
TDS	*Toronto Daily Star*
TNA	The National Archives of the United Kingdom
UAP	University of Alberta Press
UBC	University of British Columbia
UCS	*Upper Canada Sundries*

U.K.	United Kingdom
U.S.	United States
UTP	University of Toronto Press
VC	Victoria Cross
VD	Venereal Disease
WLUP	Wilfrid Laurier University Press
WO	War Office
YMCA	Young Men's Christian Association
2 I/C	Second-in-Command

CONTRIBUTORS

Dr. David Campbell completed his doctoral studies at the University of Calgary where he specialized in military history. His major area of research is the social and operational history of the Canadian Expeditionary Force during the First World War. He currently resides and teaches in Halifax, Nova Scotia.

Howard G. Coombs retired from full-time service with the Canadian Forces in 2002. He is a graduate of the Canadian Forces Staff School, Canadian Land Force Command and Staff College, and United States Army Command and General Staff College. He is currently a doctoral candidate at Queen's University studying twentieth-century Canadian military history. He is also a teaching fellow at Queen's University, a research associate of the Canadian Forces Leadership Institute, a part-time instructor at the Canadian Forces College, Toronto, and a reserve officer commanding the Princess of Wales' Own Regiment, an infantry unit based in Kingston. Most recently, he was a co-editor of *The Operational Art — Canadian Perspectives: Context and Concepts* published by Canadian Defence Academy Press in 2005, and co-author with General Rick Hillier of "Planning for Success: The Challenge of Applying Operational Art in Post Conflict Afghanistan," which appeared in the autumn 2005 edition of *Canadian Military Journal.*

Dr. Nikolas Gardner teaches history at the University of Salford, Greater Manchester, in the United Kingdom. He has written on discipline and disobedience among Canadian, British, and Indian soldiers during the First World War.

Martin Hubley earned his master of arts in war studies from King's College London and is now a doctoral student specializing in British imperial history at the University of Ottawa. His dissertation considers questions of desertion, impressment, and identity on the Royal Navy's

North American Station between 1745 and 1815. He has written reviews for several academic journals, including *The Northern Mariner/Le marin du nord, Social History/Histoire sociale,* and the *War Studies Journal.*

Dr. P. Whitney Lackenbauer is an assistant professor of Canadian history at St. Jerome's University, University of Waterloo. His current research interests focus on arctic security; aboriginal peoples and warfare; and the environmental impacts of military activities. His recent books include *Battle Grounds: The Canadian Military and Aboriginal Lands* (University of British Columbia Press, 2006) and an edited volume with Chris Madsen, *Kurt Meyer on Trial: A Documentary Record* (Canadian Defence Academy Press, 2007). He has edited three other books, authored a short monograph on military base closures, and published recent articles in *Canadian Military Journal, Journal of the Canadian Historical Association, Urban History Review,* and *Ontario History.*

Thomas Malcomson teaches at George Brown College in Toronto. At York University he is currently completing his doctoral dissertation, which focuses on control and resistance aboard the British naval vessels on the North American and West Indies station during the War of 1812. He has written several articles on maritime and naval history, co-authored *HMS* Detroit*: The Battle for Lake Erie* with his brother, Robert, and co-authored *Life-Span Development* with John Santrock, Anne MacKenzie-Rivers, and Kwan Ho Leung.

Craig Leslie Mantle graduated from Queen's University in 2002 with a master of arts in Canadian military history and has been employed by the Canadian Forces Leadership Institute as a research officer and historian ever since. He is a doctoral candidate at the University of Calgary and the editor of *The Unwilling and the Reluctant: Theoretical Perspectives on Disobedience in the Military,* published by Canadian Defence Academy Press in 2006.

Lieutenant-Colonel Ian McCulloch joined the Canadian Forces in 1977 and has held various appointments in The Royal Canadian Regiment. He holds an honours degree in journalism from Carleton University and a master of arts in war studies from the Royal Military College of Canada. Lieutenant-Colonel McCulloch has served on exchange with the 1st Battalion, Royal Regiment of Fusiliers, and as commanding officer of the Black Watch (Royal Highland Regiment) of Canada. He is an avid student of military history, and his writings have been published in many journals and books. Lieutenant-Colonel McCulloch has served as a historical consultant for the Arts and Entertainment Channel and the Canadian Broadcasting Corporation. He now serves as the principal desk officer for NATO's Military Training and Exercises program at Supreme Allied Command Headquarters — Transformation in Norfolk, Virginia.

Major James D. McKillip is an armour officer currently serving with the Directorate of History and Heritage at National Defence Headquarters in Ottawa. He has served in Germany, Iraq, Egypt, Kuwait, Afghanistan, and in many parts of Africa. He is a doctoral candidate in the Department of History at the University of Ottawa and is a previous winner of the University of Ottawa Gold Medal.

Carman Miller, who was educated at Acadia, Dalhousie, and King's College London, is a professor of Canadian history at McGill University where he has served as chair of the Department of History and dean of the Faculty of Arts. He is the author of *The Canadian Career of the Fourth Earl of Minto*; *Painting the Map Red: Canada and the South African War, 1899–1902*; and *Canada's Little War: Fighting for the British Empire in Southern Africa, 1899–1902*. Miller has also written some 30 articles or book chapters and has provided the *Dictionary of Canadian Biography* with more than 30 contributions. In 2002 he was awarded the Queen's Golden Jubilee Medal for his contributions to scholarship and the academic community.

Dr. James Paxton recently received his Ph.D. from Queen's University in Kingston, Ontario, and is now an instructor at Moravian College, Bethlehem, Pennsylvania. His dissertation focused on the Six Nations in New York and Upper Canada.

INDEX

INDEX